Nuclear Diplomacy and Crisis Management

Nuclear Diplomacy and Crisis Management

AN *International Security* READER

EDITED BY

Sean M. Lynn-Jones
Steven E. Miller
and Stephen Van Evera

THE MIT PRESS

CAMBRIDGE, MASSACHUSETTS

The contents of this book were first published in *International Security* (ISSN 0162-2889), a publication of The MIT Press under the sponsorship of the Center for Science and International Affairs at Harvard University. Except as otherwise noted, copyright in each article is owned jointly by the President and Fellows of Harvard College and the Massachusetts Institute of Technology.

John Mueller, "The Essential Irrelevance of Nuclear Weapons: Stability in the Postwar World," *IS* 13, no. 2 (Fall 1988); Robert Jervis, "The Political Effects of Nuclear Weapons: A Comment," *IS* 13, no. 2 (Fall 1988); Richard K. Betts, "A Nuclear Golden Age? The Balance Before Parity," *IS* 11, no. 3 (Winter 1986–87) © 1986 by the Brookings Institution. Reprinted with permission. Marc Trachtenberg, "A 'Wasting Asset': American Strategy and the Shifting Nuclear Balance, 1949–54," *IS* 13, no. 3 (Winter 1988/89); Roger Dingman, "Atomic Diplomacy During the Korean War," *IS* 13, no. 3 (Winter 1988/89); Scott D. Sagan, "Nuclear Alerts and Crisis Management," *IS* 9, no. 4 (Spring 1985); Gordon Chang, "To the Nuclear Brink: Eisenhower, Dulles, and the Quemoy-Matsu Crisis," *IS* 12, no. 4 (Spring 1988); H. W. Brands, Jr., "Testing Massive Retaliation: Credibility and Crisis Management in the Taiwan Strait," *IS* 12, no. 4 (Spring 1988); Marc Trachtenberg, "The Influence of Nuclear Weapons in the Cuban Missile Crisis," *IS* 10, no. 1 (Summer 1985); "Documentation: White House Tapes and Minutes of the Cuban Missile Crisis," *IS* 10, no. 1 (Summer 1985); Barry M. Blechman and Douglas M. Hart, "The Political Utility of Nuclear Weapons: The 1973 Middle East Crisis," *IS* 7, no. 1 (Summer 1982).

Selection and preface, copyright © 1990 by the President and Fellows of Harvard College and the Massachusetts Institute of Technology.

ISBN 0-262-12152-2 (hard)
        0-262-62078-2 (paper)

Library of Congress Cataloging-in-Publication Data

Nuclear diplomacy and crisis management : an International Security reader / edited by Sean M. Lynn-Jones, Steven E. Miller, Stephen Van Evera.
        p.   cm. — (International security readers)
    Includes bibliographical references
    ISBN 0-262-12152-2. — ISBN 0-262-62078-2 (pbk.)
    1. Nuclear arms control. 2. Diplomatic negotiations in international disputes. 3. Nuclear crisis management. I. Lynn -Jones, Sean M. II. Miller, Steven E. III. Van Evera, Stephen. IV. Series.
JX1974.7.N8134 1990
327.1'74—dc20

                                                                    90-5840
                                                                    CIP

Contents

The Contributors

SEAN M. LYNN-JONES is Managing Editor of *International Security* and a Research Fellow at the Center for Science and International Affairs, Harvard University.

STEVEN E. MILLER is a Senior Research Fellow at Stockholm International Peace Research Institute (SIPRI) and Co-editor of *International Security*.

STEPHEN VAN EVERA, Managing Editor of *International Security* 1984–1987, is an Adjunct Fellow at the Center for Science and International Affairs, Harvard University. He will join the faculty of the Massachusetts Institute of Technology's political science department in 1990–91.

JOHN MUELLER is Professor of Political Science at the University of Rochester.

ROBERT JERVIS is a Professor in the Department of Political Science and the Institute of War and Peace Studies at Columbia University.

RICHARD K. BETTS is a Senior Fellow at the Brookings Institution.

MARC TRACHTENBERG is Associate Professor of History at the University of Pennsylvania.

ROGER DINGMAN is Associate Professor of History at the University of Southern California.

SCOTT D. SAGAN is Assistant Professor of Political Science at Stanford University.

GORDON CHANG is Assistant Professor in the Department of History at the University of California, Irvine, and a member of Stanford University's Center for International Security and Arms Control.

H. W. BRANDS, JR. is Assistant Professor in the Department of History at Texas A & M University.

BARRY M. BLECHMAN is a Fellow at the Center for Strategic and International Studies and the Foreign Policy Institute of The Johns Hopkins University, and President of Defense Forecasts, Inc.

DOUGLAS M. HART is Assistant Vice-President for Intelligence and Targeting Applications at the Pacific-Sierra Research Corporation.

Acknowledgments

The editors gratefully acknowledge the assistance that has made this book possible. A deep debt is owed to all those at the Center for Science and International Affairs, Harvard University, who have played an editorial role at *International Security*, including Paul Doty, Joseph S. Nye, Jr., Albert Carnesale, Michael Nacht, Ashton Carter, Derek Leebaert, Melissa Healy, Lisbeth Tarlow Bernstein, Lynn Page Whittaker, Teresa Pelton Johnson, Mary Ann Wells, and Maude Fish. Lynn Eden, Lawrence Freedman, John Lewis Gaddis, Robert Jervis, John Mearsheimer, and David Rosenberg offered helpful comments on the selection of articles for inclusion in this book. Special thanks go to Lisa Grumbach and Stephen J. Stillwell, jr., for their invaluable help in preparing the volume for publication.

Preface | *Sean M. Lynn-Jones*

Since the dawn of the nuclear age at Hiroshima in 1945, statesmen have conducted diplomacy in the shadow of the bomb. Throughout this period, strategic thinkers have attempted to define, identify, and analyze the political implications of the nuclear revolution. Have nuclear weapons fundamentally changed international politics? Has a major war been averted because of or in spite of the growth in nuclear arsenals? What are the political uses of nuclear weapons? How have U.S. leaders perceived the nuclear balance? Have they acted as if nuclear superiority can be exploited for bargaining leverage? Have nuclear threats been effective in crises?

There is no consensus of opinion on most of these questions. Although many argue that nuclear weapons have made the world safer, critics charge that they pose unacceptable risks of planetary catastrophe. Some observers regard the strategic nuclear balance between the United States and the Soviet Union as critically important; the risk of war and the utility of nuclear threats are held to depend on having a clear margin of superiority. Others claim that the precise level of forces on either side becomes irrelevant as long as there is rough parity. The record of nuclear diplomacy provokes similar disagreement. In many cases, including the Korean War, there are still arguments over whether the United States actually made nuclear threats. Where there is agreement that nuclear weapons were used for diplomatic purposes, the effectiveness of implicit or explicit nuclear threats remains controversial. Several scholars have constructed elaborate theories of how nuclear risks can be manipulated for diplomatic purposes, while others suggest that nuclear weapons simply induce general caution by increasing the risks in any crisis.

The political implications of the nuclear revolution deserve continuing attention in an era in which the danger of nuclear war appears to have receded. The Gorbachev revolution in the Soviet Union and the remarkable transformation of Europe in 1989 and 1990 appear to have made a renewed era of anxiety over nuclear war unlikely. To ensure that the risk of war is kept low, it is important to understand the role nuclear weapons have played in the post-1945 international system.

Although there have been no major nuclear crises between the Soviet Union and the United States since the October 1973 Middle East war, the role of nuclear weapons in previous crises merits close examination. Not only is the political impact of nuclear threats a fascinating historical question, but the outcome of debates over the utility of nuclear weapons has important implications for current choices in arms control negotiations and decisions about acquiring nuclear or conventional weapons. Moreover, there will almost certainly be more, not fewer, nuclear powers in the future. The record of U.S. and Soviet nuclear diplomacy offers the best (and so far the only) guide to possible future attempts to extract political leverage from nuclear weapons.

This volume offers a series of perspectives on the role nuclear weapons have played in post-1945 diplomacy. Part I addresses the general political implications of the nuclear revolution, as well as U.S. perceptions of the value of nuclear weapons in the early years of the Cold War. Part II focuses on specific attempts to manipulate nuclear risks in crises.

John Mueller and Robert Jervis offer two views on the impact of nuclear weapons on postwar politics. Mueller takes issue with the conventional wisdom that nuclear weapons have, for better or for worse, transformed international relations. He argues that nuclear weapons may have influenced public debates and defense budgets, but that they have had far less impact on the course of world affairs since World War II than have nonnuclear factors. The memory of the Second World War, U.S. and Soviet contentment with the status quo, the cautious, pragmatic nature of Soviet ideology, and fears of escalation to a major conventional conflict would have sufficed to deter a Third World War even in the absence of nuclear weapons. Alliance patterns and the caution of the superpowers during crises also would have been similar without nuclear weapons. Mueller contends that the stability of the postwar world is part of a long-term trend away from war among the major developed countries.

Jervis responds to Mueller by arguing that nuclear weapons have had unique political effects because they threaten all parties to a conflict with enormous and rapid destruction. These effects are qualitatively different from those of conventional warfare. Jervis thus suggests that the stability of the postwar world cannot be attributed to conventional deterrence alone. He agrees, however, that nonmilitary dimensions of deterrence must be taken into account to explain postwar stability. Jervis nonetheless concludes that satisfaction with the status quo is not enough to prevent major war and that nuclear weapons have been necessary to make mutual security more feasible.

Turning from the general impact that nuclear weapons have had on the international system to the question of how nuclear superiority can be exploited for political purposes, the next three essays examine the diplomatic consequences of the apparent U.S. nuclear advantage in the 1950s. In 1974, Henry Kissinger asked, "What in the name of God is strategic superiority?

. . . What do you do with it?"[1] The record of nuclear diplomacy in the 1950s
may provide some answers.

Many observers regard the 1950s as a "golden age" in which the United
States enjoyed a substantial margin of superiority over the Soviet Union.
Richard Betts challenges this claim. He recognizes that the United States was
willing to use nuclear threats for political purposes, but he argues that this
willingness to approach the nuclear brink was foolhardy. Betts finds that
U.S. estimates suggested that the Soviet Union had developed the capability
to inflict unacceptable damage on the United States before the end of the
Korean War. Although estimates of U.S. vulnerability to a Soviet second
strike varied, Betts points out that U.S. leaders were aware that in a nuclear
war the United States could not escape "awesome destruction that any reasonable person should consider unacceptable." Nor could a pre-emptive first
strike by the United States limit this damage. Although the Strategic Air
Command based its plans on the assumption that U.S. forces would strike
first, the Soviet Union would have alerted and dispersed its strategic forces
in any crisis or war that might provoke a U.S. attack, thereby reducing their
vulnerability and guaranteeing that the United States could not escape massive destruction in a Soviet second strike. Betts concludes that nostalgia for
an era of U.S. nuclear superiority is unjustified and that it would be even
more foolish to resort to nuclear threats in the future.

Marc Trachtenberg assesses the impact of perceived shifts of the military
balance on U.S. strategy during the late 1940s and early 1950s. He argues
that in the early years of the nuclear era, U.S. leaders recognized that any
margin of nuclear superiority was a "wasting asset" that would disappear as
the Soviet nuclear arsenal grew. If the Soviet Union was hostile and aggressive when the United States enjoyed a nuclear monopoly, surely it would
become even more dangerous when it acquired the bomb. Trachtenberg finds
that perceptions of the nuclear balance were very important in determining
U.S. foreign policy. Drawing upon many recently declassified documents,
he argues that perceived windows of opportunity and vulnerability generated
highly aggressive thinking, including advocacy of preventive war, in the
Truman and Eisenhower administrations. These perceptions of the balance
help to explain the genesis of NSC 68, which called for an ambitious U.S.
grand strategy based on preponderant U.S. military power. The overall military balance also influenced the course of American strategy in Korea. Per-

1. Henry A. Kissinger, *Years of Upheaval* (Boston, Mass.: Little, Brown, 1982), p. 1175.

ceived U.S. vulnerability produced restraint in the winter of 1950–51, but after the balance appeared to shift in favor of the United States in late 1952, the Eisenhower administration became more willing to threaten nuclear escalation to achieve an armistice.

Roger Dingman uses many hitherto unexamined records to review the use of nuclear threats during the Korean War. It often has been argued that the Eisenhower administration resorted to atomic diplomacy to end the war after President Truman had been reluctant to rattle the nuclear saber to break the stalemate. Dingman, however, challenges this claim by tracing the Truman administration's attempts to exploit the U.S. arsenal politically throughout the Korean conflict. These nuclear feints were accompanied by threats to retaliate if the Chinese widened the war. Differing with Trachtenberg, Dingman argues that the Eisenhower administration did not emphasize nuclear threats in seeking to end the war in 1953, but attempted to rely mainly upon nonnuclear diplomacy to reach a settlement. He concludes that the record of both administrations reveals that "nuclear weapons were not easily usable tools of statecraft that produced predictable results."

Part II of this book examines the impact of nuclear weapons in selected crises. The 1948–1973 period was a veritable "age of crises," with repeated confrontations between the United States and the Soviet Union or China. At various times, war seemed imminent over the Chinese offshore islands, Berlin, Cuba, and the Middle East. The possibility of escalation to nuclear war played some role in many of these crises. As more U.S. documents on decision-making during these crises have been declassified, researchers have had the opportunity to mine a rich lode of evidence that bears on the central questions of the political utility of nuclear weapons.

The United States frequently attempted to use nuclear weapons to communicate its stakes and to manipulate the risks in crises. Nuclear alerts have been a principal means of using nuclear weapons to send political signals. Scott Sagan examines three cases of global U.S. military alerts: the May 1960 "unintended" alert that Secretary of Defense Thomas Gates ordered as a test of command and communications system during the abortive 1960 Paris summit meeting; the alert of U.S. conventional and nuclear forces to deter or compel the Soviet Union during the 1962 Cuban missile crisis; and the October 1973 alert that was meant to help avert Soviet intervention in the Yom Kippur War between Israel and Egypt and Syria. Although the evidence is ambiguous, Sagan suggests that the latter two alerts appear to have been politically effective. He notes, however, that in alerts there are many "potentially dangerous ways in which increases in military readiness for war can escape the control of central authorities." Political leaders may not recognize that the level of alert authority may be exceeded by local military command- ers, making it difficult to fine-tune an alert for political purposes. Provocative reconnaissance missions may continue or be increased in a crisis, leading to potentially dangerous incidents like the intrusion of an American U-2 spy plane into Soviet air space at the height of the Cuban missile crisis. Civilian decision-makers may have excessive confidence in the secrecy of alerts, blind- ing them to possible domestic reactions. Sagan concludes that it is critical that civilian leaders more fully understand what happens when an alert is ordered. Nuclear alerts may remain necessary diplomatic instruments, but ignorance over their operation increases the risks of inadvertent escalation.

Gordon Chang and H.W. Brands, Jr., have both drawn upon recently declassified U.S. documents to discuss the 1954–55 U.S.-China crisis over Quemoy and Matsu, two small islands off the Chinese coast that the Nation- alist Chinese retained after the Communists triumphed on the mainland in 1949. In retrospect, it seems remarkable that these seemingly insignificant islands could have become the focus of a nuclear crisis. The crisis thus provides an excellent example of an attempt to use nuclear leverage over apparently trivial stakes.

Chang argues that the 1954–55 crisis brought the United States closer to the brink of nuclear war than has generally been acknowledged. U.S. doc- uments reveal that President Eisenhower secretly pledged to defend Quemoy and Matsu against an attack from mainland China and to use nuclear weap- ons if necessary. At the peak of the crisis, Eisenhower and Secretary of State John Foster Dulles offered to blockade the Chinese coast. Chang concludes that the United States was only able to retreat from the nuclear brink because the Chinese Nationalists and the Communists independently moved to re- duce tensions in 1955.

Brands regards the crisis in the Taiwan Strait as an initial test of the Eisenhower administration's doctrine of Massive Retaliation. He credits Ei- senhower with resisting pressures to draw a nuclear line around the offshore islands, but faults him for allowing the United States to drift to the brink of war over fundamentally insignificant territories, which again became the focus of crisis in 1958. He concludes that a desire to affirm the credibility of Massive Retaliation was the driving force behind U.S. policy in the crisis.

The Cuban missile crisis of 1962 is generally regarded as the most danger- ous U.S.-Soviet nuclear confrontation. The role of nuclear weapons in the diplomacy of resolving the crisis has been an important issue in many studies of the crisis. Marc Trachtenberg identifies three schools of thought on this issue. First, some argue that nuclear weapons had little influence; U.S. and Soviet forces simply cancelled each other out. Second, others emphasize that the balance of resolve—the relative willingness of the United States and the Soviet Union to take risks over Cuba—was the decisive factor. Finally, a third school of thought claims that U.S. nuclear superiority made the critical difference in the outcome of the crisis. Trachtenberg concludes that U.S. and Soviet nuclear weapons did not cancel one another out. Concern over nuclear war definitely influenced decision-makers in Moscow and Washington. The balance of resolve favored the United States, but not overwhelmingly, and U.S. leaders did not want to manipulate nuclear risks by increasing the dangers of escalation. The strategic nuclear balance was crucial, in Trachtenberg's view, because Soviet leaders appear to have been highly conscious of the danger of an American pre-emptive strike. Even if U.S. leaders did not believe the United States had overwhelming superiority, Soviet perceptions of the balance induced restraint.

Accompanying Trachtenberg's essay are the transcripts of an October 16, 1962, meeting of the Cuban missile crisis ExComm and minutes of its meetings of October 26 and 27. These documents are an important part of the source material on which Trachtenberg bases his conclusions. They offer a glimpse into the deliberations of the highest councils of the U.S. government at the height of the crisis.[2]

Barry Blechman and Douglas Hart seek to illuminate the political role of nuclear weapons through a careful scrutiny of the U.S. nuclear alert during the October 1973 Arab-Israeli war, a case in which both sides had robust and mature nuclear forces. Prompted by a Soviet threat to send troops to rescue Egypt's encircled Third Army, the alert explicitly introduced the nuclear specter into a situation in which a superpower confrontation seemed to be brewing. Blechman and Hart discuss the several purposes that were served

---

2. The transcript of the October 27, 1962, meetings of the ExComm has been released by the John F. Kennedy Library in Dorchester, Massachusetts. An edited version has been published as McGeorge Bundy, transcriber, and James G. Blight, editor, "October 27, 1962: Transcripts of the Meetings of the ExComm," *International Security,* Vol. 12, No. 3 (Winter 1987/88), pp. 30–92. Although no Soviet or Cuban documents on the crisis have been released, several conferences among Soviet, U.S., and Cuban participants in the crisis yielded many revelations. For a summary of these findings, see Bruce J. Allyn, James G. Blight, and David A. Welch, "Essence of Revision: Moscow, Havana, and the Cuban Missile Crisis," *International Security,* Vol. 14, No. 3 (Winter 1989/90), pp. 136–172.

by the alert, foremost of which was to signal America's high stakes in the situation, to emphasize the gravity of the crisis, and—of course—to avert Soviet intervention. In their view, the nuclear threat served these purposes, as well as camouflaging the fact that the Soviet Union achieved its objectives of enforcing a cease-fire and preventing the destruction of the Egyptian Third Army. Blechman and Hart conclude that nuclear threats can help to communicate the balance of resolve and to define stakes as vital, but they may not be effective in all crises.

The articles collected here do not address all aspects of the political role of nuclear weapons. Some superpower crises, such as the several that took place over Berlin, are not examined in this volume. As more information becomes available from the U.S. archives, and possibly those of the Soviet Union and China, many of the conclusions presented in these articles will almost certainly be debated and modified. The next chapters in the history of the nuclear age have yet to be written. The editors hope that this volume will stimulate further research and thinking on these issues.

Part I:
The Political Impact
of Nuclear Weapons

The Essential Irrelevance of Nuclear Weapons

John Mueller

Stability in the Postwar World

$\mathbf{I}$t is widely assumed that, for better or worse, the existence of nuclear weapons has profoundly shaped our lives and destinies. Some find the weapons supremely beneficial. Defense analyst Edward Luttwak says, "we have lived since 1945 without another world war precisely because rational minds . . . extracted a durable peace from the very terror of nuclear weapons."[1] And Robert Art and Kenneth Waltz conclude, "the probability of war between America and Russia or between NATO and the Warsaw Pact is practically nil precisely because the military planning and deployments of each, together with the fear of escalation to general nuclear war, keep it that way."[2] Others argue that, while we may have been lucky so far, the continued existence of the weapons promises eventual calamity: The doomsday clock on the cover of the *Bulletin of the Atomic Scientists* has been pointedly hovering near midnight for over 40 years now, and in his influential bestseller, *The Fate of the Earth*, Jonathan Schell dramatically concludes that if we do not "rise up and cleanse the earth of nuclear weapons," we will "sink into the final coma and end it all."[3]

This article takes issue with both of these points of view and concludes that nuclear weapons neither crucially define a fundamental stability nor threaten severely to disturb it.

For helpful comments I would like to thank Richard Rosecrance, Karl Mueller, Robert Jervis, MacGregor Knox, Richard Betts, and the anonymous reviewers for *International Security*. This project was supported in part by the University of Rochester and by a Guggenheim Fellowship.

John Mueller is Professor of Political Science at the University of Rochester. He is the author of Retreat from Doomsday: The Obsolescence of Major War, *to be published by Basic Books in 1989.*

1. Edward N. Luttwak, "Of Bombs and Men," *Commentary*, August 1983, p. 82.
2. Robert J. Art and Kenneth N. Waltz, "Technology, Strategy, and the Uses of Force," in Robert J. Art and Kenneth N. Waltz, eds., *The Use of Force* (Lanham, Md.: University Press of America, 1983), p. 28. See also Klaus Knorr, "Controlling Nuclear War," *International Security*, Vol. 9, No. 4 (Spring 1985), p. 79; John J. Mearsheimer, "Nuclear Weapons and Deterrence in Europe," *International Security*, Vol. 9, No. 3 (Winter 1984/85), pp. 25–26; Robert Gilpin, *War and Change in World Politics* (Cambridge: Cambridge University Press, 1981), pp. 213–219.
3. Jonathan Schell, *The Fate of the Earth* (New York: Knopf, 1982), p. 231.

International Security, Fall 1988 (Vol. 13, No. 2)

The paper is in two parts. In the first it is argued that, while nuclear weapons may have substantially influenced political rhetoric, public discourse, and defense budgets and planning, it is not at all clear that they have had a significant impact on the history of world affairs since World War II. They do not seem to have been necessary to deter World War III, to determine alliance patterns, or to cause the United States and the Soviet Union to behave cautiously.

In the second part, these notions are broadened to a discussion of stability in the postwar world. It is concluded that there may be a long-term trend away from war among developed countries and that the long peace since World War II is less a peculiarity of the nuclear age than the logical conclusion of a substantial historical process. Seen broadly, deterrence seems to be remarkably firm; major war—a war among developed countries, like World War II or worse—is so improbable as to be obsolescent; imbalances in weapons systems are unlikely to have much impact on anything except budgets; and the nuclear arms competition may eventually come under control not so much out of conscious design as out of atrophy born of boredom.

The Impact of Nuclear Weapons

The postwar world might well have turned out much the same even in the absence of nuclear weapons. Without them, world war would have been discouraged by the memory of World War II, by superpower contentment with the postwar status quo, by the nature of Soviet ideology, and by the fear of escalation. Nor do the weapons seem to have been the crucial determinants of Cold War developments, of alliance patterns, or of the way the major powers have behaved in crises.

DETERRENCE OF WORLD WAR
It is true that there has been no world war since 1945 and it is also true that nuclear weapons have been developed and deployed in part to deter such a conflict. It does not follow, however, that it is the weapons that have prevented the war—that peace has been, in Winston Churchill's memorable construction, "the sturdy child of [nuclear] terror." To assert that the ominous presence of nuclear weapons has prevented a war between the two power blocs, one must assume that there would have been a war had these weapons not existed. This assumption ignores several other important war-discouraging factors in the postwar world.

THE MEMORY OF WORLD WAR II. A nuclear war would certainly be vastly destructive, but for the most part nuclear weapons simply compound and dramatize a military reality that by 1945 had already become appalling. Few with the experience of World War II behind them would contemplate its repetition with anything other than horror. Even before the bomb had been perfected, world war had become spectacularly costly and destructive, killing some 50 million worldwide. As former Secretary of State Alexander Haig put it in 1982: "The catastrophic consequences of another world war—with or without nuclear weapons—make deterrence our highest objective and our only rational military strategy."[4]

POSTWAR CONTENTMENT. For many of the combatants, World War I was as destructive as World War II, but its memory did not prevent another world war. Of course, as will be discussed more fully in the second half of this article, most nations *did* conclude from the horrors of World War I that such an event must never be repeated. If the only nations capable of starting World War II had been Britain, France, the Soviet Union, and the United States, the war would probably never have occurred. Unfortunately other major nations sought direct territorial expansion, and conflicts over these desires finally led to war.

Unlike the situation after World War I, however, the only powers capable of creating another world war since 1945 have been the big victors, the United States and the Soviet Union, each of which has emerged comfortably dominant in its respective sphere. As Waltz has observed, "the United States, and the Soviet Union as well, have more reason to be satisfied with the status quo than most earlier great powers had."[5] (Indeed, except for the dismemberment of Germany, even Hitler might have been content with the empire his arch-enemy Stalin controlled at the end of the war.) While there have been many disputes since the war, neither power has had a grievance so

---

4. *New York Times*, April 7, 1982. See also Michael Mandelbaum's comment in a book which in this respect has a curious title, *The Nuclear Revolution* (Cambridge: Cambridge University Press, 1981), p. 21: "The tanks and artillery of the Second World War, and especially the aircraft that reduced Dresden and Tokyo to rubble might have been terrifying enough by themselves to keep the peace between the United States and the Soviet Union." Also see Bruce Russett, "Away from Nuclear Mythology," in Dagobert L. Brito, Michael D. Intriligator, and Adele E. Wick, eds., *Strategies for Managing Nuclear Proliferation* (Lexington, Mass.: Lexington, 1983), pp. 148–150. And of course, given weapons advances, a full-scale *conventional* World War III could be expected to be even more destructive than World War II.
5. Kenneth N. Waltz, *Theory of International Politics* (Reading, Mass.: Addison-Wesley, 1979), p. 190. See also Joseph S. Nye, Jr., "Nuclear Learning and U.S.-Soviet Security Security Regimes," *International Organization*, Vol. 41, No. 3 (Summer 1987), p. 377.

essential as to make a world war—whether nuclear or not—an attractive means for removing the grievance.

SOVIET IDEOLOGY. Although the Soviet Union and international communism have visions of changing the world in a direction they prefer, their ideology stresses revolutionary procedures over major war. The Soviet Union may have hegemonic desires as many have argued but, with a few exceptions (especially the Korean War) to be discussed below, its tactics, inspired by the cautiously pragmatic Lenin, have stressed subversion, revolution, diplomatic and economic pressure, seduction, guerrilla warfare, local uprising, and civil war—levels at which nuclear weapons have little relevance. The communist powers have never—before or after the invention of nuclear weapons—subscribed to a Hitler-style theory of direct, Armageddon-risking conquest, and they have been extremely wary of provoking Western powers into large-scale war.[6] Moreover, if the memory of World War II deters anyone, it

---

6. Arkady N. Shevchenko, while stressing that "the Kremlin is committed to the ultimate vision of a world under its control," gives an "unequivocal no" to the question of whether "the Soviet Union would initiate a nuclear war against the United States"; instead, the Soviets "are patient and take the long view," believing "that eventually [they] will be supreme—not necessarily in this century but certainly in the next." Shevchenko, *Breaking with Moscow* (New York: Knopf, 1985), pp. 285–286. Similarly, Michael Voslensky asserts that Soviet leaders desire "external expansion," but their "aim is to win the struggle between the two systems without fighting"; he notes that Soviet military ventures before and after World War II have consistently been directed only against "weak countries" and only when the Soviets have been careful to cover themselves in advance—often withdrawing when "firm resistance" has been met. Voslensky, *Nomenklatura: The New Soviet Ruling Class* (Garden City, N.Y.: Doubleday, 1984), pp. 320–330. Richard Pipes concludes that "Soviet interests . . . are to avoid general war with the 'imperialist camp' while inciting and exacerbating every possible conflict within it." Pipes, *Survival Is Not Enough* (New York: Simon and Schuster, 1984), p. 65. William Taubman says that Stalin sought "to avert war by playing off one set of capitalist powers against another and to use the same tactic to expand Soviet power and influence without war." Taubman, *Stalin's American Policy* (New York: Norton, 1982), p. 12. MacGregor Knox argues that, for Hitler and Mussolini, "foreign conquest was the decisive prerequisite for a revolution at home," and in this respect those regimes differ importantly from those of Lenin, Stalin, and Mao. Knox, "Conquest, Foreign and Domestic, in Fascist Italy and Nazi Germany," *Journal of Modern History*, Vol. 56, No. 1 (March 1984), p. 57. In his memoirs, Nikita Khrushchev is quite straightforward about the issue: "We've always considered war to be against our own interests." He says he "never once heard Stalin say anything about preparing to commit aggression against another [presumably major] country"; and "we Communists must hasten [the] struggle" against capitalism "by any means at our disposal, *excluding war*." Khrushchev, *Khrushchev Remembers: The Last Testament*, trans. and ed., Strobe Talbott (Boston: Little, Brown, 1974), pp. 511, 533, 531, emphasis in the original. The Soviets have always been concerned about wars launched *against them* by a decaying capitalist world, but at least since 1935 they have held such wars to be potentially avoidable because of Soviet military strength and of international working class solidarity. Frederic S. Burnin, "The Communist Doctrine of the Inevitability of War," *American Political Science Review*, Vol. 57, No. 2 (June 1963), p. 339. See also Robert Jervis, *The Illogic of American Nuclear Strategy* (Ithaca: Cornell University Press, 1984), p. 156; and Michael MccGwire, "Deterrence: Problem, Not

probably does so to an extreme degree for the Soviets. Officially and unofficially they seem obsessed by the memory of the destruction they suffered. In 1953 Ambassador Averell Harriman, certainly no admirer of Stalin, observed that the Soviet dictator "was determined, if he could avoid it, never again to go through the horrors of another protracted world war."[7]

THE BELIEF IN ESCALATION. Those who started World Wars I and II did so not because they felt that costly wars of attrition were desirable, but because they felt that escalation to wars of attrition could be avoided. In World War I the offensive was believed to be dominant, and it was widely assumed that conflict would be short and decisive.[8] In World War II, both Germany and Japan experienced repeated success with bluster, short wars in peripheral areas, and blitzkrieg, aided by the counterproductive effects of their opponents' appeasement and inaction.[9]

World war in the post-1945 era has been prevented not so much by visions of nuclear horror as by the generally-accepted belief that conflict can easily escalate to a level, nuclear or not, that the essentially satisfied major powers would find intolerably costly.

To deal with the crucial issue of escalation, it is useful to assess two important phenomena of the early post-war years: the Soviet preponderance in conventional arms and the Korean War.

First, it has been argued that the Soviets would have been tempted to take advantage of their conventional strength after World War II to snap up a

Solution," *SAIS Review*, Vol. 5, No. 2 (Summer-Fall 1985), p. 122. For a study stressing the Soviet Union's "cautious opportunism" in the Third World, see Stephen T. Hosmer and Thomas W. Wolfe, *Soviet Policy and Practice toward Third World Countries* (Lexington, Mass.: Lexington Books, 1983).

7. *Newsweek*, March 16, 1953, p. 31. The Soviets presumably picked up a few things from World War I as well; as Taubman notes, they learned the "crucial lesson . . . that world war . . . can destroy the Russian regime." Taubman, *Stalin's American Policy*, p. 11.

8. Jack Snyder, *The Ideology of the Offensive* (Ithaca: Cornell University Press, 1984); Stephen Van Evera, "Why Cooperation Failed in 1914," *World Politics*, Vol. 38, No. 1 (October 1985), pp. 80–117. See also the essays on "The Great War and the Nuclear Age" in *International Security*, Vol. 9, No. 1 (Summer 1984), pp. 7–186.

9. Hitler, however, may have anticipated (or at any rate, was planning for) a total war once he had established his expanded empire—a part of his grand scheme he carefully kept from military and industrial leaders who, he knew, would find it unthinkable: see R.J. Overy, "Hitler's War and the German Economy," *Economic History Review*, Vol. 35, No. 2 (May 1982), pp. 272–291. The Japanese did not want a major war, but they were willing to risk it when their anticipated short war in China became a lengthy, enervating one, and they were forced to choose between wider war and the abandonment of the empire to which they were ideologically committed. See Robert J.C. Butow, *Tojo and the Coming of the War* (Stanford, Calif.: Stanford University Press, 1961), ch. 11.

prize like Western Europe if its chief defender, the United States, had not possessed nuclear weapons. As Winston Churchill put it in 1950, "nothing preserves Europe from an overwhelming military attack except the devastating resources of the United States in this awful weapon."[10]

This argument requires at least three questionable assumptions: (1) that the Soviets really think of Western Europe as a prize worth taking risks for;[11] (2) that, even without the atomic bomb to rely on, the United States would have disarmed after 1945 as substantially as it did; and (3) that the Soviets have actually ever had the strength to be quickly and overwhelmingly successful in a conventional attack in Western Europe.[12]

However, even if one accepts these assumptions, the Soviet Union would in all probability still have been deterred from attacking Western Europe by the enormous potential of the American war machine. Even if the USSR had the ability to blitz Western Europe, it could not have stopped the United States from repeating what it did after 1941: mobilizing with deliberate speed, putting its economy onto a wartime footing, and wearing the enemy down in a protracted conventional major war of attrition massively supplied from its unapproachable rear base.

The economic achievement of the United States during the war was astounding. While holding off one major enemy, it concentrated with its allies on defeating another, then turned back to the first. Meanwhile, it supplied everybody. With 8 million of its ablest men out of the labor market, it

---

10. Matthew A. Evangelista, "Stalin's Postwar Army Reappraised," *International Security*, Vol. 7, No. 3 (Winter 1982/83), pp. 110.
11. This assumption was certainly not obvious to Bernard Brodie: "It is difficult to discover what meaningful incentives the Russians might have for attempting to conquer Western Europe." Bernard Brodie, *Escalation and the Nuclear Option* (Princeton: Princeton University Press, 1966), pp. 71–72. Nor to George Kennan: "I have never believed that they have seen it as in their interests to overrun Western Europe militarily, or that they would have launched an attack on that region generally even if the so-called nuclear deterrent had not existed." George Kennan, "Containment Then and Now," *Foreign Affairs*, Vol. 65, No. 4 (Spring 1987), pp. 888–889. Hugh Thomas characterizes Stalin's postwar policy as "conflict which should not be carried into real war. . . . Thus, though expansion should be everywhere attempted, it should not come too close to fighting in zones where the United States, and probably Britain, would resort to arms." Hugh Thomas, *Armed Truce: The Beginnings of the Cold War, 1945–46* (New York: Atheneum, 1986), p. 102.
12. This assumption is strongly questioned in Evangelista, "Stalin's Postwar Army Reappraised," pp. 110–138. See also Adam B. Ulam, *Expansion and Coexistence* (New York: Praeger, 1968), p. 414; John J. Mearsheimer, *Conventional Deterrence* (Ithaca: Cornell University Press, 1983), ch. 6; and Barry R. Posen, "Measuring the European Conventional Balance," *International Security*, Vol. 9, No. 3 (Winter 1984/85). Among Stalin's problems at the time was a major famine in the Ukraine in 1946 and 1947. Khrushchev, *Khrushchev Remembers*, trans. and ed., Strobe Talbott (Boston: Little, Brown, 1970), ch. 7.

increased industrial production 15 percent per year and agricultural production 30 percent overall. Before the end of 1943 it was producing so much that some munitions plants were closed down, and even so it ended the war with a substantial surplus of wheat and over $90 billion in surplus war goods. (National governmental expenditures in the first peacetime year, 1946, were only about $60 billion.) As Denis Brogan observed at the time, "to the Americans war is a business, not an art."[13]

If anyone was in a position to appreciate this, it was the Soviets. By various circuitous routes the United States supplied the Soviet Union with, among other things, 409,526 trucks; 12,161 combat vehicles (more than the Germans had in 1939); 32,200 motorcycles; 1,966 locomotives; 16,000,000 pairs of boots (in two sizes); and over one-half pound of food for every Soviet soldier for every day of the war (much of it Spam).[14] It is the kind of feat that concentrates the mind, and it is extremely difficult to imagine the Soviets willingly taking on this somewhat lethargic, but ultimately hugely effective juggernaut. That Stalin was fully aware of the American achievement—and deeply impressed by it—is clear. Adam Ulam has observed that Stalin had "great respect for the United States' vast economic and hence military potential, quite apart from the bomb," and that his "whole career as dictator had been a testimony to his belief that production figures were a direct indicator of a given country's power."[15] As a member of the Joint Chiefs of Staff put it in

---

13. Despite shortages, rationing, and tax surcharges, American consumer spending increased by 12 percent between 1939 and 1944. Richard R. Lingeman, *Don't You Know There's a War On?* (New York: Putnam, 1970), pp. 133, 357, and ch. 4; Alan S. Milward, *War, Economy and Society 1939–1945* (Berkeley and Los Angeles: University of California Press, 1977), pp. 63–74, 271–275; Mercedes Rosebery, *This Day's Madness* (New York: Macmillan, 1944), p. xii.
14. John R. Deane, *The Strange Alliance* (New York: Viking, 1947), pp. 92–95; Robert Huhn Jones, *The Roads to Russia* (Norman: University of Oklahoma Press, 1969), Appendix A. Additional information from Harvey DeWeerd.
15. Adam Ulam, *The Rivals: America and Russia Since World War II* (New York: Penguin, 1971), pp. 95 and 5. In essence, Stalin seems to have understood that in Great Power wars, as Paul Kennedy put it, "victory has always gone to the side with the greatest material resources." Paul Kennedy, *The Rise and Fall of the Great Powers* (New York: Random House, 1987), p. 439. Nor is it likely that this attitude has changed much: "The men in the Kremlin are absorbed by questions of America's political, military, and economic power, and awed by its technological capacity." Shevchenko, *Breaking with Moscow*, p. 278. Edward Luttwak, while concerned that the Soviets might actually be tempted to start a war, notes the existence of "the great deterrent": the Soviet fear that "more aggressive expansion will precipitate an Alliance-wide mobilization response which could quickly erode the Kremlin's power position down to a 'natural' level—a level, that is, where the power of the Soviet Union begins to approximate its economic capacity." Edward N. Luttwak, *The Grand Strategy of the Soviet Union* (New York: St. Martin's, 1983), p. 116. Or Khrushchev: "those 'rotten' capitalists keep coming up with things which make our jaws drop in surprise." Khrushchev, *The Last Testament*, p. 532.

1949, "if there is any single factor today which would deter a nation seeking
world domination, it would be the great industrial capacity of this country
rather than its armed strength."[16] Or, as Hugh Thomas has concluded, "if
the atomic bomb had not existed, Stalin would still have feared the success
of the U.S. wartime economy."[17]

After a successful attack on Western Europe the Soviets would have been
in a position similar to that of Japan after Pearl Harbor: they might have
gains aplenty, but they would have no way to stop the United States (and
its major unapproachable allies, Canada and Japan) from eventually gearing
up for, and then launching, a war of attrition.[18] All they could hope for, like
the Japanese in 1941, would be that their victories would cause the Americans
to lose their fighting spirit. But if Japan's Asian and Pacific gains in 1941
propelled the United States into war, it is to be expected that the United
States would find a Soviet military takeover of an area of far greater importance to it—Western Europe—to be alarming in the extreme. Not only would
the U.S. be outraged at the American casualties in such an attack and at the
loss of an important geographic area, but it would very likely conclude (as
many Americans did conclude in the late 1940s even without a Soviet attack)
that an eventual attack on the United States itself was inevitable. Any Hitler-
style protests by the Soviets that they had no desire for further territorial
gains would not be very credible. Thus, even assuming that the Soviets had
the conventional capability easily to take over Western Europe, the credible
American threat of a huge, continent-hopping war of attrition from south,
west, and east could be a highly effective deterrent—all this even in the
absence of nuclear weapons.[19]

---

16. Samuel P. Huntington, *The Common Defense* (New York: Columbia University Press, 1961),
p. 46. See also Walter Millis, ed., *The Forrestal Diaries* (New York: Viking, 1951), pp. 350–351.
17. Thomas, *Armed Truce*, p. 548.
18. Interestingly, one of Hitler's "terrible anxieties" before Pearl Harbor was that the Americans
and Japanese might work out a rapprochement, uniting against Germany. Norman Rich, *Hitler's
War Aims: Ideology, the Nazi State, and the Course of Expansion* (New York: Norton, 1973), pp. 228,
231, 246.
19. In fact, in some respects the memory of World War II was *more* horrible than the prospect
of atomic war in the immediate postwar period. Western proponents of an atomic preventive
war against the USSR were countered by General Omar Bradley and others who argued that
this policy would be "folly" because the Soviets would still be able to respond with an offensive
against Western Europe which would lead to something *really* bad: an "extended, bloody and
horrible" struggle like World War II. Richard Ned Lebow, "Windows of Opportunity: Do States
Jump Through Them?" *International Security*, Vol. 9, No. 1 (Summer 1984), p. 170. See also
Hanson W. Baldwin, "War of Prevention," *New York Times*, September 1, 1950, p. 4. The
conventional threat might be more credible than atomic retaliation even in an era of U.S. nuclear

Second, there is the important issue of the Korean War. Despite the vast American superiority in atomic weapons in 1950, Stalin was willing to order, approve, or at least acquiesce in an outright attack by a communist state on a non-communist one, and it must be assumed that he would have done so at least as readily had nuclear weapons not existed. The American response was essentially the result of the lessons learned from the experiences of the 1930s: comparing this to similar incursions in Manchuria, Ethiopia, and Czechoslovakia (and partly also to previous Soviet incursions into neighboring states in East Europe and the Baltic area), Western leaders resolved that such provocations must be nipped in the bud. If they were allowed to succeed, they would only encourage more aggression in more important locales later. Consequently it seems likely that the Korean War would have occurred in much the same way had nuclear weapons not existed.

For the Soviets the lessons of the Korean War must have enhanced those of World War II: once again the United States was caught surprised and under-armed, once again it rushed hastily into action, once again it soon applied itself in a forceful way to combat—in this case for an area that it had previously declared to be of only peripheral concern. If the Korean War was a limited probe of Western resolve, it seems the Soviets drew the lessons the Truman administration intended. Unlike Germany, Japan, and Italy in the 1930s, they were tempted to try no more such probes: there have been no Koreas since Korea. It seems likely that this valuable result would have come about regardless of the existence of nuclear weapons, and it suggests that the Korean War helped to delimit vividly the methods the Soviet Union would be allowed to use to pursue its policy.[20]

---

monopoly because an American retaliatory threat to level Moscow with nuclear weapons could be countered with a threat to make a newly-captured Western city like Paris into a latter-day Lidice. And of course once both sides had nuclear capabilities, the weapons could be mutually deterring, as has often been noted in debates about deterrence in Europe. Moreover, the Soviets could use nuclear weapons to destroy a landing force, as American officials noted in 1950; see Robert Jervis, "The Impact of the Korean War on the Cold War," *Journal of Conflict Resolution*, Vol. 24, No. 4 (December 1980), p. 578.

20. Soviet military intervention in Afghanistan in 1979 was an effort to prop up a faltering pro-Soviet regime. As such it was not like Korea, but more like American escalation in Vietnam in 1965 or like the Soviet interventions in Hungary in 1956 or Czechoslovakia in 1968. For discussions of the importance of the Korean War in shaping Western perspectives on the Cold War, see John Lewis Gaddis, "Was the Truman Doctrine a Real Turning Point?" *Foreign Affairs*, Vol. 52, No. 2 (January 1974), pp. 386–401; Jervis, "The Impact of the Korean War"; and Ernest R. May, "The Cold War" in Joseph S. Nye, Jr., ed., *The Making of America's Soviet Policy* (New Haven: Yale University Press, 1984), pp. 209–230.

It is conceivable that the USSR, in carrying out its ideological commitment to revolution, might have been tempted to try step-by-step, Hitler-style military probes if it felt these would be reasonably cheap and free of risk. The policy of containment, of course, carrying with it the threat of escalation, was designed precisely to counter such probes. If the USSR ever had any thoughts about launching such military probes, the credible Western threat that these probes could escalate (demonstrated most clearly in Korea, but also during such episodes as the Berlin crisis of 1948–49) would be significantly deterring—whether or not nuclear weapons waited at the end of the escalator ride.

The Korean experience may have posed a somewhat similar lesson for the United States. In 1950, amid talk of "rolling back" Communism and sometimes even of liberating China, American-led forces invaded North Korea. This venture led to a costly and demoralizing, if limited, war with China, and resulted in a considerable reduction in American enthusiasm for such maneuvers. Had the United States been successful in taking over North Korea, there might well have been noisy calls for similar ventures elsewhere—though, of course, these calls might well have gone unheeded by the leadership.

It is not at all clear that the United States and the Soviet Union needed the Korean War to become viscerally convinced that escalation was dangerously easy. But the war probably reinforced that belief for both of them and, to the degree that it did, Korea was an important stabilizing event.

COLD WAR AND CRISIS

If nuclear weapons have been unnecessary to prevent world war, they also do not seem to have crucially affected other important developments, including development of the Cold War and patterns of alliance, as well as behavior of the superpowers in crisis.

THE COLD WAR AND ALLIANCE PATTERNS. The Cold War was an outgrowth of various disagreements between the U.S. and the USSR over ideology and over the destinies of Eastern, Central and Southern Europe. The American reaction to the perceived Soviet threat in this period mainly reflects prenuclear thinking, especially the lessons of Munich.

For example, the formation of the North Atlantic Treaty Organization and the division of the world into alliances centered on Washington and Moscow suggests that the participants were chiefly influenced by the experience of World War II. If the major determinant of these alliance patterns had been nuclear strategy, one might expect the United States and, to a lesser extent, the Soviet Union, to be only lukewarm members, for in general the alliances include nations that contribute little to nuclear defense but possess the capability unilaterally of getting the core powers into trouble.[21] And one would expect the small countries in each alliance to tie themselves as tightly as possible to the core nuclear power in order to have maximum protection from its nuclear weapons. However, the weakening of the alliances which has taken place over the last three decades has not come from the major partners.

The structure of the alliances therefore better reflects political and ideological bipolarity than sound nuclear strategy. As military economist (and later Defense Secretary) James Schlesinger has noted, the Western alliance "was based on some rather obsolescent notions regarding the strength and importance of the European nations and the direct contribution that they could make to the security of the United States. There was a striking failure to recognize the revolutionary impact that nuclear forces would make with respect to the earlier beliefs regarding European defense."[22] Or, as Warner Schilling has observed, American policies in Europe were "essentially prenuclear in their rationale. The advent of nuclear weapons had not influenced the American determination to restore the European balance of power. It was, in fact, an objective which the United States would have had an even greater incentive to undertake if the fission bomb had not been developed."[23]

CRISIS BEHAVIOR. Because of the harrowing image of nuclear war, it is sometimes argued, the United States and the Soviet Union have been notably more restrained than they might otherwise have been, and thus crises that might have escalated to dangerous levels have been resolved safely at low levels.[24]

---

21. As Michael May observes, "the existence of nuclear weapons, especially of nuclear weapons that can survive attack, help[s] make empires and client states questionable sources of security." "The U.S.-Soviet Approach to Nuclear Weapons," *International Security*, Vol. 9, No. 4 (Spring 1985), p. 150.
22. James Schlesinger, *On Relating Non-technical Elements to Systems Studies*, P-3545 (Santa Monica, Cal.: RAND, February 1967), p. 6.
23. Warner R. Schilling, "The H-Bomb Decision," *Political Science Quarterly*, Vol. 76, No. 1 (March 1961), p. 26. See also Waltz: "Nuclear weapons did not cause the condition of bipolarity. . . . Had the atom never been split, [the U.S. and the USSR] would far surpass others in military strength, and each would remain the greatest threat and source of potential damage to the other." Waltz, *Theory of International Politics*, pp. 180–181.
24. John Lewis Gaddis, *The Long Peace* (New York: Oxford University Press, 1987), pp. 229–232; Gilpin, *War and Change in World Politics*, p. 218; Coit D. Blacker, *Reluctant Warriors* (New York: Freeman, 1987), p. 46.

There is, of course, no definitive way to refute this notion since we are unable to run the events of the last forty years over, this time without nuclear weapons. And it is certainly the case that decision-makers are well aware of the horrors of nuclear war and cannot be expected to ignore the possibility that a crisis could lead to such devastation.

However, this idea—that it is the fear of nuclear war that has kept behavior restrained—looks far less convincing when its underlying assumption is directly confronted: that the major powers would have allowed their various crises to escalate if all they had to fear at the end of the escalatory ladder was something like a repetition of World War II. Whatever the rhetoric in these crises, it is difficult to see why the unaugmented horror of repeating World War II, combined with considerable comfort with the status quo, wouldn't have been enough to inspire restraint.

Once again, escalation is the key: what deters is the belief that escalation to something intolerable will occur, not so much what the details of the ultimate unbearable punishment are believed to be. Where the belief that the conflict will escalate is absent, nuclear countries *have* been militarily challenged with war—as in Korea, Vietnam, Afghanistan, Algeria, and the Falklands.[25]

To be clear: None of this is meant to deny that the sheer horror of nuclear war is impressive and mind-concentratingly dramatic, particularly in the speed with which it could bring about massive destruction. Nor is it meant to deny that decision-makers, both in times of crisis and otherwise, are fully conscious of how horribly destructive a nuclear war could be. It is simply to stress that the sheer horror of repeating World War II is not all that much *less* impressive or dramatic, and that powers essentially satisfied with the status quo will strive to avoid anything that they feel could lead to *either* calamity. World War II did not cause total destruction in the world, but it did utterly annihilate the three national regimes that brought it about. It is probably quite a bit more terrifying to think about a jump from the 50th floor

---

25. On this point, see also Evan Luard: "There is little evidence in history that the existence of supremely destructive weapons alone is capable of deterring war. If the development of bacteriological weapons, poison gas, nerve gases and other chemical armaments did not deter war before 1939, it is not easy to see why nuclear weapons should do so now." Evan Luard, *War in International Society* (New Haven: Yale University Press, 1987), p. 396. For further discussion of this issue and of the belief in many quarters after 1918 that the next war might well destroy the human race, see John Mueller, *Retreat from Doomsday: The Obsolescence of Major War* (New York: Basic Books, forthcoming in 1989).

than about a jump from the 5th floor, but anyone who finds life even minimally satisfying is extremely unlikely to do either.

Did the existence of nuclear weapons keep the Korean conflict restrained? As noted, the communist venture there seems to have been a limited probe—though somewhat more adventurous than usual and one that got out of hand with the massive American and Chinese involvement. As such, there was no particular reason—or meaningful military opportunity—for the Soviets to escalate the war further. In justifying *their* restraint, the Americans continually stressed the danger of escalating to a war with the Soviet Union—something of major concern whether or not the Soviets possessed nuclear weapons.

Nor is it clear that the existence of nuclear weapons has vitally influenced other events. For example, President Harry Truman was of the opinion that his nuclear threat drove the Soviets out of Iran in 1946, and President Dwight Eisenhower, that his nuclear threat drove the Chinese into productive discussions at the end of the Korean War in 1953. McGeorge Bundy's reassessment of these events suggests that neither threat was very well communicated and that, in any event, other occurrences—the maneuverings of the Iranian government in the one case and the death of Stalin in the other—were more important in determining the outcome.[26] But even if we assume the threats *were* important, it is not clear why the threat had to be peculiarly *nuclear*—a threat to commit destruction on the order of World War II would also have been notably unpleasant and dramatic.

Much the same could be said about other instances in which there was a real or implied threat that nuclear weapons might be brought into play: the Taiwan Straits crises of 1954–55 and 1958, the Berlin blockade of 1948–49, the Soviet-Chinese confrontation of 1969, the Six-day War in 1967, the Yom Kippur War of 1973, Cold War disagreements over Lebanon in 1958, Berlin in 1958 and 1961, offensive weapons in Cuba in 1962. All were resolved, or allowed to dissipate, at rather low rungs on the escalatory ladder. While the horror of a possible nuclear war was doubtless clear to the participants, it is certainly not apparent that they would have been much more casual about

---

26. McGeorge Bundy, "The Unimpressive Record of Atomic Diplomacy," in Gwyn Prins, ed., *The Nuclear Crisis Reader* (New York: Vintage, 1984), p. 44–47. For the argument that Truman never made a threat, see James A. Thorpe, "Truman's Ultimatum to Stalin in the Azerbaijan Crisis: The Making of a Myth," *Journal of Politics*, Vol. 40, No. 1 (February 1978), pp. 188–195. See also Gaddis, *Long Peace*, pp. 124–129; and Richard K. Betts, *Nuclear Blackmail and Nuclear Balance* (Washington, D.C.: Brookings, 1987), pp. 42–47.

escalation if the worst they had to visualize was a repetition of World War II.[27]

Of course nuclear weapons add new elements to international politics: new pieces for the players to move around the board (missiles in and out of Cuba, for example), new terrors to contemplate. But in counter to the remark attributed to Albert Einstein that nuclear weapons have changed everything except our way of thinking, it might be suggested that nuclear weapons have changed little except our way of talking, gesturing, and spending money.

Stability

The argument thus far leads to the conclusion that stability is overdetermined—that the postwar situation contains redundant sources of stability. The United States and the Soviet Union have been essentially satisfied with their lot and, fearing escalation to another costly war, have been quite willing to keep their conflicts limited. Nuclear weapons may well have enhanced this stability—they are certainly dramatic reminders of how horrible a big war could be. But it seems highly unlikely that, in their absence, the leaders of the major powers would be so unimaginative as to need such reminding. Wars are not begun out of casual caprice or idle fancy, but because one country or another decides that it can profit from (not simply win) the war—

---

27. Interestingly, even in the great "nuclear" crisis over Cuba in 1962, Khrushchev seems to have been affected as much by his memories of World War I and II as by the prospect of thermonuclear destruction. See Graham T. Allison, *Essence of Decision* (Boston: Little, Brown, 1971), p. 221. Morton Halperin argues that "the primary military factors in resolving the crisis" in the Taiwan Straits in 1954–55 were "American air and naval superiority in the area," not nuclear threats. Morton H. Halperin, *Nuclear Fallacy* (Cambridge, Mass.: Ballinger, 1987), p. 30. Alexander George and Richard Smoke note that blockade crises in Berlin in 1948–49 and in the Taiwan Straits in 1958 were broken by the ability of the Americans to find a technological solution to them. Alexander L. George and Richard Smoke, *Deterrence in American Foreign Policy* (New York: Columbia University Press, 1974), p. 383. Betts suggests that even if the American alert in 1973 was influential with the Soviets (which is quite questionable), it is "hard to argue against the proposition that the conventional force elements in it were sufficient, the nuclear component superfluous." Betts, *Nuclear Blackmail*, p. 129. As for the Soviet-Chinese confrontation, Roy Medvedev notes Soviet fears of "war with a poorly armed but extremely populous and fanatical China." Roy Medvedev, *China and the Superpowers* (New York: Basil Blackwood, 1986), p. 50; see also Shevchenko, *Breaking with Moscow*, pp. 165–166. On these issues, see also A.F.K. Organski and Jacek Kugler, *The War Ledger* (Chicago: University of Chicago Press, 1980), pp. 147–180.

the combination of risk, gain, and cost appears preferable to peace.[28] Even allowing considerably for stupidity, ineptness, miscalculation, and self-deception in these considerations, it does not appear that a large war, nuclear or otherwise, has been remotely in the interest of the essentially-contented, risk-averse, escalation-anticipating powers that have dominated world affairs since 1945.

It is *conceivable* of course that the leadership of a major power could be seized by a lucky, clever, risk-acceptant, aggressive fanatic like Hitler; or that an unprecedentedly monumental crisis could break out in an area, like Central Europe, that is of vital importance to both sides; or that a major power could be compelled toward war because it is consumed by desperate fears that it is on the verge of catastrophically losing the arms race. It is not obvious that any of these circumstances would necessarily escalate to a major war, but the existence of nuclear weapons probably does make such an escalation less likely; thus there are imaginable circumstances under which it might be useful to have nuclear weapons around. In the world we've actually lived in, however, those extreme conditions haven't come about, and they haven't ever really even been in the cards. This enhancement of stability is, therefore, purely theoretical—extra insurance against unlikely calamity.

CRISIS STABILITY, GENERAL STABILITY, AND DETERRENCE

In further assessing these issues, it seems useful to distinguish crisis stability from a more general form of stability. Much of the literature on defense policy has concentrated on crisis stability, the notion that it is desirable for both sides in a crisis to be so secure that each is able to wait out a surprise attack fully confident that it would be able to respond with a punishing counterattack. In an ideal world, because of its fear of punishing retaliation, neither side would have an incentive to start a war no matter how large or

---

28. Thus the notion that there is a special danger if one side or the other has a "war-winning" capability seems misguided; there would be danger only if a war-*profiting* capability exists. As will be discussed below, the second does not necessarily follow from the first. As Lebow argues: "History indicates that wars rarely start because one side believes it has a military advantage. Rather, they occur when leaders become convinced that force is necessary to achieve important goals." Lebow, "Windows of Opportunity," p. 149. Michael Howard says: "Wars begin with conscious and reasoned decisions based on the calculation, made by *both* parties, that they can achieve more by going to war than by remaining at peace." Michael Howard, "The Causes of Wars," *Wilson Quarterly*, Vol. 8, No. 3 (Summer 1984), p. 103. See also Luard, *War in International Society*, chs. 5, 6; Jervis, *The Illogic of American Nuclear Strategy*, ch. 6; Bruce Bueno de Mesquita, *The War Trap* (New Haven: Yale University Press, 1981), ch. 2; Gaddis, *Long Peace*, p. 232; Geoffrey Blainey, *The Causes of War* (New York: Free Press, 1973), chs. 9, 11.

desperate the disagreement, no matter how intense the crisis. Many have argued that crisis stability is "delicate": easily upset by technological or economic shifts.[29]

There is a more general form of stability, on the other hand, that is concerned with balance derived from broader needs, desires, and concerns. It prevails when two powers, taking all potential benefits, costs, and risks into account, greatly prefer peace to war—in the extreme, even to a victorious war—whether crisis stability exists or not. For example, it can be said that general stability prevails in the relationship between the United States and Canada. The United States enjoys a massive military advantage over its northern neighbor since it could attack at any time with little concern about punishing military retaliation or about the possibility of losing the war (that is, it has a full "first strike capability"), yet the danger that the United States will attack Canada is nil. General stability prevails.

Although the deterrence literature is preoccupied with military considerations, the deterrence concept may be more useful if it is broadened to include non-military incentives and disincentives. For example, it seems meaningful to suggest that the United States is "deterred" from attacking Canada, but not, obviously, by the Canadians' military might. If anyone in Washington currently were even to contemplate a war against Canada (a country, it might be noted, with which the United States has been at war in the past and where, not too long ago, many Americans felt their "manifest destiny" lay), the planner would doubtless be dissuaded by non-military factors. For example, the war would disrupt a beneficial economic relationship; the United States would have the task of occupying a vast new area with sullen and uncooperative inhabitants; the venture would produce political turmoil in the United States. Similar cases can be found in the Soviet sphere. Despite an overwhelming military superiority, the USSR has been far from anxious to attack such troublesome neighboring states as Poland and Romania. It seems likely that the vast majority of wars that never take place are caused by factors which have little to do with military considerations.[30]

---

29. The classic statement of this position is, of course, Albert Wohlstetter, "The Delicate Balance of Terror," *Foreign Affairs*, Vol. 27, No. 2 (January 1959), pp. 211–234. See also Glenn H. Snyder, *Deterrence and Defense* (Princeton: Princeton University Press, 1961), pp. 97–109.
30. Under this approach, if two nations are not at war, then it can be said that they are currently being deterred from attacking each other. That is, deterrence prevails when the expected utility for peace outweighs the expected utility for war. In this sense a deterrence relationship exists not only between the U.S. and the USSR, but also between the U.S. and Canada, and between Bolivia and Pakistan. The usefulness of this approach is that it is not limited exclusively to

Now, it would obviously be too much to suggest that general stability prevails in the relationship between the U.S. and the USSR to the same degree that it does in the relationship between the U.S. and Canada. Yet, as suggested, it is remarkably difficult to imagine how the prevailing stability between the two big powers could be upset to the point that a war could come about: both have a strong interest in peace, and none whatever in major war. Thus many of the concerns about the stability of the military balance, while valid in their own terms, miss a broader point. In the current debate over the Strategic Defense Initiative, for example, it may be the case that the proposed system will make things less stable or more stable, but this change may not alter the picture very much. It is like the millionaire who loses or gains $1000; it is true that he is now poorer or richer than before, but the important point is that his overall status has not changed very much.

If a kind of overwhelming general stability really prevails, it may well be that the concerns about arms and the arms race are substantially overdone. That is, the often-exquisite numerology of the nuclear arms race has probably had little to do with the important dynamics of the Cold War era, most of which have taken place at militarily subtle levels such as subversion, guerrilla war, local uprising, civil war, and diplomatic posturing. As Benjamin Lambeth has observed, "it is perhaps one of the notable ironies of the nuclear age that while both Washington and Moscow have often lauded superiority as a military force-posture goal, neither has ever behaved as though it really believed superiority significantly mattered in the resolution of international conflicts."[31] In their extensive study of the use of threat and force since World War II, Blechman and Kaplan conclude that, "especially noteworthy is the

---

military considerations, and that it comfortably incorporates such important deterring phenomena as satisfaction with the status quo, as well as the restraining effects of economics, morality, good will, inertia, international opinion, national self-image, etc. Thus it can deal with that multitude of cases in which a militarily superior power lives peacefully alongside an inferior one. The approach can also deal with those cases where a nation has become so distressed by the status quo that it starts a war even when it has little hope of military success. For a more formal presentation, see John Mueller, *Approaches to Measurement in International Relations: A Non-Evangelical Survey* (New York: Appleton-Century-Crofts, 1969), pp. 284–286; and Mueller, *Retreat from Doomsday*. See also note 28 above; and Richard Rosecrance, *Strategic Deterrence Reconsidered*, Adelphi Paper No. 116 (London: International Institute for Strategic Studies, Spring 1975), pp. 33–37; Lebow, "Windows of Opportunity," pp. 181–186; and Richard Ned Lebow, "Deterrence Reconsidered," *Survival*, Vol. 27, No. 1 (January/February 1985), pp. 20–28.
31. Benjamin S. Lambeth, "Deterrence in the MIRV Era," *World Politics*, Vol. 24, No. 2 (January 1972), p. 234 n.

fact that our data do not support a hypothesis that the strategic weapons balance between the United States and the USSR influences outcomes."[32]

A special danger of weapons imbalance is often cited: a dominant country might be emboldened to use its superiority for purposes of pressure and intimidation. But unless its satisfaction with the status quo falls enormously and unless its opponent's ability to respond becomes very low as well, the superior power is unlikely to push its advantage very far, and certainly not anywhere near the point of major war. Even if the war could be kept non-nuclear and even if that power had a high probability of winning, the gains are likely to be far too low, the costs far too high.[33]

STABILITY: TRENDS

Curiously, in the last twenty-five years crisis stability between the U.S. and the USSR has probably gotten worse while general stability has probably improved.

With the development of highly accurate multiple warhead missiles, there is a danger that one side might be able to obtain a first-strike counterforce capability, at least against the other side's land-based missiles and bombers, or that it might become able to cripple the other side's command and control operations. At the same time, however, it almost seems—to put it very baldly—that the two major powers have forgotten how to get into a war. Although on occasion they still remember how to say nasty things about each other, there hasn't been a true, bone-crunching confrontational crisis

---

32. Barry M. Blechman and Stephen S. Kaplan, *Force Without War* (Washington, D.C.: Brookings, 1978), p. 132. See also Jacek Kugler, "Terror Without Deterrence: Reassessing the Role of Nuclear Weapons," *Journal of Conflict Resolution*, Vol. 28, No. 3 (September 1984), pp. 470–506.
33. Betts finds "scant reason to assume . . . that the nuclear balance would be a prime consideration in a decision about whether to resort to nuclear coercion." Betts, *Nuclear Blackmail*, pp. 218–219. Hannes Adomeit sees "no congruence between increased Soviet military capabilities and enhanced Soviet propensities to take risks." Adomeit, "Soviet Crisis Prevention and Management," *Orbis*, Vol. 30, No. 1 (Spring 1986), pp. 42–43. For an able refutation of the popular notion that it was American nuclear superiority that determined the Soviet backdown in the Cuban missile crisis, see Lambeth, "Deterrence in the MIRV Era," pp. 230–234. Marc Trachtenberg has presented an interesting, if "somewhat speculative" case that Soviet behavior was influenced by Soviet strategic inferiority. His argument is largely based on the observation that the Soviets never went on an official alert, and he suggests this arose from fear of provoking an American preemptive strike. But the essential hopelessness of the tactical situation and the general fear of escalation to what Lambeth (quoting Thomas Schelling) calls "just plain war" would also seem to explain this behavior. Marc Trachtenberg, "Nuclear Weapons and the Cuban Missile Crisis," *International Security*, Vol. 10, No. 1 (Summer 1985), pp. 156–163.

for over a quarter-century. Furthermore, as Bernard Brodie notes, even the last crisis, over missiles in Cuba, was "remarkably different . . . from any previous one in history" in its "unprecedented candor, direct personal contact, and at the same time mutual respect between the chief actors."[34] Events since then that seem to have had some warlike potential, such as the military alert that attended the Yom Kippur War of 1973, fizzled while still at extremely low levels.[35] In fact, as McGeorge Bundy has noted, since 1962 "there has been no open nuclear threat by any government."[36]

It seems reasonable, though perhaps risky, to extrapolate from this trend and to suggest that, whatever happens with crisis stability in the future, general stability is here to stay for quite some time. That is, major war—war among developed countries—seems so unlikely that it may well be appropriate to consider it obsolescent. Perhaps World War II was indeed the war to end war—at least war of that scale and type.

THE HOLLANDIZATION PHENOMENON. There are, of course, other possibilities. Contentment with the status quo could diminish in time and, whatever the traumas of World War II, its lessons could eventually wear off, especially as postwar generations come to power. Somehow the fear of escalation could diminish, and small, cheap wars among major countries could again seem

---

34. Bernard Brodie, *War and Politics* (New York: Macmillan, 1973), p. 426. See also Nye, "Nuclear Learning." Betts concludes that no other Cold War crisis ever "really brought the superpowers close to war." Betts, *Nuclear Blackmail*, p. 132. At the time war did seem close, but Khrushchev's memoirs seem to support Shevchenko's conclusion that from the start the Soviets "were preoccupied almost exclusively with how to extricate themselves from the situation with minimum loss of face and prestige." Shevchenko, *Breaking with Moscow*, p. 118. New evidence demonstrates that President Kennedy was ready to end the crisis even on terms that were substantially embarrassing to the U.S., and thus it appears that, as David Welch and James Blight have concluded, "the odds that the *Americans* would have gone to war were next to zero." David A. Welch and James G. Blight, "The Eleventh Hour of the Cuban Missile Crisis," *International Security*, Vol. 12, No. 3 (Winter 1987/88), p. 27.

35. See Scott D. Sagan, "Nuclear Alerts and Crisis Management," *International Society*, Vol. 9, No. 4 (Spring 1985), pp. 127–129; and Bundy, "The Unimpressive Record of Atomic Diplomacy," pp. 50–51.

36. Bundy, "The Unimpressive Record of Atomic Diplomacy," p. 50. On the improved atmosphere after 1962, see also Brodie, *War and Politics*, p. 431. On the declining use of nuclear threats, see also Blechman and Kaplan, *Force Without War*, pp. 47–49. Public opinion data also reflect relaxed tensions: see John Mueller, "Changes in American Public Attitudes Toward International Involvement," in Ellen Stern, ed., *The Limits of Military Intervention* (Beverly Hills, Cal.: Sage, 1977), pp. 325–328; and Rob Paarlberg, "Forgetting About The Unthinkable," *Foreign Policy*, No. 10 (Spring 1973), pp. 132–140. On the flurry of concern about war in the early 1980s in response to the debate over missiles in Western Europe and to some of Ronald Reagan's rhetoric, see Josef Joffe, "Peace and Populism: Why the European Anti-Nuclear Movement Failed," *International Security*, Vol. 11, No. 4 (Spring 1987), pp. 3–40.

viable and attractive. We could get so used to living with the bomb that its use becomes almost casual. Some sort of conventional war could reemerge as a viable possibility under nuclear stalemate.[37] But, as noted, the trends seem to be substantially in the opposite direction: discontent does not seem to be on the rise, and visceral hostility seems to be on the decline.

Moreover, it might be instructive to look at some broad historical patterns. For centuries now, various countries, once warlike and militaristic, have been quietly dropping out of the war system to pursue neutrality and, insofar as they are allowed to do so, perpetual peace. Their existence tends to go unremarked because chroniclers have preferred to concentrate on the antics of the "Great Powers." "The story of international politics," observes Waltz, "is written in terms of the great powers of an era."[38] But it may be instructive for the story to include Holland, a country which chose in 1713, centuries before the invention of nuclear weapons, to abandon the fabled "struggle for power," or Sweden, which followed Holland's lead in 1721.[39] Spain and Denmark dropped out too, as did Switzerland, a country which fought its last battle in 1798 and has shown a "curious indifference" to "political or territorial aggrandizement," as one historian has put it.[40]

While Holland's bandwagon was quietly gathering riders, an organized movement in opposition to war was arising. The first significant peace organizations in Western history emerged in the wake of the Napoleonic Wars in 1815, and during the next century they sought to promote the idea that war was immoral, repugnant, inefficient, uncivilized, and futile. They also proposed remedies like disarmament, arbitration, and international law and organization, and began to give out prizes for prominent peaceable behavior.

---

37. See Edward N. Luttwak, "An Emerging Postnuclear Era?" *Washington Quarterly*, Vol. 11, No. 1 (Winter 1988), pp. 5–15.
38. Waltz, *Theory of International Politics*, p. 72.
39. They did not drop out of the great power war system merely because they were outclassed economically. With substantial effort Holland and Sweden could have struggled to stay on for a while in the ranks of the great powers, at least enough to rival the less great among them, had they so desired. In 1710 when they were dropping out, each had armies bigger than those of Britain or the Hapsburg Empire and far larger than those of Prussia. See Kennedy, *The Rise and Fall of the Great Powers*, p. 99. The sacrifices would probably have been proportionately no more than those the Soviet Union has borne in its costly effort to keep up militarily with the United States, or those Israel has borne in seeking to pursue its destiny in the Middle East, or those North Vietnam bore to expand its control into South Vietnam, or those Japan paid to enter the great power club early in this century.
40. Lynn Montross, quoted in Jack S. Levy, *War in the Modern Great Power System* (Lexington: University Press of Kentucky), p. 45. On this issue, see also Brodie, *War and Politics*, p. 314.

They had become a noticeable force by 1914 but, as one of their number, Norman Angell, has recalled, they tended to be dismissed as "cranks and faddists . . . who go about in sandals and long beards, live on nuts."[41] Their problem was that most people living within the great power system were inclined to disagree with their central premise: that war was bad. As Michael Howard has observed, "before 1914 war was almost universally considered an acceptable, perhaps an inevitable and for many people a desirable way of settling international differences."[42] One could easily find many prominent thinkers declaring that war was progressive, beneficial, and necessary; or that war was a thrilling test of manhood and a means of moral purification and spiritual enlargement, a promoter of such virtues as orderliness, cleanliness, and personal valor.[43]

It should be remembered that a most powerful effect of World War I on the countries that fought it was to replace that sort of thinking with a revulsion against wars and with an overwhelming, and so far permanent, if not wholly successful, desire to prevent similar wars from taking place. Suddenly after World War I, peace advocates were a decided majority. As A.A. Milne put it in 1935, "in 1913, with a few exceptions we all thought war was a natural and fine thing to happen, so long as we were well prepared for it and had no doubt about coming out the victor. Now, with a few exceptions, we have lost our illusions; we are agreed that war is neither natural nor fine, and that the victor suffers from it equally with the vanquished."[44]

For the few who didn't get the point, the lesson was substantially reinforced by World War II. In fact, it almost seems that after World War I the only person left in Europe who was willing to risk another total war was Adolf Hitler. He had a vision of expansion and carried it out with ruthless

---

41. Norman Angell, *After All* (New York: Farrar, Straus, and Young, 1951), p. 147. See also A.C.F. Beales, *The History of Peace* (New York: Dial, 1931); Roger Chickering, *Imperial Germany and a World Without War* (Princeton: Princeton University Press, 1975).
42. Howard, "The Causes of Wars," p. 92.
43. See the discussion in Richard Rosecrance, *Action and Reaction in World Politics* (Boston: Little, Brown, 1963), p. 163; Luard, *War in International Society*, pp. 354–365; Van Evera, "Why Cooperation Failed in 1914," pp. 89–92; Roland N. Stromberg, *Redemption by War* (Lawrence: Regents Press of Kansas, 1982); Mueller, *Retreat from Doomsday*. For a sustained and impassioned argument against such thinking, see Norman Angell, *The Great Illusion* (London: Heinemann, 1909).
44. A.A. Milne, *Peace With Honour* (New York: Dutton, 1935), pp. 9–10. See also Paul Fussell, *The Great War and Modern Memory* (New York: Oxford University Press, 1975); I.F. Clarke, *Voices Prophesying War 1763–1984* (London: Oxford University Press, 1966), ch. 5.

and single-minded determination. Many Germans found his vision appealing, but unlike the situation in 1914 where enthusiasm for war was common, Hitler found enormous reluctance at all levels within Germany to use war to quest after the vision. As Gerhard Weinberg has concluded, "whether any other German leader would indeed have taken the plunge is surely doubtful, and the very warnings Hitler received from some of his generals can only have reinforced his belief in his personal role as the one man able, willing, and even eager to lead Germany and drag the world into war."[45] Hitler himself told his generals in 1939 "in all modesty" that he alone possessed the nerve required to lead Germany to fulfill what he took to be its mission.[46] In Italy, Benito Mussolini also sought war, but only a small one, and he had to deceive his own generals to get that.[47] Only in Japan, barely touched by World War I, was the willingness to risk major war fairly widespread.[48]

Since 1945 the major nuclear powers have stayed out of war with each other, but equally interesting is the fact that warfare of *all* sorts seems to have lost its appeal within the developed world. With only minor and fleeting exceptions (the Falklands War of 1982, the Soviet invasions of Hungary and Czechoslovakia), there have been no wars among the 48 wealthiest countries in all that time.[49] Never before have so many well-armed countries spent so much time not using their arms against each other. This phenomenon surely

---

45. Gerhard Weinberg, *The Foreign Policy of Hitler's Germany* (Chicago: University of Chicago Press, 1982), p. 664.
46. Knox, "Conquest, Foreign and Domestic," p. 54.
47. MacGregor Knox, *Mussolini Unleashed 1939–1941* (Cambridge: Cambridge University Press, 1982), ch. 3.
48. On these issues, see note 9 above; Mueller, *Retreat from Doomsday*; Brodie, *War and Politics*, ch. 6; George H. Quester, *Offense and Defense in the International System* (New York: Wiley, 1977), p. 137; Luard, *War in International Society*, p. 365; the arguments by Michael Doyle about the widespread growth of liberal anti-war ideology over the last two centuries in Doyle, "Kant, Liberal Legacies, and Foreign Affairs," *Philosophy and Public Affairs*, Vol. 12, Nos. 3 and 4 (Summer and Fall, 1983); and Doyle, "Liberalism and World Politics," *American Political Science Review*, Vol. 80, No. 4 (December 1986), pp. 1151–1169. See also R.J. Rummel, "Libertarian Propositions on Violence Within and Between Nations," *Journal of Conflict Resolution*, Vol. 29, No. 3 (September 1985), pp. 419–455.
49. For a similar observation, see Luard, *War in International Society*, pp. 395–396. Wealth is per capita, calculated using 1975 data when Iraq and Iran were at their financial peak (ranking 49th and 50th). If 1985 data are used instead, more countries would be on the warless list. Countries like Monaco that have no independent foreign policy are not included in the count. The British-Argentine war over the Falklands cost less than 1000 battle deaths and thus doesn't count as a war by some standards—nor does the bloodless Soviet-Czechoslovak "war" of 1968. The Soviet invasion of Hungary was in some sense requested by the ruling politicians in Hungary and for that reason is also sometimes not classified as an international war. On these issues, see Melvin Small and J. David Singer, *Resort to Arms* (Beverly Hills, Cal.: Sage, 1982), pp. 55, 305.

goes well beyond the issue of nuclear weapons; they have probably been no more crucial to the non-war between, say, Spain and Italy than they have been to the near-war between Greece and Turkey or to the small war between Britain and Argentina.

Consider the remarkable cases of France and Germany, important countries which spent decades and centuries either fighting each other or planning to do so. For this age-old antagonism, World War II was indeed the war to end war. Like Greece and Turkey, they certainly retained the creativity to discover a motivation for war if they had really wanted to, even under an over-arching superpower balance; yet they have now lived side-by-side for nearly half a century, perhaps with some bitterness and recrimination, but without even a glimmer of war fever. They have become Hollandized with respect to one another. The case of Japan is also instructive: another formerly aggressive major power seems now to have embraced fully the virtues and profits of peace.[50]

The existence of nuclear weapons also does not help very much to explain the complete absence since 1945 of civil war in the developed world (with the possible exception of the 1944–49 Greek civil war, which could be viewed instead as an unsettled carryover of World War II). The sporadic violence in Northern Ireland or the Basque region of Spain has not really been sustained enough to be considered civil war, nor have the spurts of terrorism carried out by tiny bands of self-styled revolutionaries elsewhere in Western Europe. Except for the case of Hungary in 1956, Europeans under Soviet domination have not (so far) resorted to major violence, no matter how desperate their disaffection.[51] By one count, 43 civil wars (in addition to scores of anti-colonial wars, bloody coups, communal conflicts, and wars between regions of a country) were begun between 1945 and 1980; none of these civil wars occurred in the developed world.[52]

---

50. See also Richard Rosecrance, *The Rise of the Trading State* (New York: Basic Books, 1986).
51. Even as dedicated a foe of the Soviet regime as Alexandr Solzhenitsyn has said, "I have never advocated physical general revolution. That would entail such destruction of our people's life as would not merit the victory obtained." Quoted in Stephen F. Cohen, *Rethinking the Soviet Experience* (New York: Oxford, 1985), p. 214.
52. Small and Singer, *Resort to Arms*, chs. 12, 13. So traumatic was the Spanish Civil War of the 1930s that it inspired great restraint in the population when that country moved from dictatorship to democracy two generations later. See Edward Schumacher, "Spain Insists U.S. Cut Troops There," *New York Times*, November 20, 1985. The American Civil War seems to have had a similar effect on the United States; although General W.T. Sherman's postwar hope that there would be no war in America for "fifty years to come" proved pessimistic. Lloyd Lewis, *Sherman* (New York: Harcourt, Brace, 1958), p. 585. For the suggestion that internal stability has contrib-

As a form of activity, war in the developed world may be following once-fashionable dueling into obsolescence: the perceived wisdom, value, and efficacy of war may have moved gradually toward terminal disrepute. Where war was often casually seen as beneficial, virtuous, progressive, and glorious, or at least as necessary or inevitable, the conviction has now become widespread that war in the developed world would be intolerably costly, unwise, futile, and debased.

World war could be catastrophic, of course, and so it is sensible to be concerned about it even if its probability is microscopic. Yet general stability seems so firm and the trends so comforting that the concerns of Schell and others about our eventual "final coma" seem substantially overwrought. By themselves, weapons do not start wars, and if nuclear weapons haven't had much difference, reducing their numbers probably won't either.[53] They may be menacing, but a major war seems so spectacularly unlikely that for those who seek to save lives it may make sense to spend less time worrying about something so improbable as major war and more time dealing with limited conventional wars outside the developed world, where war still can seem cheap and tempting, where romantic notions about holy war and purifying revolution still persist and sometimes prevail, and where developed countries sometimes still fight carefully delimited surrogate wars. Wars of that sort are still far from obsolete and have killed millions since 1945.

Over a quarter century ago, strategist Herman Kahn declared that "it is most unlikely that the world can live with an uncontrolled arms race lasting for several decades." He expressed his "firm belief" that "we are not going to reach the year 2000—and maybe not even the year 1965—without a cataclysm" unless we have "much better mechanisms than we have had for forward thinking."[54] Reflecting again on the cases of the United States and Canada, of Sweden and Denmark, of Holland, of Spain and Switzerland, of France and Germany, and of Japan, it might be suggested that there is a long-term solution to the arms competition between the United States and the Soviet Union, and that it doesn't have much to do with "mechanisms."

---

uted to international stability in the developed world, see Luard, *War in International Society*, pp. 398–399.
53. See also the discussion in Jervis, *The Illogic of American Nuclear Strategy*, pp. 158, 195 n. 17.
54. Herman Kahn, *On Thermonuclear War* (Princeton: Princeton University Press, 1961), pp. 574, x, 576.

Should political tensions decline, as to a considerable degree they have since the classic Cold War era of 1945–63, it may be that the arms race will gradually dissipate.[55] And it seems possible that this condition might be brought about not principally by ingenious agreements over arms control, but by atrophy stemming from a dawning realization that, since preparations for major war are essentially irrelevant, they are profoundly foolish.

---

55. In 1817 there was an arms control agreement between the United States and British Canada about warships on the Great Lakes, but conflict, hostility, and an arms competition continued between the two neighbors for 45 years after that. By the 1870s, however, the claims and controversies had resolved themselves or been settled, and mutual disarmament gradually took place without further formal agreement. Peace happened mainly because both sides became accustomed to, and generally pleased with, the status quo. In later decades there was substantial rearmament on the Great Lakes, by agreement, because both sides found them convenient areas for naval training. See C.P. Stacey, *The Undefended Border: The Myth and the Reality* (Ottawa: Canadian Historical Association, 1955).

The Political Effects of Nuclear Weapons

A Comment

Robert Jervis

Perhaps the most striking characteristic of the postwar world is just that—it can be called "postwar" because the major powers have not fought each other since 1945. Such a lengthy period of peace among the most powerful states is unprecedented.[1] Almost as unusual is the caution with which each superpower has treated the other. Although we often model superpower relations as a game of chicken, in fact the U.S. and USSR have not behaved like reckless teenagers. Indeed, superpower crises are becoming at least as rare as wars were in the past. Unless one strains and counts 1973, we have gone over a quarter of a century without a severe crisis. Furthermore, in those that have occurred, each side has been willing to make concessions to avoid venturing too near the brink of war. Thus the more we see of the Cuban missile crisis, the more it appears as a compromise rather than an American victory. Kennedy was not willing to withhold all inducements and push the Russians as hard as he could if this required using force or even continuing the volatile confrontation.[2]

It has been common to attribute these effects to the existence of nuclear weapons. Because neither side could successfully protect itself in an all-out war, no one could win—or, to use John Mueller's phrase, profit from it.[3] Of

The author would like to thank John Mueller for comments.

Robert Jervis is a Professor in the Department of Political Science and the Institute of War and Peace Studies, Columbia University. He is the author of the forthcoming Implications of the Nuclear Revolution.

---

1. Paul Schroeder, "Does Murphy's Law Apply to History?" *Wilson Quarterly*, Vol. 9, No. 1 (New Year's 1985), p. 88; Joseph S. Nye, Jr., "The Long-Term Future of Nuclear Deterrence," in Roman Kolkowicz, *The Logic of Nuclear Terror* (Boston: Allen & Unwin, 1987), p. 234.
2. See the recent information in McGeorge Bundy, transcriber, and James G. Blight, ed., "October 27, 1962: Transcripts of the Meetings of the ExComm," *International Security*, Vol. 12, No. 3 (Winter 1987/88), pp. 30–92; and James G. Blight, Joseph S. Nye, Jr., and David A. Welch, "The Cuban Missile Crisis Revisited," *Foreign Affairs*, Vol. 66 (Fall 1987), pp. 178–179. Long before this evidence became available, Alexander George stressed Kennedy's moderation; see Alexander L. George, David K. Hall, and William E. Simons, *The Limits of Coercive Diplomacy: Laos, Cuba, Vietnam* (Boston: Little Brown, 1971), pp. 86–143.
3. "The Essential Irrelevance of Nuclear Weapons: Stability in the Postwar World," *International Security*, Vol. 13, No. 2 (Fall 1988) pp. 55–79. But as we will discuss below, it can be rational for states to fight even when profit is not expected.

International Security, Fall 1988 (Vol. 13, No. 2)
© 1988 by the President and Fellows of Harvard College and of the Massachusetts Institute of Technology.

course this does not mean that wars will not occur. It is rational to start a
war one does not expect to win (to be more technical, whose expected utility
is negative), if it is believed that the likely consequences of not fighting are
even worse.[4] War could also come through inadvertence, loss of contol, or
irrationality. But if decision-makers are "sensible,"[5] peace is the most likely
outcome. Furthermore, nuclear weapons can explain superpower caution:
when the cost of seeking excessive gains is an increased probability of total
destruction, moderation makes sense.

Some analysts have argued that these effects either have not occurred or
are not likely to be sustained in the future. Thus Fred Iklé is not alone in
asking whether nuclear deterrence can last out the century.[6] It is often
claimed that the threat of all-out retaliation is credible only as a response to
the other side's all-out attack: thus Robert McNamara agrees with more
conservative analysts whose views he usually does not share that the "sole
purpose" of strategic nuclear force "is to deter the other side's first use of its
strategic forces."[7] At best, then, nuclear weapons will keep the nuclear peace;
they will not prevent—and, indeed, may even facilitate—the use of lower
levels of violence.[8] It is then not surprising that some observers attribute
Soviet adventurism, particularly in Africa, to the Russians' ability to use the
nuclear stalemate as a shield behind which they can deploy pressure, military
aid, surrogate troops, and even their own forces in areas they had not
previously controlled. The moderation mentioned earlier seems, to some, to
be only one-sided. Indeed, American defense policy in the past decade has
been driven by the felt need to create limited nuclear options to deter Soviet
incursions that, while deeply menacing to our values, fall short of threatening
immediate destruction of the U.S.

---

4. Alternatively, to be even more technical, a decision-maker could expect to lose a war and at
the same time could see its expected utility as positive if the slight chance of victory was justified
by the size of the gains that victory would bring. But the analysis here requires only the simpler
formulation.
5. See the discussion in Patrick M. Morgan, *Deterrence: A Conceptual Analysis* (Beverly Hills, Cal.:
Sage, 1977), pp. 101–124.
6. Fred Iklé, "Can Nuclear Deterrence Last Out the Century?" *Foreign Affairs*, Vol. 51, No. 2
(January 1973), pp. 267–285.
7. Robert McNamara, "The Military Role of Nuclear Weapons," *Foreign Affairs*, Vol. 62, No. 4
(Fall 1983), p. 68. For his comments on how he came to this view, see his interview in Michael
Charlton, *From Deterrence to Defense* (Cambridge: Harvard University Press, 1987), p. 18.
8. See Glenn Snyder's discussion of the "stability-instability paradox," in "The Balance of Power
and the Balance of Terror," in Paul Seabury, ed., *The Balance of Power* (San Francisco: Chandler,
1965), pp. 184–201.

Furthermore, while nuclear weapons may have helped keep the peace between the U.S. and USSR, ominous possibilities for the future are hinted at by other states' experiences. Allies of nuclear-armed states have been attacked: Vietnam conquered Cambodia and China attacked Vietnam. Two nuclear powers have fought each other, albeit on a very small scale: Russia and China skirmished on their common border. A nonnuclear power has even threatened the heartland of a nuclear power: Syria nearly pushed Israel off the Golan Heights in 1973 and there was no reason for Israel to be confident that Syria was not trying to move into Israel proper. Some of those who do not expect the U.S. to face such a menace have predicted that continued reliance on the threat of mutual destruction "would lead eventually to the demoralization of the West. It is not possible indefinitely to tell democratic republics that their security depends on the mass extermination of civilians . . . without sooner or later producing pacifism and unilateral disarmament."[9]

John Mueller has posed a different kind of challenge to claims for a "nuclear revolution." He disputes, not the existence of a pattern of peace and stability, but the attributed cause. Nuclear weapons are "essentially irrelevant" to this effect; modernity and highly destructive nonnuclear weapons would have brought us pretty much to the same situation had it not been possible to split the atom.[10] Such intelligent revisionism makes us think about questions whose answers had seemed self-evident. But I think that, on closer inspection, the conventional wisdom turns out to be correct. Nevertheless, there is much force in Mueller's arguments, particularly in the importance of what he calls "general stability" and the reminder that the fact that nuclear war would be so disastrous does not mean that conventional wars would be cheap.

Mueller is certainly right that the atom does not have magical properties. There is nothing crucial about the fact that people, weapons, industry, and agriculture may be destroyed as a result of a particular kind of explosion,

9. Henry Kissinger, "After Reykjavik: Current East-West Negotiations," *The San Francisco Meeting of the Tri-Lateral Commission, March 1987* (New York: The Trilateral Commission, 1987), p. 4; see also ibid., p. 7, and his interview in Charlton, *From Deterrence to Defense*, p. 34.
10. Mueller, "The Essential Irrelevance." Waltz offers yet a third explanation for peace and stability—the bipolar nature of the international system, which, he argues, is not merely a product of nuclear weapons. See Kenneth Waltz, *Theory of International Politics* (Reading, Mass.: Addison-Wesley, 1979). But in a later publication he places more weight on the stabilizing effect of nuclear weapons: *The Spread of Nuclear Weapons: More May Be Better*, Adelphi Paper No. 171 (London: International Institute for Strategic Studies, 1981).

although fission and fusion do produce special by-products like fallout and electromagnetic pulse. What is important are the political effects that nuclear weapons produce, not the physics and chemistry of the explosion. We need to determine what these effects are, how they are produced, and whether modern conventional weapons would replicate them.

Political Effects of Nuclear Weapons

The existence of large nuclear stockpiles influences superpower politics from three directions. Two perspectives are familiar: First, the devastation of an all-out war would be unimaginably enormous. Second, neither side—nor, indeed, third parties—would be spared this devastation. As Bernard Brodie, Thomas Schelling, and many others have noted, what is significant about nuclear weapons is not "overkill" but "mutual kill."[11] That is, no country could win an all-out nuclear war, not only in the sense of coming out of the war better than it went in, but in the sense of being better off fighting than making the concessions needed to avoid the conflict. It should be noted that although many past wars, such as World War II for all the allies except the U.S. (and, perhaps, the USSR), would not pass the first test, they would pass the second. For example: although Britain and France did not improve their positions by fighting, they were better off than they would have been had the Nazis succeeded. Thus it made sense for them to fight even though, as they feared at the outset, they would not profit from the conflict. Furthermore, had the allies lost the war, the Germans—or at least the Nazis— would have won in a very meaningful sense, even if the cost had been extremely high. But "a nuclear war," as Reagan and Gorbachev affirmed in their joint statement after the November 1985 summit, "cannot be won and must never be fought."[12]

A third effect of nuclear weapons on superpower politics springs from the fact that the devastation could occur extremely quickly, within a matter of days or even hours. This is not to argue that a severe crisis or the limited use of force—even nuclear force—would inevitably trigger total destruction, but only that this is a possibility that cannot be dismissed. At any point, even in calm times, one side or the other could decide to launch an unpro-

---

11. Bernard Brodie, ed., *The Absolute Weapon: Atomic Power and World Order* (New York: Harcourt Brace, 1946); Thomas Schelling, *Arms and Influence* (New Haven: Yale University Press, 1966).
12. *New York Times*, November 22, 1985, p. A12.

voked all-out strike. More likely, a crisis could lead to limited uses of force which in turn, through a variety of mechanisms, could produce an all-out war. Even if neither side initially wanted this result, there is a significant, although impossible to quantify, possibility of quick and deadly escalation.

Mueller overstates the extent to which conventional explosives could substitute for nuclear ones in these characteristics of destructiveness, evenhandedness, and speed. One does not have to underestimate the horrors of previous wars to stress that the level of destruction we are now contemplating is much greater. Here, as in other areas, there comes a point at which a quantitative difference becomes a qualitative one. Charles De Gaulle put it eloquently: after a nuclear war, the "two sides would have neither powers, nor laws, nor cities, nor cultures, nor cradles, nor tombs."[13] While a total "nuclear winter" and the extermination of human life would not follow a nuclear war, the world-wide effects would be an order of magnitude greater than those of any previous war.[14] Mueller understates the differences in the scale of potential destruction: "World War II did not cause total destruction in the world, but it did utterly annihilate the three national regimes that brought it about. It is probably quite a bit more terrifying to think about a jump from the 50th floor than about a jump from the 5th floor, but anyone who finds life even minimally satisfying is extremely unlikely to do either."[15] The war did indeed destroy these national regimes, but it did not utterly destroy the country itself or even all the values the previous regimes supported. Most people in the Axis countries survived World War II; many went on to prosper. Their children, by and large, have done well. There is an enormous gulf between this outcome—even for the states that lost the war— and a nuclear holocaust. It is far from clear whether societies could ever be reconstituted after a nuclear war or whether economies would ever recover.[16] Furthermore, we should not neglect the impact of the prospect of destruction of culture, art, and national heritage: even a decision-maker who was willing

13. Speech of May 31, 1960, in Charles De Gaulle, *Discours Et Messages*, Vol. 3 (Paris: Plon, 1970), p. 218. I am grateful to McGeorge Bundy for the reference and translation.
14. Starley Thompson and Stephen Schneider, "Nuclear Winter Reappraised," *Foreign Affairs*, Vol. 64, No. 5 (Summer 1986), pp. 981–1005.
15. "The Essential Irrelevance," pp. 66–67.
16. For a discussion of economic recovery models, see Michael Kennedy and Kevin Lewis, "On Keeping Them Down: Or, Why Do Recovery Models Recover So Fast?" in Desmond Ball and Jeffrey Richelson, *Strategic Nuclear Targeting* (Ithaca: Cornell University Press, 1986), pp. 194–208.

to risk the lives of half his population might hesitate at the thought of destroying what has been treasured throughout history.

Mueller's argument just quoted is misleading on a second count as well: the countries that started World War II were destroyed, but the Allies were not. It was more than an accident but less than predetermined that the countries that were destroyed were those that sought to overturn the status quo; what is crucial in this context is that with conventional weapons at least one side can hope, if not expect, to profit from the war. Mueller is quite correct to argue that near-absolute levels of punishment are rarely required for deterrence, even when the conflict of interest between the two sides is great—i.e., when states believe that the gross gains (as contrasted with the net gains) from war would be quite high. The United States, after all, could have defeated North Vietnam. Similarly, as Mueller notes, the United States was deterred from trying to liberate East Europe even in the era of American nuclear monopoly.

But, again, one should not lose sight of the change in scale that nuclear explosives produce. In a nuclear war the "winner" might end up distinguishably less worse off than the "loser," but we should not make too much of this difference. Some have. As Harold Brown put it when he was Secretary of the Air Force, "if the Soviets thought they may be able to recover in some period of time while the U.S. would take three or four times as long, or would never recover, then the Soviets might not be deterred."[17] Similarly, one of the criteria that Secretary of Defense Melvin Laird held necessary for the essential equivalence of Soviet and American forces was: "preventing the Soviet Union from gaining the ability to cause considerably greater urban/ industrial destruction than the United States would in a nuclear war."[18] A secret White House memorandum in 1972 used a similar formulation when it defined "strategic sufficiency" as the forces necessary "to ensure that the United States would emerge from a nuclear war in discernably better shape than the Soviet Union."[19]

---

17. U.S. Senate, Preparedness Investigating Subcommittee of the Committee on Armed Services, *Hearings on Status of U.S. Strategic Power*, 90th Cong., 2d sess., April 30, 1968 (Washington, D.C.: U.S. Government Printing Office, 1968), p. 186.
18. U.S. House of Representatives, Subcommittee on Department of Defense, *Appropriations for the FY 1973 Defense Budget and FY 1973–1977 Program*, 92nd Cong., 2d sess., February 22, 1972, p. 65.
19. Quoted in Gregg Herken, *Counsels of War* (New York: Knopf, 1985), p. 266. This conception leads to measuring the peacetime strategic balance and the projected balance during a hypothetical war by looking at which side has more capability (e.g., amount of megatonnage, number

But this view is a remarkably apolitical one. It does not relate the costs of the war to the objectives and ask whether the destruction would be so great that the "winner," as well as the loser, would regret having fought it. Mueller avoids this trap, but does not sufficiently consider the possibility that, absent nuclear explosives, the kinds of analyses quoted above would in fact be appropriate. Even very high levels of destruction can rationally be compatible with a focus on who will come out ahead in an armed conflict. A state strongly motivated to change the status quo could believe that the advantages of domination were sufficiently great to justify enormous blood-letting. For example, the Russians may feel that World War II was worth the cost not only when compared with being conquered by Hitler, but also when compared with the enormous increase in Soviet prestige, influence, and relative power.

Furthermore, without nuclear weapons, states almost surely would devote great energies to seeking ways of reducing the costs of victory. The two world wars were enormously destructive because they lasted so long. Modern technology, especially when combined with nationalism and with alliances that can bring others to the rescue of a defeated state, makes it likely that wars will last long: defense is generally more efficacious than offense. But this is not automatically true; conventional wars are not necessarily wars of attrition, as the successes of Germany in 1939–40 and Israel in 1967 remind us. Blitzkrieg can work under special circumstances, and when these are believed to apply, conventional deterrence will no longer be strong.[20] Over an extended period of time, one side or the other could on occasion come to believe that a quick victory was possible. Indeed, for many years most American officials have believed not only that the Soviets could win a conventional war in Europe or the Persian Gulf, but that they could do so at low cost. Were the United States to be pushed off the continent, the considerations Mueller gives might well lead it to make peace rather than pay the

---

of warheads, numbers of warheads capable of destroying hardened targets). I have discussed the problems with this approach in "Cognition and Political Behavior," in Richard Lau and David Sears, eds., *Political Cognition* (Hillsdale, N.J.: Earlbaum, 1986), pp. 330–333; and "The Drunkard's Search" (unpublished ms.).

20. John J. Mearsheimer, *Conventional Deterrence* (Ithaca: Cornell University Press, 1983). It should be noted, however, that even a quick and militarily decisive war might not bring the fruits of victory. Modern societies may be even harder to conquer than are modern governments. A high degree of civilian cooperation is required if the victor is to reach many goals. We should not assume it will be forthcoming. See Gene Sharp, *Making Europe Unconquerable* (Cambridge, Mass.: Ballinger, 1985).

price of re-fighting World War II. Thus, extended deterrence could be more difficult without nuclear weapons. Of course, in their absence, NATO might build up a larger army and better defenses, but each side would continually explore new weapons and tactics that might permit a successful attack. At worst, such efforts would succeed. At best, they would heighten arms competition, national anxiety, and international tension. If both sides were certain that any new conventional war would last for years, the chances of war would be slight. But we should not be too quick to assume that conventional war with modern societies and weapons is synonymous with wars of attrition.

The length of the war is important in a related way as well. The fact that a war of attrition is slow makes a difference. It is true, as George Quester notes, that for some purposes all that matters is the amount of costs and pain the state has to bear, not the length of time over which it is spread.[21] But a conventional war would have to last a long time to do an enormous amount of damage; and it would not *necessarily* last a long time. Either side can open negotiations or make concessions during the war if the expected costs of continued fighting seem intolerable. Obviously, a timely termination is not guaranteed—the fitful attempts at negotiation during World War II and the stronger attempts during World War I were not fruitful. But the possibility of ending the war before the costs become excessive is never foreclosed. Of course, states can believe that a nuclear war would be prolonged, with relatively little damage being done each day, thus permitting intra-war bargaining. But no one can overlook the possibility that at any point the war could escalate to all-out destruction. Unlike the past, neither side could be certain that there would be a prolonged period for negotiation and intimidation. This blocks another path which statesmen in nonnuclear eras could see as a route to meaningful victory.

Furthermore, the possibility that escalation could occur even though neither side desires this outcome—what Schelling calls "the threat that leaves something to chance"[22]—induces caution in crises as well. The fact that sharp

---

21. George Quester, "Crisis and the Unexpected," *Journal of Interdisciplinary History*, Vol. 18, No. 3 (Spring 1988), pp. 701–703.
22. Thomas Schelling, *The Strategy of Conflict* (Cambridge: Harvard University Press, 1960), pp. 187–203; Schelling, *Arms and Influence*, pp. 92–125. Also see Jervis, *The Illogic of American Nuclear Strategy* (Ithaca: Cornell University Press, 1984), ch. 5; Jervis, "'MAD is a Fact, not a Policy': Getting the Arguments Straight," in Jervis, *Implications of the Nuclear Revolution* (Ithaca: Cornell University Press, forthcoming); and Robert Powell, "The Theoretical Foundations of Strategic Nuclear Deterrence," *Political Science Quarterly*, Vol. 100, No. 1 (Spring 1985), pp. 75–96.

confrontations can get out of control, leading to the eventual destruction of both sides, means that states will trigger them only when the incentives to do so are extremely high. Of course, crises in the conventional era also could escalate, but the possibility of quick and total destruction means that the risk, while struggling near the brink, of falling into the abyss is greater and harder to control than it was in the past. Fears of this type dominated the bargaining during the Cuban missile crisis: Kennedy's worry was "based on fear, not of Khrushchev's intention, but of human error, of something going terribly wrong down the line." Thus when Kennedy was told that a U-2 had made a navigational error and was flying over Russia, he commented: "There is always some so-and-so who doesn't get the word."[23] The knowledge of these dangers—which does not seem lacking on the Soviet side as well[24]—is a powerful force for caution.

Empirical findings on deterrence failure in the nuclear era confirm this argument. George and Smoke show that: "The initiator's belief that the risks of his action are calculable and that the unacceptable risks of it can be controlled and avoided is, with very few exceptions, a necessary (though not sufficient) condition for a decision to challenge deterrence."[25] The possibility of rapid escalation obviously does not make such beliefs impossible, but it does discourage them. The chance of escalation means that local military advantage cannot be confidently and safely employed to drive the defender out of areas in which its interests are deeply involved. Were status quo states able to threaten only a war of attrition, extended deterrence would be more difficult.

General Stability

But is very much deterrence needed? Is either superpower strongly driven to try to change the status quo? On these points I agree with much of Mueller's argument—the likely gains from war are now relatively low, thus

23. Arthur M. Schlesinger, Jr., *Robert Kennedy and His Times* (Boston: Houghton Mifflin, 1978), p. 529; quoted in Roger Hilsman, *To Move A Nation* (Garden City, N.Y.: Doubleday, 1964), p. 221.
24. See Benjamin Lambeth, "Uncertainties for the Soviet War Planner," *International Security*, Vol. 7, No. 3 (Winter 1982/83), pp. 139–66.
25. Alexander L. George and Richard Smoke, *Deterrence in American Foreign Policy* (New York: Columbia University Press, 1974), p. 529.

producing what he calls general stability.[26] The set of transformations that go under the heading of "modernization" have not only increased the costs of war, but have created alternative paths to established goals, and, more profoundly, have altered values in ways that make peace more likely. Our focus on deterrence and, even more narrowly, on matters military has led to a distorted view of international behavior. In a parallel manner, it has adversely affected policy prescriptions. We have not paid sufficient attention to the incentives states feel to change the status quo, or to the need to use inducements and reassurance, as well as threats and deterrence.[27]

States that are strongly motivated to challenge the status quo may try to do so even if the military prospects are bleak and the chances of destruction considerable. Not only can rational calculation lead such states to challenge the status quo, but people who believe that a situation is intolerable feel strong psychological pressures to conclude that it can be changed.[28] Thus nuclear weapons by themselves—and even mutual second-strike capability— might not be sufficient to produce peace. Contrary to Waltz's argument, proliferation among strongly dissatisfied countries would not necessarily recapitulate the Soviet-American pattern of stability.[29]

The crucial questions in this context are the strength of the Soviet motivation to change the status quo and the effect of American policy on Soviet drives and calculations. Indeed, differences of opinion on these matters explain much of the debate over the application of deterrence strategies toward the USSR.[30] Most of this dispute is beyond our scope here. Two points, however, are not. I think Mueller is correct to stress that not only Nazi Germany, but Hitler himself, was exceptional in the willingness to chance an enormously destructive war in order to try to dominate the world.

---

26. Mueller, "Essential Irrelevance," pp. 69–70; also see Waltz, *Theory of International Politics*, p. 190.
27. For discussions of this topic, see George, Hall, and Simons, *Limits of Coercive Diplomacy*; George and Smoke, *Deterrence in American Foreign Policy*; Richard Ned Lebow, *Between Peace and War* (Baltimore: Johns Hopkins University Press, 1981); Robert Jervis, "Deterrence Theory Revisited," *World Politics*, Vol. 31, No. 2 (January 1979), pp. 289–324; Jervis, Lebow, and Janice Gross Stein, *Psychology and Deterrence* (Baltimore: Johns Hopkins University Press, 1985); David Baldwin, "The Power of Positive Sanctions," *World Politics*, Vol. 24, No. 1 (October 1971), pp. 19–38; and Janice Gross Stein, "Deterrence and Reassurance," in Philip E. Tetlock, et al., eds., *Behavior, Society, and Nuclear War*, Vol. 2 (New York: Oxford University Press, forthcoming, 1989).
28. George and Smoke, *Deterrence in American Foreign Policy*; Lebow, *Between Peace and War*; Jervis, Lebow, and Stein, *Psychology and Deterrence*.
29. Waltz, *Spread of Nuclear Weapons*.
30. See Robert Jervis, *Perception and Misperception in International Politics* (Princeton: Princeton University Press, 1976), ch. 3.

While of course such a leader could recur, we should not let either our theories or our policies be dominated by this possibility.

A second point is one of disagreement: even if Mueller is correct to believe that the Soviet Union is basically a satisfied power—and I share his conclusion—war is still possible. Wars have broken out in the past between countries whose primary goal was to preserve the status quo. States' conceptions of what is necessary for their security often clash with one another. Because one state may be able to increase its security only by making others less secure, the premise that both sides are basically satisfied with the status quo does not lead to the conclusion that the relations between them will be peaceful and stable. But here too nuclear weapons may help. As long as all-out war means mutual devastation, it cannot be seen as a path to security. The general question of how nuclear weapons make mutual security more feasible than it often was in the past is too large a topic to engage here.[31] But I can at least suggest that they permit the superpowers to adopt military doctrines and bargaining tactics that make it possible for them to take advantage of their shared interest in preserving the status quo. Winston Churchill was right: "Safety [may] be the sturdy child of terror."

---

31. I have discussed it in the concluding chapter of *Implications of the Nuclear Revolution*.

A Nuclear Golden Age?

The Balance Before Parity

Richard K. Betts

$\mathbf{D}$oes nuclear superiority matter? More specifically, does an edge in the balance of forces offer a coercive advantage in confrontations near the brink of war? These questions have fueled spirited debate among professional strategists and policymakers in recent years. The bulk of rigorous analysis, however, has focused on the easier part of the question—the requirements for deterring a Soviet first strike on the United States. The more difficult part (estimating whether or how some margin of numerical or operational advantage in the nuclear balance confers political leverage) has more often been dealt with by obiter dicta or fast and loose assertions based on slippery evidence.

Whatever debate there is now about the political utility of nuclear superiority, the United States frequently leaned on it when it had it. NATO doctrine for defense against Soviet conventional attack rested on a nuclear counter-strike, and this solution was grasped in disputes over other areas as well. In numerous crises in the first half of the postwar era (over Berlin, Korea, the Taiwan Straits, the Middle East, and Cuba), American Presidents signalled intentions to resort to nuclear forces to counter potential conventional military initiatives by the Soviet Union or China. The signals included public rhetoric, purposeful leaks, communications through diplomatic intermediaries, and demonstrative alerts of the Strategic Air Command (SAC). Because much of the evidence is ambiguous, the precise nature, significance, or consequences of these initiatives are widely disputed—some believe the threats were serious and decisive, others see them as phony or negligible in impact. But a careful look at the record permits a reasonable argument that there was an impressive tendency of U.S. leaders to back their hands in crisis-maneuvering with threats of nuclear first use.[1] Was this nuclear reliance

This article is drawn from part of chapter 4 in *Nuclear Blackmail and Nuclear Balance* (Washington, D.C.: Brookings, 1987). For criticism of an earlier draft the author is especially grateful to Bruce Blair and Marc Trachtenberg and also to Robert Art, Barry Blechman, John Gaddis, Raymond Garthoff, Colin Gray, John Mearsheimer, Scott Sagan, and Jack Snyder.

Richard K. Betts is a senior fellow at the Brookings Institution and Visiting Professor of Government at Harvard University.

1. For detailed studies of over a dozen incidents, see chapters 2 and 3 in my forthcoming book. Where not otherwise stated, assumptions in this article are based on data and analysis in the

wise? If so, are these cases of only historical interest because the balance of nuclear power will never again permit U.S. confidence in such options?

Some observers would rationalize the past threats as reasonable tactics even if it could not have made sense to execute them, on the grounds that factors other than the balance of power guaranteed the credibility of American resolve and the adversaries would never risk calling a bluff. This article focuses on the more prevalent view that declaratory policy should not diverge far from action policy,[2] that leaders should be loath to belly up to the brink of war if they are bluffing, and that the credibility of a threat ought to rest on the plausibility of following through at acceptable cost. None see that possibility now, given nuclear parity and awesome Soviet retaliatory capability. But did the nuclear balance ever really afford that option?

The significance of U.S. superiority in the first two decades after 1945 is accepted by many on both sides of the more recent strategic debate. Some doves admit that superiority may have accorded the United States an advantage in the early years, but they focus on the point that its passing is irrevocable and invalidates any relevance of the past to the future. Some hawks, on the other hand, lament the passing of a golden age when little stood in the path of American sway,[3] a time when General Buck Turgidson in *Dr. Strangelove* could advise the President to mount an all-out attack on the USSR with the breezy qualification, "I'm not saying we wouldn't get our hair mussed, *but* . . . ." It is common to hear analysts refer to the period before 1957 (when Moscow deployed long-range bombers and demonstrated ICBM capability) as one of American invulnerability, and the period up to the mid-1960s as one of only middling vulnerability. In reality, the situation in the two decades after 1945 was never as rosy as those nostalgic for it think, because there was never a time when leaders were confident that the United States could wage nuclear war successfully—that is, parry and defeat a Soviet attack in Europe—while restricting damage of the West to "acceptable" levels.

---

book. A few points in the present article appeared in germinal form in "Elusive Equivalence," in Samuel P. Huntington, ed., *The Strategic Imperative* (Cambridge, Mass.: Ballinger, 1982), pp. 107–108, 114–115.

2. This distinction was advanced by Paul Nitze in one of the early criticisms of Eisenhower's massive retaliation policy: "Atoms, Strategy and Policy," *Foreign Affairs*, Vol. 34, No. 2 (January 1956), pp. 187–188.

3. See for example Henry A. Kissinger, "NATO: The Next Thirty Years," *Survival*, Vol. 21, No. 6 (November/December 1979), p. 266.

During the brief period of nuclear monopoly, U.S. forces lacked what would later be called "assured destruction" capability. Fission weapons were too few and too low in explosive power. SAC could have inflicted great destruction on the USSR, but there was grave doubt that atomic strikes could prevent the Soviet army from rolling to the English channel and the Pyrenees. As doubt about that passed by the early 1950s, so did the West's nuclear immunity. Even if Soviet capability against the continental United States was low, it was appreciable against the prospective bone of contention: Western Europe. Even a modest number of weapons could have devastated Britain, preventing use of the island as a base from which to move back to the continent à la 1944.[4] With more weapons, France, West Germany, and other countries could be gravely damaged. In terms of cold logic, and as Soviet strategists might have seen the issue, it would avail Washington little to fight over a prize that would have been rendered radioactive rubble. Leaving the "Hostage Europe" problem aside, what is less often recognized today is that U.S. leaders in the early period also lacked confidence that significant Soviet nuclear retaliation against the American homeland could be prevented.

If these points discredit hawkish nostalgia, they also shake some doves' categorical inferences about the irrelevance of past cases to the future. In earlier crises, *Washington leaned on the crutch of nuclear threats despite belief in significant American vulnerability to nuclear attack.* This inclination declined as the vulnerability grew, but it did not disappear, even after full parity arrived.

My argument focuses on assessments of U.S. vulnerability in the alleged golden age. Perhaps because estimates of the 1950s never reached the point of what specialists have come to see as "assured destruction," some have assumed, looking back, that they were not very inhibiting. But it is important to remember a few points about the concept of assured destruction embedded in the currency of strategic discourse by Robert McNamara's stipulated criteria (20–25 percent of population and 50 percent of industry). First, the numbers were arbitrary, selected in part because they corresponded with the point of diminishing returns from increases in U.S. capabilities. Second, they were *conservative* estimates of what would deter the *Soviets*, not necessarily what should frighten American leaders who were assumed to be less ruthless

4. Mark Edward Matthews, "The Bomb and Korea: a Reexamination of the United States' Nuclear Restraint in the Korean War 1950–1953," senior honor thesis, Harvard College, March 1981, p. 36.

and insensitive to domestic losses. And third, considering what *should* have given American Presidents pause, few ever assumed that a level of destruction of the United States that was lower by some magnitude would be an "acceptable" price to pay in war. "Unacceptable" damage is a subjective judgment, but it might best be measured relative to the stakes (anything grossly disproportionate to the territories disputed in the crises) or absolutely (say, tens of millions of fatalities). Because the domino theory prevalent in U.S. conceptions of containment inflated the significance of conflicts over small territories, American leaders might conceivably not have felt that they faced unacceptable damage in the former sense, but they did in the latter terms as early as the mid-1950s.

The exemplary estimates discussed below vary. Two distinctions should be borne in mind. First, we know better *now* that some of the early estimates were probably excessive because, with the partial exception of some CIA contributions, they tended to give insufficient allowance for the severe operational deficiencies and underdeveloped character of Soviet intercontinental capabilities. But what is better appreciated in retrospect is no excuse for assuming that what *might* have been a golden age of only modest vulnerability was believed to be such at the time, when crisis decisions were made. Second, some of the estimates cited (or the information available about them) do not give a clear indication of the assumed scenario behind them—whether the first strike was Soviet or American, or with or without warning. For judging the logic of U.S. first-use threats, Soviet second-strike capability is what matters. Later in the article we can see why, at the times of the crises discussed, a U.S. first-strike plan *under plausible circumstances* would not have pushed the assessments down to an acceptable level.

From Monopoly to Superiority

By reasonable estimates, the Soviet Union would have been unable to do devastating damage to the United States before at least the mid-1950s. Leaders contemplating war, however, ought to be reluctant to rely on best estimates. In terms of *cautious* estimates, Moscow had a finite deterrent before the end of the Korean War.

The Soviets' TU-4 bomber (a copy of the B-29) was revealed in 1947, and in September an Air Policy Board briefing noted that a large proportion of U.S. fuel storage, aircraft and plutonium production, and iron ore transshipment facilities were sited near borders (hence vulnerable to Soviet attack, while "critical targets" in the USSR lay further inland, harder to reach). The following year the Joint Intelligence Committee estimated that 200 TU-4s were deployed.[5] In 1949, the Joint Chiefs of Staff (JCS) said that the number could be 415 by mid-1950 and 1,200 by mid-1952. Without refueling, the assessment claimed, those bombers could only reach the northwestern United States if they were to return to the USSR, but could "reach every important industrial, urban and governmental control center in the United States on a one-way mission basis."[6] One-way missions could hardly have been excluded for anything as epochal as nuclear war, or for a Soviet military establishment as ruthless as believed by Americans. Even through the 1950s, it was widely assumed that many *U.S.* bombers would not be able to return in event of war.

These judgments of course did not imply impressive Soviet first-strike capability. The TU-4 force was rickety. The JCS noted Soviet operational inhibitions (lack of crew training and proper equipment, and vulnerability to interceptors). These technical uncertainties were recognized as overwhelming constraints on Soviet options. The United States had, however, virtually no air defense or early warning capability.[7] In the year following the first Soviet nuclear test, nevertheless, NSC-68 said, "The Soviet Union now has aircraft able to deliver the atomic bomb," and reported intelligence estimates that the Russians would have 10–20 bombs by mid-1950, 200 by mid-1954, and accuracy on target comparable to that of the U.S. being "40–60 percent of bombs sortied." This was the basis for NSC-68's identification of 1954 as the year of maximum danger, "for the delivery of 100 atomic bombs on targets in the United States would seriously damage this country."[8]

The report qualified the estimate by stipulating Soviet surprise attack against "no more effective opposition than we now have programmed."[9] By

---

5. Harry R. Borowski, *A Hollow Threat* (Westport, Conn.: Greenwood Press, 1982), pp. 99–100; and JIC 380/2, cited in Joseph T. Jockel, "The United States and Canadian Efforts at Continental Air Defense, 1945–1957," Ph.D. dissertation, Johns Hopkins University, 1978, p. 18.
6. JCS 2801/1 quoted in Jack H. Nunn, *The Soviet First Strike Threat: The U.S. Perspective* (New York: Praeger, 1982), p. 95.
7. Ibid., p. 96.
8. NSC-68, in U.S. Department of State, *Foreign Relations of the United States: 1950* (Washington, D.C.: U.S. Government Printing Office, 1977), Vol. 1, p. 251; series hereinafter noted as "FRUS."
9. Ibid., p. 266. Judging from similar language, NSC-68 apparently drew on the CIA's "Estimate of the Effects of the Soviet Possession of the Atomic Bomb Upon the Security of the United States and Upon the Probabilities of Direct Soviet Military Action," ORE 91–49, April 6, 1950, pp. 1, 3, 6 (Carrolton Press collection). The State Department, Army, Navy, and Air Force representatives dissented vigorously from the paper's benign estimate of Soviet intent, but did not challenge the estimate of capabilities.

late 1950, an assessment by the Weapons System Evaluation Group (WSEG) warned that deficiencies in the hastily inaugurated "Lashup" air defense system made it possible that *all* Soviet bombers might penetrate to targets.[10] With defense programming liberated by the Korean War, air defense did improve, but did not outpace Soviet offensive capability. (Truman did not even authorize building a radar net that would provide 3–6 hours tactical warning until December 1952.)[11] Soviet detonation of a hydrogen bomb before the 1954 year of maximum danger also represented destructive capability beyond that envisioned in the estimate of 100 fission bombs on target as the level at which damage would be "serious."

Other estimates in 1949 cited modest numbers of bombs as a major danger (if taken in isolation they would seem more alarming than if one assumed realistically that a countervalue first strike would be nonsensical). An Army Intelligence briefing to the NSC indicated that just eighteen weapons on nine critical targets would "wipe out one-third of U.S. steel and iron production, cripple governmental operations in Washington, and hamper and delay mobilization and retaliatory efforts,"[12] and the Air Force argued that delivery of 50 bombs could prevent effective mobilization for the defense of Europe.[13]

The 1951 MacArthur hearings included secret testimony deleted from the public record which indicated that the Soviets already had the capability to deliver great nuclear damage against U.S. cities.[14] In 1952, although national intelligence estimates cited only 50 bombs and 800 TU-4s in the Soviet inventory at the time, CIA Scientific Intelligence Reports were saying that Soviet technology had advanced to the point that "military requirements rather than technical limitations" would determine the stockpile.[15]

In January 1953, as Eisenhower was about to become President, several studies pointed to mounting vulnerability. The secretaries of State and Defense reported that since mid-1952, "probably 65–85% of the atomic bombs

---

10. Jockel, "United States and Canadian Efforts," p. 114.
11. David Alan Rosenberg, "The Origins of Overkill," *International Security*, Vol. 7, No. 4 (Spring 1983), p. 31.
12. Steven L. Rearden, *History of the Office of the Secretary of Defense* (Washington, D.C.: Historical Office, OSD, 1984), Vol. 1, p. 525.
13. Jockel, "United States and Canadian Efforts," p. 95.
14. John Edward Wiltz, "The MacArthur Inquiry, 1951," in Arthur M. Schlesinger, Jr. and Roger Bruns, eds., *Congress Investigates* (New York: Chelsea House/R.R. Bowker, 1975), Vol. 5, p. 3633.
15. NSC 135/1 Annex, "NSC Staff Study on Reappraisal of United States Objectives and Strategy for National Security," August 22, 1952, in *FRUS 1952–54*, Vol. 2, Part 1, p. 105; JCS 2101/75, NIE 64, and NIE 64–66, cited in Rosenberg, "Origins of Overkill," p. 23; CIA reports quoted in Nunn, *Soviet First Strike Threat*, p. 93.

launched by the USSR could be delivered on target in the United States," U.S. civil defense "is only 10% to 15% effective at the present time," and current programs would "no more than double this effectiveness by the end of 1954."[16] NSC-141 estimated that by 1955 Moscow would have 300 bombs and possibly as many as 600, and Secretary of State Acheson's Policy Planning Staff director, Paul Nitze, told him that the study "makes clear . . . that the net capability of the Soviet Union to injure the United States must *already* be measured in terms of many millions of casualties." A report by a prestigious panel of consultants also prefigured the essential criticism of the massive retaliation doctrine, even before it was adopted:

Two additional characteristics of present American policy increase the significance of the current commitment to immediate and massive retaliatory action. First is that . . . this is not simply one way of dealing with the Soviet Union in the event of war; it appears to be the only way now seriously considered. . . . Second, this intensive preoccupation with the development of a massive capacity for atomic attack is not matched by any corresponding concern for the defense of the U.S. in case of a similar attack on the part of the Soviet Union. Indeed both the public and the responsible military authorities appear to be persuaded that the important characteristic of the atomic bomb is that it can be used against the Soviet Union; much less attention has been given to the equally important fact that atomic bombs can be used by the Soviet Union against the United States. This situation results partly from . . . an apparent reluctance to face the simple but unpleasant fact that *the atomic bomb works both ways.*[17]

Undeterred, Eisenhower moved to implement the New Look.

From Superiority to Sufficiency

One rationale for optimism could have been that better defenses would negate the nascent Soviet offensive capability, but defensive improvements lagged behind Soviet offensive gains. The special consultants' panel reporting in January 1953 argued that under current conditions "we should be lucky

---

16. "Report by the Secretaries of State and Defense and the Director for Mutual Security on Reexamination of United States Programs for National Security," January 16, 1953, in *FRUS 1952–54*, Vol. 2, Part 1, p. 214.
17. Nitze quotation in "Memorandum by the Director of the Policy Planning Staff (Nitze) to the Secretary of State," January 12, 1953, in ibid., p. 203 (emphasis added). See also Jockel, "United States and Canadian Efforts," pp. 159–160. Report quotation in "Armaments and American Policy," Report by the Panel of Consultants of the Department of State to the Secretary of State, January 1953, in *FRUS 1953–54*, Vol. 2, Part 2, p. 1071 (emphasis added).

to get one in five" of attacking bombers. Subsequent studies and exercises demonstrated this to be optimistic. In mid-May (just before an NSC decision of May 20 on escalation in Korea if negotiations did not conclude), the NSC's Special Evaluation Subcommittee said that by mid-1953 U.S. air defenses could "'kill,' before bomb-release line, about 7 percent of the attacking bomber force"; in two years the percentage would rise to 27 percent, but the attacking force would be larger by then.[18] This estimate was similar to the one produced by Air Defense Command war games the year before, which predicted potential attrition of 23–37 percent by 1955.[19]

On July 11, 1953, Operation Tailwind simulated Soviet strikes on U.S. cities as a test. By SAC's account, the drill was a disaster: defenses "only scored one-half of a 'kill' before bomb release and only one 'kill' after bomb release."[20] NSC 159 concluded:

The present continental defense programs are not now adequate either to prevent, neutralize or seriously deter the military or covert attack which the USSR is capable of launching, nor are they adequate to insure the continuity of government, the continuity of production, or the protection of the industrial mobilization base and millions of citizens in our great and exposed metropolitan centers.[21]

In August 1953, the Soviets detonated a hydrogen bomb. On October 7, the NSC met to discuss the draft of NSC 162, which established the New Look massive retaliation doctrine. Three nuances of alternate wording bearing on the degree of damage a Soviet nuclear attack could exact were discussed—whether the adverb "very" should precede "serious damage"; whether the phrase "or shortly will have" should be deleted from the sentence stating "The USSR has or shortly will have sufficient bombs and air-

---

18. "Armaments and American Policy," in *FRUS 1953–54*, Vol. 2, Part 2, p. 1067; and "Report of the Special Evaluation Subcommittee of the National Security Council," in ibid., Part 1, pp. 337–338. See also DCI Dulles's comments (pp. 356–357), increasing the estimate of Soviet TU-4s in 1953 to 1,600, with production continuing at 35 per month, thus allowing "the Soviet Long-Range Air Force to expend planes relatively plentifully on one-way missions." On the May 20 NSC decision, see *FRUS 1952–54*, Vol. 15, Part 1, pp. 1065–1068; and Dwight D. Eisenhower, *The White House Years*, Vol. I: *Mandate for Change* (New York: Doubleday, 1963), p. 180.
19. Jockel, "United States and Canadian Efforts," p. 160.
20. "Memorandum Op-36C/jm, 18 March 1954," reprinted in *International Security*, Vol. 6, No. 3 (Winter 1981/1982), p. 24.
21. Cited in "Continental Defense," Draft Statement of Policy Proposed by the NSC, February 11, 1954, in *FRUS 1952–54*, Vol. 2, Part 1, p. 613.

craft" to inflict such damage; and whether the degree of damage should be characterized as "possibly crippling." In all cases the more severe wording was selected.[22] Although these may seem trivial distinctions today, it is notable that U.S. leaders were not premising stronger reliance on nuclear forces on optimistic notions of U.S. immunity even in the short term.

"Very serious damage," of course, did not mean the level of destruction taken for granted in recent decades. Depending on plausible variations in the scenario, however, it was still quite extensive. NSC-141 in January 1953 posited an attack with 100 bombs of 50 kilotons (recognizing that the Soviets could produce higher-yield bombs) and calculated total casualties of 22 million.[23] The May 15, 1953 NSC estimate assumed a Soviet surprise attack against U.S. bomber bases, with leftover assets targeted against population. This would destroy 24 percent of U.S. nuclear delivery capability at the time, and about 30 percent in 1955; cause "initial paralysis" of a third of total industrial production in 1953, and two-thirds two years later; and could "produce a maximum of 9 million casualties in 1953, and 12.5 million in 1955, one-half of which might result in deaths." The report suggested the probable casualties might be as low as half of the figures cited, and noted that failure of strategic surprise or improvement in tactical warning "would greatly reduce the damage indicated."[24] If the fate of Europe were at stake, this "very serious damage" might seem acceptable, but two points should have been grounds for considering possibly higher damage.

First, the above estimate assumed that almost half of Soviet bombs were expended against airbases. A principal scenario that has concerned strategists is that the Soviets would launch a conventional invasion while holding their nuclear force in reserve to deter U.S. escalation. With Soviet nuclear weapons programmed for retaliation rather than a first strike, it would have been reasonable to assume that a much larger fraction of them could be aimed at cities. When the study considered this as a secondary possibility, estimated casualties rose to 24 million in 1953 and 31 million in 1955. Second, the May 1953 NSC estimate assumed 300 Soviet bombs of about 80 kilotons by mid-1955. The hydrogen bomb which arrived on the scene just a few months later represented a markedly different threat. A year later, national intelli-

---

22. "Memorandum of Discussion at the 165th Meeting of the National Security Council, Wednesday, October 7, 1953," in ibid., p. 531.
23. Cited in Jockel, "United States and Canadian Efforts," p. 159.
24. "Report of the Special Evaluation Subcommittee," pp. 332–334.

gence estimates (NIEs) cited more than a fourfold increase in total Soviet megatonnage from the previous year's judgment (from 6 to 25 megatons).[25]

In a scenario in which most Soviet weapons were targeted on cities, even with *planned* improvements in air defense, and assuming some bombers failed to reach targets for other reasons, these estimates suggest that thoughtful leaders should have considered the possibility that war could bring down a total of five to ten megatons (in simplistic terms, 400–800 times the explosive power of the Hiroshima bomb)[26] on population centers in the course of 1954 or 1955, and possibly more. In February 1953 a research group calculated hypothetical results of a Soviet attack on 100 urban targets with just 100 bombs including eleven of one megaton, and concluded that there would be 19 million fatalities.[27]

The number of variables, uncertainties, and organizations making calculations yielded varied judgments. In early 1954, a special national intelligence estimate put more weight on Soviet operational inhibitions (due to reliance on the TU-4 and undeveloped forward basing) and calculated that no more than 250 Soviet bombers (some of which might not be bomb-carriers) could reach targets—and the number would probably be fewer.[28] In that year and the next, however, the Soviets revealed two new bombers, including the turbojet Bison. Deployed American interceptors (F-86, F-89, and F-94) were not judged capable of dealing with jet bombers. Although Khrushchev's memoirs cite lack of confidence in the Bison due to test and range problems, these doubts were not well recognized in the United States, as reflected in the "bomber gap" controversy which ensued in the intelligence community.[29]

25. Ibid., pp. 334, 343, 347, 725.
26. Analysis later made clearer that gross megatonnage in an arsenal of high-yield weapons cannot be equated with the sum of explosive power of a larger number of low-yield weapons, because effects attenuate as yield increases. (To account for this, the concept of "equivalent" megatonnage was invented and a semi-arbitrary formula became accepted: equivalent megatonnage equals yield to the power of two-thirds.) In the early period, however, most observers still thought in terms of gross megatonnage, and the Soviet stockpile would have been fractionated anyway.
27. MIT Lincoln Laboratory, "Final Report of Summer Study Group," February 10, 1953, Vol. I, cited in Jockel, "United States and Canadian Efforts," p. 157.
28. SNIE 11-2-54, "Soviet Capabilities for Attack on the U.S. Through 1957," February 1954 (declassified June 1978), p. 8. For 1957, the estimate was 700 (pp. 8–9).
29. Jockel, "United States and Canadian Efforts," p. 163; and Strobe Talbott, ed. and trans., *Khrushchev Remembers: The Last Testament* (Boston: Little, Brown, 1974), p. 39. On the bomber gap, see Lawrence Freedman, *U.S. Intelligence and the Soviet Strategic Threat* (Boulder, Colo.: Westview Press, 1977), pp. 65–67; and John Prados, *The Soviet Estimate* (New York: Dial Press, 1982), chapter 4.

Concern about new bombers was still directed toward the future, but vulnerability in 1955 was nonetheless great enough to worry decision-makers when they confronted it. In June, a high-level exercise was conducted. Operation Alert—complete with a cabinet meeting at an alternate national command post—simulated decision problems under nuclear attack. Fifty-three cities were assumed bombed, with 8.5 million *immediate* fatalities, 8 million injured, unknown numbers of fallout casualties, and 25 million homeless people in need of food and shelter. The cabinet secretary's minutes recount, "The President's one comment was: staggering." Eisenhower discussed the results of the exercise at a news conference the following month.[30] Confidence continued to rest more on high deterrence than on low vulnerability. The official 1955 "Net Evaluation" projected that, "As of 1958, the estimated Soviet nuclear stockpile and delivery capability will be inadequate to 'knock out' the United States." This was couched not in terms of acceptable damage to the United States so much as the greater American capacity for a counterblow: "Although the USSR could damage the United States on a scale unprecedented in human experience, it could not prevent the delivery of an even more devastating retaliatory attack."[31]

Of course, even the enthusiasts for the New Look had recognized from the beginning that U.S. nuclear superiority was a wasting asset. An Eisenhower memo to Dulles in August 1953 noted that when Moscow got the H-bomb it might be able to cripple the United States, whereupon American deterrence would have to rest on the ability "to inflict greater loss against the enemy than he could reasonably hope to inflict upon us."[32] So it is not surprising that between 1955 and 1956 the Administration shifted to a policy emphasizing "sufficiency" rather than the Air Force's version of superiority.[33]

But would there be a point at which absolute U.S. vulnerability made the relative difference in Soviet vulnerability insufficient comfort for deterrence?

---

30. Maxwell M. Rabb, "Minutes of the Second Plenary Meeting of the Interim Assembly Ravenrock Conference Room, 11:00–12:15 A.M., Friday, June 15, 1955," pp. 5, 7, in Dwight D. Eisenhower Library/Ann Whitman File [DDEL/AWF], Cabinet Series, Box 5; *Public Papers of the Presidents: Dwight D. Eisenhower, 1955* (Washington, D.C.: U.S. Government Printing Office, 1959), pp. 671–672.

31. Quoted in Arthur Radford, Memorandum for the Special Assistant to the President, National Security Affairs, "Implications of the Revised Estimate of Soviet Nuclear Capabilities with Respect to the Conclusions of the 1955 Net Evaluation," May 31, 1956, p. 1, in DDEL/White House Office [WHO], Office of the Special Assistant for National Security Affairs, NSC Series, Policy Papers Subseries, Box 17.

32. Quoted in Rosenberg, "Origins of Overkill," p. 33.

33. Jerome H. Kahan, *Security in the Nuclear Age* (Washington, D.C.: Brookings Institution, 1975), pp. 31–34.

This remained a matter of theoretical debate until near the end of the decade, and did not impinge as powerfully as it might have until then because the threats Eisenhower made involved the Soviets only indirectly (Korea and the Taiwan Straits) or in cases where there were few grounds for concern that the crisis might escalate (Suez and Lebanon). Yet the later 1950s showed that while the President did not change his reliance on the nuclear threat to deter Soviet action, his grounds for seeing nuclear war as at all manageable declined still further.

From Sufficiency to Overwhelming Vulnerability

Eisenhower kept a personal diary. Given inconsistencies in what he told colleagues and the public and Machiavellian interpretations by revisionist scholars of the reasons for such contradictions, this source—written at the time, and not aimed at anyone involved in policy at the time—might be most indicative of his "real" thinking. A January 23, 1956 entry goes on at length quite remarkable for a busy chief executive about an Air Force briefing on nuclear damage projected for two war scenarios occurring in mid-year. In one scenario of surprise attack, Eisenhower wrote:

. . . the United States experienced practically total economic collapse. . . . a new government had to be improvised by the states. Casualties were enormous. . . . something on the order of 65% of the population would require some kind of medical care, and in most instances, no opportunity whatsoever to get it. . . . While these things were going on, the damage inflicted by us against the Soviets was roughly three times greater.[34]

The second scenario assumed that the Soviets attacked after a month of strategic warning, and concentrated against U.S. air bases rather than the continental United States alone. "Nevertheless," the President wrote, "there was *no significant difference* in the losses we would take." This was three years before the second Berlin crisis, when Eisenhower hinted in public and made clear in secret meetings that war over Berlin would be all-out nuclear war.[35]

---

34. "Jan '56 Diary," pp. 1–2, in DDEL/AWF, DDE Diaries, Box 12.
35. John S.D. Eisenhower, "Memorandum of Conference With the President, March 6, 1959, 10:30 AM," March 6, 1959, p. 6, and John S.D. Eisenhower, "Memorandum of Conference With the President, March 6, 1959–5:00 PM," March 7, 1959, pp. 3–6, 9–10, in DDEL/WHO, Office of the Staff Secretary, International Series, Box 6; A.J. Goodpaster, "Memorandum of Conference With the President, March 9, 1959," March 10, 1959, p. 1, in DDEL/AWF, DDE Diaries, Box 29; *Executive Sessions of the Senate Foreign Relations Committee (Historical Series)*, 86th Cong., 1st sess., 1959 (Washington, D.C.: U.S. Government Printing Office, 1982), pp. 220–221, 225, 229, 231,

Wording in the immediate threat estimate in June in NSC 5606, a Planning Board report, was not quite as apocalyptic as Eisenhower's musings (perhaps because it was not solely an Air Force product, as the briefing discussed in the diary was). NSC 5606 cited "some time in 1958" or "possibly as early as 1957" as the date at which the USSR would develop the capability for "a crippling blow."[36] And there are indications that the President remained concerned with uncertainties about the precise amount and forms of damage the United States would suffer in nuclear war, and whether the country could stand it in some sense. At the end of 1956, he told the NSC that given "the picture of terrific destruction," analysis should be done to see how much the United States could "absorb and still survive."[37] As late as mid-1959, after the Berlin Deadline crisis, he was asking for studies "to see what this country would look like five days or so following a nuclear attack . . . just what the situation would be."[38]

Defensive improvements, earlier hoped to retard Soviet striking capability, were languishing. Technological breakthroughs in radar and data-handling were not being exploited, and innovation slowed, due to administration economies. In February 1955, a specially constituted Technological Capabilities Panel (TCP) reported continuing deficiencies in the number and quality of air defense systems, including serious gaps in radar coverage and major inadequacies in interceptors and other weapons.[39] In mid-year, another panel produced a pessimistic analysis of Soviet gains in technology, which could

---

233–234; *Public Papers of the Presidents of the United States: Dwight D. Eisenhower, 1959* (Washington, D.C.: U.S. Government Printing Office, 1960), pp. 244–245, 249, 252; and Thomas W. Wolfe, *Soviet Power and Europe* (Baltimore: Johns Hopkins University Press, 1970), p. 91n.

36. NSC 5606, "Continental Defense," June 5, 1956, Annex A, p. 22, in DDEL/WHO, Office of the Special Assistant for National Security Affairs, NSC Series, Policy Papers Subseries, Box 17. The estimate noted that "over 71 percent of the Defense-supporting industry (59 percent of all manufacturing industry) and 54 percent of the workers engaged in manufacturing are located in 59 large metropolitan centers." Ibid., Annex B, pp. 28–29.

37. J. Patrick Coyne, Memorandum, "Discussion at the 306th Meeting of the National Security Council, Thursday, December 20, 1956," December 21, 1956, pp. 3–4, in DDEL/AWF, NSC Series, Box 8.

38. Gordon Gray, "Memorandum of Meeting with the President," May 7, 1959, in DDEL/WHO, Office of Special Assistant for National Security Affairs, Special Assistant Series, Presidential Subseries, Box 4. Quotation from A.J. Goodpaster, "Memorandum of Conference With the President," July 27, 1959, p. 2, in DDEL/WHO, Office of Staff Secretary, Subject Series, DoD Subseries, Box 4.

39. Technological Capabilities Panel, Science Advisory Committee, "Meeting the Threat of Surprise Attack," February 14, 1955, Vol. 2, Part 4, p. 75, in DDEL/WHO, Office of Special Assistant for National Security Affairs, NSC Series, Subject Subseries, Box 11; and Jockel, "United States and Canadian Efforts," p. 17.

soon surpass the United States[40]—a dire prediction predating by over two years the alarm surrounding Sputnik and the Gaither Committee. By the following year, Air Force Secretary Donald Quarles admitted that in coping with vulnerability, "we lost ground."[41] NSC 5606 reaffirmed the air defense deficiencies outlined by the TCP and noted that improvements in continental defense were consistently negated by increases in the Soviet nuclear stockpile and delivery capability.[42] This problem was never overcome.

Assessments by the Continental Air Defense Command in 1957, based on optimistic assumptions, estimated defenses as only capable of preventing the Soviets from bombing 40 percent of their targets.[43] By the end of the decade, the President's Science Advisory Committee cited the SAGE air defense system as only "far better than nothing," and noted "that perfectly feasible plans of air attack could be devised which would make it inoperable."[44] An NSC briefing in late 1960 summed up the record of the race between offense and defense: "As the enemy capability increased, it became necessary to build [air defense] weapons of increasing capability. The modern interceptor . . . is not more effective in coping with this kind of threat than the early fighters were in coping with an earlier threat."[45] And by then, the ICBM threat had eventuated, even if large numbers were only on the horizon.

Damage estimates continued to climb, even before the missile gap controversy. In May 1957, Eisenhower cited a Net Evaluation figure of 25 million dead and 60 million needing hospitalization. A June 1957 JCS study, which included fallout effects, referred to between 46 and 117 million fatalities, though it assumed all bombs were aimed at population targets. A Federal Civil Defense Administration estimate assuming a third of the targets would be military installations nevertheless cited 82 million dead Americans as the result.[46] The NIE in November 1957, however, emphasized continuing re-

---

40. Ellis Johnson, "The Comparative Military Technology of the U.S. and USSR," Annex A, Tab 2, Report of the Quantico Vulnerabilities Panel, reprinted in W.W. Rostow, *Open Skies: Eisenhower's Proposal of July 21, 1955* (Austin: University of Texas Press, 1982).
41. Quoted in Nunn, *Soviet First Strike Threat*, pp. 116–121.
42. NSC 5606, Annex B, pp. 25–26.
43. The CONAD assessment projected improvements to 60 and 80 percent for 1960 and 1963, but only considered bombers, ignored degradation of defenses by electronic countermeasures, and assumed substantial improvements in air defense. JCS 1899/339, cited in Jockel, "United States and Canadian Efforts," pp. 165, 166n.
44. July 28, 1959 meeting, reported in George B. Kistiakowsky's diary, *A Scientist at the White House* (Cambridge: Harvard University Press, 1976), p. 24.
45. "Continental Defense," Minutes of Briefing to NCS by John H. Rubel, September 15, 1960, in DDEL/WHO, Office of Staff Secretary, Subject Series, Alphabetical Subseries, Box 19.
46. Fred I. Greenstein, *The Hidden-Hand Presidency* (New York: Basic Books, 1982), p. 48; and

strictions on efficacy of Soviet forces, such as "the relatively small numbers of operational heavy bombers, the status of support facilities at Arctic bases, and the lack as yet of a substantial inflight refueling capability," though it also mentioned Soviet ability to employ "small numbers of both bomber-launched air to surface missiles and submarine-launched surface-to-surface missiles."[47]

Although the post-Sputnik ICBM scare remained a political football through the 1960 election, the controversy within the executive branch was more or less resolved in favor of more relaxed near-term estimates by the end of 1958—and the President had never taken the "gap" seriously anyway. In secret testimony in January 1959, military representatives reported revised estimates which pushed possible Soviet deployment of 100 ICBMs back to 1960 or 1961; lowered the number, quality, and range of submarine-launched cruise missiles; and cited no more than 125 heavy Bear and Bison bombers.[48] Thus U.S. nuclear superiority in the *balance of forces* was clearly still over-whelming and Moscow certainly had no meaningful *first*-strike option. Many then (and today) saw this as grounds for the credibility of nuclear leverage. This view might be supportable in regard to a couple of cases such as the 1958 Taiwan Straits crisis (in which China would have been the target of U.S. nuclear first use and the Soviets would have had to use nuclear weapons before being struck themselves if they supported the Chinese in war), or the 1962 missile crisis (in which U.S. strategy did not rely on first use but on deterrence of *Soviet* escalation). But in other cases, such as the contest over Berlin, the balance of forces should have offered less comfort, since *population* vulnerability to Soviet second-strike retaliation would have been the crucial factor.

The ratio of American to Soviet vulnerability may have improved briefly in the early 1960s because the Soviets dawdled in development of modern delivery systems while U.S. offensive forces spurted sharply upward. Exactly what this meant, however, depended on the issue considered. The principal U.S. advantage accruing from the Kennedy buildup was in counterforce capability against unready Soviet forces. Depending on the scenario, U.S.

JCS 1899/339 and FCDA study cited in Jockel, "United States and Canadian Efforts," pp. 163–165.
47. NIE 11-4-57, "Main Trends in Soviet Capabilities and Policies 1957–1962," November 12, 1957, p. 37 (Carrolton Press collection).
48. *Executive Sessions of the Senate Foreign Relations Committee (Historical Series)*, Vol. 11, 86th Cong., 1st sess., 1959 (Washington, D.C.: U.S. Government Printing Office, 1982), pp. 19–23.

population vulnerability remained quite high. The limits to how comforting the U.S. first-strike option should have been are discussed subsequently.

A 1960 Air Force study which projected war three years later reportedly indicated that an indiscriminate Soviet first strike would kill 150 million Americans, and even Soviet *retaliation* after an indiscriminate U.S. first strike would kill 110 million.[49] This may have been due to Air Force inflation of projected Soviet forces, but the figure of 150 million American dead has been cited as what President Kennedy took away from his first briefing by the JCS (though he heard privately from the Air Force that losses would be far lower if the U.S. struck first). At the height of the 1961 Berlin crisis, the Air Force advised that a U.S. first strike might keep losses down to ten million (although this was glaringly inconsistent with SAC's position in other forums that Moscow might have many undetected, and therefore untargeted, missiles). Civilian staff planners working separately under Paul Nitze developed a Berlin-related counterforce plan in great secrecy which projected bounds of 2–15 million U.S. fatalities.[50] Without an effective first strike, however, other estimates said even the full *planned* civil defense shelter program would not reduce U.S. fatalities below 39–56 million if a fair number of high-yield Soviet weapons were aimed at cities (62–100 million without shelters); "as few as 15 missiles diverted to the attack of cities will cause between 10 and 20 million fatalities" with full civil defense.[51]

A major intelligence assessment produced shortly before the 1962 missile crisis said that from then through five years later "*even in the most favorable case* with restraints in targeting on both sides, civil casualties in the United States and Western Europe could be on the order of ten million each," and up to 100 million or more each without restraints.[52] In neither of the two

---

49. Richard Fryklund, *100 Million Lives: Maximum Survival in a Nuclear War* (New York: Macmillan, 1962), pp. 3–4, 21–22. The study supported discriminating counterforce; it projected U.S. and Soviet fatalities as three and five million respectively in a "no cities" exchange (pp. 13–14).
50. Fred Kaplan, *The Wizards of Armageddon* (New York: Simon and Schuster, 1983), pp. 294–301; and Gregg Herken, *Counsels of War* (New York: Knopf, 1985), p. 161.
51. These estimates, from studies by SRI, Rand, ORO, and WSEG, assumed a 350 megaton Soviet attack, but with most weapons aimed at military targets; a smaller retaliatory attack, but aimed primarily at cities, would probably have produced comparable casualties. A *counterforce* version of the 350 megaton strike was predicted to yield 11–40 million dead without the shelter program in place. See Carl Kaysen, Memorandum for Bundy, "Berlin Crisis and Civil Defense," July 7, 1961, Appendix, pp. 2–3, in John F. Kennedy Library/National Security Files [JFKL/NSF], Countries Series, Box 81.
52. "Report of the Special Inter-Departmental Committee on Implications of NIE 11-8-62 and Related Intelligence," reprinted in Raymond L. Garthoff, *Intelligence Assessment and Policymaking: A Decision Point in the Kennedy Administration* (Washington, D.C.: Brookings Institution, 1984), p. 44 (emphasis added).

confrontations over Berlin or Cuba, however, were there sound reasons for assuming "favorable" conditions. The planned shelter program never got very far, and only theory—not evidence about Soviet views or plans—suggested that Moscow might restrain targeting of civilian assets.

Limits of the U.S. First-Strike Option

The main counterargument to the relevance of early vulnerability estimates would be that their pessimism was skewed because some avoided factoring in the full meaning of U.S. counterforce capability. It is no secret that a first-strike option was integral to U.S. policy through much of the postwar period; indeed, it was the essence of massive retaliation, and in more ambiguous form remained part of flexible response. This mitigates the implications of the previous section only slightly, however, if one considers evidence about limitations of both U.S. intentions and capabilities.

The option of preemption was recommended by the JCS from the beginning of the postwar era. (A *preemptive* strike is one made in immediate anticipation of enemy attack; a surprise attack against an enemy who is not yet preparing his own attack may be *preventive,* but not preemptive.)[53] In September 1945, they said "that the U.S. must be ready 'to strike the first blow if necessary,'" and two years later they "recommended that Congress be asked to redefine 'acts of aggression' to include 'the readying of atomic weapons against us,' and to authorize the President" to retaliate in anticipation. NSC-68 rejected preventive war but tentatively embraced preemption.[54]

SAC Commander and later Air Force Chief of Staff Curtis LeMay is legendary for his enthusiasm for a first strike. His memoirs contain thinly veiled arguments in favor of preventive war and a later book published in the year of his American Independent Party candidacy for the Vice Presidency endorsed first-strike capability as "absolutely necessary."[55] The most impressive claim about LeMay's attitude is a reported encounter between the General and Robert Sprague, deputy head of the Gaither Committee. LeMay allegedly

---

53. See Richard K. Betts, *Surprise Attack* (Washington, D.C.: Brookings Institution, 1982), pp. 145–147.
54. Rosenberg, "Origins of Overkill," pp. 17, 25.
55. Gen. Curtis LeMay with Mackinlay Kantor, *Mission With LeMay* (Garden City: Doubleday, 1965), pp. 418–482, 559–561; and Gen. Curtis LeMay with Maj. Gen. Dale Smith, *America Is In Danger* (New York: Funk & Wagnalls, 1968), p. 63.

told Sprague he was not worried about SAC's vulnerability (against which Rand analyst Albert Wohlstetter was crusading at the time) because if he received warning of Soviet massing from U.S. reconnaissance and signals intelligence (SIGINT), "I'm going to knock the shit out of them before they take off the ground." When the stunned Sprague said that was not national policy, LeMay allegedly responded that he didn't care: "It's my policy. That's what I'm going to do."[56] (Although this is hard to believe, Sprague confirmed the essence of Kaplan's account in a letter to Marc Trachtenberg. It is unclear how command and control arrangements could have permitted a large-scale coordinated attack in peacetime without presidential authorization, but there are indications that authority may have been delegated for situations in which communication broke down.)[57]

In 1960, Air Force Chief of Staff Thomas White testified in Congress against finite deterrence because it did not take account of "the possibility of reaction on our part to strategic warning."[58] Four years later, Defense Secretary McNamara testified against a new manned bomber and in favor of emphasizing missiles because "The quicker our retaliatory force can reach the opponent, the more chance we have of catching a substantial part of his force on the ground."[59]

These examples only reflect general planning considerations not geared to any specific crisis with all the attendant political confusion, uncertainty, and awesome immediacy. What did Commanders in Chief, those most responsible for acting in such circumstances, think about a first strike? There is no way to ascertain their most private thoughts, but there are other indications. Ironically, the clearest reluctance and moral handwringing were Truman's during the Berlin Blockade; when the United States faced no Soviet retaliatory capability, the nuclear signal in the crisis (dispatching to Europe B-29 groups which the Russians might have known did not carry nuclear ordnance) was

---

56. Kaplan, *Wizards of Armageddon*, pp. 132–134.
57. McGeorge Bundy warned Kennedy just ten days into his administration that a review of "existing papers" suggested the possibility of "a situation today in which a subordinate commander faced with a substantial Russian military action could start the thermonuclear holocaust on his own initiative if he could not reach you (by failure of communication at either end of the line)." Memorandum to the President, "Policies Previously Approved in NSC Which Need Review," January 30, 1961, JFKL/NSF, Meetings and Memoranda Series, Box 313. I thank Marc Trachtenberg for calling my attention to this document and to Sprague's confirmation.
58. Quoted in Robert E. Osgood, *NATO: The Entangling Alliance* (Chicago: University of Chicago Press, 1962), p. 202.
59. Quoted in Robert Frank Futrell, *Ideas, Concepts, Doctrine* (Montgomery, Ala.: Maxwell Air Force Base, June 1971), Vol. 2, p. 679.

nearly the weakest and most cautious of any undertaken. For Kennedy, there is no public evidence of whether or how he thought about a first-strike option in the two biggest crises of the Cold War (Berlin 1961, Cuba 1962) which occurred in his administration. Eisenhower, the President associated with the largest number of tacit U.S. nuclear threats, seemed to tilt in opposite directions at different times. In his private diary entry of January 23, 1956, he wrote:

The only possible way of reducing these losses would be for us to take the initiative some time during the assumed month in which we had the warning of the attack and launch a surprise attack against the Soviets. This would not only be against our traditions but it would appear to be impossible that any such thing would occur.[60]

On the other hand, when the Gaither Committee briefed him the next year, he agreed that the Soviets should not be allowed to strike first, and records show that in his last year in office he was briefed by the JCS Chairman on issues related to preemption after warning.[61]

There is one fundamental set of problems in connecting a planning principle of this sort with likely action in a crisis where some U.S. nuclear threat had been made. Statements cited above appear oriented to a situation of unprovoked Soviet preparation of a nuclear attack out of the blue. If the Soviets were to be observed readying their nuclear force *after* a U.S. nuclear signal aimed at deterring conventional action—such as the limited SAC alerts in the Suez and Lebanon crises of the 1950s and the 1973 Middle East War, or the complete DEFCON-2 posture of October 1962—the situation would be markedly different. This question never arose, because the Soviets never countered such U.S. signals with comparable action, so this criticism can only rest on logic or inference from cases of conventional conflict. In such a case, however, U.S. leaders would face more than one choice. They could decide that Moscow meant to strike, and authorize preemption. This is the standard concern of deterrence theory about crisis stability and spiraling reactions. If political experience and common sense are considered, however, it is at least as likely that the President would see the Soviet alert as a precautionary counter to the American alert.[62] Even in the dark days of the 1950s, it is not easy to imagine leaders resolving such an uncertainty in favor

60. "Jan. '56 Diary," p. 2.
61. Herken, *Counsels of War*, p. 127.
62. See the arguments in Betts, *Surprise Attack*, chapters 4–6.

of preemption very quickly, before Moscow's alert had modified the vulnerability of its nuclear force.

To pose a similar and ultimately more telling problem, the theoretical option of a disarming strike envisioned by some of the Berlin contingency planners in 1961 appears based on inconsistent assumptions about plausible intentions and capabilities. To succeed in keeping U.S. fatalities down to the low millions, the strike reportedly planned on catching the Soviet forces in their normal unready posture (missiles and bombers separated from warheads, concentrated on regular bases, and screened by a faulty early warning network which U.S. bombers could circumvent). But to provoke the U.S. nuclear riposte in the first place, the Soviets would have had to initiate military action to take West Berlin. Would Moscow conceivably move to the unprecedented step of starting conventional combat without putting some reasonable portion of its nuclear force close to launch-on-warning status? That is, the Soviets' own decision to go to conventional war would be the functional equivalent to them of strategic warning of U.S. nuclear attack. Thus primed (and probably dispersed), the force would be less likely to be caught flatfooted everywhere even if leaky radars let many U.S. bombers close to target before alarm. Under these circumstances, American missiles might more effectively catch alert bombers or soft ICBMs on the ground, since the Soviets were then only beginning to construct the Hen House radars for tactical warning of ballistic missile attack. It is at least questionable, however, that the U.S. SIOP (Single Integrated Operational Plan) up to 1962 could have programmed a reliable number of ballistic missile warheads (which then numbered only in the hundreds) against *all* of the dispersal airfields in the vast expanse of the USSR. Even if only, say, 10 percent of the 200-odd Soviet bombers managed to fly out through the attack and penetrate U.S. air defenses, several tens of megatons might still come down on American cities. In short, a U.S. disarming preemptive strike after conventional war had begun would be less feasible, while a more feasible preventive surprise attack before conflict erupted—an American Pearl Harbor—was politically unthinkable.

For the sake of further argument, leave that logic aside for the moment. Some of the population vulnerability estimates cited previously might be dismissed as excessive on grounds that analysts outside the Air Force were not privy to the extent of U.S. first-strike capability. Bureaucratic-politics interpretations of the role of estimates, however, cut both ways. Many of the Air Force estimates of civilian damage were even higher than the others.

Could these be explained away as disingenuous data games meant to support higher budgets? If so, the game could not work unless the data were believed by their consumers. Logically, moreover, a budget politics motive for the Air Force could have backfired by encouraging diversion of resources from the offensive forces sought by the service to air defense assets which it wanted much less. Indeed, at the end of 1956, Eisenhower reacted to damage assessments from the Net Evaluation Subcommittee by asking "why we should put a single nickel into anything" but concentrating on better defenses and reduction of force vulnerability.[63]

Like air defense improvements, growth in offensive forces raced against growth in Soviet forces. Splendid U.S. first-strike capability was often seen as within reach, but still in the future. Revelations about the extraordinary quality of U.S. SIGINT and substantial American and British aerial and balloon reconnaissance of the USSR have underwritten nostalgia by showing much greater ability to locate and target Soviet forces than might have been publicly assumed at the time. This overshoots, however, because high confidence and total coverage did not exist until the advent of satellite surveillance after 1960. The U-2 did not begin flying until mid-1956 and could not cover all of the Soviet interior; and between early 1958 and April 1960 few deep-penetration flights were mounted.[64]

As early in the period of U.S. superiority as March 1954, a WSEG report projecting war in July 1955 discussed a U.S. attack on Soviet bloc airfields, but noted that it did not cover all *known* fields to which Soviet aircraft could be dispersed: "at least 240 unstruck and uncontaminated emergency airfields would be available to the Soviets . . . even under the improbable assumptions only 5 percent of the aircraft survived, seventy-five weapons could be lifted against the U.S."[65] Later, at the apex of U.S. counterforce capability and eight months before the Cuban missile crisis, Secretary McNamara testified secretly that "Soviet-inflicted damage to the civil societies of the Alliance could be very grave indeed. *Even if we attempted to destroy the enemy nuclear strike capability at its source,* using all our available resources, some portion of the Soviet force would survive to strike back."[66]

---

63. Coyne memorandum of 306th NSC Meeting, pp. 3–4.
64. Paul Worthman letter in Rostow, *Open Skies*, p. 193. Results of balloon reconnaissance were very poor.
65. "Briefing of WSEG Report No. 12," reprinted in *International Security*, Vol. 6, No. 3 (Winter 1981/1982), p. 32.
66. *Executive Sessions of the Senate Foreign Relations Committee Together With Joint Sessions With the*

Such studies might be deflated by arguing that accounting of U.S. first-strike coverage was artificially cautious or that Soviet operational constraints were too often ignored. (In the same year as the above WSEG report, a special national intelligence estimate had said that the Soviets might need up to a month to deliver their entire nuclear stockpile.)[67] Three considerations still negate the notion that leaders would have had much more confidence than implied by the estimates of appreciable U.S. population vulnerability.

First is the simple point that there were numerous pessimistic estimates serving as the currency of assessment, and these were not less widely purveyed than any confident views that could have prevailed within SAC's inner sanctums. In 1955, for instance, the TCP reported, "*Neither* the U.S. nor the Soviets can mount an air strike against the other that would surely be decisive," with the definition of decisive including "ability to strike back essentially eliminated." The report foresaw a U.S. capability to "mount a decisive air strike" only in the future.[68] And in 1956 a CIA contribution to the NSC Planning Board's report even said, "it is possible that the USSR, if it sought full strategic surprise, could launch an attack on the continental U.S. without undertaking any observable preparations which would provide strategic warning."[69]

Second, to discredit the impact of pessimistic estimates, one would have to assume that the Air Force whispered its closely held confidence in first-strike capability into the President's ear. Leaving aside his numerous statements reflecting no confidence in low vulnerability, Eisenhower's private diary entry offers no grounds for believing this had happened. Moreover, it would have made a mockery of the Air Force's *own* pessimistic estimates.

Third, before the Kennedy Administration, the Air Force was not even oriented to maximizing absolutely the counterforce priority in the first-strike option. In the mid-1950s, target planners compromised counterforce aim points in order to gain "bonus" damage against civil targets, and the first SIOP was based on an "Optimum Mix" of Soviet civilian and military targets. In 1960, Chief of Naval Operations Arleigh Burke criticized it as falling between two stools: "counterforce receives higher precedence than is war-

---

Senate Armed Services Committee (Historical Series), Vol. 14, 87th Cong., 2d sess., 1962 (Washington, D.C.: U.S. Government Printing Office, 1986), p. 149 (emphasis added). By that time, the administration estimated not only 200 Soviet bombers that could be launched for round-trip missions, but 30 submarines rigged to deliver 90 missiles. Ibid., p. 145.
67. Draft SNIE 11-8-54, cited in Rosenberg, "Origins of Overkill," p. 34.
68. TCP, "Meeting the Threat of Surprise Attack," pp. 72–73 (emphasis added and deleted).
69. NSC 5606, Annex B, p. 25.

ranted for a retaliatory plan, and less precedence than is warranted for an initiative plan."[70] (Considering the overwhelming percentage of weapons allocated to military targets, however, the limitations on counterforce optimization may seem trivial to some.) When McNamara arrived at the Pentagon, the Air Force had not yet been convinced of the desirability of maximizing counterforce in the terms envisioned by civilian analysts, and a WSEG briefing for the secretary argued against such a strategy by saying that nontargetable weapons would be able to deliver 1–2,000 megatons, killing half the American population.[71] It took time and effort by the new corps of civilian analysts to make counterforce the complete priority in the early 1960s, and then it proved to be a fleeting priority.

Could one argue that none of the internal vulnerability estimates discussed mattered for crisis coercion, on grounds that U.S. leaders convinced Moscow that they were not intimidated by the prospective consequences of initiating nuclear war? The threats themselves, and frequent reliance on them, were meant to communicate preference for nuclear war over conventional defeat, but Presidents' statements never suggested that the U.S. homeland would not suffer unimaginably. And if anything, prevalent discourse in the country, especially after Sputnik, reflected a more devastating impression of nuclear war than that of secret government estimates. This was the era of popular apocalyptic literature like Nevil Shute's *On the Beach*, Walter M. Miller, Jr.'s *A Canticle for Liebowitz*, and Pat Frank's *Alas, Babylon*. The latter novel ends a year after nuclear war, as remnants of national authority begin to reestablish communication with surviving rural communities. Paul Hart, an Air Force officer landing in a Florida town, explains:

"We're a second class power now. Tertiary would be more accurate. I doubt if we have the population of France—or rather as large as France used to be. . . ." Randy said, "Paul, there's one thing more. Who won the war?"

Paul put his fist on his hips and his eyes narrowed. "You're kidding! You mean you really don't know?"

"No . . . Nobody's told us."

"We won it. We really clobbered 'em!" Hart's eyes lowered and his arms drooped. He said, "Not that it matters."

---

70. CNO cable to commands, quoted in Rosenberg, "Origins of Overkill," pp. 7–8; and Kaplan, *Wizards of Armageddon*, pp. 211–212.
71. Ibid., pp. 258–259. The principal Air Force resistance, however, was not to improving counterforce but to withholding strikes on urban-industrial targets. The WSEG report also was probably based on a projected situation a few years later.

The engine started and Randy turned away to face the thousand-year night.[72]

Which was further from the mark—the popular imagination, or the belief of some professionals that Americans could weather nuclear war with consequences not radically worse than having their "hair mussed"?

Did the Bomb Work "Both Ways"?

Why shouldn't the Soviets' retaliatory capability have deterred the United States from initiating nuclear combat? Were U.S. leaders in crisis decisions nonchalant about accepting tens of millions of casualties if nuclear threats failed to accomplish their purpose and war broke out? No, but case studies of the crises concerned suggest that they refused to face this question decisively, banking that deterrence or compellence would not fail. For a pure strategist devoted to rationalism, certainty, and careful planning, and uncomfortable with relying on bluffs, the fit between U.S. doctrine, capabilities, and specific crisis initiatives appears uncomfortably loose. If we appreciate the ambiguity of evidence about what animated Presidents' thinking on these questions, speculation about Soviet thinking appears doubly adventurous. Some attempt is necessary, though, since a strategic equation has two sides.

So what were the Russians—the objects of nuclear threats—to think? Were U.S. leaders foolishly blind to the risks of avoidable devastation of their society? Were they bluffing? Did Soviet leaders believe the latter about U.S. doctrine in normal periods but suspect the former when faced with nuclear threats in crises? Were they bluffing about their own retaliatory capability, believing it weaker than U.S. estimates did? Or was it all beside the point, because they did not intend to take the conventional military actions that the U.S. nuclear signals aimed to deter? The answer could be: all of the above.

The Soviets' rhetoric inflated their capabilities against the continental United States, but in terms of notions about what *should* deter escalation by a rational and prudent American President, some elements of Soviet rhetoric and action were consistent. Khrushchev justified his cuts in conventional forces in the late 1950s on grounds that "The number of troops and rifles and bayonets is no longer decisive. . . . our ability to deter imperialist aggres-

---

72. Pat Frank, *Alas, Babylon* (New York: Bantam, 1960), pp. 278–279.

sion depends on our nuclear and thermonuclear fire power." He also spoke often in terms of simple nuclear countervalue capability and overkill.[73] In 1960 he announced cutbacks in production of certain missiles because rockets "are not cucumbers, you know—you don't eat them—and more than a certain number are not required to repel aggression."[74] Although this represented a bluff about existing ICBM capability, it reflected a notion of the adequacy of finite deterrence. Soviet analysts often criticized U.S. doctrine for "what they regarded as an American lack of recognition of the consequences of Soviet retaliation in any attempted U.S. blitzkrieg by surprise nuclear attack."[75] In 1959, for example, Defense Minister Rodion Malinovsky said in *Pravda*, "playing down the effective capacity of the U.S.S.R. to deal a counterblow to the aggressor and exaggeration of their transoceanic capabilities . . . do not testify to the presence of common sense among the U.S. military."[76]

Moscow was relying primarily on its capability to destroy Western Europe. Claims about how much damage it could inflict on the U.S. homeland, in what ways, were only vaguely stated, but statements in regard to Europe were very specific and frequent. Khrushchev's memoirs confess greater pessimism about Soviet intercontinental bomber capabilities than showed up in the American estimates. Official rhetoric before the late 1950s did not explicitly suggest that the socialist camp would come out of war better off than the West, but it did claim that both Western Europe and the United States would receive unacceptable damage, and by the late 1950s the official view was clear "that the heartlands of all states would suffer," so that "as a result, the West was deterred."[77]

Khrushchev's boldest bluffs did not come until this latter post-Sputnik period (he made the first mention that the USSR was producing ICBMs just two days after issuing the deadline that touched off the second Berlin crisis). Several months later, Khrushchev stated that the Soviet Union had "no less force and capabilities" than the United States, and by 1960 Moscow was making the first claims of military superiority. (In the most extreme variants,

73. *Khrushchev Remembers*, pp. 516, 517.
74. Quoted in Arnold Horelick and Myron Rush, *Strategic Power and Soviet Foreign Policy* (Chicago: University of Chicago Press, 1965), p. 72.
75. Raymond Garthoff, *The Soviet Image of Future War* (Washington, D.C.: Public Affairs Press, 1959), p. 81.
76. Quoted in Horelick and Rush, *Soviet Strategic Power*, p. 53.
77. William Zimmerman, *Soviet Perspectives on International Relations* (Princeton: Princeton University Press, 1969), p. 173.

Soviet statements touted their air defenses as negating the U.S. bomber threat. Referring to the downing of the U-2, Khrushchev said in May 1960, "then of course, not a single bomber could get through to its target.")[78]

These bluffs energized debate in the U.S. body politic but did not worry Eisenhower. His successor was reluctant to rely on nuclear weapons and pushed NATO toward more effort at conventional defense. This could not help West Berlin, though, isolated as it was behind Soviet lines, and in October 1961 Kennedy handled the last Berlin crisis by communicating to Moscow U.S. knowledge of how inferior Soviet nuclear capability really was.[79] The reversal of Soviet confidence was reflected that month when Marshal Malinovsky, in the first such statement by a major official since 1957, hinted that under some circumstances the Soviets might preempt.[80]

Implications

The U.S. vulnerability estimates cited previously suggest that the argument for a golden age of U.S. leaders' confidence in ability to limit damage to a remotely acceptable level (say, total blast and fallout fatalities under 10 percent of the population) may be supportable for at best two brief periods: before the mid-1950s and, less certainly, in the early 1960s. With better evidence available about the Soviets' lethargy in developing a bomber force in which *they* had confidence, the actual U.S. capability to limit damage with some effectiveness probably persisted throughout most of the first two decades after World War II. But the logic of deterrence rests on beliefs about the situation at the time. Unless Eisenhower were to have dismissed most of the U.S. vulnerability estimates discussed as hysterical eyewash—and his statements show he did not—for most of his administration he may have had confidence in deterrence, but could not have had confidence that a need to follow through and implement nuclear threats would have yielded more than a Pyrrhic victory.

It is conceivable that if forced to decide, U.S. authorities might have judged that the death of 10 percent or more of the American people, as well as the

78. Ibid., p. 175; and Horelick and Rush, *Soviet Strategic Power*, pp. 50, 74, with Khrushchev quoted on pp. 53, 75.
79. Robert M. Slusser, *The Berlin Crisis of 1961* (Baltimore: Johns Hopkins University Press, 1973), pp. 223, 372–375; Desmond Ball, *Politics and Force Levels* (Berkeley: University of California Press, 1980), p. 98; and Roger Hilsman, *To Move a Nation* (Garden City: Doubleday, 1967), pp. 163–164.
80. Zimmerman, *Soviet Perspectives on International Relations*, p. 187.

serious injury of as many and the wreckage of a large fraction of the economic and social fabric, might be a price worth paying to prevent the absorption of all of Europe into Soviet dominion. The nuclear threats that came closest to being associated with such a prospective contingency were those over Berlin. The reported staff estimate in September 1961 of 2–15 million American fatalities if the United States struck first would be consistent with the above notion of acceptable damage, but 1957 figures of 25–117 million would not. Yet the available sources suggest that Eisenhower was more serene about relying on the nuclear threat in the second Berlin crisis than Kennedy was in the third. In either case, however, the rationalistic cost-benefit standard for acceptable damage did not apply. The U.S. threats were directed not against a likely Soviet invasion of NATO territory, but against occupation of half a city. The rationale might be salvaged by the prevalent domino theory: if today Berlin, then tomorrow Bonn and Paris. Yet deliberate nuclear escalation over Berlin still appears hard to justify in terms of cold rationality.

In the second half of the postwar era, attention to these problems waned. With the advent of nuclear parity, and arms control negotiations aimed at codifying it, the United States gave up attempting to maintain even marginal superiority. In the détente period, the easing of political tension made the possibility of war with the USSR seem utterly remote, so concern with the military logic and credibility of strategic doctrine eased as well.

In that context, there were still bitter and politically salient disputes about the nuclear balance of power, but for the most part they concerned how *parity* should be defined and how *mutual* nuclear deterrence should be preserved. Throughout most of the 1970s, the focus of U.S. strategic debate was on this symmetrical aspect of the military competition. It almost became bad form to recall that decades earlier, "deterrence" was hardly meant to be mutual at all, that prevalent usage of the term in the West had referred to the threat of a nuclear offensive to counter a conventional Soviet or Chinese military initiative.[81] Nor was it fashionable to dwell on the fact that despite acceptance of nuclear parity and arms control, the United States still remained committed to deliberate escalation (including first use of central strategic

---

81. Theorists differentiated the concept fairly early, coining the modifiers "active," "extended," or "Type II" to denote nuclear deterrence of conventional attack, and "passive," "basic," or "mutual" to refer to deterrence of nuclear attack. See Osgood, *NATO: The Entangling Alliance*, pp. 60–61, 132–134; and Herman Kahn, *On Thermonuclear War* (Princeton: Princeton University Press, 1960), pp. 126, 282. For some time, however, especially in Europe and the Eisenhower Administration, normal parlance focused on deterrence of conventional aggression.

forces under some circumstances), which implicitly means that the Soviets' nuclear retaliatory deterrent would not always deter us.[82]

As détente died and the possibility of war seemed a bit less remote, old concerns about the rationality and credibility of reliance on escalation resurfaced. If the viability of first-use commitments rests on capacity to limit damage from Soviet retaliation, parity obviously foreclosed the option, so many hawks nostalgic for the putative golden age joined anti-nuclear doves in the search for a strategic alternative to flexible response. None emerged with enough persuasiveness to stir majority support for a shift.

The preceding review, however, suggests that there was no real golden age, and that earlier Presidents' willingness to spar around the nuclear brink did not depend on confidence that if they tumbled over it, the United States could escape awesome destruction that any reasonable person should consider unacceptable. Moreover, Presidents proved willing to invoke risks of nuclear war in disputes over territories whose intrinsic significance was far less than that of Western Europe, the stake that animated development of the theory and policy of extended deterrence. Why did Khrushchev's finite deterrent not enforce greater prudence on American leaders? Other explanations have been offered that rationalize relying on first-use threats despite vulnerability to retaliation, but they are not quite satisfactory.

One view, for example, is that in a competition in risk-taking the balance of resolve is governed by the balance of interests between the contenders—their relative stakes in the dispute—rather than by the balance of nuclear power. The defensive, status quo party in the conflict has the inherent advantage in credibility over which side will first shrink from the brink. Since the Soviets or Chinese were the aggressors in the crises at issue, in this view, American nuclear threats could be sensible tactics.[83] And since this theory

---

82. After the 1960s, some Americans mistakenly came to assume that the first-use commitment was limited to tactical or theater nuclear weapons, perhaps because the consensus of U.S. strategic analysts had rejected full-scale "coupling" as suicidal. That intellectual rejection, however, was not matched politically. Although NATO's flexible response doctrine envisions graduated escalation, it is still based on the principle of a "seamless web" of nuclear forces, and allied governments reject the notion of a separate "Eurostrategic" balance.

83. Echoing the work of Thomas Schelling, variations on these themes can be found among Robert Jervis, "Why Nuclear Superiority Doesn't Matter," *Political Science Quarterly*, Vol. 94, No. 4 (Winter 1979–80), p. 628; Jervis, *The Illogic of American Nuclear Strategy* (Ithaca: Cornell University Press, 1984), pp. 134, 153–154; Kenneth Waltz, *The Spread of Nuclear Weapons: More May Be Better*, Adelphi Paper No. 171 (London: International Institute for Strategic Studies, Autumn 1981), p. 1; and Richard Ned Lebow, "The Cuban Missile Crisis: Reading the Lessons Correctly," *Political Science Quarterly*, Vol. 98, No. 3 (Fall 1983), p. 448.

makes the balance of nuclear forces irrelevant, it suggests that parity should not negate the option. Indeed, muted nuclear threats were resurrected twice in crises after the acknowledged arrival of parity (the DEFCON-3 alert of SAC in October 1973, and several leaks in early 1980 about nuclear options for countering further Soviet advances toward the Persian Gulf).

Reflection upon the record, however, suggests that this "balance of resolve" theory is more useful for explaining the U.S. decisions to attempt nuclear leverage than it is for explaining Soviet reactions to the ploy. (There are insufficient grounds for assuming that Soviet beliefs corresponded with the reality apparent to Americans—that is, that the Soviets saw themselves as aggressors and recognized that U.S. stakes in the disputes were greater than their own.)[84] The success of deterrence depends on the perception and judgment of the deterree, not on "objective" reality or the intent of the deterrer. The balance of resolve explanation thus offers little reason to assume either that U.S. leaders in the future will refrain from attempts to use nuclear leverage *or* that Moscow will react as favorably as in past cases. (The post-parity instances of U.S. threats were not tested to the degree that some earlier ones were, since Moscow was not forced to concede anything. In 1973, both sides got what they wanted—a truce without either further Israeli advance or Soviet intervention—and in 1980 there is no evidence that the Soviets intended to march beyond Afghanistan.)

Another idea for rationalizing first-use threats is Eisenhower's, cited earlier—that after Moscow achieved the capacity to inflict devastating damage on the United States in an absolute sense, deterrence could rest on the continuing disparity that still guaranteed relatively greater damage to the USSR. In a game of "chicken," as it were, the bigger car could expect the smaller one to swerve first, even if a crash would wreck both. This view resembles what theorists called escalation dominance. If it is any more persuasive in accounting for Soviet willingness to accommodate in earlier crises, however, this notion offers no comforting warrant for the future, since disparity is long gone.

Perhaps these questions are not crucial—for example, if past cases of U.S. reliance on nuclear threats were as dubious in significance as some critics claim,[85] or if the reduced incidence of direct U.S.–Soviet military confronta-

---

84. For elaboration, see the first part of chapter 4 in my forthcoming book.
85. For example, McGeorge Bundy, "The Unimpressive Record of Atomic Diplomacy," in Gwyn Prins, ed., *The Choice: Nuclear Weapons versus Security* (London: Chatto & Windus, 1984).

tions since 1962 is a permanent change in the nature of the global competition. The world is certainly not the same as it was in the first half of the postwar era. Looking back at estimates of vulnerability to Soviet nuclear power in that era, however, suggests that change in the nature of strategic dilemmas and anxieties about first use has been more incremental than epochal. If reliance on a policy of deliberate first use is crazy now, as many critics believe, it was only marginally more prudent then. For the commitment to NATO, there are good grounds for maintaining the policy of extended deterrence despite doubts about its rationality, because the U.S. interest in Europe is clearest and most obviously intense, the superpower conflict has stabilized there anyway, and military alternatives for deterrence are politically infeasible.[86] It is doubtful, however, that the risk is any longer worthwhile in regard to secondary or tertiary interests such as most of the ones that evoked U.S. threats in the first half of the postwar era.

Did it really make sense before the fact to take the risks in the past cases, or were American leaders just lucky that Moscow never chose to call their hand? However that uncertainty is judged, nostalgia for a phony golden age of invulnerability is not as dangerous as the inference some might draw from exposure of the myth—that facile resort to nuclear threats would necessarily be as safe a tactic now as then. There is enough of the record available on this side to show that less has changed than meets the eye in Americans' sense of nuclear vulnerability. But about thinking in the inner sanctums of the other side there is no reliable evidence, although Soviet spokesmen in the 1970s cited military parity as the development that had compelled American acceptance of détente. In any case, in the future there is no basis for blithely assuming Soviet willingness to accept unfavorable outcomes in crisis rather than call what reasonable judgment would say must be an American bluff.

---

86. Richard K. Betts, "Compound Deterrence vs. No First Use: What's Wrong Is What's Right," *Orbis*, Vol. 28, No. 4 (Winter 1985).

A "Wasting Asset"

American Strategy and the Shifting Nuclear Balance, 1949–1954

Marc Trachtenberg

$\mathbf{I}$n January 1946, General Leslie Groves, the wartime commander of the Manhattan Project, prepared a memorandum on the military implications of the atomic bomb. "If we were ruthlessly realistic," he wrote, "we would not permit any foreign power with which we are not firmly allied, and in which we do not have absolute confidence, to make or possess atomic weapons. If such a country started to make atomic weapons we would destroy its capacity to make them before it had progressed far enough to threaten us."[1]

In the late 1940s and well into the early 1950s, the basic idea that the United States should not just sit back and allow a hostile power like the Soviet Union to acquire a massive nuclear arsenal—that a much more "active" and more "positive" policy had to be seriously considered—was surprisingly widespread. The American government, of course, never came close to implementing a preventive war strategy. As far as the public as a whole was concerned, the idea seems to have had only a limited appeal.[2] What ran deep, however, was a tremendous sense of foreboding. If the Soviets were allowed to develop nuclear forces of their own, there was no telling what might

The author is grateful to the MacArthur Foundation, the Social Science Research Council, and to his colleagues and friends at MIT and elsewhere for their support. An earlier version of this article was presented to a conference held in May 1988 under the auspices of the American Academy of Arts and Sciences Committee on History, the Social Sciences, and National Security Affairs. The author would especially like to thank those who took part in that meeting for their comments and criticism.

Marc Trachtenberg is Associate Professor of History at the University of Pennsylvania. This article was written while he was a MacArthur/SSRC Fellow in International Peace and Security in the Defense and Arms Control Studies Program at MIT's Center for International Studies.

---

1. General Leslie Groves, "Statement on the atomic bomb and its effect on the Army," appendix to JCS 1477/6, January 21, 1946, in CCS 471.6 (8-15-45), sec. 2, Record Group (RG) 218, United States National Archives (USNA), Washington, D.C. There is a slightly different version, dated January 2, 1946, in U.S. Department of State, *Foreign Relations of the United States* (*FRUS*), 1946, Vol. I, pp. 1197–1203. Eisenhower, who thought Groves's views were "perhaps extreme in some respects," nevertheless had a high regard for the paper as a whole. See Louis Galambos, ed., *The Papers of Dwight David Eisenhower*, Vol. VII, pp. 760–761, 641–642, n. 7. See also James Schnabel, *The History of the Joint Chiefs of Staff*, Vol. I, 1945–47 (Washington, D.C.: U.S. Government Printing Office [U.S. GPO], 1979), pp. 281–282.
2. Thus in September 1954 a Gallup poll asked: "Some people say we should go to war against Russia now while we still have the advantage in atomic and hydrogen weapons. Do you agree or disagree with this point of view?" Thirteen percent of the sample agreed, 76 percent disagreed, 11 percent had no opinion. Similarly in July 1950, right after the outbreak of the Korean War, 15 percent of a Gallup sample thought the United States "should declare war on Russia now." Hazel Gaudet Erskine, "The Polls: Atomic Weapons and Nuclear Energy," *Public Opinion Quarterly*, Vol. 27 (1963), p. 177; George Gallup, *The Gallup Poll: Public Opinion 1935–1971* (New York: Random House, 1972), Vol. 1, p. 930.

International Security, Winter 1988/89 (Vol. 13, No. 3)

happen. If they were so hostile and aggressive even in the period of America's nuclear monopoly, what would they be like once this monopoly had been broken? There was no reason to assume that a nuclear world would be stable; wouldn't the Soviets some day try to destroy the one power that prevented them from achieving their goals by launching a nuclear attack on the United States? The clouds of danger were gathering on the horizon. Was the West, through its passivity, simply drifting toward disaster? Wasn't some sort of more "positive" policy worth considering?

The basic goal here is to study how people dealt with these problems—how they came to terms with the dramatic shifts in the military balance and the extraordinary changes in the overall military environment that were taking place in the first decade of the nuclear age. The nuclear revolution, the loss of the American atomic monopoly, and the coming of thermonuclear weapons in the early 1950s were all of enormous importance to the formation of American policy. It had been clear from the very beginning of the nuclear age that America's nuclear monopoly, even its nuclear superiority, was inevitably a "wasting asset."[3] But what did this imply in terms of foreign and military policy?

Most of the analysis here will focus on the purely historical problem of how this set of concerns worked its way through the political system. But two important points emerge from re-examination of this period. The first has to do with the role of trends in the military balance. Concerns about the way the balance was changing—about the expected opening and closing of "windows of vulnerability"—carried a good deal of political weight; indeed, they turned out to be far more important than I ever would have imagined.[4] The whole concept of "windows," it became clear, was not simply an abstract, academic construct, artificially imposed on historical reality. Although the term itself was not used at the time, one is struck by how real the "window" concept was; its impact on actual policy was both enormous and pervasive. In particular, concerns about anticipated shifts in the military balance played a critical role in shaping not only grand strategy, but also policy on specific issues, especially during the Korean War. The reluctance to escalate during the winter of 1950–51 was due to a sense among "insiders" familiar with the true state of the military balance that a window of vulnerability had opened up, and that the Soviets might be tempted to strike before the United States was able to close it. It followed that this was not the time to run risks. By 1953 the situation had altered dramatically as a result of the extraordinary buildup of American military power then taking place; this shift in the balance led to a greatly increased willingness to escalate in Korea if the war could not be ended on acceptable terms. America's window of vulnerability had been shut; and a window of opportunity opened. A key question during the early Eisenhower

---

3. The term "wasting asset" was quite common at the time. See, for example, Schnabel, *History of the Joint Chiefs of Staff*, Vol. I, pp. 258–259.
4. For a discussion of some of the theoretical issues relating to this question, see especially Stephen Van Evera, "Causes of War" (Ph.D. dissertation, University of California at Berkeley, 1984), chap. 2, and pp. 89–94, 330–339; see also Jack Levy, "Declining Power and the Preventive Motivation for War," *World Politics*, Vol. 40, No. 1 (October 1987), pp. 82–107.

period, therefore, was whether this new situation could be exploited before it too disappeared.

The second major point to emerge from the study is that aggressive ideas were taken very seriously in the American government in the early 1950s, even at the highest levels of the administration. This aggressive mood was in part rooted in concerns about the shifting military balance. This is not to say that an aggressive policy was ever implemented. The real question is not whether such a policy was ever adopted, but what sort of political weight this kind of thinking carried.

This article, therefore, has the following structure. A brief survey of "preventive war" thinking in the first section simply sets the stage: It turns out that support for a highly aggressive strategy was much more widespread than has ever been recognized. But these explicit calls for a showdown with the Soviets "before it was too late" were just the tip of the iceberg, a surface manifestation of a much more pervasive, but also more amorphous, set of concerns about what the loss of America's nuclear advantage might lead to.

But was all of this just talk, or did these anxieties have a real impact on policy? This issue will be addressed in two parts. First, I examine the sort of thinking that took shape as high government officials grappled with these issues on a fairly abstract and general level. The analysis in the second section will therefore focus on statements of grand strategy, and especially on NSC 68. The test, however, of how seriously such documents are to be taken is whether the sort of thinking they reflected had any impact on specific issues. The third section, therefore, examines how concerns about the shifting balance affected actual policy, especially during the Korean War. The fourth section takes the story to its conclusion by looking at how preventive war arguments were finally confronted and laid to rest during the early Eisenhower period, in the Solarium exercise and its aftermath in 1953–54. I end by exploring some of the implications of the argument for understanding the overall course of American foreign and military policy in the early 1950s, in the Far East, Central Europe, and elsewhere around the globe.

"Preventive War" Thinking, 1945–53

The sort of argument that General Groves made in 1946 was quite common in the early atomic age. The idea that the United States had to take some sort of action before its nuclear edge was neutralized was by no means limited to the lunatic fringe. William L. Laurence, for example, the science correspondent for the *New York Times* and then America's leading writer on nuclear issues, wanted to force the Soviets in 1948 to accept nuclear disarmament, through an ultimatum if necessary. If they turned down this American demand, their atomic plants should be destroyed before bombs could be produced. If that meant war, he said, it would be one forced on America by Soviet "insistence on an atomic-armament race which must inevitably lead to war anyway. Under the circumstances, it would be to our advantage to have it while we are still the sole possessors of the atomic bomb."[5]

Those who wanted a more "positive" policy often argued that an unrestricted nuclear arms race would "inevitably" lead to war. Groves also assumed that "the world could not long survive" an "armament race in atomic weapons."[6] Senator Brien McMahon, the influential chairman of the Joint Committee on Atomic Energy, thought that "almost nothing could be worse than the current atomic armaments race and that victory in a future war, whatever its sequel in other respects, would at least assure effective international control over weapons of mass destruction."[7]

This argument for a more "positive" policy was a favorite theme of a number of scientists and intellectuals. Bertrand Russell had advocated a Laurence-style ultimatum in 1946.[8] By 1948, he was calling for preventive war pure and simple.[9] The famous physicist Leo Szilard had evidently argued for preventive war at the very beginning of the atomic age: it was "from the lips of Leo Szilard," Bernard Brodie wrote, that he had "heard, in October of 1945, the first outright advocacy in [his] experience of preventive war."[10]

Preventive war was a very live issue among the civilian strategists at the RAND Corporation well into the early 1950s, and there is some evidence that the Navy was interested in the question in 1948.[11] At the State Department, even moderates like

---

5. William L. Laurence, "How Soon Will Russia Have the A-Bomb?" *Saturday Evening Post*, November 6, 1948, p. 182.

6. Groves, "Statement on the atomic bomb."

7. Senator Brien McMahon to Harry S Truman, November 21, 1949, *FRUS*, 1949, Vol. I, p. 591. Note also McMahon's remarks in a top secret hearing held on January 20, 1950, Stenographic Transcript of Hearings before the Joint Committee on Atomic Energy, January 20, 1950, Vol. I, "Projected Development of Super Weapons" (TS), CD 471.6 A-Bomb, RG 330, USNA, quoted in Samuel Williamson (with Steven Rearden), "The View from Above: High-Level Decisions and the Soviet-American Strategic Arms Competition, 1945–50," p. 199 (unpublished manuscript, October 1975, available from Office of the Secretary of Defense, Freedom of Information Office); and also *The Journals of David E. Lilienthal*, Vol. II, pp. 584–585. For additional information on preventive war thinking in the Senate, see n. 62 below.

8. See Bertrand Russell's statement in the *Bulletin of the Atomic Scientists*, Vol. 2, No. 7–8 (October 1946), pp. 19–21.

9. See the report of Bertrand Russell's speech of November 20, 1948, at the New Commonwealth School, London, in the *New York Times*, November 21, 1948, p. 4.

10. Bernard Brodie's recollection is in Brodie to Thomas Schelling, January 8, 1965, enclosure, Brodie Papers, Box 2, University of California at Los Angeles (UCLA) Library. See also the last paragraph of Leo Szilard to Vannevar Bush, January 14, 1944, in Gertrude Weiss Szilard and Spencer Weart, eds., *Leo Szilard: His Version of the Facts* (Cambridge, Mass.: MIT Press, 1978), p. 163. Szilard's article, "Calling for a Crusade," *Bulletin of the Atomic Scientists*, Vol. 3, No. 4–5 (April–May 1947), p. 103, while not of course an argument for preventive war, nonetheless betrays a certain attraction to the idea. See also the Fermi-Rabi statement of October 1949 opposing the development of the hydrogen bomb: the last sentence seemed to take it for granted that the United States could retaliate even against Soviet *production* of a "Super." *FRUS*, 1949, Vol. I, p. 573.

11. The mathematician John Williams, then one of the leading figures at RAND, was the principal champion there of a preventive war strategy. He and Brodie had a very interesting memorandum debate on the issue in 1953 and 1954. See John Williams, "In Response to Paxson's

Charles Bohlen and George Kennan were worried about what would happen if matters were allowed to drift and the Soviets began to build large nuclear forces of their own. "We were not now in the military phase of our relations with the Russians," Bohlen pointed out at a State Department meeting in April 1949, but America had to "look ahead" and think in long-range terms. Suppose that by 1953 Russia had recovered from the war and was "in possession of the atomic bomb." The United States might then wonder: "What should we have done in 1949?"[12] As for Kennan, he thought in 1950 that a war that the Soviet Union stumbled into at that point, before she had really built up an impressive nuclear force, might in the long run "be the best solution for us."[13]

Or take the case of Winston Churchill. In 1946, he predicted that there would be a war with Russia in perhaps seven or eight years. How, he was asked, could Britain take part in an atomic war? "We ought not to wait until Russia is ready," he replied. "I believe it will be eight years before she has these bombs."[14] He argued repeatedly in 1948 for a showdown with the Russians—for "bringing matters to a head" before the American nuclear monopoly was broken. If this led to a war, he told the House of Commons at the beginning of the year, having it then offered "the best chance of coming out of it alive."[15] If the Soviets were so aggressive now, he argued in October, when only America had the bomb, imagine what they would be like "when they got the atomic bomb and have accumulated a large store." Matters could not be allowed to drift; a more active policy was necessary; "no one in his senses can believe we have a limitless period of time before us."[16] Thus Churchill, even before the Berlin

---

Memo on the Probability of War," February 3, 1953, and "Regarding the Preventive War Doctrine," July 27, 1953, unpublished RAND papers. The memoranda that Brodie, Williams, and others exchanged on the question are in the folder "Strategic Objectives Committee," in James Digby's personal files at RAND; I am grateful to Mr. Digby for allowing me to consult them. On Navy interest in the idea, see the "Agenda for [Navy] General Board Serial 315. Study of Nature of Warfare within Next Ten Years and Navy Contributions in Support of National Security," March 30, 1948, CD 23-1-10, RG 330, 1947–50 series, USNA, especially question 119. The study itself, evidently written by the future Chief of Naval Operations (CNO) Arleigh Burke, is apparently still classified.
12. Record of the Undersecretary's Meeting, April 15, 1949, *FRUS*, 1949, Vol. I, p. 284.
13. "Memorandum of National Security Council Consultants' Meeting," June 29, 1950, *FRUS*, 1950, Vol. I, p. 330. See also John Lewis Gaddis, *Strategies of Containment* (New York: Oxford University Press, 1982), p. 48n. Note also some information that came out during the John Paton Davies affair of November 1954: when Davies was dismissed as a security risk, he defended himself (among other ways) by presenting evidence that he had called in 1950 for a "preventive showdown with the Soviet Union." *The New York Times*, November 6, 1954, pp. 8, 9.
14. This is an extract from Lord Moran's diary, *Winston Churchill: The Struggle for Survival, 1940–1965* (London: Constable, 1966), p. 315; note also pp. 505, 545.
15. *Parliamentary Debates*, House of Commons, January 23, 1948, p. 561.
16. Winston S. Churchill Llandudno speech, October 9, 1948, *New York Times*, October 10, 1948, p. 4. These speeches made a big impression on political scientist Hans Morgenthau, who also stressed the dangers of a policy of drift and agreed with Churchill that matters needed to be brought "to a head" with the Soviets. See Morgenthau, "The Conquest of the United States by Germany," *Bulletin of the Atomic Scientists*, Vol. 6, No. 1 (January 1950), esp. pp. 23–26. Morgenthau complained that the American government ignored the tremendous significance of the breaking of the U.S. nuclear monopoly, but he was reacting simply to the blasé image that

blockade, privately urged the American government to present the Soviets with an ultimatum: they must either withdraw from East Germany or see their cities destroyed by atomic attack.[17]

The real heart of preventive war thinking at this time, however, lay within the U.S. Air Force. The preventive war policy was, as Brodie pointed out in 1953, "for several years certainly the prevailing philosophy at the Air War College."[18] General Orvil Anderson, the commanding officer at that institution, had in fact "been in the habit of giving students at the college a completely detailed exposition, often lasting three or four hours, on how a preventive war through strategic airpower could be carried out." "Give me the order to do it," he said, "and I can break up Russia's five A-bomb nests in a week. . . . And when I went up to Christ—I think I could explain to Him that I had saved civilization."[19]

General Anderson's views were evidently shared by other high-ranking Air Force officers, including General George Kenney, the first commander of the Strategic Air Command, and his successor, General Curtis LeMay.[20] General Nathan Twining, Air

---

American officials were deliberately trying to project: see, for example, the instructions on how to react to the Soviet atomic test in the William Frye memo, September 23, 1949, P & O 091 Russia (sec. 1), RG 219, Military Records Branch, USNA.

17. Lewis Douglas to Robert Lovett, April 17, 1948, *FRUS*, 1948, Vol. II, p. 895. 1948 was also the year that Churchill published *The Gathering Storm* (Boston: Houghton Mifflin, 1948), his account of the origins of the Second World War. This book can be viewed as the intellectual pivot linking the interwar period with the nuclear age. The political message of the book certainly has to be interpreted in the light of the other things that Churchill was saying that year. Note especially the "theme of the volume": "how the English-speaking peoples through their unwisdom, carelessness, and good nature allowed the wicked to rearm," and the extraordinary passage on pp. 346–348 (pp. 310–311 in the Bantam paperback edition), a powerful argument for acting before it was too late.

18. Bernard Brodie, "A Commentary on the Preventive-War Doctrine," RAND paper, June 11, 1953, p. 1. See also his Air War College talk of April 17, 1952, "Changing Capabilities and National Objectives," Brodie Papers, Box 12, UCLA, p. 23ff; both, in Marc Trachtenberg, ed., *The Development of American Strategic Thought* (New York: Garland, 1988), vol. 3.

19. *The New York Times*, September 2, 1950, p. 8.

20. The point about Kenney is based on William Kaufmann's personal recollections; it came out in a conversation the author had with him in 1986. Kaufmann knew Kenney quite well in the late 1940s. Kenney, however, was more discreet than Anderson in his public remarks, and did not go beyond an argument about the inevitability of war. See "White Star vs. Red," *Newsweek*, May 17, 1948, pp. 30–32. As for LeMay, he pointed out much later that there had been a time, before the Soviets had accumulated a stockpile of atomic bombs, when the U.S. could have destroyed the entire Soviet capability to wage war "without losing a man to their defenses." He denied that he had ever formally advocated a preventive war strategy, but he did admit that he might have said to some people at SAC, "We've got this capability. Maybe the Nation ought to do it." Curtis E. LeMay with MacKinlay Kantor, *Mission with LeMay* (Garden City, N.Y.: Doubleday, 1965), pp. 481–482. Note also the discussion in the book by LeMay's successor as SAC commander, General Thomas S. Power, who discussed the idea at some length and took a "balanced" approach to the subject: "the concept of 'preventive war'," he said, "is too complex to justify conclusive opinions either for or against it." Thomas Power, *Design for Survival* (New York: Coward McCann, 1965), pp. 79–84. See also the transcript of a series of discussions held in Princeton in late 1953 and early 1954, pp. 1317–1319, Acheson Papers, Box 76, Harry S Truman Library (HSTL), hereafter cited as "Princeton Seminar." According to Nitze, there was a group,

Force Chief of Staff and then Chairman of the Joint Chiefs of Staff (JCS) under Eisenhower, was also sympathetic to Anderson's point of view. In the mid-1960s, a good ten years after preventive war had essentially died out as an issue, he wrote that Anderson had been a "brilliant officer," and his difficulty "lay in his outspoken evaluation of the basic moral issue involved in our confrontation of the Communist conspiracy." For Anderson, preventive war had simply been the lesser of two evils, but his views, Twining complained, "were never given a fair hearing by the State Department, or for that matter, by the military establishment."[21]

The Loss of Monopoly: NSC 68 and American Strategy, 1950–52

The most important government officials at the time were quite hostile to the "preventive war" thesis. But this is not to say that they were not concerned with the problems that would result from the ending of America's nuclear monopoly. The Soviet explosion of an atomic device in late 1949, in fact, led to a major rethinking of American strategy. NSC 68, the basic document here, was written mainly by Paul Nitze, Kennan's successor as head of the State Department's Policy Planning Staff. The report also reflected the views of Secretary of State Dean Acheson, its chief defender in high government circles; it can in fact be seen as a kind of fleshing out of the Acheson strategy of creating "situations of strength."[22] Contrary to what is commonly believed, the strategy called for in NSC 68 was *not* essentially defensive in nature, and the aggressive thrust of the document was probably linked to concerns about long-term trends in the strategic balance. Indeed, it turns out that window thinking had an important impact on American grand strategy, especially in the period after the outbreak of the Korean War.

The authors of NSC 68 believed that America's atomic monopoly was the one thing that had balanced Soviet superiority in ground forces; they were concerned, therefore, that with growing Soviet atomic capabilities, America's nuclear edge was being neutralized more rapidly than conventional forces could be created to fill the gap: hence

---

centering on elements in or connected with the Air Force, that was convinced in 1950 that general war was inevitable, and that this notion had implied something like a preventive war strategy. The group (as he recalled it) included Colonel Herschel Williams of the Air Force; apparently James Burnham (the name is garbled in the transcript) was the major figure in the group.

21. Nathan F. Twining, *Neither Liberty Nor Safety: A Hard Look at U.S. Military Policy and Strategy* (New York: Holt, Rinehart and Winston, 1966), pp. 18–19. See also pp. 49, 56, 60, 276. Note also the August 1953 Air Force study "The Coming National Crisis," discussed in David Alan Rosenberg, "The Origins of Overkill: Nuclear Weapons and American Strategy, 1945–1960," *International Security*, Vol. 7, No. 4 (Spring 1983), p. 33. This study, Rosenberg says, argued that "the time was approaching when the U.S. would find itself in a 'militarily unmanageable' position. Before that time arrived, the nation would have to choose whether to trust its future to 'the whims of a small group of proven barbarians' in the USSR, or 'be militarily prepared to support such decisions as might involve general war.'"

22. See, for example, Dean Acheson's "total diplomacy" speech of February 16, 1950, *Department of State Bulletin*, March 20, 1950.

the sense of a danger zone. But they did not believe that, once American ground forces had been built up and an overall balance had been restored, that would be the end of the problem: they did not believe that the threat of retaliation would be an adequate deterrent to nuclear attack. The Soviets, it was predicted, would be able to deliver a hundred atomic bombs on target by 1954. This did not mean that the Soviets could wipe out American industry as such, for this was still the early atomic age, but they could destroy America's "*superiority* in economic potential." The Soviets could thus prevent the United States from "developing a general military superiority in a war of long duration." Even if they had to absorb an American retaliatory attack, it was "hardly conceivable that, if war comes, the Soviet leaders would refrain from the use of atomic weapons unless they felt fully confident of attaining their objectives by other means."[23] In fact, as a Policy Planning Staff paper emphasized in mid-1952, NSC 68 did not hold that "the existence of two large atomic stockpiles" would result in a nuclear stand-off, but instead had predicted that it might well "prove to be an incitement to war."[24]

Because of the advantages of getting in the first blow, there would be a constant danger of surprise attack: the incentive to preempt would be a permanent source of instability. The need, therefore, was not simply to cover a gap; the concern was not limited to the next four or so years. The real problem was more far-reaching, but what could be done about it?

NSC 68 explicitly ruled out a strategy of preventive war, in the sense of an unprovoked surprise attack on the Soviet Union.[25] But a number of the document's key points echoed the standard preventive war arguments: the developing situation was not stable, the country was moving into a period of enormous danger, and this situation could not last indefinitely. Nitze and Acheson took it for granted that America was dealing not with an ordinary adversary, but with a ruthless enemy intent on world domination, and ultimately on the destruction of the United States.[26]

---

23. NSC 68, April 7, 1950, *FRUS*, 1950, Vol. I, pp. 251, 266, 268. Emphasis added. See also a Policy Planning Staff paper written in mid-1952, *FRUS*, 1952–54, Vol. II, p. 62, para. 9.

24. Enclosure in Paul Nitze to H. Freeman Matthews, July 14, 1952, *FRUS*, 1952–54, Vol. II, p. 62. These were all very controversial issues within the government, especially in 1950. Nitze himself had earlier leaned toward the line that nuclear forces tended to neutralize each other (*FRUS*, 1950, Vol. I, p. 14), and it is not clear to what extent NSC 68 marked a genuine shift in opinion on his part, as opposed to an accommodation to those, especially in the military, who took the opposite line. For a fascinating inside account of these disputes, see Harvey to Armstrong, June 23, 1950, Records of the Policy Planning Staff, Box 7, folder "Atomic Energy—Armaments 1950," RG 59, USNA. For the views of the military, see JIC 502, January 20, 1950, CCS 471.6 USSR (11-8-49), "Implications of Soviet Success in Achieving Atomic Capability," sec. 1, in RG 218, USNA; this document was their contribution to the process that culminated in NSC 68. For a Central Intelligence Agency (CIA) contribution, see ORE 91-49, February 10, 1950, file CD 11-1-2, Box 61, RG 330 (1947–50 series), USNA.

25. *FRUS*, 1950, Vol. I, pp. 281–282. According to General Twining, however, in the discussions leading to NSC 68, the preventive war option was "advocated with much more vigor" than all but one of the three other policies considered in the report. Twining, *Neither Liberty nor Safety*, p. 49.

26. *FRUS*, 1950, Vol. I, pp. 207–208, 145.

It was widely assumed in official circles that it might not be possible to work out a satisfactory *modus vivendi* with the Soviets. One high official in the State Department went even further and "suggested that in the last analysis we may find that we have to drive out the rulers of the Kremlin completely."[27] Acheson himself argued that we already were in a "real war" with them, although the American people still did not realize it.[28] And Robert Lovett, then a consultant to the NSC, developed the point: the United States should "start acting exactly as though we were under fire from an invading army. In the war in which we are presently engaged, we should fight with no holds barred. We should find every weak spot in the enemy's armor, both on the periphery and at the center, and hit him with anything that comes to hand. Anything we do short of an all-out effort is inexcusable."[29]

The most important point about NSC 68 is that this was *not* a defensive-minded, status quo–oriented document.[30] For Acheson and Nitze, the fundamental aim of American policy was quite ambitious: to bring about a "retraction" of Soviet power—to force the Soviets to "recede" by creating "situations of strength."[31] The policy of NSC 68 was, in its own terms, a "policy of calculated and gradual coercion"; the aim was "to check and to roll back the Kremlin's drive for world domination." To support such a policy, it was important to go beyond merely balancing Soviet power, and to build up "clearly superior overall power in its most inclusive sense."[32]

What was the point of such an ambitious policy? The document itself presented two rationales, but neither is entirely satisfactory. First, it argued that a merely

---

27. R. Gordon Arneson, special assistant to the undersecretary of state for atomic energy policy, from the Record of the Meeting of the State-Defense Policy Review Group, February 27, 1950, *FRUS*, 1950, Vol. I, p. 174.

28. Ibid., p. 207; see also ibid., p. 293.

29. Record of the Meeting of the State-Defense Policy Review Group, March 16, 1950, ibid., p. 198. Lovett had been undersecretary of state until January 1949; he was appointed deputy secretary of defense in September 1950, and the following year succeeded Marshall as secretary of defense.

30. The large literature on the subject assumes that NSC 68 called for an essentially defensive policy. The early account by Paul Hammond, "NSC-68: Prologue to Rearmament," in Warner Schilling, Paul Hammond and Glenn Snyder, *Strategy, Politics, and Defense Budgets* (New York: Columbia University Press, 1962), was written before the text of the document became available. The more recent literature is therefore more interesting in this connection. See in particular Samuel F. Wells, Jr., "Sounding the Tocsin: NSC 68 and the Soviet Threat," *International Security*, Vol. 4, No. 2 (Fall 1979), pp. 116–158; and Steven Rearden, *The Evolution of American Strategic Doctrine: Paul Nitze and the Soviet Challenge* (Boulder, Colo.: Westview, 1984) esp. pp. 22–26. The chapter on NSC 68 in Gaddis, *Strategies of Containment*, is as close to a standard account as we have. Gaddis (p. 100) repeats his earlier judgment (in "NSC 68 and the Problem of Ends and Means," *International Security*, Vol. 4, No. 4 [Spring 1980], p. 168) that the military buildup called for in the document was intended "to be defensive in nature."

31. For Acheson, see Memorandum of Conversation, March 24, 1950, *FRUS*, 1950, Vol. I, p. 208. The term "retraction" appears in many documents from this period. See especially NSC 68, April 7, 1950, *FRUS*, 1950, Vol. I, pp. 252, 289. Note also a Nitze memorandum of July 14, 1952, in *FRUS*, 1952–54, Vol. II, pp. 58–59.

32. *FRUS*, 1950, Vol. I, pp. 253, 255, 284. Note also the reference to the H-bomb in ibid., p. 267: "If the U.S. develops a thermonuclear weapon ahead of the U.S.S.R., the U.S. should for the time being be able to bring increased pressure on the U.S.S.R."

defensive policy was inadequate because the "absence of order among nations [was] becoming less and less tolerable." The enormous tensions of the Cold War could not continue for long and would eventually be replaced by "some kind of order," either on their terms or on ours.[33] But an argument of this sort seems much too abstract and academic to be the real taproot of thinking about basic policy.

The other argument was that a "process of accommodation, withdrawal and frustration" was needed in order to bring about "the necessary changes in the Soviet system." The Kremlin could be "a victim of its own dynamism": if its "forward thrusts" were frustrated, and the Soviets had to deal with a "superior counterpressure," "the seeds of decay within the Soviet system would begin to flourish and fructify."[34] This is quite similar to the argument Kennan had made in July 1947 in the famous "X-article" in *Foreign Affairs*, but there the claim was that an essentially defensive strategy would be sufficient to produce these results. Why did NSC 68 propose to go further? Why was a more aggressive American strategy more likely to bring about these changes in the Soviet system? Despite its length, NSC 68 contained no answer to this basic question. One is therefore left with the suspicion that some unarticulated motive was the real basis for the aggressive strategy called for in NSC 68.

It seems that concerns about the shifting balance played a major role in shaping the policy outlined in NSC 68. The report assumed that in time a Soviet surprise attack on the United States might well be militarily decisive. An American buildup "might put off for some time" the date when the Soviets would be able to launch such an attack. But when that time came—and the document seemed to assume that it would come eventually—the Soviets "might be tempted to strike swiftly and with stealth."[35] The assumption that the Soviets were intent on world domination and thus on the destruction of American power, and the belief that they were absolutely ruthless and that their policy was "guided only by considerations of expediency," implied that they would strike when they had developed this capability.[36] In that case, it did not make sense to opt for a strategy of simply "buying time," in the hope that there might be a basic transformation of the Soviet system in the next few years.[37] Taken to their logical conclusion, these arguments pointed to a much more extreme policy than the one called for in NSC 68—perhaps to a strategy of "bringing matters to a head" with the Russians before it was too late. But this was not the strategy that people like Nitze and Acheson seem to have been reaching for. One has the sense instead that the architects of NSC 68 could scarcely bring themselves to accept the conclusions that followed from their own arguments. It seems instead that they settled, as a kind of psychological compromise, for the lesser strategy of "rollback"

---

33. *FRUS*, 1950, Vol. I, pp. 241, 263.
34. *FRUS*, 1950, Vol. I, pp. 248, 287.
35. Ibid., pp. 266–267.
36. The quotation is from Paul Nitze, "Recent Soviet Moves," February 8, 1950, ibid., p. 145.
37. On "buying time," see a Policy Planning Staff document of December 9, 1950, *FRUS*, 1950, Vol. I, p. 464; also see NSC 68, ibid., p. 287.

and forcing a "retraction of Soviet power," and for the buildup that might make these possible.

This is not to argue that NSC 68 had a hidden agenda and that the real goal of the aggressive strategy was to generate situations that might lead to a war before America's nuclear advantage was lost forever. It is clear, in fact, that neither Nitze nor Acheson actually wanted a war, above all, not in 1950. What they wanted was to create such overwhelming power that the United States could achieve its goals without actually having to fight. But such a military strategy was extremely ambitious. As Nitze put it in mid-1952, it would take "clearly preponderant power" to make progress by peaceful means, "probably more power than to win military victory in the event of war."[38]

At the end of the Truman administration, Nitze would complain that even the extraordinary buildup of military power that had taken place during the Korean War had been inadequate. The defense budget might have tripled, but the "situations of strength" that national policy had called for had never been created. In January 1953, he worried that the United States was becoming "a sort of hedge-hog, unattractive to attack, but basically not very worrisome over a period of time beyond our immediate position"; Nitze was upset that the goals laid out in documents like NSC 68 were not being taken "sufficiently seriously as to warrant doing what is necessary to give us some chance of seeing these objectives attained."[39]

A war itself was never desired, but it does seem clear that Nitze was willing to accept a real risk of a nuclear conflict, but only *after* the trends had been reversed and American power had been rebuilt. For the time being, he wrote in 1950, the United States was weak and needed above all "to build a platform from which we can subsequently go on to a successful outcome of this life-and-death struggle" with the Kremlin. "We must," he stressed, "avoid becoming involved in general hostilities with the USSR in our present position of military weakness if this is at all possible without sacrificing our self-respect and without endangering our survival."[40] But then? The clear implication is that when "our position of weakness" turns into a "position of strength," it would become less necessary to tread cautiously.[41].

In the meantime, however, the country was going to have to cross a danger zone. With the outbreak of the Korean War and the rearmament decisions that were made in its wake, the argument was extended to take note of another danger: the risk that the Soviets might strike preemptively, in order to head off the shift in the balance of military power that American rearmament would bring about. The assumption was

---

38. Paul Nitze to H. F. Matthews, July 14, 1952, *FRUS*, 1952–54, Vol. II, p. 59.
39. Nitze to Dean Acheson, January 12, 1953, *FRUS*, 1952–54, Vol. II, p. 205.
40. *FRUS*, 1950, Vol. I, p. 464. This sort of thinking was fairly common during the late Truman period.
41. Note also in this context Acheson's complaints in May and June 1953 about the "weakness" of the Eisenhower policy, and the new administration's failure to follow through on Truman's policy of "building strength." Acheson to Truman, May 28, 1953, Box 30, folder 391, and Acheson Memorandum of Conversation, June 23, 1953, Box 68, folder 172, both in the Dean Acheson Papers, Sterling Library, Yale University, New Haven, Connecticut.

that a "window" favoring the Soviets had opened, and that the American attempt to close it might well lead to a war.

Such window thinking is a recurrent theme in the published *Foreign Relations* documents. NSC 73/4 of August 25, 1950, for example, argued that the Korean events might be "the first phase of a general Soviet plan for global war." In that case, the Soviets would avoid war until they had calculated that "the United States had reached the point of maximum diversion and attrition of its forces-in-being," or until the USSR had developed its nuclear forces "to the point which it deemed desirable for a general attack on the West." As long as America's forces were being drawn increasingly into the fighting in Korea, "the Kremlin might not hasten the outbreak of general hostilities since the USSR would be increasing its own capabilities as those of the U.S. diminished." But this could change, the document warned, "at the point where the Kremlin estimated that our maximum weakness had been reached, and that further passage of time leading to the material strengthening of the relative position and military posture of the United States would not work to Soviet advantage."[42]

A CIA memorandum a few weeks later was even more specific about dates: "In the belief that their object cannot be fully attained without a general war with the Western Powers, the Soviet rulers may deliberately provoke such a war at the time when, in their opinion, the relative strength of the USSR is at its maximum. It is estimated that such a period will exist from now through 1954, with the peak of Soviet strength relative to the Western Powers being reached about 1952."[43] Window arguments of this sort were very common, especially in 1951.[44]

The sense that a great window of vulnerability had opened up helps explain why the U.S. government as a whole, and especially those officials who really understood military matters, were so afraid of general war in late 1950 and 1951: for the time being, the military balance favored the Soviets, who might therefore soon choose to precipitate a war with the West. For the same reason, the West had to move with great caution during this period. Indeed, these assumptions had begun to take shape in early 1950, even before the outbreak of the Korean War. It had been predicted that the shift in the balance resulting from the ending of the American nuclear monopoly would embolden the Soviets and lead to an increase in communist aggressiveness.[45] The events in Korea seemed to confirm this prophecy, and thus to vindicate this

42. *FRUS*, 1950, Vol. I, p. 378. See also *FRUS*, 1950, Vol. VII, p. 523.
43. NIE-3 of November 15, 1950, *FRUS*, 1950, Vol. I, p. 415. Even more specific is the estimate of the "Moscow-Peiping Time-Table for War," written by the Director of the State Department's Office of Chinese Affairs (O. Edmund Clubb), December 18, 1950, ibid., p. 478ff. See also CIA Director Walter Bedell Smith's memo of December 11, 1950, *FRUS*, 1951, Vol. I, p. 3.
44. See *FRUS*, 1951, Vol. I, pp. 40, 111, 126, 131, 153, 198–199, for various documents with similar "window" themes. Note also an interesting variation in an NSC staff document of August 12, 1952, *FRUS*, 1952–1954, Vol. II, p. 74, para. 3: this was a "bringing matters to a head" argument in reverse.
45. For a typical example of such a prediction prior to the outbreak of the Korean War, see the Policy Planning Staff paper, "The Current Position in the Cold War," April 14, 1950, *FRUS*, 1950, Vol. III, esp. pp. 858–859; note also Nitze's comments in *FRUS*, 1950, Vol. I, p. 143.

whole way of viewing things; a good part of the reason the Korean War had such an extraordinary impact on American policy in this period is that the ground had been prepared in this way. Indeed, what the Korean War seemed to show was that the situation was even more serious than NSC 68 had assumed. The fact that the Soviets had been willing to accept the risk of war with America—first, in approving the North Korean attack, and then in supporting China's intervention in the war—showed how strong they thought their position now was, and thus how far they might now be prepared to go, not just in the Far East, but in Europe as well.[46]

It followed that the central goal of diplomacy, as Bohlen put it in 1951, was to steer the country through the danger zone: "It is axiomatic that when one group of powers seeks to close a dangerous disparity in its armed strength in relation to another group of powers, a period of danger by that factor alone is to be anticipated. The diplomatic arm of the United States should be utilized in this period in such a fashion as to minimize rather than intensify the danger of a general war resulting from a Soviet response to what they might regard as an increasing threat to their existence."[47]

It was, therefore, important to be discreet about America's real long-term aims. There was a great danger, according to a 1952 Policy Planning Staff paper, that if the Soviets thought war was unavoidable, they might initiate a war that would push the United States "back to the Western hemisphere" and allow them to take over the vast resources of Eurasia. To achieve this goal, which would put them in a commanding position for the final phases of the world struggle, they might even be willing to absorb "whatever damage we can inflict" through atomic bombardment. It was thus important at present to avoid giving them the impression that war was inevitable. Talk of rollback was ill-advised at a time when a period of stability was needed to enable the West to develop its power, and in particular to build up its forces in Europe. It followed that public pronouncements for the time being had to

---

46. See Acheson's remarks in the special NSC meeting held on November 28, 1950, especially the passage summarized on p. 15 of Elsey's notes of this meeting; Elsey Papers, Box 72, "Korea. National Security Council Meeting, 3:00 p.m., November 28, 1950," HSTL. "Time is shorter than we thought, Mr. Acheson said. We used to think we could take our time up to 1952, but if we were right in that, the Russians wouldn't be taking such terrible risks as they are now." (There is a less revealing record of this meeting in *FRUS*, 1950, Vol. VII, pp. 1242ff.) Note also NIE-15, "Probable Soviet Moves to Exploit the Present Situation," December 11, 1950, president's secretary's files (PSF), Box 253, HSTL, especially the first paragraph in this document. Finally, see Acheson's later discussion of all this in the Princeton Seminar, p. 906. None of this, of course, should be taken as implying that there was no hard evidence that fed into these assessments. There were in fact important indications from intelligence sources of a general increase in Soviet aggressiveness and preparations for war. See in this regard Kennan's comments in the Princeton Seminar, pp. 1189–1190, and the memorandum of an intelligence briefing requested by the secretary of defense on "Soviet Activity in Europe During the Past Year Which Points Toward Offensive Military Operations," October 26, 1950, CD 350.09, RG 330 (July–December 1950 series), USNA.
47. Bohlen memorandum, September 21, 1951, *FRUS*, 1951, Vol. I, p. 172. The last phrase hints at a sense of the "security dilemma" aspect of the situation; the first sentence echoes Tirpitz's pre–World War I arguments about a "danger zone."

be strictly defensive in tone. "It seems dangerous," the paper argued, "to adopt the political posture that we must roll back the Iron Curtain" at a time when the West was not yet able to defend even the present line of demarcation.[48]

Policy in Practice: Korea, and Elsewhere

In this section, I want to show first how the sort of thinking described in the previous section was related, (a) to the decision not to escalate in Korea during the terrible winter of 1950–51; and (b) to the extraordinary rearmament decisions made in late 1950. Second, I examine how the dramatic buildup of American military power that eventually did take place, and the shift in the strategic balance that this brought about, affected the course of American strategy, especially in Korea, but elsewhere as well.

The first point to make about the Korean War is that the United States never really opted for a "limited war" strategy in that conflict. American policy was *not* shaped by a belief that as a matter of principle any escalation of the fighting was to be avoided. Rosemary Foot's conclusion about the "thinness of the dividing line between a limited and an expanded conflict" is correct.[49] It was taken for granted that a serious Soviet intervention in the war would lead to World War III, and not just to a local U.S.–Soviet war in the Far East.[50] As for a Chinese intervention, there was originally

---

48. Policy Planning Staff paper, n.d., *FRUS*, 1952–54, Vol. II, pp. 67–68. Once again, the parallels with pre–World War I Germany are striking. Paul Kennedy gives some amazing examples of German frankness (among themselves) about the importance of concealing their ultimate goals from the outside world while German naval power was being built up. For example, when Prince Henry of Prussia visited Britain in 1903, he "informed Tirpitz that 'the cat is out of the bag,' and regretfully added that 'we would have been much further than we are now, had we understood the art of keeping quiet.'" Paul Kennedy, *The Rise of the Anglo-German Antagonism, 1860–1914* (London: George Allen and Unwin, 1980), pp. 257–258. Note also the examples of the German recognition of the need for discretion in "Strategic Aspects of the Anglo-German Naval Race," in Kennedy, *Strategy and Diplomacy, 1870–1945* (London, Boston: Allen & Unwin/ Fontana, 1984), pp. 132, 159–160.
49. Rosemary Foot, *The Wrong War: American Policy and the Dimensions of the Korean Conflict, 1950–1953* (Ithaca: Cornell University Press, 1985), p. 37. Later on, however, she implies that there was a more or less definitive decision to fight a limited war. A "crucial turning point" was reached in early 1951: unless the administration soon opted for "expanded operations against China," she says, the Americans would be settling "for a limited conflict" (p. 120).
50. This was a very common assumption in the documents. For the JCS views, see the Bradley memoranda of July 10, 1950 (circulated as NSC 76), and November 9, 1950, *FRUS*, 1950, Vol. VII, pp. 346 and 1121. The more guarded official State Department view is reflected in NSC 76/ 1 of July 25, 1950, ibid., pp. 475–477. Formal policy was reflected in NSC 73/4 of August 25, 1950, *FRUS*, 1950, Vol. I, pp. 375ff; see esp. p. 386. The less formal documents are more revealing: see esp. the "Summary of United States–United Kingdom Discussions," July 20–24, 1950, *FRUS*, 1950, Vol. VII, p. 463, para. 8; and Memorandum of Conversation, August 25, 1950, ibid., p. 647. For the views of important officials, see the record of U.S.–Canadian discussions, May 25 and June 14, 1951, *FRUS*, 1951, Vol. I, pp. 841, 850 (Nitze and Acheson); and the minutes of meeting between high State and Defense Department officials, August 6, 1951, ibid., p. 878 (Lovett). The one piece of evidence I saw that points in the opposite direction is the record of high-level meeting held in late June. When General Vandenberg pointed out that American air power would only be effective against North Korean armor if Soviet jets did not intervene,

no intention to fight a war limited to the Korean peninsula; the initial impulse was to respond to a Chinese attack by a certain widening of the conflict.[51] In fact, American officials at this point even considered the possibility that the United States should respond to a Chinese intervention with an attack on the Soviet Union itself.[52]

This extreme idea was quickly ruled out. But reading the documents, one does detect a certain undercurrent of emotion—an impulse to escalate, held in check only by considerations of expediency. As CIA Director Walter Bedell Smith put it at an NSC meeting in November 1950, the Chinese intervention had raised "the question as to what point the U.S. will be driven to, to attack the problem at its heart, namely Moscow, instead of handling it on the periphery as at present."[53] The implication was that this point was not that far off, that the United States could only be pushed so far and was rapidly reaching that limit. The same kind of thinking is reflected in a Joint Chiefs of Staff paper of January 3, 1951, which argued that it was "militarily foolhardy" to get involved in a land war against China while the "heart of aggressive COMMIE power remained untouched."[54]

President Truman himself was also attracted, at least on a visceral level, to the idea of bringing matters to a head with the Russians. He warned publicly in July 1950 that new acts of aggression "might well strain to the breaking point the fabric of world peace."[55] On September 1 (that is, two months before the Chinese intervened), he issued another warning that fighting in Korea might "expand into a general war" if "Communist imperialism" drew new armies and governments into the Korean conflict. The warning was given despite the fact that Truman had just approved NSC 73/4, which argued for localization of any new conflict.[56] Perhaps the president's warning was essentially a bluff, or perhaps it is to be understood in domestic political terms as a response to Republican pressure, since leading Republican politicians had been loudly calling for threats of this sort.[57] But it seems that something visceral was

---

Truman asked about America's ability to knock out Soviet bases in the area, and then ordered the Air Force to "prepare plans to wipe out all Soviet air bases in the Far East." Memorandum of Conversation, June 25, 1950, *FRUS*, 1950, Vol. VII, pp. 157–161.
51. Foot, *Wrong War*, pp. 82–84.
52. "Summary of United States–United Kingdom Discussions," July 20–24, 1950, *FRUS*, 1950, Vol. VII, p. 463, para. 9; see also p. 465.
53. Minutes of the 71st Meeting of the National Security Council (November 9, 1950). Available on microfilm: "Minutes of Meetings of the National Security Council," University Publications of America, reel 1 (hereafter MNSC).
54. JCS 1776/180, January 3, 1951, "Records of the Joint Chiefs of Staff," University Publications of America microfilm publication (1979), Part II (1946–53), Section C (Far East), reel 9, frame 832 (henceforth cited in the form: RJCS/II/C/9/832). Emphasis in original.
55. *Public Papers of the Presidents of the United States: Harry S Truman*, 1950, pp. 527–537; cited in *FRUS*, 1951, Vol. I, p. 837.
56. *New York Times*, September 2, 1950, p. 4. NSC 73/4 would limit the American response to a Chinese intervention to "appropriate air and naval action" against China. A widening of the war to include, in such a case, an attack on the Soviet Union itself was not even considered in the document, which generally took the line that in dealing with Communist moves "over the next two or three months" conflicts were to be localized. *FRUS*, 1950, Vol. I, pp. 375ff, esp. 385–388.
57. *New York Times*, August 16, 1950, pp. 1:7, 17:1.

being expressed, something that also comes out in Truman's famous diary reflections written a year and a half later, where he considered issuing a nuclear ultimatum to the Soviets as a way of ending the war.[58]

The late summer of 1950 also saw a flurry of articles in the public press dealing with preventive war. The secretary of the navy, Francis Matthews, gave a speech on August 25 calling for the United States to initiate a "war of aggression." Americans, he said, should become the world's first "aggressors for peace."[59] This was followed by a report by the *New York Times*'s well-informed military correspondent, Hanson Baldwin, that Matthews was launching a trial balloon, and that his speech reflected the thinking of Secretary of Defense Louis Johnson, "who has been selling the same doctrine of the preventive war in private conversations around Washington."[60] A day later, the same day that Truman's warning about a "general war" was printed, the *Times* published an account of General Orvil Anderson's advocacy of preventive war.[61] (Truman then dismissed Anderson for going public with the idea.) Even before the Korean War, the preventive war idea had some support in the Congress, and now Senator John McClellan spoke out in favor of the policy.[62]

---

58. The passages are quoted and commented on in Foot, *Wrong War*, p. 176, and in two articles by Barton Bernstein: "Truman's Secret Thoughts on Ending the Korean War," *Foreign Service Journal*, Vol. 57, No. 10 (November 1980); and "New Light on the Korean War," *International History Review*, Vol. 3, No. 2 (April 1981). Note also General Douglas MacArthur's "Memorandum on Ending the Korean War," in his *Reminiscences* (New York: McGraw Hill, 1964), pp. 410–412; and Bob Considine's related interview with MacArthur, published immediately after MacArthur's death, *New York Times*, April 9, 1964, p. 16.

59. *New York Times*, August 25, 1950, p. 1:6.

60. *New York Times*, September 1, 1950, p. 4:2; republished in part in the *Bulletin of the Atomic Scientists*, Vol. 6, No. 10 (October 1950), p. 318; a similar report had appeared in Marquis Childs' column in the *Washington Post* on August 31. Note also Truman's objection to the last paragraph in the Defense Department's proposed directive to MacArthur in an NSC meeting held on June 28, 1950, which, he said, seemed to imply that "we were planning to go to war with Russia." Memorandum for the President, June 30, 1950, MNSC, reel 1. On this, see also Harry Truman, *Memoirs*, Vol. II, *Years of Trial and Hope* (Garden City: Doubleday, 1956), p. 341. Given his general approach, it is astonishing that Johnson as late as July 1949 had been unwilling to increase the budget for analyzing the intelligence on Soviet nuclear capabilities that had been gathered, an increase that had been strongly recommended to him by a committee that had looked into this issue. Memorandum of July 8, 1949, CD 11-1-2, Box 61, RG 330 (1947–50 series), USNA.

61. It is sometimes implied (e.g., by Dean Acheson, in *Present at the Creation* [New York: Norton, 1969], p. 478) or claimed (e.g., by Barton Bernstein, in "Truman's Secret Thoughts," p. 31) that Matthews, like Orvil Anderson, was removed from his position for taking this line. But in fact when he offered to resign Truman simply told him to "forget about it" and in spite of his general incompetence was allowed to continue in office for another year. George Elsey, "Memorandum for File," October 2, 1950, Elsey Papers, Box 72, HSTL.

62. McFall memorandum, January 26, 1950, *FRUS*, 1950, Vol. I, pp. 140–141; and *Newsweek*, February 13, 1950, p. 20, where Congressman Henry M. Jackson was linked to the "preventive war" idea. McClellan's remarks are quoted in "Both Parties Back Truman Arms Call," *New York Times*, September 3, 1950, p. 11:1. Another Senator (Millikin) is identified as a supporter of preventive war in Williamson, "The View from Above," p. 195. On the mood in the country at the time, note the discussion between Secretary Acheson and a group of senators and congress-

The Matthews and McClellan speeches appear to be the most extreme outcroppings of a somewhat inchoate but very widespread wave of feeling: that the aggressive thrust of Soviet policy reflected in the North Korean attack was something the United States could not live with forever, and that perhaps the time was coming when it would have to be dealt with directly, before matters got completely out of hand. What kept this in check was not an abstract commitment to the philosophy of limited war, but rather a sense for America's current military weakness. Major rearmament decisions were made in late 1950, but it would be a long time before the actual military balance could be reversed. The CIA, for example, assumed that the period from 1950 through 1954 would thus be a time when "the strength of the Soviet Union vis-à-vis the Western Powers is at a maximum"; this sort of assumption was then quite common within the government.[63] It was therefore the Soviets who might deliberately provoke a war during this period; for the United States to plunge into a general war, or take actions which ran a serious risk of it, might actually play into Russian hands. A general war that broke out in 1950 or 1951 might well be a disaster for the West. As General Omar N. Bradley, chairman of the Joint Chiefs of Staff, pointed out at an NSC meeting in November 1950, if a global war broke out, "we might be in danger of losing."[64]

To understand this fear, it is necessary to probe a bit more deeply into how global warfare was understood at this time. This was still not a period when it was taken for granted that all-out war meant the destruction of whole societies. The Harmon and Hull reports of 1949 and 1950 had made it clear that the initial "atomic blitz" could not be counted on to destroy the war-making power of the Soviet Union.[65] By the same token, a Soviet atomic attack in the early 1950s would have had only a

men on August 10, 1950, in *FRUS*, 1950, Vol. III, pp. 197–204. Here Senator Estes Kefauver insisted that "sentiment throughout the country was building up" in the direction of preventive war; pp. 204, 199. See in this context Demaree Bess, "How Close is War with Russia?" *Saturday Evening Post*, November 24, 1951, esp. p. 107; and also Senator Paul Douglas's view, reported in *Time*, December 18, 1950, pp. 20–21, that in the event of new communist aggression, the U.S. should "unleash such power as we have directly upon Russia itself." The fact that Douglas was one of the most liberal members of Congress shows just how far this sort of thinking extended at the time. The leading newspapers generally reacted negatively to the Matthews speech, but some important journalists supported the navy secretary. See, for example, David Lawrence, "Matthews Speech is Realistic If Not in Line With Policy," *Washington Star*, August 28, 1950. Note finally a short article in *Time*, September 18, 1950, p. 30: "Background for War: War Now? Or When? or Never?" This article called for a buildup followed by a "showdown" with the Russians by 1953.
63. CIA memorandum, October 12, 1950, *FRUS*, 1950, Vol. VII, pp. 937–938.
64. Minutes of the 71st Meeting of the National Security Council, November 9, 1950, MNSC, reel 1.
65. Harmon Report: JCS 1953/1, May 12, 1949, CCS 373 (10-23-48), RG 218, USNA, analyzed in David Alan Rosenberg, "American Atomic Strategy and the Hydrogen Bomb Decision," *Journal of American History*, Vol. 66, No. 1 (June 1979). Hull Report: JCS 1952/11, February 10, 1950, same file, discussed in Richard Rowe, "American Nuclear Strategy and the Korean War" (M.A. thesis, University of Pennsylvania, 1984), pp. 26ff. See also the second paragraph in section C of NSC 68, *FRUS*, 1950, Vol. I, p. 281.

limited effect on the American war economy: it could not prevent the United States from mounting a major military effort.[66] The reason was that unlike the high-yield weapons being developed in the early 1950s, the early fission bombs were weapons of relatively limited power. As Edward Teller pointed out in 1947, even if a large number of such bombs—"say a thousand or ten thousand"—were launched against America, "many millions" would die, but if certain elementary precautions were taken, the country as a whole "could survive heavy atomic bombardment" and go on to win the war. This would not be the case with the new weapons already on the horizon.[67]

It was thus taken for granted in the early 1950s that a third world war would be long.[68] In the first few weeks of the war, the United States would be swept off the continent of Europe, at least up to the Pyrenees. America would then begin to mobilize its resources and mount a sustained bombing campaign with atomic bombs and aircraft produced after the outbreak of the war. The Soviets, who now had the great resources of Western Europe to draw on, would at the same time be conducting their own air offensive against the United States and its bases and allies overseas. This would be a war of endurance, and the intensity with which this air war was conducted would be an important determinant of its outcome. The ability to base forces overseas (so that a much more intense bombing campaign could be conducted with medium bombers) was therefore still very important. It was for this reason that the bulk of the bomber fleet was composed of medium bombers, B-29s and B-50s; the B-36 intercontinental bomber, which became operational in 1947 (and which, like the B-29, could carry just one fission bomb), made up only a small fraction of the bomber force. At the end of 1950, for example, there were only 38 B-36s in the Air Force, in contrast to 477 medium bombers. Such a small force could scarcely operate effectively by itself.[69]

---

66. See the report of the Special Evaluation Subcommittee of the National Security Council (Edwards Committee), NSC 140/1, May 18, 1953, *FRUS, 1952–54*, Vol. II, p. 343.

67. Edward Teller, "How Dangerous Are Atomic Weapons?" *Bulletin of the Atomic Scientists*, Vol. 3, No. 2 (February 1947), pp. 35–36.

68. The JCS mobilization guidance, for example, assumed that it would last at least five years. "National Stockpiling Program," prepared by the Defense Department and the Office of Defense Mobilization, October 12, 1951, *FRUS, 1951*, Vol. I, p. 211.

69. For the figures, see Walter Poole, *History of the Joint Chiefs of Staff*, Vol. IV, 1950–52, p. 168. My conclusion that effectiveness of air warfare with such a small force would be limited is based on the following considerations. Soviet air defenses would be proportionately more effective against a B-36 attack; a more massive strike that used both medium and heavy bombers would be better able to saturate the air defense network. Attrition of the B-36 force might therefore be significantly higher, and the Air Force might be forced to adopt tactics—night bombing, for example—that reduced attrition, but sacrificed a degree of accuracy. But since the goal was to destroy war-sustaining industrial installations which, as a rule, were located on the outskirts of cities, a loss of accuracy could seriously affect the ability of the air offensive to achieve its goals. Because the shock wave from the bomb spreads over three dimensions, the blast effect falls off roughly in proportion to the cube of the distance from the center of the explosion—a doubling of the average error, for instance, would mean that overpressure would be cut on the average by a factor of eight. Given the limited power of the early fission bombs, this meant that an air offensive with B-36s in late 1950 might have had only a very limited impact on Soviet war

America was therefore highly dependent on the use of bases in Britain, and the implications of this point were well understood by many American officials in this period.[70] This dependence on Britain was a source of weakness for both military and political reasons. The bases that the Strategic Air Command (SAC) planned to use in Britain were considered "exceedingly vulnerable to air attack." In early 1950, none of them even had any "organized ground defenses."[71] Beyond such technical consider-ations, there was a persistent and pervasive fear that the Soviet ability to bring the British isles under air attack might well lead to a "neutralization" of the United Kingdom, and thus to the loss of these bases, even if Britain itself could not actually be conquered.[72]

In a long war, there were many uncertainties, and no one could be sure what the outcome would be. To those familiar with America's military problems, it was also clear that the outbreak of the Korean War had exacerbated an already dangerous situation. As the JCS's Joint Strategic Plans Committee (JSPC) pointed out on July 14, 1950, the allocation of forces to Korea had "drastically reduced" America's "ca-pability to implement our plans for global war." It followed from that, the JSPC argued, that top priority had to be placed on the "regaining of our ability to implement our plans for a global war." This point would be stressed in many important docu-ments from the period.[73]

Concerns about current weakness lay at the heart of the Nitze strategy. Nitze's analysis, and especially the assumptions about a danger zone that the country would

---

potential. Even the bombs (admittedly less powerful) dropped on a completely unprepared and undefended Hiroshima had left the bulk of the city's industrial plant intact. According to the U.S. Strategic Bombing Survey (USSBS), factories "responsible for nearly three-fourths of Hi-roshima's industrial product could have resumed normal operation within thirty days of the attack, had the war continued." USSBS, *The Effects of Atomic Bombs on Hiroshima and Nagasaki* (Washington, D.C.: U.S. GPO, 1946), reprinted in David MacIsaac, ed., *The United States Strategic Bombing Survey* (New York: Garland, 1976), Vol. VII. This analysis had a major impact on thinking about strategic air warfare in the early atomic age.

70. Thus when Truman in December 1950 alluded (accurately, as we now know) to the fact that nuclear weapons were being considered for use in Korea, Prime Minister Clement Attlee quickly came over to Washington to try to make sure that nothing of that sort would happen. Acheson commented in this connection that British views could not be ignored "since we can bring U.S. power into play only with the cooperation of the British." Memorandum for the President, December 12, 1950, MNSC, reel 1.

71. This was the judgment of the Hull Report, paragraph 79 (see n. 65).

72. Even before the Soviets had tested their first atomic bomb, this fear of a "neutralization" of Britain through air attack was very real. In BROILER, the Joint Outline War Plan for 1949, it was noted that the plan "depends critically on the use of the U.K. as an operational base," and it had been assumed in the plan that this would be possible. But the Joint Intelligence Group, the document pointed out, had noted that "neutralization of the U.K. by air and guided missile attacks and partial air and submarine blockade would probably be a Soviet capability in 1948" (Enclosure to JSPG 496/4, March 8, 1948, p. 3). BROILER is available on microfilm in RJCS/II/A/ 4/353ff. With the Soviet atomic bomb, these fears became much more intense: see for example JIC 435/36 of October 5, 1949, RJCS/II/A/3/257ff., and JIC 435/52, February 7, 1951, "Estimate of the Scale and Nature of a Soviet Attack on the United Kingdom between now and mid–1952," RJCS/II/A/6/849ff.

73. JCS 1924/20, July 14, 1950, RJCS/II/C/9/135, 138, 159.

have to cross, had (as noted above) led him in early 1950 to expect an increase in Soviet aggressiveness.[74] The North Korean attack, and then the Chinese intervention, seemed to support the idea that the Soviets were willing to accept, at the very least, an increased risk of war during this period of America's relative weakness. But by the same token it was important that America avoid a war with Russia at this time. The United States therefore had to avoid action that might increase the risk of such a war, such as crossing the 38th Parallel, or (after the Chinese intervention) expanding the war into Manchuria. It was for this reason that Nitze then took a relatively dovish line on issues relating to the escalation of the war. In this he was joined by officers like General Bradley who, while obviously extremely frustrated by the situation, were nevertheless convinced that this was not the time to take risks.[75]

The turnabout of John M. Allison, director of State Department's Office of Northeast Asian Affairs, provides a good example of the link between this sense of weakness and the reluctance to escalate in Korea. On July 24, 1950, Allison had attacked Nitze's line as "a policy of appeasement," "a timid half-hearted policy designed not to provoke the Soviets to war." He argued instead for the conquest of North Korea. "That this may mean war on a global scale is true," he said, but "when all legal and moral right is on our side why should we hesitate?" "The free world," he concluded, "cannot any longer live under constant fear."[76]

But by mid-August he had changed his mind. He now recognized the need to avoid a global war as a limiting factor, and it is clear that a new sense for America's current military weakness played the key role in bringing about this shift in position. The argument in the memorandum where Allison registered his new opinion turned on a key passage from NSC 73/1: "The United States is not now capable of conducting immediately a general military offensive against the USSR because our forces are either not appropriately positioned or are so inadequate as to be incapable of effective action."[77]

The Allison example illustrates in a particularly striking way the important distinction between the views of "outsiders" and "insiders" on these issues. 1950 may have marked the high tide of "preventive war" agitation, but those who called for such highly aggressive strategies were for the most part simply ignorant of military realities. The "insiders" were acutely conscious of American weakness at that point. Indeed, what they were afraid of was that the Soviets would take advantage of the opportunity that had opened up for them and would deliberately pursue aggressive policies that

---

74. Paul Nitze, "Recent Soviet Moves," February 8, 1950, *FRUS*, 1950, Vol. I, p. 147. Korea was mentioned as one of the places where Soviet moves might be made.
75. Policy Planning Staff memo, July 22, 1950, *FRUS*, 1950, Vol. VII, pp. 449–454; "Chinese Communist Intervention in Korea," NIE-2, November 8, 1950, ibid., p. 1102; JCS memo, November 9, 1950, ibid., p. 1121; memoranda of State–Defense Department meetings, December 1 and 3, 1950, ibid., p. 1279 (for Bradley's caution) and p. 1330 (for his frustration); Minutes of Truman-Attlee talks, December 7, 1950, ibid., p. 1457 (for Secretary Marshall's frustration). See also Foot, *Wrong War*, p. 117.
76. Allison memorandum, July 24, 1950, *FRUS*, 1950, Vol. VII, pp. 460–461.
77. Allison memorandum, August 12, 1950, *FRUS*, 1950, Vol. VII, pp. 571–572.

might lead to war with the United States. The Soviets might even choose to initiate their own preventive war before the balance began to turn against them.

For the insiders, both civilian and military, it was therefore clear by the end of the year that a major escalation which ran the risk of Soviet involvement, and thus of global war, had to be ruled out, even though the military situation in Korea was extremely bleak. The one partial exception among top military officers was General Hoyt Vandenberg, the Air Force Chief of Staff. In a discussion with high Defense Department officials in December 1950, he pinpointed August 1951 as the "point of greatest danger," the point at which the Soviets were most likely to "initiate an early war." If this was correct, he said, the next eight months "would not work in our favor since we would not improve our ground potential significantly but would in that period have given the Soviets a chance to produce additional atomic bombs." "He did not say so specifically," according to the record of the meeting made by Assistant Secretary of State Dean Rusk, "but the implication was that it would be better for us to precipitate hostilities at an early date in order to prevent further USSR atomic buildup."[78]

It is striking that the most forceful advocates of air power were the ones who took the most aggressive line at this time. Stuart Symington, for example, secretary of the Air Force from September 1947 to April 1950 and then chairman of the National Security Resources Board, was a great champion of air power. Although in two memoranda written during this bleak period of the war he denied that he wanted to expand the Korean conflict into a general war with Russia, these memoranda sounded the standard themes of the preventive war thesis. The United States was already at war with the Soviets, he said, and the country was currently losing this life-or-death struggle, because it had opted for the purely defensive policy of containment; it had sought always to "localize" aggression, and had drawn back from dealing with the problem at its heart. A "clear and positive" policy had to replace the policy of drift, because, with the development of Soviet nuclear capabilities, time was "running out far more rapidly" than most Americans realized. Symington argued for a strategy of withdrawal from Korea, and replacement of the ground war by an air and naval war against China; if this led to Soviet involvement, the result (announced in advance) would be "the atomic bombardment of Soviet Russia itself."[79]

---

78. Dean Rusk, Memorandum of Conversation, December 19, 1950, *FRUS*, 1950, Vol. VII, pp. 1572–1573. In general, the Air Force's access to inside information was more than balanced by what can only be called its nonrational attachment to air power, which led it to overestimate the effectiveness both of a Soviet air strike on the U.S. and of a U.S. air attack on the USSR; the two arguments together greatly strengthened in the minds of many Air Force officers the case for a "positive" policy. The nonrationality of Air Force thinking on this issue—what the Army liked to refer to as the Air Force's "subjectivity"—comes out very clearly in the documents recording the extraordinary debate on basic strategy that took place at the JCS level from 1948 to 1950. See the portion of the file CCS 373 (10-23-48) in RG 218 at the National Archives covering this period; and the file P & O 373 TS for 1949 and P & O Hot Files for 1950–51, Box 11, RG 319. On Air Force "subjectivity," see General Ray Maddocks, Memoranda for the Army Chief of Staff, February 8 and (especially) March 16, 1949, P & O 373 TS, RG 319, USNA.
79. NSC 100, January 11, 1951, and Symington memo, n.d., *FRUS*, 1951, Vol. I, pp. 7–18, 21–

The general response to Symington's arguments was quite hostile, and shows that the more extreme "air power" position then had very limited appeal.[80] President Truman's personal reaction was quite negative. He characterized a long series of Symington's points as "bunk" or "drivel"; and he drafted (but evidently did not send) a short note to Symington: "My dear Stu, this is [as] big a lot of Top Secret malarky as I've ever read. Your time is wasted on such bunk as this. HST."[81]

The mainstream position, shared by the Joint Chiefs and the State Department, was that the United States could not run the risk of escalation *at that point*. It was currently too weak to take on a global war. The top priority was therefore to build up American power first. As Admiral Forrest Sherman, the Chief of Naval Operations (CNO), put it in a memorandum which was to become the basis of the official JCS position, the crucial thing was to "*delay* a general war with Russia until we have achieved the necessary degree of military and industrial mobilization."[82] General J. Lawton Collins, the Army Chief of Staff, was even more precise as to when escalation might be possible: "Since the United States is not now prepared to engage in global war, and will not be ready before 1 July 1952, we should take all honorable means to avoid any action that is likely to bring Russia into open conflict with the United States prior to that date."[83]

Once the general thinking about trends in the global military balance is understood, many of these documents relating to Korean War strategy take on new meaning. Phrases that one might otherwise overlook, or dismiss as merely pro forma, are suddenly seen in a new light—for example, General Bradley's comment on December 1, 1950, that if Chinese air came in, the United States might have to "defer" striking back, or the military view in February 1951 that "retaliatory action against China," because it might lead to Soviet intervention, "would involve excessive risks *at this time*.[84]

---

33. See also Foot, *Wrong War*, pp. 115–116. According to Harriman in the Princeton Seminar, Symington "under [Bernard] Baruch's influence," took the position that there was going to be a war with Russia, and that total mobilization was therefore necessary. It was taken for granted in the discussion that followed that these arguments were closely related to the preventive war idea. Princeton Seminar, p. 1317ff. Harriman's account is substantiated by the file of correspondence with Symington in Box 95 of the Baruch Papers at the Seeley G. Mudd Library in Princeton. See for example Bernard Baruch to Stuart Symington, November 21, 1950, Symington to Baruch, November 24, 1950, and especially Baruch to Symington, December 5, 1950.
80. See Foot, *Wrong War*, pp. 115–116.
81. *FRUS*, 1951, Vol. I, pp. 21–33. The Truman note is on p. 33.
82. Sherman memo on "Courses of Action Relative to Communist China and Korea," JCS 2118/5, January 3, 1951, JCS Records, II/C/2/677. Emphasis added. The final document recording the JCS position (JCS 2118/10 of January 12, 1951) was revised to take account of General Collins's memo, cited below. The text was circulated as NSC 101; *FRUS*, 1951, Vol. VII, p. 71.
83. JCS 2118/9, January 12, 1951, RJCS/II/C/2/688. The July 1, 1952, date corresponded to official policy. As a result of the new crisis created by the Chinese intervention in the Korean War, the target date for completing the military buildup needed to support the goals laid out in NSC 68 was advanced from mid–1954 to June 30, 1952. The new date was set in NSC 68/4 of December 14, 1950; *FRUS*, 1950, Vol. I, pp. 467ff. For related documents, see ibid., pp. 466–467, 474–475; and *FRUS*, 1951, Vol. I, pp. 131–132.
84. Memorandum of Conversation, December 1, 1950, *FRUS*, 1950, Vol. VII, p. 1279; Record of Department of State–JCS meeting, February 13, 1951, *FRUS*, 1951, Vol. VII, p. 177. Emphasis added.

General Bradley's famous comment, in particular, that a war with China would be "the wrong war, at the wrong place, at the wrong time, and with the wrong enemy," takes on a whole new dimension of meaning when seen in this context. This remark has come to be taken as a symbol of the "limited war" policy—of America's desire to avoid an expansion of the conflict. But what Bradley was implying was that if the United States were forced to fight the Communists, the *right war* was a war against Russia itself, and the *right place* to fight it was not at the periphery, but at the heart of Soviet power. Most importantly, it implied that if it had to be fought at all (Bradley of course hoped it could be avoided), there was a *right time* for fighting it, namely, after American power had been built up. Indeed, he went on to point out that the United States was "not in the best military position to seek a showdown," and that he would not support any policy that would "rush us headlong into a showdown before we are ready."[85] Similar themes were reflected in many documents of the period. Acheson, for example, commented in December 1950 that the "great trouble is that we are fighting the wrong nation. We are fighting the second team, whereas the real enemy is the Soviet Union."[86]

State Department views were not far removed from those of the military. It was taken for granted that the United States should avoid an extension of the Korean conflict and prevent "the development of general war, particularly during the period in which the United States and its allies are in the process of achieving the requisite degree of military and industrial mobilization."[87] A month later, Acheson reiterated the point: a general advance north of the 38th Parallel, he wrote Secretary of Defense George Marshall, was to be avoided because of the "risk of extending the Korean conflict to other areas and even into general war at a time when we are not ready to risk general war."[88]

It was absolutely crucial, therefore, to build up America's military power, and one of the most important themes stressed in these documents was the vital importance of such a buildup.[89] In fact, the rate of American military spending was to triple during this period, and only a small fraction of this was due to the Korean campaign as such.[90]

---

85. 82nd Cong., 1st sess., Senate Committees on Armed Services and Foreign Relations, *Military Situation in the Far East* (Washington, D.C.: U.S. GPO, 1951), pp. 1917–1920.
86. Memorandum of Conversation, December 3, 1950, FRUS, 1950, Vol. VII, p. 1326.
87. "U.S. Action to Counter Communist Chinese Aggression," January 17, 1951, FRUS, 1951, Vol. VII, pp. 1515–1516.
88. Acheson to Marshall, February 23, 1951, enclosure, FRUS, 1951, Vol. VII, p. 193. Emphasis added. Note also Truman to MacArthur, January 13, 1951: "*pending the build-up of our national strength*, we must act with great prudence in so far as extending the area of hostilities is concerned." In Truman, *Years of Trial and Hope*, pp. 435–436; reprinted in James F. Schnabel and Robert J. Watson, *History of the Joint Chiefs of Staff*, Vol. III, *The Korean War* (Wilmington, Del.: Glazier, 1979), p. 420. Emphasis added.
89. See, for example, JCS memo, July 13, 1951, Schnabel and Watson, *History of the JCS*, p. 667; Position Paper for Washington Foreign Ministers' Meeting and British talks, September 8, 1951, ibid., p. 889.
90. The ending of the Korean War, it was assumed in 1953, would result in a $2 billion saving in a projected $41 billion defense budget. FRUS, 1952–54, Vol. II, pp. 279, 284, 311.

The result was an extraordinary buildup of military strength, which acted like an acid, gradually eating away at all those constraints that had kept the United States from escalating at the end of 1950 and in early 1951. The key to the history of the Korean War, in fact, is America's increasing willingness to escalate the conflict. This shift took place in two phases. First, in 1951, it gradually became clear that the government's worst fears about Soviet aggressiveness had been exaggerated: East Germany did not invade the Federal Republic, there was no new Berlin Crisis, Yugoslavia was not attacked, Soviet forces did not move into Iran.[91] As fears of a great risk of war with the Soviets began to fade, the American government felt somewhat freer to act in the Far East.

The second and more dramatic phase began with the resurgence of American military power in late 1952 and 1953. This led to a much greater willingness to escalate, if that was needed to bring the Korean conflict to a successful conclusion. The decisions of the Eisenhower period, with regard both to the war in Korea and to global strategy as a whole, have to be understood as the climax of a process begun years before in the Truman administration.

The relatively small issue of the bombing of Rashin, a port near North Korea's border with the Soviet Union, provides one early indicator of this increasing willingness to escalate the war. In 1950, the State Department blocked plans for the bombing of Rashin; it feared that such action "might entail the gravest consequences." As one high official put it, "both the Defense Establishment and the State Department feel very strongly that we do not want active Soviet participation in the Korean war or the commencement of worldwide hostilities *this year*. We believed that if the Soviet authorities are undecided or are hesitating as to whether to move on a wider basis now, the bombing of Rashin or similar moves might well prove an important deciding factor."[92] But the Truman administration reversed the decision as early as August 1951.[93]

There was a striking evolution of American policy more generally on the extension of the air war. JCS 2118/4 of January 12, 1951, had provided for air strikes against China only if the Chinese Communists attacked American forces "outside of Korea."[94] But in April 1951, General Matthew Ridgway, the U.S. Commander in the Far East, was authorized to attack enemy air bases in Manchuria and the Shantung peninsula "in the event of a major enemy air attack from outside Korea."[95] In November and December the terms were extended a bit further. The JCS wanted American planes to be able to attack air bases in China "whenever the scale of enemy air activity is

---

91. These fears are reflected in many documents from the early Korean War period. See, for example, "Meeting of the NSC in the Cabinet Room of the White House," June 28, 1950, Acheson Papers, Box 65, "Memoranda of Conversation, May–June 1950," HSTL; and especially NIE-15, "Probable Soviet Moves to Exploit the Present Situation," December 11, 1950, PSF, Box 253, HSTL. Note also Acheson's and Nitze's later comments in the Princeton Seminar, pp. 906, 908.
92. Matthews memorandum, August 14, 1950, *FRUS*, 1950, Vol. VII, p. 574. Emphasis added.
93. See Foot, *Wrong War*, pp. 76, 149–150.
94. Schnabel and Watson, *History of the JCS*, p. 419.
95. JCS to Ridgway, April 28, 1951, *FRUS*, 1951, Vol. VII, p. 386.

such as seriously to jeopardize the security of United States forces in the Korean area."[96] This meant that *preemptive* action would be authorized if the Chinese built up their bomber force to a level that might jeopardize the security of American forces.[97] The proposal was approved, with the provisos that such action would have to be "specifically authorized by the President," and that if there was time, the key allies would be informed of the decision in advance.[98] These conditions somewhat limited the effect of the decision, but it is nonetheless clear that the Truman administration was becoming increasingly willing to escalate the war.

These early shifts, however, were minor compared with what would come later when the mobilization effort finally made itself felt in terms of increasing military end-products. For example, General Vandenberg pointed out in September 1951 that the production curve for fighters would begin to go up in the spring, but "we won't really get rolling until next fall."[99] Overall output did increase dramatically in 1952. "U.S. monthly production of military end items," one document reported in August 1952, "is five or six times as large as it was June 1950. Between July 1951 and May 1952 the monthly deliveries of military end items have risen from an annual rate of $6.4 billion to $17.8 billion, and the trend is sharply upward."[100]

The American military buildup was particularly dramatic in the nuclear weapons area. Since 1950, there had been a great expansion in the production of fissionable material, and there had been very important qualitative changes as well, especially with regard to tactical nuclear weapons.[101] By early 1952, the Atomic Energy Com-

96. JCS memo, November 3, 1951, *FRUS*, 1951, Vol. VII, p. 1108.
97. Johnson memo, November 7, 1951, *FRUS*, 1951, Vol. VII, p. 1094.
98. Ibid., pp. 1261, 1383. For some indication of the seriousness with which the matter of preemption in the Far East was taken at the highest political level, see Churchill to Acheson, February 18, 1952 (with enclosure), and Acheson to Churchill, February 19, 1952, Acheson Papers, Box 63, folder "Churchill, Winston S.," HSTL. Note also Admiral Blandy's reference (in this context) to "anticipatory retaliation" on the "Longines-Wittnauer Chronoscope," June 11, 1951, videotape T76:0145, Museum of Broadcasting, New York. Blandy, who had recently retired from the Navy, had long been close to nuclear weapons matters and had, for example, been the commander at the Crossroads tests in 1946.
99. Notes of Department of State–JCS meeting, September 25, 1951, *FRUS*, 1951, Vol. VII, p. 943.
100. NCS 135/1, Annex, August 22, 1952, *FRUS*, 1952–54, Vol. II, p. 106. Some of the reasons mobilization was taking so long are discussed in NSC 114/1, August 8, 1951, enclosure, *FRUS*, 1951, Vol. I, p. 137; and in NSC 114/3, enclosure 1, May 10, 1952, *FRUS*, 1952–54, Vol. II, pp. 29–30. For a detailed description of the mobilization program, see Annex 1 to NSC 114, July 27, 1951, in Documents of the National Security Council (University Publications of America microfilm publication), Supplement 1, reel 1 (hereafter DNSC). There are frequent references in the documents to the depressingly slow pace of industrial mobilization. See, for example, the summaries of discussion at the 103rd and 105th meetings of the NSC, September 27 and October 18, 1951, PSF, Box 220, HSTL. Note also the discussion at the Princeton Seminar, p. 1314.
101. See Rosenberg, "The Origins of Overkill," esp. pp. 23–24, and the sources cited there. Note also C. Savage, "Increase in Production of Fissionable Material," September 26, 1950, Records of the Policy Planning Staff, Box 6, folder "Atomic Energy—Armaments, 1950," RG 59, USNA: "This program to increase the production of fissionable material calls for an expansion of production at a rate as rapid as the limiting factor of ore permits, without resorting to extreme

mission had developed atomic bombs small and light enough to be used by "such fighter aircraft as the F-84 and some Navy carrier planes." As a result, "between May 1951 and July 1953 the Air Force moved rapidly to build a tactical atomic force."[102] By 1952, "techniques and procedures" for the use of atomic weapons on the battlefield had been worked out.[103] At about the same time, the stockpile of bombs had become so large that, from the JCS point of view, scarcity no longer carried any weight as an argument against the use of nuclear weapons in Korea.[104]

The result of this buildup was an increasing willingness in 1952 and early 1953 to escalate the war in Korea if no armistice agreement could be reached. By early 1953, it was clear that the use of nuclear weapons had become an integral part of an overall policy of escalation.[105] Expansion of the war would involve, at the very minimum, an attack on air bases in Manchuria; nuclear weapons would provide a very effective way of destroying those targets.[106] It should be noted that this shift was not due solely to the change of administration. It was the same JCS that had been so cautious at the end of 1950 and in early 1951 that now advocated a nuclear escalation: the thinking in JCS circles in this regard had obviously begun to shift before the new Eisenhower administration took over.[107]

By the beginning of 1953, it was clear that the overall balance had shifted dramatically in America's favor. The United States, said Secretary of State John Foster Dulles

---

measures of diminishing returns. The rate of production under it probably could not be appreciably increased even if we were *sure* that war was inevitable." Emphasis in original.

102. George F. Lemmer, "The Air Force and Strategic Deterrence, 1951–1960," pp. 14–15. A sanitized, declassified version is available at the Office of Air Force History, Bolling Air Force Base, Washington. For some indication of the increasing size of nuclear forces deployed to Europe in support of NATO in this period, see JCS 2220/4, January 31, 1952, "Information for General Eisenhower on Availability of Atomic Weapons," RJCS/II/G/3/1077; and JCS 2220/19, May 6, 1953, "Revision of Information for General Ridgway on Availability of Atomic Weapons," RJCS/II/G/4/54ff.

103. Rowe, "American Nuclear Strategy," pp. 61–64. The tactics and operational techniques were developed partly through tests conducted in Korea in October and November 1951 involving "actual atomic bombs, less nuclear components." Ibid., p. 62.

104. Ibid., p. 64. Note also Nitze's comments in a memo to Acheson of January 12, 1952, *FRUS*, 1952–54, Vol. II, p. 204.

105. Joint Strategic Plans Committee (JSPC), "Future Courses of Action in Connection with the Situation in Korea (Estimate)," JSPC 853/145, January 26, 1953, RJCS/II/C/11/1041ff, esp. frames 1051, 1052; JCS memo of March 28, 1953, "Future Courses of Action in Connection with the Situation in Korea," White House Office Papers, NSC series, Policy Papers subseries, Box 2, Dwight D. Eisenhower Library, Abilene, Ks. (DDEL), discussed in Rowe, "American Nuclear Strategy," pp. 66–68; JCS memo, May 19, 1953, *FRUS*, 1952–54, Vol. XV, pp. 1059–1064; and esp. minutes of May 20, 1953, NSC meeting, ibid., pp. 1064–1068.

106. JCS memo, May 19, 1953, *FRUS*, 1952–54, Vol. XV, p. 1061; memorandum of Department of State–JCS meeting, March 27, 1953, ibid., p. 818 (Vandenberg's remarks). Note also General Hull's comment in the May 13, 1953, NSC meeting, ibid., p. 1014, General Clark's June 1952 request for nuclear-capable F-84s for the counter-air mission, and General Collins's favorable answer, anticipating that they would be sent by November, in RJCS/II/C/10/1102, 1106.

107. Eisenhower was sworn in as president on January 20, 1953. JSPC 853/145, the document on which the JCS based its recommendations, was circulated just six days later; it was based on a report by the Joint Strategic Plans Group, JSPC 853/142, the work for which had been done considerably earlier.

in early 1953, could now get better armistice terms in Korea than had earlier been possible "in view of our much greater power and the Soviet Union's much greater weakness currently."[108]

The shift in the military balance between 1950 and 1953 had a major impact on American policy not just in Korea but elsewhere around the globe. There was a striking change in U.S. policy on Berlin in this period. In the policy documents on Berlin from the end of the blockade through early 1951, caution had been the keynote: if the blockade were reimposed, there should be no "probe"; the JCS thought the Western powers were too weak to undertake a ground action of this sort. In February 1951, the JCS was reluctant to recommend any major military action, even if Soviet forces attacked West Berlin: "Only the Berlin garrison, augmented by the West Berlin police, should be used to resist the attack, pending further consideration at the highest governmental level." The United States had, of course, undertaken to defend West Berlin; the problem was, as the Joint Strategic Plans Committee bluntly pointed out, that the country neither had, nor would soon have, "the military capability to carry out completely our commitments in this regard."[109]

By the spring of 1952, however, high officials had already begun to rethink American policy on the use of force in any new Berlin crisis: "We were opposed to it before," General Bradley said on May 14, "but it should be reconsidered now."[110] And in fact, by mid-1952, the U.S. line on Berlin had completely swung around to a much tougher position: in NSC 132/1 of June 12, 1952, a military probe was accepted, and it was now taken for granted that an attack on Berlin would almost certainly lead to general war. The American position on Berlin became even tougher during the early Eisenhower period; and the JCS documents make it clear that it was, at least from their point of view, the improved military situation that had made possible this dramatic shift of policy.[111]

---

108. Notes of NSC meeting, April 8, 1953, *FRUS*, 1952–54, Vol. XV:1, p. 894.

109. See especially NSC 24/3, "Possible U.S. Courses of Action in the Event the USSR Reimposes the Berlin Blockade," June 14, 1949, DNSC, reel 1; Marshall to Lay, October 18, 1950, in NSC 89, *FRUS*, 1950, Vol. IV, pp. 893–894; JCS 1907/62, January 24, 1951, RJCS/II/G/5/418ff. This last document was the basis for the official JCS memorandum to Secretary of Defense George Marshall, February 7, 1951, *FRUS*, 1951, Vol. III, p. 1892ff. During the blockade itself, the American attitude was surprisingly weak: Truman was unwilling even to shoot down a barrage balloon if that had proved necessary to maintain access to Berlin, because that might have led to a war for which "the U.S. did not have enough soldiers." Williamson, "The View from Above," p. 104.

110. *FRUS*, 1952–54, Vol. VII, p. 1241.

111. The basic document on Berlin for the late Truman period was NSC 132/1 of June 12, 1952 (*FRUS*, 1952–54, Vol. VII, p. 1261ff), much of which was evidently carried over into NSC 5404/ 2, the key Berlin policy document for the early Eisenhower period. This latter document has not been declassified, but one can learn a good deal about it from the Operations Coordinating Board Progress Reports on it of January 7, 1955 and May 17, 1956, DNSC, Supplement 2, reel 1, and Supplement 4, reel 1, respectively. For the military view that the shift in the balance had made all this possible, see the Joint Strategic Survey Committee (JSSC) report on NSC 173, JCS 1907/101 of December 5, 1953, in RJCS/II/G/5/909ff. Note especially the JSSC's contrast with the earlier period "when the military posture of the Allies was too weak to permit of forceful measures in the assertion of the Allied right of surface entry into Berlin." This text was carried

There was a parallel shift in American policy on Indochina during this period. In 1950, the military felt that the United States was too weak to risk escalation of the conflict even if the Chinese intervened in force in the area; by 1952, the American strategy for the defense of Indochina was based on the idea that if the Chinese moved in, the Western powers would have to widen the war and attack China itself.[112]

This examination of the effect of the shifting balance on American foreign and military policy is important because of the light it sheds on the way nuclear forces influence political behavior. It was the overall strategic balance that was crucial, not specific, isolated gestures like particular deployments of nuclear-capable bombers at various points in time. What counted was the actual willingness to escalate, rather than overt threats or ultimata, which the Eisenhower administration was in fact anxious to avoid.[113]

A Time for Decision: "Preventive War" under Eisenhower

In May 1953, when the Eisenhower administration was making its final decisions about the Korean War, Vice President Richard Nixon argued at an NSC meeting that these choices should be made "only in the context of the longer-term problem which would confront us when the Soviet Union had amassed a sufficient stockpile of atomic weapons to deal us a critical blow and to rob us of the initiative in the area of foreign policy." The President "agreed with the views of the Vice President, and

---

over into the JCS Memorandum of January 19, 1954 on NSC 5404, which pressed for a toughening of the text with the argument that there was "no question, all factors considered, but that the Western Powers are now in a stronger military position relative to the Soviet Bloc than they were in 1949." Declassified Documents Collection, 1984/828. Comparing this document with, for example, the corresponding JCS documents from the beginning of 1951, one cannot help but be struck by an extraordinary difference in tone: the virtual defeatism of early 1951 was replaced by an attack on "temporizing measures" and an insistence that the West not hesitate to take "positive action" as soon as its position in Berlin was challenged.

112. See "The History of the Joint Chiefs of Staff. The Joint Chiefs of Staff and the War in Vietnam. History of the Indochina Incident, 1940–1954," JCS Historical Division, 1971, Military Records Branch, USNA, pp. 190, 194–198, 225, 241–258, 294–295, 388, 453–454. A number of the documents summarized here have been published in *FRUS* and in the *Pentagon Papers*, but some of the most important ones are still classified.

113. As early as November 1950, Bedell Smith, then CIA director, argued against laying down an ultimatum, and spoke instead of "quiet exploration with implied threats." Memorandum for the President, November 10, 1950, MNSC, reel 1. Smith, one of Eisenhower's closest associates from World War II, became undersecretary of state in 1953. He soon took a hand in a diplomatic initiative aimed at getting the Soviets to help bring about a Korean armistice. Once again, the theme is avoidance of the appearance of "a threat or ultimatum" and just setting forth a "simple statement of facts" as to what was likely to happen if an arrangement was not worked out. *FRUS*, 1952–54, Vol. XV, p. 915; see also pp. 1081, 1096, 1103, 1110–1111. This is in fact one of the basic techniques of coercive diplomacy: the pose of an impartial observer objectively pointing out—even regretfully—how matters were likely to evolve. Another related technique is the ruling out of alternative possibilities—that is, pointing out what the U.S. was *not* going to do.

explained that Project Solarium was being initiated with this precise problem in mind."[114]

The result of the Korean War buildup had been to transform America's "window of vulnerability" into a "window of opportunity." Would the United States take advantage of it, or would it allow its strategic edge simply to waste away as the Soviets built up their nuclear forces? The aim of this section is to tell how this issue was handled during the early Eisenhower period. What is striking here is, first, how seriously this problem was taken: the most aggressive strategies were never simply dismissed out of hand, but instead had broad appeal, even at the highest political level. But it is also important to note that the impulse to pursue a "dynamic" and "positive" policy was contained; a more or less final decision to rule out such a policy was reached at the end of 1954.

It was during the Solarium exercise of 1953 and its aftermath in 1954 that the Eisenhower administration confronted the issues raised by the shifting nuclear balance. But it was not just asymmetries in military capabilities that were important; the military environment as a whole was changing dramatically at this time. In the early atomic age, a full-scale nuclear war was still actually fightable.[115] An attack that resulted in even a million deaths would of course have been an appalling catastrophe; but the level of devastation that such a figure represents was still quite modest compared with what would be possible a few years later.[116] And these estimates assumed a Soviet surprise attack; if the United States struck first, a Soviet retaliatory attack might have had a much more limited impact. Thus even as late as 1953 or 1954 fighting and, in some meaningful sense, winning an air-atomic war was still "thinkable." It would probably be a long war, and the devastation would be terrible, but the United States would survive as a functioning society.

The extraordinary advances in nuclear weapons technology taking place in the early 1950s were to shatter this image of what a general atomic war would be like. The coming of high-yield weapons, and especially of thermonuclear weapons, was of fundamental importance. As Edward Teller had predicted, a single weapon could now devastate "three or four hundred square miles," instead of just three or four square miles, and the radiological effect might be even more devastating than the increased yield.[117] It was clear, even from the open sources, that these new weapons could generate vast amounts of lethal fallout.[118] The combination of increased yields

---

114. Minutes of NSC meeting, May 13, 1953, *FRUS*, 1952–54, Vol. XV, p. 1016.
115. If war had broken out in 1953, for example, the American estimates implied that a surprise Soviet nuclear attack might have caused something on the order of 3,000,000 deaths; the casualty estimates could perhaps be cut in half if the U.S. took some rudimentary civil defense measures. This is based on information provided in *FRUS*, 1951, Vol. I, pp. 187, 225; and *FRUS*, 1952–54, Vol. II, pp. 334–335, 337, 344–345.
116. See the chart in *FRUS*, 1952–54, Vol. II, p. 651.
117. Teller, "How Dangerous Are Atomic Weapons?" p. 36.
118. Hans Bethe, "The Hydrogen Bomb," *Bulletin of the Atomic Scientists*, Vol. 6, No. 4 (April 1950), pp. 99–104, 125. The passage referred to is on p. 101, and is immediately followed by a reference to the Teller article cited above, which, Bethe said, had already described this threat. Because Bethe here seemed to hint at the way the H-bomb was actually being designed, this

and fallout meant that the new hydrogen bomb was truly an area weapon. The United States could scarcely survive an attack with even a relatively small number of these bombs.

For some people in the government, the increased potential for devastation simply underscored the importance of not allowing the enemy to strike first. This emphasis on getting in the first blow was not new: from the beginning of the atomic age, preemption had been considered very important, especially in military circles.[119] By 1952, the idea had worked its way up to the presidential level: "startled" by a briefing on U.S. vulnerability he had received in September of that year, Truman concluded that "there wasn't much of a defense in prospect except a vigorous offense."[120] Under Eisenhower, this point became absolutely central to American strategy. As David Rosenberg says, "massive retaliation" really meant massive preemption—certainly at the level of military operations, but also, in a more ambiguous way, at the level of general strategy.[121]

It was understood that the question of how dangerous this new world was going to be turned on the issue of the vulnerability of strategic forces, or more precisely on the tractability of the vulnerability problem, which ultimately would determine how much of an incentive there would be to preempt. As an NSC study pointed out in 1952, "the controlling relationship in the atomic equation appears not to be that of

article "caused a memorable storm" in the AEC. On the AEC reaction, see the editorial note by Eugene Rabinowitch, "The 'Hydrogen Bomb' Story," *Bulletin of the Atomic Scientists*, Vol. 8, No. 9 (December 1952), p. 298. A basic description of the link between fallout and bomb design was laid out in J. Rotblat, "The Hydrogen-Uranium Bomb," *Bulletin of the Atomic Scientists*, Vol. 11, No. 5 (May 1955), pp. 171–172, 177.
119. The "principle of pre-emptive attack," characterized by the author of the official JCS history as a "strange, new strategic concept for U.S. military planners," had emerged in late 1945. See Schnabel, *History of the Joint Chiefs of Staff*, Vol. I, p. 278, summarizing JCS 1477/1, October 30, 1945, a study of the military implications of the atomic bomb, and p. 148, summarizing JCS 1518 of October 9, 1945, the basic JCS "strategic concept and plan"; see ibid., p. 305, for the effect of this line of thinking on JCS basing policy. See also ibid., pp. 58, 311. Note finally the Compton Board's argument for a strategy of preemption, and thus for the need to "redefine" what constituted an "aggressive act," an idea that General LeMay quickly picked up on. "The Evaluation of the Atomic Bomb as a Military Weapon. The Final Report of the Joint Chiefs of Staff Evaluation Board for Operation Crossroads," June 30, 1947, PSF, Box 220, Subject File, "NSC—Atomic—Atomic Test—Crossroads," HSTL. For LeMay's thinking, see Lemmer, "Air Force and Strategic Deterrence," p. 35.
120. Minutes of NSC meeting, September 3, 1952, *FRUS*, 1952–54, Vol. II, p. 121.
121. A strategy of preemption is implied in a large number of documents from the Eisenhower period. See, for example, A. J. Goodpaster, Memorandum of Conference with the President, December 22, 1954, pp. 1, 3, Ann Whitman File (AWF), Ann Whitman Diary (AWD), Box 3, ACW Diary, December 1954 (2), DDEL. Note also Eisenhower's remarks at an NSC meeting on July 29, 1954, especially the allusion to Clausewitz's principle of "diminishing as much as possible the first blow of an enemy attack," and his comment at another NSC meeting in early 1957 that since a massive Soviet nuclear attack would cause casualties "on the order of 50,000,000 people . . . the only sensible thing for us to do was to put all our resources into our SAC capability and into hydrogen bombs." It is obvious that the only way this additional capability could make a difference was if the U.S. struck first. Discussion at 208th and 312th meetings of the National Security Council, AWF, NSC series, Boxes 5 and 8, DDEL.

stockpiles to each other, but rather the relationship of one stockpile, plus its deliv-
erability, to the number of key enemy targets, including retaliatory facilities, which
must be destroyed in order to warrant an attack."[122] In 1951, the Air Force believed
that the Soviets had already achieved the capability "critically to hamper" America's
ability to strike back after an attack.[123] The Policy Planning Staff therefore wondered
whether it was possible to build forces that could survive a surprise attack and go on
to launch a heavy retaliatory strike. If this turned out to be impossible, a fundamental
"reconsideration of national strategy" would be required.[124]

The "reappraisal" of strategy thus turned in large part on issues related to what
would now be called the stability of deterrence. One State Department official outlined
some of the basic questions in May 1952: "Does currently approved U.S. national
strategy remain valid in the light of apparently rapidly growing atomic, and possibly
thermonuclear, capacity of the USSR? In other words, is time of the essence? Can we
really hope to 'contain' the Soviet Union even if we maintain a high-level military
strength indefinitely? Or must we adopt a more 'aggressive' policy?"[125] The argument
for a new and more aggressive strategy was based on the assumption that there was
no way, short of striking first, of preventing the Soviets from developing forces able
essentially to destroy America's retaliatory capability in a surprise attack.

But this was only part of the problem. The extraordinary changes in the nature of
general nuclear warfare taking place in the early 1950s were raising a whole series of
fundamental questions about national policy. Should the nation simply accept this
new world of thermonuclear weapons and nuclear plenty? Should it resign itself to
an almost inevitable loss of strategic superiority, and to living in a world where an
absolutely devastating surprise attack might be a very real risk? Gordon Dean, the
recently retired Chairman of the Atomic Energy Commission, did not mince words
on this issue: "Can we as a nation and can the nations of the now free world permit
the Soviet to reach the position where, if it chooses, it can completely annihilate this
country?"[126] The implication was that the United States might have to do something
about this developing situation before it was too late, while it still had enough of a
strategic edge to take some sort of "decisive action."

Project Solarium was the key device the new administration used to bring such
basic policy issues into focus. The idea for this unusual exercise in the making of
grand strategy came from Secretary of State Dulles, and Eisenhower himself took it
very seriously.[127] Three task forces were set up. Each was to elaborate and defend a

---

122. "NSC Staff Study on Reappraisal of United States Objectives and Strategy for National
Security," August 22, 1952, FRUS, 1952–54, Vol. II, p. 111.
123. Memorandum by the Policy Planning Staff to the Secretary of State, FRUS, 1951, Vol. I,
pp. 224–225, 227. See also Nitze to Acheson, January 12, 1953, FRUS, 1952–54, Vol. II, p. 203:
"I do not think that there is, even now, a general understanding in the U.S. government that
vulnerability to Soviet attack may prevent SAC from ever leaving the ground."
124. October 16, 1951 memo, FRUS, 1951, Vol. I, p. 227.
125. Schwartz to Bohlen, May 12, 1952, FRUS, 1952–54, Vol. II, p. 14.
126. Quoted in a lead article in Time, October 5, 1953, p. 24. For a fuller text, see Gordon Dean's
"Tasks for the Statesmen," Bulletin of the Atomic Scientists, Vol. 10, No. 1 (January 1954).
127. See Robert Cutler, No Time For Rest (Boston: Little, Brown, 1966), p. 307ff.

different line of strategy. Even the most cautious strategy, Alternative A, called for the United States "to assume the strategic offensive in its conflict with Soviet Communism." Rollback was to be a basic goal.[128] Alternative B, which called for drawing a line and threatening massive retaliation if the Soviets should cross it, was more a strategy than a policy—a means of supporting the goal of containment, rather than an alternative to it.

Alternative C was by far the most extreme position: "The U.S. cannot continue to live with the Soviet threat. So long as the Soviet Union exists, it will not fall apart, but must and can be shaken apart."[129] This task force concluded that "time has been working against us. This trend will continue unless it is arrested, and reversed by positive action."[130] The idea was to take American *war* objectives—ending Soviet domination outside Russia, "curtailing Soviet power for aggressive war," reducing the strength of "Bolshevik elements left in Soviet Russia"—as the "*true* objectives of the United States," to be achieved through Cold War, "although admittedly running greater risk of general war." There is no doubt that this line of policy proposed to rely not just on the usual instruments of Cold War strategy—covert operations, propaganda, economic measures—but on military power as well. One of its basic principles was to "exploit to the fullest, use of military forces as instruments of national policy to achieve political, propaganda and prestige objectives by both military and diplomatic means." The one limitation was that the country should not *initiate* a general war, but it should be perfectly willing to risk one. To support this strategy, a massive expansion in the military budget was called for.[131]

In setting its timetable for action, Task Force C's "basic problem was to correlate the timing of actions by the United States against the time when the Soviet Union will be capable of dealing a destructive blow to the United States (five years)." Its fundamental assumption "was that under current policies, or under those of A and B, time will be working against us to the point where the Soviet threat will soon become unbearable and the survival of the United States problematical."[132] During this period, there would be a war with China, perhaps growing out of a new war in Korea. By 1958, the United States would have dealt "a severe blow to Chinese prestige through the administration of a sound military defeat and the destruction of some of

---

128. *FRUS*, 1952–54, Vol. II, pp. 400–401, 406.
129. "Summary of Points Made in Discussion Following Presentation by Task Forces, July 16, 1953," *FRUS*, 1952–54, Vol. II, p. 434. The full Solarium reports were declassified in 1987 (with portions exempted), and are available in Office of the Special Assistant for National Security Affairs (OSANSA), NSC series, Subject subseries, Box 9, DDEL, and also in the NSC files at the USNA, Judicial-Social-Fiscal Branch.
130. The rest of this section is deleted from the published version of the document, probably indicating it is even more extreme than what was left in. That the censors sometimes "sanitize" out the more extreme passages of this sort is clear from a comparison of a reference to a report by Arthur Flemming, Director of Defense Mobilization, during an NSC meeting in November 1954, and the "sanitized" text of the report. *FRUS*, 1952–54, Vol. II, pp. 791, 782–783.
131. "Summaries Prepared by the NSC Staff of Project Solarium Presentations and Written Reports," transmitted July 22, 1953, *FRUS*, 1952–54, Vol. II, pp. 417–418, 422.
132. Ibid., p. 416; "Project SOLARIUM. Summary of Basic Concepts of Task Forces," July 30, 1953, NSC Meeting Files, No. 157, Tab D, NSC Records, USNA.

her industrial centers," presumably through atomic bombardment.[133] The two basic long-term goals, to be achieved after 1965, were the "overthrow of the Communist regime in China" and "the reduction of Soviet power and militancy and the elimination of the Communist conspiracy."[134]

It was against the backdrop of the Solarium discussions that Eisenhower and Dulles came to grips with the basic dilemma of the New Look: the sense that nuclear forces had become a fact of life, and that policy had to be built on a nuclear basis, but on the other hand, that the nuclearization of global politics might generate a fear of nuclear war that might shatter the Western alliance. It was clear, especially to Eisenhower, that primary reliance would have to be based on nuclear forces, particularly on the Strategic Air Command. It was not that the president viewed nuclear weapons as a godsend, in that only they allowed the West to neutralize the massive military manpower of the Soviet bloc. In fact, he thought it unfortunate that nuclear weapons even existed, since in any nonnuclear war, "he was certain that with its great resources the United States would surely be able to whip the Soviet Union."[135] But the clock could not be turned back, and there was no way that any agreement could be worked out that would assure with certainty that these weapons could be abolished.

The basic realities of this new world had to be faced without sentimentality. Eisenhower was never able to accept the argument about a nuclear stalemate and the possibility that a general war might be fought with only conventional weapons.[136] Nuclear weapons dominated all lesser forms of weaponry, and it was obvious to him that in a major conflict they would, in the final analysis, be used. His thinking was right out of the first few pages of Clausewitz: war has an innate tendency to become absolute. Winning was the only thing that mattered. "In such a war," he said, "the United States would be applying a force so terrible that one simply could not be

---

133. This was obviously closely related to the debate that had just come to a head on an expansion of the war in Korea. The discussion can be followed in *FRUS*, 1952–54, Vol. XV:1.

134. *FRUS*, 1952–54, Vol. II, pp. 423, 430–431.

135. Notes of NSC meeting, June 23, 1954, ibid., p. 1469. Eisenhower repeated the point the next day: "he would gladly go back to the kind of warfare which was waged in 1941 if in 1945 the A-bomb had proved impossible to make." Notes of NSC meeting, June 24, 1954, ibid., p. 688.

136. General Ridgway, at an NSC meeting in December, had argued that if the U.S. did not resort to nuclear attack, the Russians might not use nuclear weapons either. But Eisenhower "said he did not believe any such thing." Notes of NSC meeting, December 3, 1954, ibid., p. 804. This sort of argument, he said in another meeting, was "completely erroneous." Notes of NSC meeting, June 24, 1954, ibid., p. 689. Eisenhower held to this view throughout his administration. For example, in a conversation with Robert Bowie in August 1960, Eisenhower "said that he agreed that we are not going to have a tactical nuclear war in Western Europe. In fact, he said he cannot see any chance of keeping any war in Europe from becoming a general war. For this reason he thought we must be ready to throw the book at the Russians should they jump us. He did not see how there could be such a thing as a limited war in Europe, and thought we would be fooling ourselves and our European friends if we said we could fight such a war without recourse to nuclear weapons. If massive land war operations such as the Ludendorff offensive in early 1918 in World War I were to occur, he was sure that nations would use every weapon available to them." A.J. Goodpaster, "Memorandum of Conference with the President," August 19, 1960, Declassified Documents Collection, 1987/1139.

meticulous as to the methods by which the force was brought to bear."[137] Thus for Eisenhower, the fundamental role of nuclear weapons was something permanent and ultimately inescapable.

It was, however, also simply a fact of international life that the nuclearization of great power politics was generating fears that might well lead to a neutralization of front-line allies in Europe and the Far East.[138] The United States, however, could not go it alone in the world. Secretary Dulles hammered away at this theme again and again. "No single country," he said, "not even the United States, could, out of its own resources, adequately match the strength of a powerful totalitarian state. We were in no position to extract from our people what tyrannical rulers could extract from their people. The attempt to do so would 'bust us.' Accordingly, the only way the free world could hope to maintain sufficient strength so that each of its members did not 'go broke,' was the pooling of resources." Isolation, he warned, "would cost the United States dearly in the long run."[139]

Dulles laid out the basic problem in an important memorandum of September 6, 1953. On the one hand, the United States was going to shift its military policy in the direction of increased emphasis on nuclear capabilities and the withdrawal of ground forces from Europe. But with the growth of Soviet nuclear forces, he wrote, "the NATO concept [was] losing its grip" in Europe. SAC bases overseas were coming to be seen more as "lightning rods" than as "umbrellas." America was becoming so vulnerable to Soviet retaliatory attack that the Europeans were beginning to believe "that we might stay out if Europe were attacked first. And if the U.S. were attacked first, Europe might prefer to stay out." The American strategy of redeployment and a build-up of continental defense would, moreover, be interpreted "as final proof of an isolationist trend and the adoption of the 'Fortress America' concept." Dulles doubted "that any eloquence or reasoning on our part would prevent disintegration and deterioration of our position, with our growing isolation through the reaction of our present allies. The resources of the free world would then no longer be in a common fund to be drawn on for community security, and the balance of world power, military and economic, would doubtless shift rapidly to our great disadvantage." A basic conclusion followed: "we cannot avoid a major reconsideration of collective security concepts." For Dulles, there was only one answer to the dilemma: détente with the Soviet Union, "a spectacular effort to relax world tensions on a global basis."[140]

---

137. Notes of NSC meeting, March 25, 1954, *FRUS, 1952–54*, Vol. II, pp. 639–641.
138. The fear of a nuclear-generated neutralization of Europe and the Far East was a minor theme in the *Foreign Relations* documents as early as 1950; see, for example, a passing reference to this prospect in NSC 68, *FRUS, 1950*, Vol. I, p. 265. By 1953, it had become considerably more important: see Nitze's comments, *FRUS, 1952–54*, Vol. II, p. 203 (where he called this "a subject of utmost delicacy"); the National Intelligence Estimate of October 23, 1953, para. 4(a), ibid., p. 552; State Department Paper, November 15, 1954, ibid., p. 773; Allen Dulles paper, November 18, 1954, ibid., p. 777.
139. Notes of NSC meeting, August 27, 1954, ibid., p. 452.
140. Dulles memorandum, September 6, 1953, ibid., pp. 457–460. According to Dulles, the "line of thinking" initiated here ended in Eisenhower's "Atoms for Peace" speech of December 1953.

But for Eisenhower, détente was not the only solution. He reacted to Dulles's argument by briefly considering the idea of preventive war. He and his secretary of state discussed the issue at length on September 7, and on September 8 he summed up his views in a memorandum to Dulles. If there was to be a "real revision in policies—some of which may temporarily, or even for a very extended time, involve us in vastly increased expenditures," he said, we would have to start educating the American people now. Given the power of nuclear weapons, and the fact that the Soviets blocked international control, the only reasonable assumption was that they were "contemplating aggressive use." America's policy therefore "could no longer be geared" toward simply avoiding "disaster during the early 'surprise' stages of a war." The United States would instead "have to be constantly ready, on an instantaneous basis, to inflict greater loss upon the enemy than he could reasonably hope to inflict upon us." This, he said, "would be a deterrent—but if the contest to maintain this relative position should have to continue indefinitely, the cost would either drive us to war—or into some form of dictatorial government." "In such circumstances" he concluded, "we would be forced to consider whether or not our duty to future generations did not require us to *initiate* war at the most propitious moment that we could designate."[141]

This was not the only instance of Eisenhower's interest in preventive war at the time. Lord Moran, for example, recalled in his diary an encounter between Churchill and Eisenhower at the Bermuda conference in December 1953: "'Of course,' said the P.M. pacing up and down the room, 'anyone could say the Russians are evil minded and mean to destroy the free countries. Well, if we really feel like that, perhaps we ought to take action before they get as many atomic bombs as America has. I made that point to Ike, who said, perhaps logically, that it ought to be considered.'"[142] And when Dulles, in an NSC meeting in June 1954, pointed out that most of America's allies would not support a tough policy, Eisenhower said that "if this were indeed the situation, we should perhaps come back to the very grave question: Should the United States now get ready to fight the Soviet Union? The President pointed out that he had brought up this question more than once at prior Council meetings, and that he had never done so facetiously."[143]

Why then was a preventive war strategy, in any of its variants, never adopted as policy? It was not that Eisenhower was shocked or appalled by this way of thinking.[144]

Dulles, Memorandum for the President, May 12, 1954, Dulles Papers, White House Memoranda Series, Box 1, "White House Correspondence, 1954 (1)," DDEL.
141. Eisenhower to Dulles, September 8, 1953, *FRUS*, 1952–54, Vol. II, p. 461. Emphasis in original. Note also Dulles, "Memorandum for Mr. Bowie," September 8, 1953, Dulles Papers, White House Memoranda series, Box 1, "White House Correspondence 1953 (2)," DDEL. The reference to "vastly increased expenditures" suggests a link to Alternative C from the Solarium Study, which had recently been discussed at the NSC level.
142. Moran, *Winston Churchill: The Struggle for Survival*, p. 505.
143. Notes of NSC meeting, June 24, 1954, *FRUS*, 1952–54, Vol. II, p. 696.
144. See, for example, his reaction to the Solarium presentations, *FRUS*, 1952–54, Vol. II, pp. 397–398, 438. What the president wanted was a blending of all three alternatives, but to his annoyance those who had worked on the project rejected this as impossible. Note also his

But with a decision of this magnitude, many other considerations had to be taken into account, and one in particular was always decisive: even if a general war was won in any meaningful sense, the problems that would have to be faced in the postwar period would be staggering. There was one point, Eisenhower said, that he, as president, had to live with all the time, "namely, what do you do with the world after you have won victory in such a catastrophic nuclear war?"[145] "The colossal job," he said, "of occupying the territories of the defeated enemy would be far beyond the resources of the United States at the end of such a war."[146] He in fact doubted "whether any nations as we now know them would continue to exist at the conclusion of this war."[147] At one point he even made the startling comment that "the only thing worse than losing a global war was winning one."[148]

As a result, very little of Alternative C from the Solarium project ended up in NSC 162/2, the carefully worked out statement of basic national security policy adopted on October 29, 1953. The sense of a need to act before America's nuclear lead had been lost was reduced to a fairly anodyne sentence in paragraph 45: "In the face of the developing Soviet threat, the broad aim of U.S. security policies must be to create, prior to the achievement of mutual atomic plenty, conditions under which the United States and the free world coalition are prepared to meet the Soviet-Communist threat with resolution and to negotiate for its alleviation under proper safeguards."[149]

By 1954, what was left of Alternative C was simply a strong feeling that perhaps the United States ought to take advantage of her fading nuclear superiority before she lost it completely. Those, especially in the military, who argued along these lines at the time predicted that the loss of America's nuclear edge would lead to a dangerous upsurge in Soviet aggressiveness. In such a case, the only alternative to appeasement would be an enormously destructive war, one that the nation could scarcely hope to win in any meaningful sense. But they did not argue that the United States should therefore try to provoke a war before this situation came to pass. Instead, they called simply for a more "active," "dynamic" or "positive" policy, without spelling out precisely what they had in mind.

As in Solarium, the interest in a more "aggressive" strategy was clearly linked to concerns about the shifting nuclear balance. This is illustrated by two memoranda presented by the new Joint Chiefs of Staff in 1954.[150] The first was a JCS attack, dated June 23, 1954, on the whole idea of negotiation with the Soviet bloc. The enemy was unrelenting, it argued, and would settle for nothing less than total victory. From the

---

reaction to the "preventive war" briefing by the JCS's Advanced Study Group, 200th Meeting of the NSC, June 4, 1954, AWF, NSC series, Box 5. For more on this briefing, which had earlier been presented to Eisenhower, see Rosenberg, "Origins of Overkill," p. 34.

145. Notes of NSC meeting, December 3, 1954, *FRUS*, 1952–54, Vol. II, p. 804. See also Eisenhower's comments to some military officers in June 1954, in R. H. Ferrell, ed., *The Diary of James Hagerty* (Bloomington: Indiana University Press, 1983), p. 69.

146. Notes of NSC meeting, March 4, 1954, *FRUS*, 1952–54, Vol. II, p. 636.

147. Notes of NSC meeting, March 25, 1954, ibid., p. 642.

148. *FRUS*, 1952–54, Vol. II, p. 397.

149. *FRUS*, 1952–54, Vol. II, p. 595.

150. For the context, see Robert J. Watson, *History of the Joint Chiefs of Staff*, Vol. V, 1953–54, (Washington, D.C.: U.S. GPO, 1986), chap. 2, esp. pp. 45–46, 48–52.

U.S. standpoint, things were already bad, and, with the development of Soviet nuclear capabilities, could only get worse: "the engulfment of a large segment of the world and its people by the Soviets has been accomplished during the period in which the United States first held a monopoly and then a significant superiority in atomic weapons and in the means for their delivery. It may properly be assumed that, unless the Soviet attitude is altered by outside influences, the aggressive and irresponsible tactics pursued with success by the Soviets thus far will be only a prelude to the proportions which such tactics will attain once the present atomic superiority of the United States has been neutralized." The United States, the Chiefs argued, had to exploit its present nuclear superiority by taking "positive actions": the Soviets had to be made to see that failure on its part to make concessions would "involve grave risks to the maintenance of their regime."[151]

The JCS contribution to the annual review of basic national security policy, dated November 22, 1954, similarly argued that the world conflict was now in a "critical" stage, and within a few years would "probably reach a decisive state."[152] It, too, pointed out that the allies were drifting away: the fear of atomic war was driving them toward neutralism. (One thinks of the Kaiser on the eve of World War I complaining about how his allies were falling away "like rotten pears.") And then the call for action:

The non-Communist world, if it takes positive and timely *dynamic* countermeasures, presently has ample resources to meet this situation, and with high chance of maintaining world peace without sacrifice of either vital security interests or fundamental moral principles, or in the event of war being forced upon it, of winning that war beyond any reasonable doubt. On the other hand, failure on the part of the free world and particularly of the United States to take such timely and dynamic action could, within a relatively short span of years, result in the United States finding itself isolated from the rest of the free world and thus placed in such jeopardy as to reduce its freedom of action to two alternatives—that of accommodation to Soviet designs or contesting such designs under conditions not favorable to our success.

Complaining that the government had not acted with the proper sense of urgency, and that policy had been too passive and reactive, the JCS called for a policy "of unmistakably positive quality." The nation should not be "required to defer" to the most cautious allies. The United States, they argued, had to be ready "to undertake certain risks inherent in the adoption of dynamic and positive security measures."[153]

What sort of "timely and dynamic action" could possibly solve the problems resulting from the growth of Soviet nuclear power? Perhaps the JCS had a hidden agenda that they did not dare to set out explicitly; perhaps they were forced to speak in "code language" because the preventive war option had been ruled out in 1953. There is some evidence that the Chiefs, and especially JCS Chairman Radford, were

151. JCS to Wilson, June 23, 1954, FRUS, 1952–54, Vol. II, pp. 680–686.
152. Taken literally, what this implied was that matters were coming to a head, and the struggle would be *decided* one way or the other. Admiral Radford, in an NSC meeting at which these issues were discussed, said specifically that unless communist action was forestalled, the United States could not "hope for anything but a showdown with Soviet Communists by 1959 or 1960." Notes of NSC meeting, November 24, 1954, ibid., p. 792.
153. Wilson to Lay, November 22, 1954, ibid., pp. 785–787. Emphasis in original.

indeed thinking in these terms.[154] But this evidence is by no means conclusive, and it is certainly possible that top military leaders at the time had never really worked this issue through in their own minds: they knew what they did not like, namely, the growth of Soviet nuclear capabilities, and felt very strongly that a policy of drift might lead to catastrophe, but were not quite sure what could be done about it.

In any case, the JCS soon got a hearing: the issue of a more "positive policy" came to a climax in the NSC at the end of 1954. In these discussions it was Dulles, a hawk during the discussions about ending the Korean War, the man who had called during the presidential campaign for a "policy of boldness," who now took the lead in arguing for a relatively mild policy.[155] What, he asked, was the point of the aggressive strategy that the Chiefs had recommended? The problem was not simply that the allies would not follow us; this was an important consideration, but if the policy was

---

154. Radford, it is now clear, was in favor of a highly aggressive strategy that would have forced the Soviets both to disarm and to abandon their empire in Eastern Europe; a rejection of these demands would have led to a discriminate counterforce attack and perhaps ultimately to full-scale war. This was the basic strategy called for in the Air Force's Project Control, a major study conducted out of the Air War College in 1953–54; when Radford was briefed on the project in August 1954, these ideas received his enthusiastic support. "If the U.S. did not adopt and successfully follow through on a course of action similar to Project Control," he said, it was his belief "that in the period mid 1957–1960 there would be either an all-out atomic war or the U.S. would be forced into an agreement which would mean victory for the U.S.S.R." Radford commented that this strategy would face political obstacles; the idea would, he thought, be resisted by both the State Department and the allies. In fact, when Project Control was briefed to the State Department, Robert Bowie, the head of the Policy Planning Staff, opposed it as "simply another version of preventive war." This is based on Tami Davis Biddle, "Handling the Soviet Threat: Arguments for Preventive War and Compellence in the Early Cold War Period," draft manuscript presented at conference of the Society for Historians of American Foreign Relations, Washington, D.C., June 9–11, 1988, pp. 44–45 (the Project Control strategy), pp. 61–62 and n. 148 (Radford and Bowie). Note also her discussion of the official Air Force reaction, pp. 55–57, and an excerpt from a 1953 book by Air Force General Dale Smith, quoted in George Lowe, *The Age of Deterrence* (Boston: Little, Brown, 1964), p. 54. As for the other Chiefs, note some rather suggestive passages in CNO Admiral Carney's speech in May 1954. In dealing with the communists, Carney argued, the United States should not simply "rush around plugging the dike" with localized military actions, but should have the "guts" to take the "rougher road" that at least gave some hope of a decent outcome. The choice had to be made quickly; "we're traveling at high speed and I don't believe much time will be vouchsafed us." According to Lowe (p. 56), Carney was "widely thought to be suggesting a preventive war." The text of the speech is in the *New York Times*, May 28, 1954, p. 2. Air Force Chief of Staff Twining's sympathy for this sort of thinking is suggested by the passages quoted above from his book: if Twining took this line in public even in the mid-1960s, one imagines that the line he took in private around 1954 must have been considerably stronger, especially given the kind of thinking common in Air Force circles at the time. Even General Ridgway, Army Chief of Staff and by far the strongest advocate of the "limited war" philosophy in the JCS, had by 1954 evidently moved very far toward the idea of hitting the enemy at his heart: if the U.S. were to intervene militarily in the Indochina conflict, it should avoid getting bogged down in a local war and should instead initiate mobilization and "neutralize the sources of Viet Minh strength" by taking military action against China. JCS Historical Division, "History of the Indochina Incident," p. 388.
155. On Dulles's line at the start of the Eisenhower administration, see especially his handwritten notes of his comments at a high-level meeting on December 11, 1952, Dulles Papers, Subject File, Box 8, "S.S. Helena Notes," DDEL.

right, Dulles said, he would go along with it anyway.[156] The real problem was that it did not make any strategic sense. There was only one respect in which the United States was facing a deterioration in its global position, "namely, the forthcoming achievement of atomic plenty and a nuclear balance of power between the U.S. and the USSR." "But how," Dulles asked in a key NSC meeting in November 1954, "were we to prevent the Soviet Union from achieving such a nuclear balance of power without going to war with the USSR? Certainly no actions on the periphery of the Soviet Union would stop the growth of the atomic capabilities of the Soviet Union."[157] Eisenhower himself had long had doubts about "how much we should poke the animal through the bars of the cage."[158]

Dulles now appeared comfortable with present American policies, which he described in surprisingly Kennanesque terms: "Our alliance system has staked out the vital areas of the world which we propose to hold even at the risk of general war. These vital areas include currently all the areas of immediate strategic value to us or which possess significant war potential. The NATO area is by all odds the greatest single U.S. asset."[159] Dulles stressed his personal sympathy for the JCS position. He reminded them that he himself had called for a more dynamic policy during the 1952 presidential campaign, and even after taking office, had supported a policy of bringing about "the disintegration of Soviet power."[160] But, he noted in the December 1954 NSC meeting, his views had changed: Experience showed that beyond a certain point, the "dynamic" policy could not be translated into specific courses of action.[161]

The general mood at this NSC meeting was in harmony with Dulles's more relaxed views. Treasury Secretary George Humphrey and Defense Secretary Charles Wilson were essentially willing to accept coexistence (although the latter did not particularly like the word). As for Eisenhower, he was not opposed to the idea of negotiation with the Soviets. Even the old idea that all outposts had to be held, which Dulles had supported at the beginning of the Eisenhower period, was now abandoned: Indochina, Dulles said, was not terribly significant to us, and Eisenhower had already pointed out at an earlier meeting that if people did not want to be free, and would not fight for their freedom, there was not very much the United States could do about it.[162]

The December 21, 1954, NSC meeting marks, in a sense, the end of an era. The period had begun with the Soviet atomic test in late 1949. The tensions generated by that event had played an important role in the American policy debates of the early

---

156. Notes of NSC meeting, June 24, 1954, *FRUS*, 1952–54, Vol. II, pp. 694–695.
157. Notes of NSC meeting, November 24, 1954, ibid., pp. 789–790. The kind of minor aggressions that had been proposed were "such projects as the detachment of Albania or an assault on Hainan Island." Notes of NSC meeting, October 29, 1953, ibid., p. 569.
158. Cutler to Dulles, September 3, 1953, ibid., p. 457.
159. Notes of NSC meeting, December 21, 1954, ibid., pp. 833–834.
160. Notes of NSC meeting, March 31, 1953, ibid., p. 267.
161. Ibid., p. 833.
162. Ibid., p. 837 (for Humphrey); p. 840 (for Wilson); p. 843 (Eisenhower on negotiations); p. 266 (for Dulles's domino argument in early 1953); p. 835 (for his later, milder views on the subject); p. 709 (for Eisenhower, on people not willing to fight for their freedom).

1950s, but by the end of 1954 had essentially worked themselves out. This is not to argue that "preventive war" thinking disappeared without a trace: even as late as 1959, Eisenhower was still wondering whether America "should start fighting now" instead of "waiting to go quietly down the drain."[163] And in 1960, fed up with "Khrushchev and his threats," the President "strongly intimated that he wished there was no moral restriction that prevented him from one night pushing the proper button and sending all of our atomic bombs in the direction of the Communist bloc."[164]

But these were now merely isolated expressions of frustration. It was too late for anything like this to be seriously considered as a real policy option. Dulles's reaction in 1958 to an argument that the United States should consider taking some action before it lost its strategic edge over the Soviet Union probably comes much closer to capturing the heart of Eisenhower administration thinking on this issue in the late 1950s. The question of preventive war, of course, had been around for a long time: Dulles recalled how in June 1946 he and Senator Vandenberg had "speculated" on whether force would be justified if the Soviets refused to accept international control of nuclear weapons. But this was no longer an open question: "No man," Dulles felt, "should arrogate to himself the power to decide that the future of mankind would benefit by an action entailing the killing of tens of millions of people."[165]

Conclusion

The nuclear revolution was like a great earthquake, setting off a series of shock waves that gradually worked their way through the world political system. The basic aim here was to study one part of this process, the way people dealt with the problem

---

163. Bryce Harlow, Memorandum for the Record, March 26, 1959, AWF, DDE Diaries, Staff Notes, March 1–15, 1959 (1), DDEL; also Declassified Documents Collection, 1978/118C.
164. Notes for Files, September 25, 1960, AWF, AWD, Box 11, DDEL.
165. Dulles's interlocutor was Robert Sprague, in 1954, consultant to the NSC on continental defense, in 1957, chief architect of the Gaither Report. In his 1958 conversation with the secretary of state, Sprague argued that for the next two and one-half years, "the U.S. position vis-à-vis the Soviet Union will be at its strongest," and that "during this period we can knock out the Soviet Union's military capability without taking a similar blow from the Soviet Union." He had therefore asked the president to appoint a study group to consider "what the U.S. should do during the few years in which we will retain a margin of advantage." Memorandum of Conversation, January 3, 1958, Dulles Papers, General Correspondence and Memoranda Series, Box 1, "Memoranda of Conversation—General—S(1)," DDEL. A few years earlier, Sprague, in briefing the NSC on continental defense, had evidently referred to preventive war as an option open to the U.S.; in another NSC meeting a few weeks later, he argued that the U.S. could not afford "to leave in Soviet hands the question of whether they should or should not attack us" in the near future. "Discussion at the 205th Meeting of the National Security Council, Thursday, July 1, 1954," (allusion by Dulles, p. 19); and "Discussion at the 208th Meeting of the National Security Council, Thursday, July 29, 1954," p. 4, both in AWF, NSC series, Box 5, DDEL. (Incidentally, in November 1957, three members of the Gaither Committee urged reconsideration of the whole idea of preventive war.) David Alan Rosenberg, "Toward Armageddon: The Foundations of United States Nuclear Strategy, 1945–1961" (Ph.D. dissertation, University of Chicago, 1983), p. 236.

of the shifting strategic balance, and especially the loss of the American nuclear monopoly, in the period from 1949 to 1954. This story is of interest because of the light it sheds on the problem of how the world came to terms with nuclear weapons—how they were absorbed into the international system, and how people accommodated to the basic realities of the nuclear age.

What surprised me the most as I went through these sources was that so much attention was given to the extraordinary *shifts* then taking place, both in the military balance and in the military environment as a whole. It was a surprise that such window thinking loomed as large as it did; it was perhaps not quite so surprising that the global balance, as such, played an important role in shaping policy. But once this became clear, all kinds of other things began to fall into place.

In this concluding section, I want to explore some of the implications of the argument here in three areas, specifically: (a) American military policy; (b) American foreign policy; and (c) global politics as a whole. The sort of thinking discussed above was obviously not *directly* translated into policy, but this set of concerns did enter into the matrix out of which policy developed, and the *indirect* effects were of considerable importance.

MILITARY POLICY. The sort of thinking that was emerging in response to concerns about the shifting nuclear balance was clearly one of the major elements factored into the Eisenhower strategy. The New Look took it for granted that if the Soviets turned out to be totally impossible to live with, that if they insisted on pursuing highly aggressive policies and sought relentlessly to force a retreat of American power especially from Europe and the Far East, then the United States would have to go to war with them. In such a war, the goal would be to destroy Soviet power totally, once and for all. If the Soviets were in fact this bad, and if as a result such a war had to be fought, it might be dangerous to try too hard to avoid a showdown. Given the way the military balance was bound to shift, the United States would be well-advised to make its stand sooner rather than later. Moreover, if general war was a real possibility, then it was obviously important that the United States be able to strike quickly, so that any Soviet counter-attack could be blunted.

This thinking helps explain the emphasis that American military policy in the 1950s placed on preemption, as well as the targeting philosophy based on destroying "the heart of Soviet power." All of these ideas were cut from the same cloth, and tended, at least in a psychological sense, to be mutually reinforcing. They all added up to a way of looking at the world that carried a certain political weight—influencing, for example, how broadly the conditions for preemption were defined.[166] This body of evidence thus helps support the conclusion that the Eisenhower strategy has to be taken seriously, that it was not at bottom (as some people argue) simply a gigantic bluff. Ideas of this sort, in their pure form, were never able to dictate policy, but they certainly affected the way the policy balance was struck.

---

166. The term "preemption" was not used in the NSC documents, which generally referred instead to the conditions under which the United States would have to assume that general war was imminent.

FOREIGN POLICY. How did these concerns about trends in the military balance relate to American foreign policy as a whole in this period? The strategy of building up American and allied power, especially the dramatic shift in late 1950 on the German question—that is, the opting for the rearmament of West Germany—clearly has to be understood in this context.

In the Far East, concerns about the balance played an important direct role in foreign policy. In the winter of 1950–51, they acted as a force for restraint. But after the balance had shifted in late 1952, the tenor of high-level American policy discussions became noticeably more hawkish.[167] The evidence is spotty, but one suspects that the increasing pressure for a more aggressive American policy in East Asia was linked to the sort of thinking reflected in documents like the Solarium Task Force C report. From the point of view of people like Admiral Radford, the China area must have seemed like the best place in the world to try to implement a "dynamic" and "positive" policy.[168] Indeed, for some military officers, a general war with China was attractive precisely because it might have led to an all-out war with the Soviet Union as well, before it was too late. General K.D. Nichols, who for years had been one of the most important officers concerned with nuclear matters, argued at the end of 1952 for the deliberate use of nuclear weapons in the war against China. One goal, he said, was to "precipitate a major war," evidently against the USSR, "at a time when we have greatest potential for winning it with minimum damage to the U.S.A."[169]

By the end of 1954, however, American policy as a whole was drawing back from what was referred to even in internal documents as an "aggressive" strategy against China; from that point on, the United States sought in practice simply to support the status quo in the Far East.[170] This was probably linked to what was going on at the level of general policy making at exactly this time—the defeat of the JCS in the NSC, also in late 1954, and the opting for a policy of coexistence with the Soviets.

<hr>

167. This can be followed in some detail in FRUS, 1952–54, Vol. XIV; there is also some relevant material in Vol. XII.
168. Even in 1952 (when he was U.S. commander in the Pacific), Radford was pressing for a more aggressive U.S. policy in the China area. See the report by General Merrill to the Policy Planning Staff, April 17, 1952, Records of the Policy Planning Staff, Box 32, "Policy Planning Staff Meetings (1950)," RG 59, USNA. Radford was thinking in terms of the seizure of Hainan Island by the Chinese Nationalists (with U.S. support), and maybe even a "lodgment" in "one of the coastal provinces."
169. Memorandum quoted in K.D. Nichols, The Road to Trinity (New York: William Morrow, 1987), p. 12; see also p. 291.
170. The JCS were informed on September 28, 1954, that the president had "suspended" the policy of supporting Chinese Nationalist raids on the mainland. JCS Memorandum for the Secretary of Defense, October 1, 1954, File for NSC Meeting, No. 216, Tab C, NSC Records, USNA. Another important development a little later was the conclusion of the Mutual Defense Treaty with the government on Taiwan. This had been considered earlier, but the U.S. had preferred in 1954 not to negotiate such a pact "primarily because a defensive pact might have the effect of tying the hands of the GRC." NSC Operations Coordinating Board, Progress Report on United States Objectives and Courses of Action with Respect to Formosa and the Chinese National Government, July 16, 1954, p. 5, NSC 146 File, NSC Records, USNA.

GLOBAL POLITICS, 1949–54. Finally, the shifting balance seems to have had an important bearing on the course of global politics as a whole in the period down to 1954. The Soviets were deeply concerned with what was going on in the United States in this period. The harsh anti-communist rhetoric coming out of Washington was bad enough; but now, on top of this, the West had taken a series of extraordinary moves to build up its military power. In this context, certain signals were especially important. Remarks that seemed to indicate that influential elements in the U.S. government thought that the emerging military situation was intolerable, and that a more "positive" strategy might be necessary, were bound to alarm the Soviets. Thus, for example, Senator William Knowland's call in late 1954, for a basic change in U.S. policy before time ran out and the communists were able to resume their advance under cover of an "atomic stalemate," was just one of many pronouncements that might have been taken as indications of the way official thinking was moving in the United States. Knowland was the Republican leader in the Senate; although the administration publicly distanced itself from his views, the Soviets may well have wondered whether this was because Knowland was more radical than Eisenhower and Dulles, or simply less discreet.[171]

Statements coming from more authoritative sources were worrisome enough. In August of 1954, General Twining had made the somewhat ambiguous point that the proof of America's peaceful intentions was that "there is already sufficient reason for war, if we are seeking war."[172] Eisenhower himself, in his first State of the Union address in early 1953, also made a comment that was susceptible to more than one interpretation: he warned that the "free world cannot indefinitely remain in a posture of paralyzed tension." It is unlikely that such remarks passed unnoticed in the USSR. Indeed, as Eisenhower himself put it, the Russians must have been "scared as hell" at this time.[173]

It seems quite clear that the USSR accommodated to the new thrust of American policy. The most important shift was on Soviet policy on the German question. There were three great steps along the road to a full resurgence of German power: the creation of the Federal Republic, the rearmament of West Germany, and the nuclearization of the Bundeswehr. The first and third led to crises: The decisions taken at the London Conference in 1948 made it clear that a West German state would soon be brought into being, and the Soviets reacted by blockading West Berlin in 1948–49. Similarly in the late 1950s, when it seemed that West German armed forces were well on their way toward acquiring nuclear forces of their own, the Soviets also provoked a very serious Berlin crisis.[174] But the second phase in this process, the rearmament

171. "Knowland Warns of Policy Danger; Calls for Review," *New York Times*, November 16, 1954, p. 1. The text of the statement is on p. 18.
172. Quoted in the *New York Times*, August 21, 1954, p. 5.
173. *Public Papers of the Presidents: Eisenhower*, 1953, p. 13; notes of NSC meeting, June 4, 1953, *FRUS*, 1952–54, Vol. II, p. 369.
174. See Marc Trachtenberg, "The Berlin Crisis," in Charles F. Brower, ed., *The Theory and Practice of American National Security, 1960–68* (forthcoming).

of West Germany, did not lead to anything comparable, in spite of the fact that a very sharp Soviet reaction was widely expected at the time.[175]

This, in other words, was a Berlin crisis that did not happen. Instead of responding aggressively to what was going on, the Soviets opted for a conciliatory policy. The series of moves culminating in the famous Soviet note on Germany of March 10, 1952, is best understood in the context of these Soviet fears and anxieties.[176] The Soviets, in other words, had accommodated to the shift in the balance that had taken place in the early 1950s.

This, in any case, was the view the Soviet leaders themselves came to have of this period. Nikita Khrushchev, for example, later referred with apparent distaste, evidently to the period around 1952 to 1954, as a time when the West really did have the upper hand strategically. "It is high time," Khrushchev said in his speech of

---

175. The key decisions on the American side were made in late 1950 after the outbreak of the Korean War. Even before Korea, the Soviet reaction to German rearmament was a source of great anxiety, not just in Western Europe but also in the United States. "The rearmament of Germany," U.S. High Commissioner John McCloy wrote in early June 1950, "would undoubtedly speed up any Soviet schedule for any possible future action in Germany and would, no doubt, be regarded by them as sufficiently provocative to warrant extreme countermeasures." McCloy to Acheson, June 13, 1950, PSF, Box 178, "Germany. Folder 2," HSTL. After the war in Korea broke out, these fears became more intense, although they were counterbalanced by fears about what would happen if the West did nothing while its nuclear advantage gradually disappeared. The CIA, for example, in early 1951 thought that there was a better than fifty-fifty chance that West German rearmament would lead to war with the Soviets. Memorandum for the President, January 25, 1951, p. 4, MNSC, reel 1. See also the CIA study, "Probable Soviet Reactions to a Remilitarization of Western Germany," NIE-17, December 27, 1950, PSF, Box 253, HSTL, esp. paragraphs 7 and 9. In 1952, when the agreements creating a framework for German rearmament were finally signed, there was again a great fear that the Soviets would react by provoking a new Berlin crisis. But again, the American government, somewhat to its surprise, was struck by the fact that no aggressive moves were taken around Berlin; the situation on the access routes remained normal in 1952–53. *FRUS*, 1952–54, Vol. VII, pp. 1239, 1236, 1272, 1294, 1373.

176. There was, and to a certain extent still is, a tendency in the West to dismiss the Soviet offers as being purely tactical in their purpose, the aim supposedly having been to derail the process leading to the military integration of West Germany into the NATO bloc. The best scholarship, however, demonstrates that this was not the case. A superb dissertation by Paul Willging provides a very effective analysis of this issue: Paul R. Willging, "Soviet Foreign Policy in the German Question: 1950–1955" (Ph.D. dissertation, Columbia University, 1973). This work can now be supplemented by, for example, important documents from British, French and American archival sources, which show that many Western statesmen believed at the time that these Soviet moves reflected a real shift in policy on the German question. There was a parallel shift in the tone of official East German utterances. In late 1950, East German Prime Minister Otto Grotewohl quite clearly threatened that what had happened in Korea might well be repeated in Germany, and communist party leader Walter Ulbricht said the regime had decided against building a new seaport "since soon 'democratic Germany' would have Hamburg and Lubeck." Cited in Thomas Schwartz, "From Occupation to Alliance: John J. McCloy and the Allied High Commission in the Federal Republic of Germany, 1949–1952" (Ph.D. dissertation, Harvard University, 1985), p. 303; see also p. 354, n. 14. By early 1952, however, the East Germans increasingly emphasized defense. The parallel with Korea, still a theme in Grotewohl's remarks, was now much more ambiguous. It was no longer an East German invasion of the West that was threatened; instead, Grotewohl spoke simply of the "great danger" of a "fratricidal war of Germans against Germans." Quoted in McCloy to State Department, May 16, 1952, *FRUS*, 1952–54, Vol. VII, p. 341.

November 10, 1958, "to realize that the times when the imperialists could act from 'positions of strength' with impunity have gone never to return, and try as they may, the imperialists will not be able to change the balance of forces in their favour."[177] These shifts on the Soviet side, especially the turn toward conciliation during the late Stalin and early post-Stalin periods, in turn had a major impact on the policy of the Western powers, and all this was part of a much broader process whereby the fate of Germany, and with it the structure of power in Europe, was worked out.

We as a society suffer today from what can only be called an extraordinary case of collective nuclear amnesia. A picture of the past has taken shape that has very little to do with what our nuclear past was really like.[178] It is now often taken for granted that even in the 1950s nuclear war was simply "unthinkable" as an instrument of policy; that nuclear forces were never "usable" and served only to "deter their use by others"; and that the threat of "massive retaliation" was at bottom just pure bluff, because the United States would never be the first to launch a nuclear strike. This picture has taken shape because it serves important political purposes for both the left and the right, but one cannot immerse oneself in the sources for this period without coming to the conclusion that something very basic has been forgotten. The historical documents themselves give a very different picture.

It is important to see the past as it really was, to understand that thirty-five years ago people lived in a much more frightening world than anything we know today. Out of that world a stable peace eventually took shape. How this happened is a problem of more than just historical interest. The one thing that is now clear is that this is an extremely interesting problem to explore, and one where historical scholarship has barely begun to scratch the surface.

177. This speech, of course, marked the beginning of the great Berlin crisis of 1958–62. For the text, see U.S. Senate Committee on Foreign Relations, *Documents on Germany, 1944–1961* (Washington, D.C.: U.S. GPO, 1961), p. 339. There is an even more striking admission in Khrushchev's August 11, 1961, speech. "There was a time," he said, "when American Secretary of State Dulles brandished thermonuclear bombs and followed a position of strength policy with regard to the socialist countries. . . . That was barefaced atomic blackmail, but it had to be reckoned with at the time because we did not possess sufficient means of retaliation, and if we did, they were not as many and not of the same power as those of our opponents." Ibid., pp. 718–719. A series of other retrospective comments by East German and Soviet leaders are quoted in Willging, "Soviet Foreign Policy." Note finally, for what it is worth, Khrushchev's comment in his memoirs that Stalin "lived in terror of an enemy attack." Nikita Khrushchev, *Khrushchev Remembers*, ed. and trans. by Strobe Talbott (Boston: Little, Brown, 1970), p. 393.
178. For a couple of interesting examples, see Paul Nitze, "Assuring Strategic Stability in an Era of Détente," *Foreign Affairs*, Vol. 54, No. 2 (January 1976), p. 211; and Henry Kissinger, "A New Era for NATO," *Newsweek*, October 12, 1987, p. 60. Kissinger wrote here that he has "argued for 30 years that the threshold at which nuclear weapons have to be used should be raised much higher." But exactly thirty years earlier, he had published *Nuclear Weapons and Foreign Policy*, the book that established his reputation, in which he argued for a limited war strategy based on tactical nuclear weapons. These, he wrote, needed to be employed more freely than was possible in a strategy based on massive retaliation. The Eisenhower strategy had locked us into a posture that was much too defensive in nature; strategy instead needed to be oriented toward such "positive goals" as the reunification of Germany and the liberation of Eastern Europe. Needless to say, all this is forgotten today. See Henry Kissinger, *Nuclear Weapons and Foreign Policy* (New York: Harper/Council on Foreign Relations, 1957).

Atomic Diplomacy During the Korean War

Roger Dingman

In January 1956, *Life* magazine published an article that purportedly explained how the Eisenhower administration had ended the Korean War. Secretary of State John Foster Dulles revealed that he had conveyed an "unmistakable warning" to Beijing that the United States would use nuclear weapons against China if rapid progress toward a negotiated settlement was not made. He asserted that it was "a pretty fair inference" that this nuclear threat had worked. Dulles made this claim in defense of the notion that nuclear weapons were useful, indeed essential, tools of statecraft: When nuclear capability was combined with communication of intent to use it if necessary, deterrence— and even compellence—worked.[1]

Dulles spoke in response to partisan critics at the beginning of an election year, but his words influenced policy and history long after the 1956 contest ended. They defined the parameters of a debate about the political and diplomatic utility of nuclear weapons generally and the outcome of the Korean War in particular.[2] However, the secretary of state's claim was doubly deceptive. It focused analysts' attention on the six months of Republican conflict management, to the neglect of the preceding two and one-half years of Democratic stewardship. Moreover, Dulles's claim prompted a debate over

This essay was prepared for a conference on the study of nuclear weapons held at Columbia University with the support of the John D. and Catherine T. MacArthur Foundation. I am especially indebted to Roger M. Anders, Dennis Bilger, William H. Cunliffe, David Haight, Brigadier General John W. Huston, USAFR, and Edward Reese for archival guidance; to Robert Jervis, Franklin D. Mitchell, and colleagues at the School of Modern Asian Studies, Griffith University, Brisbane, Australia, for comments on earlier draft portions of the manuscript; and to the U.S. Naval War College and the Department of History, University of Southern California, for financing my travels to necessary archives. I alone bear responsibility for the arguments advanced herein.

Roger Dingman is Associate Professor of History at the University of Southern California. He has also served as Professor of Strategy at the U.S. Naval War College and is Distinguished Visiting Professor of History at the U.S. Air Force Academy for 1988–89.

1. James Shepley, "How Dulles Averted War," *Life*, January 16, 1956, pp. 70–72ff.
2. Edward C. Keefer, "President Dwight D. Eisenhower and the End of the Korean War," *Diplomatic History*, Vol. 10, No. 3 (Summer 1986), pp. 267–268, summarizes the historiographical debate triggered by Dulles's claim. A recent restatement of Dulles's argument, based primarily upon published sources, is Daniel Calingaert, "Nuclear Weapons and the Korean War," *Journal of Strategic Studies*, Vol. 11, No. 2 (June 1988), pp. 177–202.

International Security, Winter 1988/89 (Vol. 13, No. 3)
© 1988 by the President and Fellows of Harvard College and of the Massachusetts Institute of Technology.

the effects of Washington's atomic diplomacy that deflected attention from its substance and character. The result was to reinforce an essentially partisan interpretation of what occurred and to leave unconsidered more fundamental questions as to how, when, and why the United States tried to use nuclear weapons to its advantage in managing a limited war.

This article attempts to answer those basic questions. It focuses on Washington's attempts to derive political and diplomatic rather than tactical military advantage from the possession and deployment of nuclear weapons. What follows differs from earlier explorations of this subject in three vital respects. First, it reviews the entire war to demonstrate that atomic diplomacy was an element of American statecraft throughout the conflict and not just in its concluding months. Secondly, the story rests upon a deeper and broader documentary foundation than earlier treatments of this subject. The availability of previously top-secret documents from the papers of key individuals, the several armed services, the State and Defense Departments, the National Security Council (NSC), and Atomic Energy Commission (AEC) permits a more detailed analysis of Washington's attempts to use nuclear weapons as tools of conflict management.[3] Finally, the examination goes beyond words to deeds. By tracing military and diplomatic actions as well as parsing political intentions, the narrative that follows seeks to provide fresh insight into the history of United States Korean War policies and the evolution of American thinking about the utility of nuclear weapons.

Attitudes and Assumptions

American statesman and military professionals brought three basic assumptions about nuclear weapons to the task of conflict management during the Korean War. They believed that the United States enjoyed clear, but qualified nuclear superiority over the Soviet Union. They assumed that such superiority ought, somehow, to be usable. They also thought that the combination

---

3. Two sorts of previously unavailable archival materials proved most useful in the development of this essay. The papers of senior U.S. Air Force and Atomic Energy Commission (AEC) officials, most notably those of General Curtis E. LeMay, General Hoyt S. Vandenberg, and AEC Chairman Gordon A. Dean, include not only individual diaries but also official papers unavailable elsewhere. Many of the personal daily schedules of ranking officials—most notably those of Dean G. Acheson, Omar N. Bradley, J. Lawton Collins, Louis A. Johnson, and Hoyt S. Vandenberg—contain notations of visitors and telephone conversations. When used in conjunction with departmental documents, these materials facilitated detailed reconstruction of patterns of decision and action.

of restraint and resolve in atomic diplomacy during the Berlin Blockade of 1948–49 had worked and could prove effective in future crises. Because these three ideas profoundly influenced the decisions of both the Truman and Eisenhower administrations, they deserve further explication.

In June 1950, Washington had a clear but qualified nuclear advantage over Moscow. America had nearly three hundred atomic bombs in its stockpile, and more than two hundred sixty aircraft capable of putting them on Soviet targets.[4] The Soviet Union had exploded its first nuclear device only ten months earlier and could strike the United States only by one-way bomber missions or by smuggling nuclear weapons into American harbors aboard merchant vessels.[5] While both powers dramatically increased their nuclear stockpiles and improved their delivery systems during the Korean War, this balance favoring the United States did not change fundamentally between 1950 and 1953.[6]

But American decision-makers recognized that their nuclear superiority was qualified in two respects. First, despite flaws in enemy delivery capabilities, the grim truth was that Moscow's ability to strike the American heartland was growing.[7] Secondly, Washington acknowledged real limitations in America's ability to put nuclear weapons on enemy targets. Although

---

4. David Alan Rosenberg, "U.S. Nuclear Stockpile 1945 to 1950," *Bulletin of the Atomic Scientists*, Vol. 38, No. 5 (May 1982), p. 26.
5. Central Intelligence Agency (CIA), Intelligence memorandum 323-SRC, August 25, 1950, intelligence file, president's secretary's file (PSF), Box 250, Harry S Truman papers, Truman Library, Independence, Missouri (hereafter "Truman papers, HSTL").
6. Executive Secretary, National Security Council (NSC), to Chairman, AEC, December 6, 1950, NSC atomic weapons file, PSF, Box 202, Truman papers, HSTL; Briefing: Air Estimate of the Situation, 1951–1954, U.S. Air Force Commanders' Conference, October 30, 1951, item 168.7026-9, Charles Cabell papers, Simpson Historical Research Center, Maxwell Air Force Base, Alabama (hereafter "Cabell papers"). The briefing document puts Soviet nuclear strength at less than half the estimated American stockpile as of January 1951. *New York Times*, October 2, 1951; Office of the Historian, Strategic Air Command (SAC), *Development of Strategic Air Command, 1946–1976* (Omaha: U.S. Air Force SAC, 1976), pp. 20, 27, 33, 35, 38; Secretary of Defense to Executive Secretary, NSC, June 8, 1953, Office of Special Assistant for National Security Affairs (OSANSA), NSC subject file, atomic energy series, Box 1, Dwight D. Eisenhower papers, Dwight D. Eisenhower Library, Abilene, Kansas; Office of the Historian, Strategic Air Command, Status of Strategic Air Command, January–June 1953, Volume 1, frame 0481, reel K4263, Office of Air Force History, Bolling Air Force Base, Maryland.
7. President Truman publicly acknowledged American vulnerability to Soviet attack in April 1951; *Public Papers of the President, 1951* (Washington, D.C.: U.S. Government Printing Office [U.S. GPO], 1965), pp. 225–226. This series will hereafter be cited as *Truman Public Papers*, with dates and pages. By early 1953, President Eisenhower's advisers were debating the extent, not the possibility, of damage from Soviet nuclear strikes. See *Foreign Relations of the United States* (hereafter "*FRUS*"), 1952–1954, Volume 2, *National Security Affairs* (Washington, D.C.: U.S. GPO, 1984), pp. 203, 213–214, 232–233.

war plans called for launching an atomic blitzkrieg against the Soviet Union in the event of general war, not one nuclear-configured aircraft was deployed outside the continental United States when the Korean fighting began.[8] Strategic Air Command (SAC) planners estimated that it would take three months to bomb Moscow into submission, given the inadequacy of forward bases and overseas fuel supplies.[9] By 1953 the probability of swifter, successful strikes against the Soviet Union had increased thanks to the introduction of jet bombers, the development of overseas bases, and the deployment of aircraft carriers modified so as to be capable of carrying nuclear weapons.[10] But the Pentagon did not have custody of any complete atomic bombs, and the State Department had not begun negotiations for their deployment to foreign soil.[11] That meant that Washington had no immediately usable nuclear force near Korea.

Despite these limitations, President Truman, President Eisenhower, many of their key advisers, and probably most politicians along with a majority of the general public believed that nuclear superiority *ought* to be usable.[12] While the two presidents were sensitive to the moral dilemmas posed by the indiscriminate destructiveness of atomic weapons, both, as trained military men, placed them at the top of the hierarchy of usable force. Within days of the outbreak of fighting in Korea, both men alluded to the possibility of using atomic arms.[13] By early July 1950, Pentagon staff officers and the commander

8. SAC, *Development of SAC*, pp. 20–21; David Alan Rosenberg, "The Origins of Overkill," *International Security*, Vol. 7, No. 4 (Spring 1983), pp. 15–18, 25.

9. Office of the Historian, Strategic Air Command, "History of the Strategic Air Command: January–June 1950," Volume 2, chapter 7 (declassified by author's Freedom of Information Act request); Major General S.E. Anderson, Director of Plans, U.S. Air Force, to Secretary of the Air Force Stuart Symington, April 11, 1950, Box 100, Office of Secretary of the Air Force papers, Record Group (RG) 330, U.S. National Archives (hereafter "NA").

10. SAC, *Development of SAC*, pp. 35, 38; Status of Strategic Air Command, January–June 1953, Volume 1, frame 0502, reel K4263, Volume 7, frame 0946, reel K4264, Office of Air Force History, Bolling Air Force Base.

11. James Lay to Truman, December 5, 1950, Secretary of Defense to Executive Secretary, NSC, May 1, 1951, NSC atomic file, PSF, Truman papers, HSTL; Atomic Energy Commission, "Weapons Custody and Use," April 25, 1961, AEC 867/49, file 1442, folder 2, Atomic Energy Secretariat papers, Department of Energy (hereafter AEC, "Weapons Custody and Use"); Herbert B. Loper to Clinton P. Anderson, November 10, 1960, "Memorandum on History of Atomic Weapons Custody," Minutes, Box 5, Records of Joint Committee on Atomic Energy (JCAE), RG 128, NA (hereafter cited as "Loper memorandum").

12. Carlton Savage to George Kennan, memorandum, "Preliminary Study of Attitudes of U.S. Population about U.S. Use of Atomic Bomb in War," December 21, 1949, Box 50, Paul Nitze file, Policy Planning Staff files, Department of State papers, RG 59, NA.

13. David E. Lilienthal, *Journals: The Atomic Energy Years 1945–1950* (New York: Harper and Row, 1964), p. 391; Robert Ferrell, ed., *The Eisenhower Diaries* (New York: Norton, 1981), pp. 175–176; *FRUS*, 1950, Volume 7, *Korea*, pp. 159–160.

in chief of the Pacific fleet surmised that, if the situation in Korea became desperate, Congress and the public would demand the use of atomic weapons.[14]

The change of administrations in January 1953 strengthened official Washington's belief that nuclear weapons were usable tools of statecraft. The new secretary of state, John Foster Dulles, had argued in 1948 that the public would demand a resort to nuclear arms if the situation appeared to require their use.[15] His May 1952 *Life* magazine article, entitled "A Policy of Boldness," prefigured the Eisenhower administration's "New Look" strategy by championing reliance on nuclear weapons and strong alliances as deterrents to future communist aggression.[16] Thus the question confronting American statesmen as the war neared its end, just as at its beginning, was not whether, but how and when, to employ nuclear weapons for conflict management.

Democratic and Republican statesmen looked back to the dispatch of two squadrons of B-29s to Western Europe during the Berlin Blockade of 1948–49 for guidance on how best to use American nuclear superiority. Although the press described the flight of these aircraft, similar to those that had dropped atomic bombs in 1945 but not actually configured to do so, as a training mission, their deployment was widely interpreted as a demonstration of resolve in the face of Soviet pressure.[17] In fact, President Truman and his diplomatic advisers practiced restraint at the same time, rejecting Pentagon requests for custody of nuclear weapons and avoiding negotiating tactics that might back Moscow into a corner from which there was no face-saving escape.[18] In the summer of 1948, American statesmen doubted that the B-29 deployment contributed directly to settlement of the Berlin Blockade crisis.[19]

14. Commander in Chief Pacific Fleet (CINCPACFLT Radford) to Chief of Naval Operations (CNO Sherman), 080941Z, July 8, 1950, enclosure to JCS 1776/25 in Ops TS Korea file, Box 34a, section 14, cases 41–60, Assistant Chief of Staff, Operations, U.S. Army papers, RG 319, NA; Cabell memorandum, "Action to Prevent a Dunkirk in Korea," shown to General Norstad, July 12, 1950, TS 189327, Cabell papers.
15. James V. Forrestal diary, October 10, 1948, cited in Avi Shlaim, *The United States and the Berlin Blockade, 1948–1949* (Berkeley: University of California Press, 1983), p. 359.
16. John Foster Dulles, "A Policy of Boldness," *Life*, May 19, 1952, pp. 151–158; Stephen E. Ambrose, *Eisenhower*, Vol. 2 (New York: Simon and Schuster, 1984), pp. 33–34.
17. *New York Times*, June 19, 1948, July 16, 18, 26, 28, 1948; Shlaim, *The United States and the Berlin Blockade*, pp. 235–239, 337–341; Harry Borowski, *A Hollow Threat: Strategic Air Power and Containment before Korea* (Westport, Conn.: Greenwood, 1982), pp. 125–130.
18. *Truman Public Papers*, 1948, p. 415; AEC, "Weapons Custody and Use"; Loper memorandum; Ronald Pruessen, *John Foster Dulles: The Road to Power* (New York: Free Press, 1982), pp. 376–377.
19. Lilienthal, *Journals*, Vol. 2, p. 391; Robert Ferrell, ed., *Dear Bess* (New York: Norton, 1983), pp. 554–555.

But as time hazed over the particulars of this episode, they came to believe that atomic arms could be instruments of "force without war."[20] Their credibility might even exceed their actual capability if they were used, without overt threats, for purposes of deterrence rather than compellence.[21] Thus American statesmen and soldiers brought to the Korean War the conviction that atomic arms, if properly employed, could be extremely valuable tools for conflict management.

From Resolve to Restraint, June 1950–June 1951

During the first year of the war, a pattern in the use of nuclear weapons took shape in Washington. Forced repeatedly by battlefield circumstance to consider their tactical use in and around Korea, the Truman administration time and again turned away from such action. Driven by the same circumstances to consider how atomic weapons might help manage the political and diplomatic aspects of the conflict, the administration came to appreciate their utility in dealing with its enemies, the Soviet Union and the People's Republic of China (PRC); with its principal ally, Britain; and with its partisan foes at home. How and why President Truman and his senior advisers developed what might even be termed a strategy for the use of nuclear weapons can be seen by analyzing their behavior at four moments of crisis during the first year of the Korean conflict. Two of those moments came early in the fighting, in July 1950. A third followed at the end of November, when massive Chinese intervention confronted the United States with "an entirely new war."[22] The fourth and most serious of these crises struck Washington in April 1951.

FIRST USE: BOMBERS TO BRITAIN
The possibility of using nuclear weapons tactically came up during President Truman's very first wartime meeting with his senior advisers at Blair House on Sunday evening, June 25, 1950. The president raised the issue by asking Air Force Chief of Staff Hoyt S. Vandenberg if American planes could "take out" Soviet bases near Korea. The general replied affirmatively, but said it

20. The phrase "force without war" is the title of a book by Barry Blechman and Stephen S. Kaplan (Washington, D.C.: Brookings, 1978); Shlaim, *The United States and the Berlin Blockade*, p. 359.
21. John Lewis Gaddis, *The Long Peace* (New York: Oxford University Press, 1987), pp. 108–110.
22. *FRUS*, 1950, Vol. 7, *Korea*, p. 1237.

would require atomic bombs. That response prompted Truman to order the preparation of plans for launching an atomic attack in the event the Soviet Union entered the fighting.[23]

During the next three weeks, however, the president and his advisers came to see more diplomatic and political than military utility in nuclear weapons. That perception grew out of developments surrounding the first engagements between American and North Korean forces. Washington intervened in Korea to defend the principle of collective security and America's leadership of the non-communist world.[24] Policy-makers hoped for "resounding military success achieved by demonstrably overwhelming power."[25] But neither bombing North Korea nor blocking key roads slowed the enemy juggernaut plunging southward. In their first encounters, it was American troops rather than Pyongyang's soldiers who retreated.[26] Alarmed by these results, General Douglas MacArthur begged Washington to double the force at his disposal so that he might hold at least the southern tip of the Korean peninsula.[27]

But his superiors were not prepared to make definitive choices at this point. Meeting with the Cabinet on July 7, 1950, the president groped for some way to "let the world know we mean business." Central Intelligence Agency (CIA) Director Roscoe Hillenkoetter proposed seeking United Nations sanction for use of the atomic bomb even if doing so could not guarantee that Moscow would restrain Pyongyang and Beijing. Although he remained skeptical of Soviet intentions, Truman declined to make so overt a threat. Downplaying the immediate danger, he insisted that the Soviets were "seventy percent bluffers."[28] Then, making a Solomonic choice between the Pen-

---

23. Ibid., pp. 159–160. It should be noted that no one present voiced the slightest objection to the president's order.
24. Ernest R. May, *"Lessons" of the Past* (New York: Oxford University Press, 1973), pp. 75–78; William Stueck, Jr., *The Road to Confrontation* (Chapel Hill: University of North Carolina Press, 1981), pp. 191–192, 255–257.
25. *FRUS*, 1950, Vol. 7, *Korea*, p. 278.
26. Roy K. Flint, "Task Force Smith and the 24th Division: Delay and Withdrawal, 5–19 July 1950," in Charles E. Heller and William A. Stofft, eds., *America's First Battles 1776–1965* (Lawrence: University Press of Kansas, 1986), pp. 266–299; Clay Blair, *Forgotten War: America in Korea 1950–1953* (New York: Times Books, 1987), pp. 101–111.
27. D. Clayton James, *The Years of MacArthur*, Vol. 3 (Boston: Houghton Mifflin, 1985), pp. 441–442; James F. Schnabel and Robert J. Watson, *The History of the Joint Chiefs of Staff: The Joint Chiefs of Staff and National Policy*, Volume 3, *The Korean War*, part I (Washington, D.C.: Joint Chiefs of Staff [JCS], 1978), pp. 179–185.
28. Cabinet meeting notes, July 7, 1950, Box 1, Matthew J. Connelly papers, Truman Library; "Memorandum on psychological use of the Atomic bomb in Korea Conflict," July 6, 1950,

tagon's desire to call one hundred thousand men to arms and the Treasury's fear of the economic effects of full-scale mobilization, he let it be known that the Defense Department could exceed its current budget and use the draft.[29]

Two days later, the Joint Chiefs of Staff (JCS) postponed a decision on General MacArthur's troop request and set aside Chairman Omar Bradley's suggestion to put atomic weapons at MacArthur's disposal.[30] Their choice reflected doubts about MacArthur's judgment, unwillingness to allow Korea to disrupt Europe-first strategic priorities, and hesitancy to use nuclear weapons in a manner that seemed less than likely to be decisive.[31] They then decided that two of their number should visit General MacArthur in Tokyo and the battlefield in Korea before further decisions on force levels and deployments were made.[32]

In the interim, the Truman administration decided that nuclear strength must be used to demonstrate its determination to prevail in Korea. On July 8, 1950, SAC Commander Curtis LeMay was ordered to repeat, in effect, the Berlin Blockade B-29 feint of 1948.[33] The order grew out of General Vandenberg's desire to do *something* to counter the impression of ineffectiveness conveyed by the meager results of American bombing in Korea.[34] Sending aircraft to Britain carrying "Russian target materials" also implemented President Truman's previously expressed desire for expedited planning for attacks against the Soviet Union. LeMay, hoping to improve the readiness of his force still further, proposed that the B-29s carry everything but the fissionable cores of nuclear weapons.[35] If they did, and if this deployment was rounded out by the dispatch of ten nuclear-configured B-29s across the Pacific

Hillenkoetter memorandum to the president, July 7, 1950, intelligence file, PSF, Box 249, Truman papers, HSTL.

29. *New York Times*, July 8, 1950.

30. Schnabel and Watson, *JCS History*, Vol. 3, pp. 185–186; July 9, 1950 memorandum, Historical Record, June–July 1950 folder, Box 16, Matthew B. Ridgway papers, U.S. Army Military History Institute, Carlisle Barracks, Pennsylvania.

31. Ibid.; Gruenther to Bolte, July 9, 1950, CCS 383.21 Korea (3-19-45), section 23, Joint Chiefs of Staff papers, RG 218, NA; James, *MacArthur*, Vol. 3, p. 443; Schnabel and Watson, *JCS History*, Vol. 3, p. 185.

32. Ibid., pp. 185–186.

33. LeMay telecon with Commanding General, 3rd Air Division, July 8, 1950, summarized in LeMay diary, July 8, 1950, Curtis E. LeMay papers, Library of Congress. (A telecon was an exchange of teletype messages, flashed upon a screen so that they might be viewed simultaneously by more than one person.)

34. Memorandum of Norstad-LeMay telephone conversation, July 2, 1950, Box 7/10, Lauris Norstad papers, Modern Military Records Branch, NA.

35. LeMay diary, July 8, 1950, LeMay papers. "Russian target materials" presumably referred to maps and charts, prioritized target lists, radar scope information, etc.

and the overseas prepositioning of tankers and support aircraft, the time needed to commence and wage atomic war against the Soviet Union would be dramatically reduced.[36]

The JCS gave only qualified approval to the modified proposal, probably out of fear that its nuclear aspect might create diplomatic difficulties. Initial British reactions confirmed that concern, for the Royal Air Force, arguing that the proposed deployment had "wide consequences" and might be regarded as "an unfriendly act" by Moscow, refused to accede to the American request without prior agreement at the political level.[37] By nightfall on July 9, 1950, however, Air Force Vice Chief of Staff Lauris Norstad had persuaded Air Marshal Lord Tedder, who headed the British Joint Liaison Mission in Washington, to support the proposal; Norstad had also obtained clearance "at the highest level" to seek the approval of the British Chiefs of Staff for it.[38]

Much more significantly, Secretary of State Dean Acheson approved the deployment as a demonstration of resolve. While he may have shared Soviet expert Charles Bohlen's belief that "some measure" beyond military and economic mobilization was necessary to keep the Soviets from intervening in Korea or stirring up trouble elsewhere,[39] Acheson was more immediately concerned to impress the British with America's determination to prevail in Korea. The secretary of state was unhappy with London's recognition of the PRC and its dissent from interposition of the United States Seventh Fleet in the Taiwan Strait.[40] Although he had been assured that Britain would not seek a return to the *status quo ante* in Korea by letting the PRC have Taiwan, he worried lest London promote a peace settlement requiring withdrawal of American forces from the peninsula. His doubts were not dispelled by talks with British Ambassador Sir Oliver Franks on Sunday afternoon, July 9.[41] The next day Acheson sent London a note that rejected paying a price for disengagement in Korea and called for Anglo-American solidarity on ques-

---

36. Ibid., July 10, 1950.
37. General Joseph Lawton Collins daily schedule, July 9, 1950, Box 40, Collins papers, Eisenhower Library; Norstad to LeMay, July 9, 1950; Commanding General 3rd Air Division to Chief of Staff, U.S. Air Force, 091200Z, July 9, 1950, Box 86, Hoyt S. Vandenberg papers, Library of Congress.
38. Chief of Staff, USAF, to Commanding General 3rd Air Division, 092016Z July 9, 1950; Norstad to LeMay, July 9, 1950, Box 86, Vandenberg papers.
39. *FRUS*, 1950, Vol. 7, *Korea*, pp. 326–327.
40. Ibid., pp. 330–331, 340.
41. Ibid., pp. 331, 337; Acheson daily schedule, July 9, 1950, Box 45, Dean G. Acheson papers, Truman Library.

tions "of the gravest importance" certain to arise when the "fiction" of Soviet and Chinese non-involvement wore thin.[42] Sending B-29s to Britain was simply one more way to underline the gravity of the situation, demonstrate America's resolve, and elicit the cooperation of its most important ally.

The next morning the American ambassador in London called Prime Minister Clement Attlee out of a Cabinet meeting to put the deployment proposal before him. Recalling the events of 1948, Attlee suspected that Washington wanted to make the B-29 movement a demonstration of strength for Moscow's benefit. He was convinced that it would be wrong to do so. When he asked if the planes would carry atomic bombs, the ambassador confessed that they would "probably" have everything but the nuclear cores aboard. Attlee then took the American proposal to his Cabinet colleagues who, after considerable debate, approved it with one proviso: London and Washington must coordinate publicity so as to make the deployment appear purely routine.[43]

That requirement did not trouble President Truman, who readily gave formal approval to the proposed deployment on July 11.[44] The president had every reason to do so. The movement of B-29s across the Atlantic would enhance strategic readiness as he had ordered on June 25. Already reported in that morning's *New York Times* as a "normal rotation,"[45] the deployment might remind Moscow of America's nuclear strength without provoking the Soviets. Putting nuclear-configured B-29s in Britain also underlined the need for renewed Anglo-American solidarity. But the deployment neither risked a wider war nor loosened Truman's control over atomic weapons, for their nuclear cores would remain in the United States.[46] Finally, the president may have perceived domestic political advantages in sending bombers to Britain.

42. *FRUS*, 1950, Vol. 7, *Korea*, pp. 347–352.
43. Commanding General 3rd Air Division to Vice Chief of Staff, U.S. Air Force, July 10, 1950, Box 86, Vandenberg papers.
44. Norstad to LeMay, XG 68/102205, July 10, 1950, ibid., indicated that the AEC and Defense Department had agreed to present to the president their request to send nuclear "hardware" to Britain; Truman schedule, July 11, 1950, indicates that the president conferred early that morning with W. Averell Harriman, his newly designated special assistant for mutual security affairs. Harriman, a former ambassador to the Soviet Union, may have advised Truman on what to do at this point; Johnson schedule, July 11, 1950, Louis A. Johnson papers, University of Virginia Library, Charlottesville, and Gordon A. Dean diary, July 11, 1950, confirm their meeting with the president that afternoon; Norstad to Commanding General 3rd Air Division, 111729Z, July 11, 1950, Box 86, Vandenberg papers.
45. *New York Times*, July 11, 1950.
46. Gordon Dean to Truman, July 10, 1950, Box 4931, RG 326, U.S. Department of Energy Archives.

Cooperation in this endeavor might ease frictions between his secretaries of state and defense and thus deprive Republican critics of grounds for attacking the administration's management of the war.[47]

DETERRING THE CHINESE—AND THE REPUBLICANS

Less than three weeks after he sent nuclear-configured bombers across the Atlantic, Truman dispatched ten similar aircraft across the Pacific to Guam. His decision to do so took shape at a moment of uncertainty and crisis. While his advisers pondered tactical use of atomic weapons in Korea, they were deeply divided over whether, when, and how to do so. One Pentagon staff study argued that the general deterrent value of atomic weapons unused far exceeded the benefits that might flow from their employment with indeterminate results on the remote Korean peninsula.[48] Yet senior Operations Division officers suggested that Army Chief of Staff J. Lawton Collins query General MacArthur about possible use of nuclear weapons in Korea.[49] At the State Department, a Policy Planning Staff (PPS) study concluded that atomic bombs should be used in Korea only if Moscow or Beijing entered the fighting, and their employment promised decisive military success.[50] But after hearing the director of the Armed Forces Special Weapons Project, which managed the nuclear stockpile, say that the bomb might be used to prevent American forces from being pushed off the peninsula by North Korean forces

47. Eben Ayers diary, June 29, 1950, July 3, 10, 1950, Eben Ayers papers, Truman Library, indicates that the president knew that his defense secretary had telephoned congratulations to Republican Senator Robert A. Taft of Ohio on his speech calling for Secretary Acheson's resignation. Ayers on July 10 noted Truman's sensitivity to what he perceived as excessive Republican partisanship.
48. Report by an Ad Hoc Committee, Plans Division, "Employment of Atomic Bombs in Korea," July 12, 1950, Ops 091 TS Korea (July 12, 1950), RG 319, NA. Assistant Secretary of Defense Stephen Early made a similar argument, on grounds that the Soviet public would never be made aware of American use of the bomb in Korea. See Johnson to Truman, July 6, 1950, CIA Memoranda 1950–52 folder, intelligence file, PSF, Box 249, Truman papers.
49. Bolte to Gruenther, July 25, Ops 091 TS Korea (July 24, 1950), section 6; D.D. Dickson to Bolte, with enclosures, July 17, file 333 Pacific, case 3, Army General Staff Operations Division papers, RG 319, NA. The recommendation that Collins raise the question of tactical use of nuclear weapons with General MacArthur may have been designed to elicit the latter's opinions on arguments in a study titled "Employment of Atomic Weapons against Military Targets," prepared by Lt. Col. Harry L. Hillyard of the Joint War Plans Branch of the Army Operations Division, June 30, 1950, Hot Files, Box 11, Army General Staff Operations Division papers, RG 319, NA. It argued that atomic attacks might soften up ports prior to an amphibious assault, and it called for the use of penetration-type bombs against enemy forward air bases.
50. Carleton Savage to Paul Nitze, July 15, 1950, Atomic Energy–Armaments folder, 1950, Box 7, Policy Planning Staff Papers, RG 59, NA.

alone, Paul Nitze, the new PPS director, hinted to Secretary of State Acheson that the door for tactical use of atomic weapons in Korea remained open.[51]

By the beginning of the last week of July, however, such divergence of opinion became an unaffordable luxury. Washington suddenly faced circumstances that suggested that the atomic bomb might have to be used as a deterrent to limit the scope and determine the outcome of the fighting in Korea. There the enemy had squeezed American forces into a ninety-mile perimeter around Pusan. Within five days, despite General MacArthur's insistence that there be no further retreat, the North Koreans pushed Yankee and South Korean defenders back into an area that was two-thirds its previous size.[52] At the same time, it appeared that Washington's effort to isolate the Korean battlefield by interposing the Seventh Fleet in the Taiwan Strait might collapse. Its commander complained that he could not fight in Korea and stop a PRC invasion at the same time.[53] When the CIA reported a buildup of Chinese amphibious and paratroop forces opposite Taiwan, President Truman rejected the pleas of Jiang Jieshi (Chiang Kai-shek) for a pre-emptive strike against them.[54] Yet the NSC could not agree on providing military aid to the Nationalist leader.[55] On top of all this, Dean Acheson's efforts to enlist Britain's sympathy, if not support, for denying Taiwan to PRC control proved fruitless.[56]

Amidst fears that the line that Washington had drawn across Korea and in the Taiwan Strait might crumble, a proposal to send nuclear-configured

51. Nitze to Acheson, July 17, 1950, ibid. Nitze was reacting to both General Kenneth D. Nichols' thought that the bomb might have to be used short of a war with the Soviet Union, and Hanson Baldwin's *New York Times* column of July 17, 1950, that argued that the bomb must not be used in Korea under any circumstances.
52. *New York Times*, July 26–30, 1950; James, *MacArthur*, Vol. 3, p. 446.
53. Memorandum of Rusk-Burns-Orem meeting, July 24, 1950, Box 18, Office of Chinese Affairs papers, RG 59, NA; Commander Seventh Fleet (Joy) to Chief of Naval Operations (Sherman), 250256Z, July 25, 1950, Commander in Chief Pacific Fleet (Radford) to Chief of Naval Operations, 251224Z, July 25, 1950, Navy Department Top Secret Message Files, reel 50, Naval Historical Center, Washington, D.C.; and Commander in Chief Far East (CINCFE) to Joint Chiefs of Staff, CM In 15682, July 26, 1950, cited in G-3 Operations Log, 1950, tab 5, 091 Korea TS, Section I-1, Book I, RG 319, NA; these detail the Army-Navy dispute on this matter; James A. Field, Jr., *The United States Navy in the Korean War* (Washington, D.C.: U.S. GPO, 1962), pp. 108–110, 115–116, 119–120, 125.
54. CIA memorandum 312, July 26, 1950, cited in Clubb to Rusk, August 3, 1950, file 306.00111, Office of Chinese Affairs papers, RG 59, NA; Truman to Acheson, and Clubb to Rusk, ibid., July 18, 1950.
55. Acheson memorandum on NSC meeting, July 27, 1950, Box 65, Acheson papers.
56. *FRUS*, 1950, Vol. 7, *Korea*, p. 330; Dean G. Acheson, *Present at the Creation* (New York: Norton, 1969), p. 543.

bombers across the Pacific took shape. Air Force Chief of Staff Vandenberg was the driving force behind it. When he and General Collins met General MacArthur in Tokyo, the Army Chief of Staff declined to raise questions about possible use of nuclear weapons in Korea as his subordinates had suggested. But when Vandenberg asked MacArthur about how he might cut off Chinese communist forces if they entered the fighting, the old general replied that he saw "a unique use for the atomic bomb" in isolating them in North Korea. If Vandenberg would "sweeten up" the B-29 force at his disposal, the job could be done. The air force general immediately promised to do so.[57]

When Vandenberg returned to Washington, however, this scheme was modified to meet the needs of the increasingly desperate military situation. Convinced that "things were in a hell of a mess," Vandenberg suggested to JCS Chairman Bradley that SAC B-29s should be sent to destroy North Korean cities.[58] Cool to the idea at first, Bradley warmed to it when he met the chiefs on Friday July 28. His colleagues, who were increasingly concerned about the situation in the Taiwan Strait, recommended approval for Chinese Nationalist "offensive-defensive" actions there, despite President Truman's previous rejection of that course of action.[59]

The next morning the chiefs added ten nuclear-configured B-29s to the SAC task force about to cross the Pacific.[60] Doing so made perfect sense from their point of view. The deployment answered their subordinates' earlier call for prepositioning nuclear strike forces abroad. It probably seemed a more potent and less controversial response to the threat of Chinese action against Taiwan than allowing Jiang Jieshi to attack the mainland. The movement of the bombers implied agreement with General MacArthur's ideas; and even though he would not have operational control over them, their dispatch could be taken as an indication of resolve which would soften his unhappi-

---

57. Minutes of MacArthur-Collins-Vandenberg conference, July 13, 1950, Ops 333 Pacific (1950–1951), case 3, RG 319, NA.

58. Memoranda on LeMay-Norstad and Ramey-LeMay telephone conversations, July 29, 1950, LeMay diary.

59. Ibid.; General Omar N. Bradley, Chairman Joint Chiefs of Staff, Diary (hereafter "Bradley schedule"), July 28–29, 1950, Box 107, Omar N. Bradley papers, U.S. Military Academy Library, West Point, New York; Collins schedule, July 28–29, 1950; Vandenberg daily diary (hereafter "Vandenberg schedule"), July 28–29, 1950, Box 4, Vandenberg papers; Johnson schedule, July 29, 1950; Acheson memorandum on NSC meeting, July 27, 1950, Box 65, Acheson papers.

60. LeMay-Norstad and Ramey-LeMay telephone conversations, July 29, 1950, LeMay diary.

ness over Washington's unwillingness to approve his Inchon counteroffensive.[61]

Secretary of Defense Louis Johnson readily approved the chiefs' proposal for the deployment, and he may have told the president about it even before Truman boarded the *Williamsburg* for a weekend cruise.[62] When the yacht returned on Sunday afternoon, July 30, Johnson met the president at the Navy Yard pier and made what must have been a potent argument for resorting to nuclear arms.[63] Although he had publicly denied three days earlier that he was considering using the atomic bomb in Korea, Truman readily approved transfer of its nonnuclear components to military custody for deployment to Guam.[64]

Why did he do so? What did he expect to achieve through this action? In the absence of detailed records of this decision, answers to those questions must remain speculative. Truman may simply have seen the deployment as a contingent response to the North Korean offensive, launched that very day, which sought to force American troops out of Korea.[65] He may have regarded it as an expression of resolve that, if known to Beijing, would deter the Chinese in Korea and the Taiwan Strait. Almost certainly, that was how Dean Acheson regarded the deployment. One of his China experts had previously suggested that "a calculated indiscretion"[66] by the American ambassador in New Delhi about the dire consequences of Chinese military action would be passed on to Beijing.[67] Acheson had used that channel to emphasize Washington's hope that the PRC would stay out of the fighting. But now he reverted to the mode of communication used three weeks earlier and in 1948: Within hours after Acheson was informed of the proposed deployment, a *New York Times* reporter knew about it. The next day's newspaper printed

---

61. Ibid., July 30, 1950; James, *MacArthur*, Vol. 3, pp. 443–444; Schnabel and Watson, *JCS History*, Vol. 3, pp. 204–207.
62. Richard G. Hewlett and Francis Duncan, *A History of the United States Atomic Energy Commission* (University Park: Pennsylvania State University Press, 1969), Vol. 2, pp. 524–525; Truman and Johnson schedules, July 29, 1950.
63. Johnson schedule, July 30, 1950.
64. *Truman Public Papers*, 1950, p. 562; Hewlett and Duncan, *History of the United States Atomic Energy Commission*, Vol. 2, p. 525.
65. *New York Times*, July 31, 1950.
66. John Paton Davies memorandum, "Calculated Indiscretion by Ambassador Henderson," Box 19, Office of Chinese Affairs papers, RG 59, NA.
67. *FRUS*, 1950, Vol. 7, *Korea*, pp. 488–489.

news of the impending movement of B-29s across the Pacific for all, including the enemy, to read.[68]

Truman may also have acted in anticipation of the need to demonstrate toughness to blunt Republican attacks on his Korean policies. The day after the president approved the deployment of nuclear bombers westward, the Chairman of the Republican National Committee criticized the administration's "fumbling, stumbling ineptness" in managing the war.[69] In what may have been an attempt to shut Republican mouths, Truman then sent Secretary Johnson and Chairman Bradley to testify before the Joint Committee on Atomic Energy (JCAE), whose membership included Senators William F. Knowland and Bourke Hickenlooper, two of the most vociferous critics of administration East Asian policies.[70]

Did the second B-29 deployment achieve any of the goals Washington may have had in mind? The aircraft took no part in the bombing of North Korea, and they returned to the United States before Chinese forces began crossing the Yalu.[71] Despite the *New York Times* article about their dispatch and the newspaper accounts that speculated that nuclear weapons might be aboard one of the planes that crashed near San Francisco,[72] there can be no certainty that either Chinese or Soviet intelligence picked up the "resolve" implicit in their capabilities. Nor can it be argued that the deployment changed Moscow's and Beijing's intended courses of action. The PRC did not invade Taiwan but moved crack military units to the northeast where they began preparation for action in Korea in August.[73] Republican criticism of admin-

---

68. Acheson schedule, July 31, 1950. The fact that Acheson, alone among those who knew of the proposed deployment, met with someone likely to have spoken directly to the press (i.e., State Department press spokesman Michael McDermott), suggests that he was probably responsible for the leak; *New York Times*, August 1, 1950.
69. *New York Times*, August 1, 1950.
70. Truman, Johnson, and Bradley schedules, August 1–2, 1950; White House telephone logs, August 1, 1950, Truman papers, HSTL; see *Congressional Record*, 81st Cong., 1st sess., pp. 9641, 9754–9755, 9910–9911, 10054, 10065–10066, 10174, 10926–10927, for details of Republican criticism. *Congressional Directory*, 81st Cong., 2d sess. (Washington, D.C.: U.S. GPO, 1950), p. 219, indicates committee memberships.
71. Evidence on the return of nuclear-configured B-29s to continental United States in "History Strategic Air Command: July–December 1950," Volume 1, frame 482; and LeMay diary, September 13, November 8, 1950.
72. On August 3, 1950, one of the nuclear-configured B-29s crashed shortly after takeoff from Fairfield-Suisun (later renamed Travis) Air Force Base, killing the prospective commander of the nuclear strike force. The huge explosion that resulted was compared with a nuclear one, but none of the press photographs of the wreckage showed that all of the component parts except the fissionable core of an atomic weapon were aboard the aircraft. LeMay diary, August 3–6, 1950; *New York Times*, August 7, 1950.
73. Jonathan Pollack, "The Korean War and Sino-American Relations," unpublished paper

istration Korean policies proved neither as fierce nor as focused on conduct of the war as the White House feared.[74] But opposition restraint may have arisen as much from Republican fears of seeming to undercut American troops and their popular commander as from awareness of the president's dispatch of nuclear-configured bombers across the Pacific.

What, then, was the significance of this second attempt to use nuclear weapons in managing the Korean conflict? The decisions of late July 1950 demonstrated the strength of Washington's belief that such weapons, even if deployed without explicit statements of intent, could serve as deterrents. They also intensified the Truman administration's determination to be ready in the event that atomic arms might again be needed. Before the B-29s returned to their bases, State Department officials began to consider how best to help the Air Force select targets in the PRC.[75] Even more importantly, the president's senior advisers recognized that the highly personal, *ad hoc* style of decision-making that produced this second deployment of nuclear-configured bombers might not be adequate for the future. They proposed, and President Truman accepted, formation of a special NSC subcommittee on atomic matters to consider principles and procedures for future transfers of nuclear weapons to military custody.[76] If another crisis arose, the administration intended to be better prepared to consider whether or not atomic arms should be used to resolve it.

NEITHER DETERRENCE NOR COMPELLENCE

The next, more serious crisis hit Washington late in November 1950, when Chinese troops poured across the Yalu, halting the United Nations forces' conquest of North Korea. That disaster triggered talk of atomic bombs. President Truman told reporters that he would take "whatever steps are neces-

prepared for conference of Chinese and American historians, Beijing, October 1986, pp. 6–10, uses interviews and recently published official Chinese military histories to reconstruct Beijing's decisions of late July and early August pointing toward intervention in Korea.

74. Ayers diary, August 3–4, 1950. My generalizations about the mildness and relative paucity of Republican attacks on the administration's Korean War policies are based upon the *Congressional Record* and *New York Times* for August 3–11 and 26–30, 1950, periods immediately following the decision to send B-29s across the Pacific, General MacArthur's visit to Taipei, and President Truman's insistence that the general withdraw planned remarks about China and Taiwan to the Veterans of Foreign Wars.

75. Clubb to Stuart, August 8, 1950, Box 18, Office of Chinese Affairs papers, RG 59, NA.

76. The membership of the NSC's special committee on atomic energy was to include the secretaries of state and defense and the chairman of the Atomic Energy Commission. Truman to Gordon A. Dean, August 15, 1950, NSC personnel file, PSF, Box 220, Truman papers.

sary" to deal with the situation and indicated that the use of nuclear weapons had "always been [under] active consideration." When he added that the military commander in the field would be "in charge of" their use, the president ignited a political and diplomatic crisis of the first order.[77] Despite White House "clarification" of Truman's remarks, British Prime Minister Clement Attlee announced that he was flying to Washington for talks with the president, presumably to get Truman's finger off the nuclear trigger.[78] Four days later, on December 4, Truman and his senior advisers reluctantly began a series of summit talks.[79] Amidst these dramatic developments, SAC Commander Curtis LeMay thought his nuclear bombers might be ordered westward once again at a moment's notice.[80] But those orders never came.

That they did not reflected restraint in Washington born of changes in military, psychological, and political circumstances since July 1950. The Pentagon did not propose repeating the B-29 deployments of the preceding summer for two reasons. First, experts' sense of how atomic weapons might be used tactically in Korea had narrowed in a most unpleasant manner. Before the Chinese intervention crisis broke, senior staff officers had stopped short of recommending that the joint chiefs seek approval to deploy atomic bombs across the Pacific.[81] Their reluctance then probably mirrored doubts about Beijing's intentions and uncertainty about the utility of air-burst weapons against small units of enemy forces. Once large numbers of Chinese troops were in Korea, however, the Joint Strategic Planning Committee con-

77. *Truman Public Papers*, 1950, pp. 725–728.
78. *New York Times, Washington Post*, both, December 1, 1950.
79. *New York Times, Washington Post*, both, December 5, 1950; *FRUS*, 1950, Vol. 7, *Korea*, pp. 1361–1374; Acheson, *Present at the Creation*, p. 618. Roger Dingman, "Truman, Attlee, and the Korean War Crisis," *International Studies* (London School of Economics: International Centre for Economics and Related Disciplines, 1982), Vol. 1, pp. 1–42; and Rosemary Foot, "Anglo-American Relations in the Korean Crisis: the British Effort to Avert an Expanded War, December 1950–January 1951," *Diplomatic History*, Vol. 10, No. 3 (Winter 1986), pp. 43–51, offer detailed discussions of the summit talks.
80. LeMay to Vandenberg, December 2, file B-8852/2 and LeMay memorandum for the record, December 6, 1950, file B-8706/1, Box B-196, LeMay papers. It should be noted that LeMay, in the first message, expressed opposition to actual use of nuclear weapons in Korea.
81. Major General Charles Bolte to Collins, November 16, 1950; Collins to JCS, November 20, 1950; Secretaries of Joint Staff to JCS, November 21, 1950; JCS 2173, Plans and Operations Division, Korea TS file, Box 34a, Section III, cases 41–60, RG 319, NA. The fact that the Joint Strategic Survey Committee recommended redeployment of nuclear-configured B-29s to the vicinity of Korea without preparing the usual draft letter from the Joint Chiefs to the secretary of defense and without advising the chiefs to seek approval for "certain preparatory measures" for such a deployment hints at lingering doubts or dissent about this recommendation among Committee members.

cluded that defense, rather than deterrence or compellence, was the only logical reason for using nuclear arms there.[82] Thus the JCS recommended that British Prime Minister Attlee be told that the United States had "no intention" of using nuclear weapons in Korea unless they should be needed to protect evacuation of UN forces or to prevent a "major military disaster."[83]

Secondly, the chiefs were not certain that the situation in Korea was so desperate as to make their only options nuclear. Spurred, perhaps, by Chief of Naval Operations Forrest Sherman's doubts about the accuracy of General MacArthur's reports, they decided to send General Collins, previously a skeptic about tactical use of nuclear weapons, and Air Force Intelligence Chief General Charles Cabell, a vigorous advocate of their use in war against the Soviet Union, to Tokyo.[84] They found the UN Commander guardedly optimistic. While he had previously discussed nuclear targeting in China with his staff, he now felt that the ground situation in Korea was stabilizing, and advised postponing any nuclear decisions.[85] Reassured, General Collins announced publicly that he saw no need to use atomic bombs in Korea.[86]

The soldiers' caution was matched by restraint at the State Department. In mid-November, second-level officials there had considered but rejected using nuclear weapons in Korea. They argued with cool logic that the probable costs of doing so—measured in terms of shattered UN unity, decreased respect in Asia, and possible war with China—far outweighed any possible military gains.[87] The psychology of the situation early in December reinforced the strength of that argument for Secretary of State Dean Acheson. He feared for reason on all sides at this point. Truman had spoken imprudently about using nuclear weapons. Prime Minister Attlee had rashly invited himself to

82. Bolte to Collins, December 3, 1950, G-3 AWPB/71684, comments on JCS 2173/2, Operations Division, Hot Files, tab 67, Box 11, RG 319, NA.
83. Bradley to Secretary of Defense, with enclosures, December 4, 1950, JCS 2173/3, Plans and Operations Division, Korea TS file, Box 34A, Section III, cases 41–60, RG 319, NA.
84. Joy to Sherman, 010702Z, December 1, 1950, Navy Top Secret files, reel 50; *FRUS, 1950,* Vol. 7, *Korea,* p. 1278. Collins' views on possible responses to the Chinese intervention were also strongly colored by his low estimate of Korea's strategic value. See ibid., p. 1279; *New York Times,* December 4, 1950.
85. Lieutenant General George E. Stratemeyer diary, December 1 and 7, 1950, George E. Stratemeyer papers, Simpson Historical Research Center (SHC), Maxwell Air Force Base, Alabama. This first-hand account casts doubt on Dean Acheson's later claim that General MacArthur, according to Collins' first report, thought atomic weapons might have to be used in North Korea unless there was a ceasefire or a new policy authorizing air attacks on and naval blockade of the PRC. See Acheson, *Present at the Creation,* p. 616.
86. *Pacific Stars and Stripes,* December 6, 1950; *Washington Post,* December 6, 1950.
87. *FRUS, 1950,* Vol. 7, *Korea,* pp. 1098–1100.

Washington. Acheson's own political enemies were sharpening their knives.[88] Moreover, he had wildly overestimated the rationality of the Chinese leaders in assuming that they would accept Washington's protestations of innocent intent during the UN drive toward the Yalu.[89] If Beijing had misread his calculus of deterrence then, could he be certain now that the Chinese would respond rationally to any intimation of intent to resort to nuclear arms? The secretary of state thought not. It was definitely a time to keep his powder dry.[90]

President Truman was drawn to that conclusion for the same reasons that his diplomatic and military advisers were. But domestic political conditions quite different from those of the preceding July also counseled nuclear inaction during the first weeks of December 1950. Then, nuclear action had offered at least some prospect of strengthening his leadership. Now, having apparently erred in his November 30 remarks about possible use of atomic weapons, the president could best demonstrate leadership by resisting forces pulling him in opposite directions. Administration representatives succeeded in silencing those who spoke of atomic war on Capitol Hill.[91] The president also knew that he must resist pressures from "the Limeys" to share command and control over both Korean operations and any possible use of nuclear weapons.[92] Self-control and inaction became, in short, the preferred ways of demonstrating and defending presidential leadership.

Thus Truman and his most senior advisers never seriously considered using nuclear weapons during the first grim weeks of December 1950. This third crisis, nevertheless, helped crystallize Washington's thoughts about their utility in two important respects. First, by narrowing the prospect for tactical use of the weapons to covering the retreat of UN forces from Korea, this episode reduced the bomb's attractiveness to military professionals. Late in January 1951, General MacArthur refused even to consider a proposal for forward deployment of nuclear weapons for that purpose.[93] Second, the

---

88. *New York Times, Washington Post*, both, December 5, 1950; Acheson, *Present at the Creation*, p. 627.

89. *FRUS*, 1950, Vol. 7, *Korea*, pp. 1142, 1158; Stueck, *Road to Confrontation*, pp. 248–250.

90. *FRUS*, 1950, Vol. 7, *Korea*, pp. 1323–1332.

91. Dingman, "Truman, Attlee, and the Korean War Crisis," pp. 51–52, details the administration's efforts to prevail over congressional foes at this point.

92. George Elsey minutes and memoranda, n.d. (but internal evidence clearly indicates that it was written during the December 1950 Truman-Attlee summit), Box 164, PSF, Truman papers, HSTL; *FRUS*, 1950, Vol. 7, *Korea*, pp. 1431–1432.

93. CGEUSAK (Commanding General Eighth U.S. Army, Korea, Ridgway) to CINCFE, January

events of December 1950 reinforced senior civilian officials' distaste for atomic threats, without destroying their openness to other methods of using nuclear weapons. When National Security Resources Board Chairman Stuart Symington insisted that the atomic bomb was America's "political ace," Truman let Dean Acheson retort that it was a "political liability" whose threatened use would "frighten our allies to death" without worrying the Soviets. But that exchange within the NSC did not preclude other, more subtle uses for atomic weapons. Speaking at the president's request, CIA Director Walter Bedell Smith told the NSC that nuclear superiority was a wasting asset best used before the Soviet stockpile grew to such a point that Moscow would be willing to risk atomic war.[94] That no one objected to that argument suggested that the Truman administration intended to keep nuclear weapons among its tools for conflict management.

Deterrence Without Compellence, April–June 1951

Early in April 1951, President Truman picked up his nuclear tools for a third and final time. He did so in the gravest circumstances. The Korean fighting seemed about to take a dangerous new turn. While UN troops were poised to cross the 38th Parallel in force, the Chinese appeared to be readying a massive ground offensive.[95] Moreover, Washington had indications that Moscow had moved three divisions into Manchuria and had positioned other forces for an attack on Japan.[96]

The administration faced this situation divided within itself and at odds with its allies. The State and Defense Departments had barely agreed on a Jesuitical distinction between immediate military and long-term political objectives in Korea.[97] Although some diplomats doubted that the enemy could

---

18, 1951; CINCFE to CGEUSAK, January 30, 1951; both, Korea special file, Box 20, Ridgway papers.

94. NSC meeting minutes, January 25, 1951, NSC file, PSF, Box 220, Truman papers, HSTL.

95. J.M. Elizalde report on Rusk briefing to Elpidio Quirino, February 18, 1951, Elizalde-Quirino special correspondence, Elpidio Quirino papers, Ayala Museum, Makati, Manila, Philippines; *New York Times*, March 30, 1951, and April 1, 1951.

96. Gordon A. Dean diary, April 5, 1951, AEC Secretariat papers, RG 126, Department of Energy Archives, Germantown, Maryland. This document is reprinted in Roger M. Anders, ed., *Forging the Atomic Shield* (Chapel Hill: University of North Carolina Press, 1987), p. 127.

97. *FRUS*, 1951, Vol. 7, *Korea and China*, pp. 189–194, 203–206, 233, and 285–286, details civil-military differences over defining the objective to be achieved in the Korean fighting. Also see Executive secretary, NSC, to NSC Senior Staff, "United States National Objectives and Policy in Asia," March 15, 1951, CCS 092 Asia (6-25-48), sec. 11, RG 218, NA.

be compelled to negotiate,[98] the Joint Chiefs and General MacArthur believed that maintaining a strong position in Korea and imposing direct military and economic pressures on China could lead to a negotiated end to the fighting.[99] Efforts to resolve these differences only made matters worse. While Washington struggled to draft an appropriate presidential statement calling for cease-fire talks, General MacArthur warned Beijing that the UN might abandon its "tolerant effort" to limit the fighting to Korea.[100] The general's remarks infuriated the president's senior civilian advisers. But noting the Joint Chiefs' refusal to condemn what MacArthur had said and the popular appeal of his words, they advised President Truman simply to issue what the press subsequently termed a "mystifying clarification" of his policy.[101]

The mildness of his response to what appeared to be a challenge by General MacArthur proved doubly troublesome to the president. Britons began to fear that "the mad satrap" in Tokyo was about to drag them into "full-scale war."[102] Protests in London spiraled: the Chiefs of Staff opposed any major advance beyond the 38th Parallel; the Cabinet decided to press for a new, more restrictive directive to MacArthur; and the House of Commons tabled a motion of no confidence in the general.[103] Furthermore, President Truman appeared weak and indecisive at home. His popularity fell to a new low,[104] and pundit Walter Lippman termed his relations with Congress "a danger to national security."[105] Even though the Senate approved his request to send additional divisions to Europe, it attached conditions widely regarded as infringements on his prerogatives as commander in chief.[106] Summing things up, the assistant secretary of state for public affairs concluded that the people lacked confidence in their leaders' ability to end the Korean War.[107]

98. *FRUS*, 1951, Vol. 7, *Korea and China*, pp. 249–251.
99. JCS 1776/199, 200, March 19 and 23, 1951, CCS 383.21 Korea (3-19-45), section 44, RG 218, NA.
100. *FRUS*, 1951, Vol. 7, *Korea and China*, pp. 254, 263–266.
101. Lovett-Acheson telephone conversation memorandum, March 24, 1951, Box 66, Acheson papers; Acheson, *Present at the Creation*, pp. 668–669; *New York Times*, March 25, 1951.
102. Gladwyn Jebb to Foreign Office, No. 368, March 26, 1951, Foreign Office (FO) 371/92061/f1017/10; Jebb to Foreign Office, No. 400, April 6, 1951, FO 371/92061/f1017/11, Public Record Office (PRO), London.
103. Chuter Ede to Herbert Morrison, April 6, 1951, FO 371/92815/fk1096/41; Cabinet minute 23–51, April 2, 1951, CAB 128/19, PRO.
104. *Washington Post*, April 1, 1951; Truman's popularity dropped from 36 percent to a mere 26 percent approval level between January and mid-March, 1951. See George H. Gallup, comp., *The Gallup Poll, 1935–1971*, Vol. 2 (New York: Random House, 1972), pp. 958, 970.
105. *Washington Post*, April 5, 1951.
106. Ibid., April 6, 1951; *New York Times*, April 3, 1951.
107. Undersecretary's meeting minutes, April 4, 1951, UM-N327, Records of the Executive Secretariat, RG 59, NA.

On April 4, the situation reached crisis proportions. UN troops plunged across the 38th Parallel,[108] but Washington sank into deeper discord. The JCS gave preliminary approval to a memorandum that opposed any ceasefire in Korea that would tie down American troops there; they also urged immediate preparation for air and naval action against China.[109] The Department of State remained silent, trapped between Dean Acheson's desire to talk tough to the Soviets and his fear that doing so would alarm allies and ruin chances for any peace talks that might be initiated in Moscow.[110] Policy Planning Staff (PPS) Director Nitze made matters still worse by telling the joint chiefs that a proposed Seventh Fleet sortie along the south China coast was too provocative.[111] His objections probably swept away the last of their doubts on the necessity of forceful, even unilateral, action to bring the Korean fighting to an end.[112]

While his advisers quarrelled, Truman tried to bolster his sagging leadership. In a defensive, almost paranoid gesture, he had recently ordered the Cabinet to mobilize to counteract what he regarded as an organized campaign to discredit the presidency.[113] Now, on April 4, 1951, he summoned three of the "Big Four" congressional leaders, hoping to get their help in alerting Capitol Hill and the public to the dangers confronting the nation.[114] Shortly after that meeting, House Speaker Sam Rayburn warned that the country was "in greater danger of an expanded war today than . . . at any time since . . . 1945."[115]

But those words had little effect. In Tokyo, MacArthur's headquarters denied the existence of a Soviet buildup and yet claimed that the general was authorized to retaliate against a Soviet attack.[116] In Washington, Republicans scoffed at Rayburn's warning. Minority Leader Joseph Martin of Massachusetts read in public a letter from General MacArthur. It implied that

---

108. *New York Times, Washington Post*, both, April 4, 1951.
109. Decision on JCS 1776/202, April 4, 1951, CCS 335.14 (6-6-42), sec. 7, RG 218, NA; Schnabel and Watson, *JCS History*, Vol. 3, pp. 470–471.
110. Undersecretary's meeting minutes, April 4, 1951, UM-N327, Records of the Executive Secretariat, RG 59, NA.
111. *FRUS*, 1951, Vol. 7, *Korea and China*, pp. 1616–1619.
112. JCS 1776/202, April 5, 1951, CCS 383.21 Korea (3-19-45), sec. 45, RG 218, NA; Dean diary, April 5, 1951, hints that the JCS had virtually finalized a decision to request transfer of atomic weapons to military custody by the evening of April 4. See Anders, *Forging the Atomic Shield*, p. 134.
113. Cabinet meeting notes, April 2, 1951, Box 1, Connelly papers.
114. Truman schedule, April 4, 1951; *New York Times*, April 5, 1951.
115. *Congressional Record*, 82d Cong., 2d sess., p. 3311.
116. *New York Times, Washington Post*, both, April 5, 1951.

Washington misunderstood the global strategic significance of the Korean conflict and proclaimed that there was "no substitute for victory" in the fighting.[117] Taking those words as an unmistakable challenge to his leadership, President Truman launched the train of events that would culminate in his relieving General MacArthur of command.[118]

But before that decision became final, the president decided to send B-29s carrying complete atomic weapons across the Pacific. That choice took shape on Friday, April 6, 1951. That morning General Bradley brought him the latest reports on the enemy buildup and the chiefs' recommendation that General MacArthur be authorized to retaliate against air bases and aircraft in Manchuria and Shantung in the event of "a major attack" on UN forces originating outside the Korean peninsula.[119] The president then conferred with CIA Director Smith, perhaps to get confirmation of reported concentrations of men and aircraft, perhaps to consider whether pre-emptive rather than retaliatory action was required.[120] After meeting with the Cabinet, he spoke with his innermost circle of advisers on national security matters about relieving General MacArthur and perhaps about preventing enemy escalation of the Korean fighting as well.[121] By mid-afternoon, his mind made up, Truman telephoned AEC Chairman Dean and asked him to come to the White House immediately.[122]

The president painted an ominous picture when Dean entered the Oval Office. Enemy planes were parked wingtip to wingtip on Manchurian airfields; Soviet submarines were concentrated at Vladivostok; and a sizable Soviet force had moved south on Sakhalin. Moscow might be about to try a one-two knock-out blow, striking UN forces by air in Korea and cutting them off at sea from their Japanese bases. To check this threat, Truman had decided to send complete nuclear weapons and SAC bombers across the Pacific. The bombs were not to be frittered away indecisively on the Korean peninsula, and he was not giving the Air Force a green light to drop them. Saying he

117. *Congressional Record*, 82d Cong., 2d sess., pp. 3373–3380; *FRUS*, 1951, Vol. 7, *Korea and China*, pp. 298–299.
118. White House telephone log, April 5, 1951; Bradley schedule, April 5, 1951; Schnabel and Watson, *JCS History*, Vol. 3, pp. 535–536.
119. Truman schedule, April 6, 1951; *FRUS*, 1951, Vol. 7, *Korea and China*, p. 309.
120. Truman schedule, April 6, 1951.
121. Ibid.; Cabinet meeting notes, April 6, 1951, Box 1, Connelly papers; Robert H. Ferrell, ed., *Off the Record: The Private Papers of Harry S. Truman* (New York: Penguin Books, 1982), pp. 210–211.
122. White House telephone log, April 6, 1951, Truman papers, HSTL.

hoped the need to do so would never arise, Truman promised that he would consult the NSC's special committee on atomic energy before taking any such decision. That convinced Dean, who upon returning to his office immediately telephoned General Vandenberg about transferring nine complete atomic bombs to Air Force custody.[123]

But was the situation in and around Korea as desperate as the president implied? His senior military and diplomatic advisers thought so—for a moment. While the president spoke with Dean, they sought Britain's agreement for retaliatory bombing beyond Korea if UN forces were attacked from outside the peninsula.[124] The next day, April 7, the 99th Medium Bomb Wing was ordered to pick up atomic bombs for transshipment to Guam.[125]

But by that time, the sense of military and diplomatic urgency attending the president's order weakened. The task force was ordered to wait on Guam, rather than to proceed as originally planned to Okinawa for "possible action against retardation targets," that is, Soviet forces poised to strike Korea or Japan. While nuclear weapons would be prepositioned on Okinawa, the prospective strike force commander would remain at SAC headquarters near Omaha instead of going to Tokyo.[126] General Bradley also held up a directive to General MacArthur, just approved by President Truman and Secretary Acheson, that authorized retaliatory strikes against air attackers from outside the Korean peninsula.[127] In marked contrast to his behavior the preceding July, Dean Acheson did not immediately refute British challenges to Washington's assessment of the threat or press London to concur in proposed responses to it.[128]

---

123. Dean diary, April 6, 1951, reprinted in Anders, *Forging the Atomic Shield*, p. 137. What the president said on this occasion was considerably more alarming than the flow of incoming intelligence reports suggested. General MacArthur's G-2 reports suggested that the enemy buildup of an "international volunteer force" and his massing of aircraft was ominous but not necessarily indicative of immediate intent to attack. See Far East Command (FECOM) G-2 intelligence reports 31263131, April 16, 1951, Box 388, Record Group 338, Modern Military Records Field Branch, National Archives, Suitland, Maryland. The daily NSC/CIA memoranda to the president for this period made no mention of an enemy buildup. See CIA daily intelligence summaries, April 16, 1951, intelligence files, PSF, Box 250, Truman Library papers.
124. *FRUS*, 1951, Vol. 7, *Korea and China*, pp. 307–309; Bradley schedule, April 6, 1951.
125. 9th Medium Bomb Wing, Travis Air Force Base, History, April 1–30, 1951, frame 1060, reel 2325, SHC; LeMay diary, April 7, 1951.
126. LeMay diary, April 7–8, 1951; LeMay to Vandenberg, April 8, 1951, B-10526-3, Box B-197, LeMay papers; LeMay to Vandenberg, April 8, 1951, B-10526/1, Box 22, Vandenberg papers.
127. Bradley schedule, April 8, 1951; Schnabel and Watson, *JCS History*, Vol. 3, pp. 485–486; Omar N. Bradley and Clay Blair, *A General's Life: An Autobiography* (New York: Simon and Schuster, 1983), pp. 630–631.
128. Acheson schedules, April 7–15, 1951; *FRUS*, 1951, Vol. 7, *Korea and China*, pp. 316–319,

But the sense of domestic political danger that informed the president's decision did not dissipate. Sending the nuclear bombers and approving a directive that conditionally authorized their use were essential to winning the joint chiefs' support for his decision to relieve General MacArthur. The chiefs were at first loath to do so.[129] But by deploying nuclear weapons Truman made clear the distinction between his disapproval of MacArthur's public statements and his acceptance of the strategic concepts underlying them. The president also strengthened the argument for relieving MacArthur on grounds of "confidence"; if nuclear operations were pending, it was absolutely essential that Washington have the utmost trust in its field commander. General Bradley used that argument with his colleagues, and they concluded, late Sunday afternoon April 8, that they must support the president's decision to bring MacArthur home.[130]

At this point, Truman may not have intended to make more explicit political use of the decision to deploy nuclear bombers abroad. But circumstances beyond his control all but forced him to do so. The president tried, but failed, to persuade AEC Chairman Dean to keep secret the transfer of nuclear weapons to military custody. When Dean reminded him that the JCAE had to be informed, Truman persuaded him to let Senator Brien McMahon of Connecticut, author of the legislation requiring such disclosure and a more politically potent spokesman than Dean, do so.[131] McMahon, in turn, tried unsuccessfully to limit knowledge of the atomic deployment to the most senior members of the JCAE. But its ranking Republicans insisted that the full committee be told of the president's decision.[132] Thus by Tuesday morning, April 10, eighteen legislators, including some of the sharpest critics of administration East Asian policies, knew that Truman was sending nuclear weapons abroad for the first time since 1945.[133]

327–334, chronicle consultations with representatives of other nations with forces in Korea. These conversations revealed allies' reservations but did not prompt immediate State Department efforts to overcome them.

129. Bradley schedules, April 5–8, 1951; "Events in Connection with Change of Command in Far East," April 24, 1951, CCS 013.36 (4-20-51), RG 218, NA.

130. Ibid.; Bradley and Blair, *A General's Life*, pp. 631–635.

131. Truman schedule, April 9, 1951; Dean diary, April 9, 1951, reprinted in Anders, *Forging the Atomic Shield*, pp. 137–139.

132. Anders, *Forging the Atomic Shield*, pp. 139–140; Truman to McMahon, April 10, 1951, chronological name file, PSF, Truman papers, HSTL.

133. *Congressional Directory*, 82d Congress, 2d sess. (Washington, D.C.: U.S. GPO, 1951), p. 220.

The next evening, they and the nation heard Truman deliver a speech carefully crafted to defend his relief of General MacArthur and his management of the Korean conflict. The president attacked his unruly subordinate, insisting that it would be "wrong, tragically wrong" for the United States to widen the war. Then he warned Moscow and Beijing that they would be "foolhardy" to escalate the fighting in Korea. The communists, he insisted, must "choose and bear the responsibility" for what might occur if they altered the rules of engagement by launching air attacks against UN forces.[134] That veiled threat, which made no mention of the nuclear-armed B-29s just ordered to cross the Pacific, was meant to convey a message of resolution, tempered by reasoned restraint, to all who heard him.

In the highly charged atmosphere following General MacArthur's relief, such carefully balanced phrases proved inadequate for managing conflict at home and abroad. Eight days after Mr. Truman spoke, General MacArthur electrified Congress and the nation with an emotional speech in which he claimed that the joint chiefs concurred in his belief that expansion and escalation could bring victory in Korea.[135] Two weeks later, the general became the star witness in a protracted Senate inquiry into his dismissal and the policies that led to it.[136] In Korea, the Chinese, undeterred by anything the president had said or done, launched their largest ground offensive to date.[137]

Realizing that more must be done to deter and restrain its enemies, the administration made subtle use of atomic weapons in three ways over the next ninety days. First, the Pentagon managed the nuclear deployment so as to suggest that it might become something far more serious than a training exercise or deterrent feint. Late in April, following the renewed enemy ground offensive in Korea, Truman approved a second movement westward of nuclear-configured aircraft.[138] SAC sent a command and control team to Tokyo; its commander remained there to coordinate operational plans for possible atomic strikes.[139] Washington also sent to General Ridgway, Mac-

134. *New York Times*, April 12, 1951; *Truman Public Papers*, 1951, pp. 223–227.
135. *New York Times*, April 20, 1951; James, *MacArthur*, Vol. 3, pp. 612–617.
136. *New York Times*, May 4–6, 1951; James, *MacArthur*, Vol. 3, pp. 621–633.
137. *New York Times*, May 16, 1951; Pollack, "The Korean War and Sino-American Relations," p. 36; Bradley and Blair, *A General's Life*, pp. 640–641. Blair, *The Forgotten War*, pp. 822–855, 874–893, provides the most recent, detailed account of these offensives.
138. LeMay diary, April 28–29, 1951; 9th Medium Bomb Wing, Travis Air Force Base, History, April 1951, frame 1061, reel 2325, SHC.
139. Thomas S. Power to LeMay, 020755Z, May 2, 1951, item B-10856/2; LeMay to Major General Thomas D. White, May 7, 1951, item B-10934/4; both, Box B-197, LeMay papers.

Arthur's successor, a directive that gave him qualified authority to launch
atomic strikes in retaliation for a major air attack originating from beyond
the Korean peninsula.[140] While the nuclear weapons remained on Guam, the
bombers logged training flight time to prepare for using them.[141] Early in
June, in a departure from previous practice that the enemy might interpret
as a prelude to expanded fighting, reconnaissance aircraft overflew airfields
in Manchuria and Shantung to obtain target data.[142]

Second, Washington sent a secret envoy to Hong Kong with what could
be interpreted as a nuclear message for Beijing. Although earlier pourparlers
had proven fruitless, PPS member Charles Burton Marshall's mission was to
contact persons capable of getting that message to PRC leaders.[143] On the
eve of his departure, he met with Dean Acheson. Although he was not
informed of the nuclear deployment,[144] it appears that Marshall was instructed in the secretary of state's method of warning an adversary without
overtly threatening him. What he told putative messengers to Beijing bore
ominous hints of American nuclear power. Marshall warned the PRC not to
misread MacArthur's relief and the administration's rejection of his call for
expanded fighting as signs of weakness or timidity. There were limits to
American patience and restraint, and Chinese leaders should be aware of
Washington's ability to set their nation's development back for decades.[145]
Those words were strong enough to raise doubts in Chinese minds about

---

140. Schnabel and Watson, *JCS History*, Vol. 3, pp. 488–489; *FRUS*, 1951, Vol. 7, *Korea*, pp. 386–387, 394–398.
141. Precisely what the nuclear-configured bombers sent to Guam did during the early part of their deployment remains somewhat unclear because the 9th Aviation Squadron History for May 1951 is presently unavailable. However, the absence of any indications of combat-related activity in the LeMay diary and correspondence or in the diaries of officers at Far East Air Force Headquarters who worked with the SAC Liaison Officer, together with the routine character of reports in the June 1951 squadron history, suggests that training operations may have been all that occurred. See 9th Aviation Squadron History, June 1951, frame 1471, reel 2325, SAC Histories, SHC.
142. Colonel Winton R. Close to Major General T.S. Power, June 6, 19, 1951, items B-11651, B-11843, Box B-197; CGFEAF (Commanding General, Far East Air Force) Tokyo to HQUSAF (Headquarters, U.S. Air Force), 080810Z, June 8, 1951, item B-11501, Box B-198, LeMay papers.
143. This mission was preceded by months of pourparlers between University of Washington Professor George A. Taylor and a former Chinese employee of the U.S. Army who had remained in the People's Republic after 1949. Taylor, who engaged in intelligence activities in China before and during World War II, had served as a consultant to the CIA. His unofficial status made him an ideal go-between at this point in the war. These contacts are detailed in *FRUS*, 1951, Vol. 7, *Korea and China*, pp. 1476–1503, 1519–1521, 1530–1535, 1542–1548, 1550–1552, 1557–1562, 1583–1584, 1588–1589. Interview with George A. Taylor, Seattle, Washington, April 14, 1984.
144. Interview with Charles Burton Marshall, January 29, 1983.
145. *FRUS*, 1951, Vol. 7, *Korea and China*, pp. 1658–1663.

American nuclear intentions, yet they by no means constituted an overt atomic threat.

Third, the administration when dealing with domestic foes gave hints of its willingness to use nuclear weapons. By the time the Senate investigation got under way early in May 1951, the State Department, which had incorporated ideas strikingly similar to MacArthur's into revisions for the basic NSC East Asian policy paper, sought ways of expressing them without seeming to have stolen them from the general.[146] One way of doing so—and of crushing MacArthur politically—was to express determination to retaliate if the enemy widened the war. Administration spokesmen did so repeatedly in their testimony, Secretary of Defense Marshall no less than eleven times.[147] But his words carried a special meaning for the chairman and four other members of the investigating committee who also sat on the JCAE.[148] Knowing that President Truman had sent atomic bombs and bombers to the Western Pacific, could they doubt the administration's determination, or its insistence that the issue was MacArthur's behavior rather than the administration's conduct of the war?

What effect did this third Truman nuclear feint have upon his enemies and on his subsequent conduct of the war? Its impact upon foreign foes remains unclear. While the threat of air attacks from outside Korea never became reality, that threat may itself have been nothing more than a deterrent gesture. Despite the fact that Marshall's ominous words reached Beijing, it is not clear that PRC leaders also knew of the deployment of the nuclear-armed B-29s to East Asia.[149] It seems much more likely that the failure of the

---

146. Minutes of Undersecretary's Advisory Committee, May 1, 1951, Korea Project Files, Box 28, RG 59, NA. *FRUS*, 1951, Vol. 6, *East Asia and the Pacific*, pp. 33–63, reprints NSC 48/5 in its final form.

147. U.S. Congress, Senate Committee on Armed Services and Committee on Foreign Relations, 82d Cong., 1st sess., "Inquiry into the Military Situation in the Far East and the Facts Surrounding the Relief of General of the Army Douglas MacArthur from His Assignments in That Area," (Original) Report of Proceedings, microfilm edition, reel 1, pp. 808, 848, RG 146, NA; ibid., reel 2, pp. 908, 1007, 1017, 1081–1082, 1091, 1272, 1300–1303, 1650, 1752 (hereafter cited as "MacArthur Hearings," with appropriate reel and page data).

148. *Congressional Directory*, 82d Cong., 1st sess., pp. 195–196, 220.

149. *FRUS*, 1951, Vol. 7, *Korea and China*, p. 1697, reveals C.B. Marshall's belief that his "message" got through to Chinese leaders. No evidence is currently available that might indicate whether signals intelligence could have provided Beijing with a clue as to the presence of nuclear-armed B-29s on Guam. It is possibe that PRC leaders read American RB-45 reconnaissance overflights of Manchuria early in June 1951, which met with Chinese attacks, as evidence of American intent to expand and possibly escalate the fighting. CGFEAF to HQUSAF, 080810Z, June 8, 1951, item B-11501, Box B-198, LeMay papers, provides detail on this incident.

two major Chinese ground offensives launched after the bombers moved westward prompted Beijing's shift from an offensive to a defensive strategy in Korea.[150]

So, too, the nuclear deployment had at best an indeterminate effect on the president's domestic political enemies. Senate Republicans did not probe weaknesses in the administration's conduct of the war as vigorously or thoroughly as they might have. But their reluctance to do so did not derive exclusively from their knowledge of the nuclear movement. Some Republicans were loath to tie their political fates to that of General MacArthur.[151] Others were reluctant to weaken the bipartisan anti-communist consensus during a war.[152] Truman's opponents may also have been simply outmaneuvered by Senator Richard Russell, the crafty chairman of the investigating committee. His insistence on limited questioning on a rotating basis inhibited pursuit of any argument to its logical conclusion.[153]

The impact of this third episode of atomic diplomacy on the Truman administration's thinking about how best to use nuclear weapons is, however, much clearer. Rather than making senior officials eager to employ them, it reinforced their reluctance to do so. President Truman never again sent nuclear-armed bombers abroad. Nor did he use his power to do so to gain political advantage at home; he apparently saw his actions in the spring of 1951 as one-time measures justified only by the gravity of the situation. The Truman administration also stopped short of concluding that the nuclear deployment had compelled its foreign foes to negotiate an armistice in Korea. The B-29s and their nuclear cargoes returned home late in June 1951, just before the Soviet UN delegate delivered a speech that opened the door to armistice negotiations.[154] When they heard it, President Truman and his senior advisers reacted with surprise, rather than confidence that the nuclear deployment had forced the enemy to the negotiation table.[155]

---

150. Bradley and Blair, *A General's Life*, pp. 641–642; Pollack, "The Korean War and Sino-American Relations," p. 38.
151. *Washington Post*, April 17, 1951; *New York Times*, April 20, 1951, and May 1, 1951.
152. Senator H. Alexander Smith diary, April 18, May 9, 17, June 1, 15, 1951, in H. Alexander Smith papers, Seeley G. Mudd Library, Princeton University, Princeton, New Jersey; Thomas E. Dewey to Annie L.T. Dewey, April 11, 1951, Thomas E. Dewey papers, University of Rochester Library, Rochester, New York; Blair, *Forgotten War*, p. 812.
153. MacArthur Hearings, reel 1, pp. 10, 61.
154. 9th Aviation Squadron History, June 1951, frames 1471, 1478, reel 2325, Strategic Air Command History, SHC; *FRUS*, 1951, Vol. 7, *Korea and China*, pp. 546–547; *New York Times*, June 24, 1951.
155. *FRUS*, 1951, Vol. 7, pp. 547–554; Ferrell, *Off the Record*, p. 214.

But this final episode of Truman's atomic diplomacy does appear to have strengthened the administration's belief in the persuasive power of nuclear weapons. They could be used to convince enemies to respect and allies to support an armistice in Korea. When truce talks showed signs of success, Washington tried to commit its allies to the so-called Greater Sanctions Statement, an agreement which threatened the enemy with war beyond Korea if he violated truce terms.[156] Implying that retaliation might be nuclear, Dean Acheson at that time argued that atomic weapons had been useful tools in prodding Beijing and Pyongyang into armistice talks.[157] Such a posture suggested that the Truman administration continued to believe that nuclear superiority, when used with subtlety and restraint, could help manage the Korean War to an acceptable conclusion.

From Deterrence to Compellence? January–July 1953

In January 1953, a new administration, bringing a desire and an intent but not the design to end the Korean War, came to power in Washington. For its first six months, the Eisenhower administration searched for a strategy to end the fighting. Despite retrospective claims to the contrary,[158] coercive atomic diplomacy was not a component of that strategy. Instead, the new administration acted even more cautiously than had its predecessor in using nuclear weapons to help bring the Korean War to an end.

The new Republican leaders proceeded slowly and circumspectly for at least three reasons. First, they faced the same constraints—qualified nuclear superiority, growing Soviet retaliatory capability, and a lack of forward-deployed atomic arms—that limited their predecessors. Second, neither Dwight Eisenhower nor his secretary of state–designate, John Foster Dulles,

---

156. *FRUS*, 1951, Vol. 7, *Korea and China*, pp. 1156–1157, 1191, 1238–1239, 1249–1250, 1256, 1261–1262, 1350–1351, 1397, 1453.
157. Ibid., pp. 897–898. Acheson, as always, veiled the reference to atomic diplomacy in telling British Foreign Secretary Sir Anthony Eden that "it was possible to reach the conclusion" that Moscow had called for truce negotiations because Soviet leaders "foresaw" that otherwise the Korean fighting "might easily spread and endanger" their position.
158. Sherman Adams, *Firsthand Report* (New York: Harper, 1961), pp. 48–49; Adams claimed that "atomic missiles" were moved to Okinawa in the spring of 1953; he stated that Dulles "deliberately planted" a nuclear message for Beijing in New Delhi, and recalled Eisenhower's later saying that an "atomic threat" had brought peace in 1953. The president implied that a hint of intent "to move decisively without inhibition in our use of weapons" produced agreement at the Panmunjom truce negotiations. See Dwight D. Eisenhower, *The White House Years: Mandate for Change, 1953–1956* (Garden City, N.Y.: Doubleday, 1963), p. 181.

had honed their general ideas about nuclear weapons into a practical plan for ending the war. Their words and deeds during the 1952 campaign and in the weeks between election and inauguration were deliberately opaque and imprecise. Eisenhower went to Korea, as he had promised, but he studiously avoided discussing Op-Plan 8-52, which called for the use of nuclear weapons in and beyond Korea in conjunction with an advance to the narrow waist of the peninsula, with UN Commander Mark W. Clark.[159] The president-elect and Dulles met with General MacArthur, but neither would endorse the deposed general's proposal to use atomic bombs to isolate enemy forces already on the peninsula in the event Moscow refused neutralization for a united Korea.[160]

Third, caution and circumspection made good political sense at home and abroad. Domestically, they precluded a split within the Republican Party between those who thought along MacArthurian lines and the more knowledgeable and conservative legislators who feared that using atomic weapons in Korea might reduce the American nuclear stockpile to the point of weakening global deterrence.[161] Internationally, circumspect actions and imprecise words kept adversaries and allies uncertain of the new administration's intentions and fostered an impression of toughness which Dulles thought potentially useful in negotiations.[162]

But once in office, the new leaders had to think, speak, and act in more concrete terms. From the second week of February through the end of May 1953, they used the NSC as a forum in which to consider alternative ways to end the Korean fighting. Some analysts have interpreted their discussions, which touched on options ranging up to military use of atomic weapons in and beyond the peninsula, as a prologue to attempted nuclear compellence. They link the NSC's approval of contingency plans for the use of nuclear arms to John Foster Dulles's "signaling" that intention to Beijing by way of

---

159. Ambrose, *Eisenhower*, Vol. 1, p. 569; Vol. 2, pp. 30–31. Op-Plan 8-52 was prepared by General Mark Clark as CINCFE in response to JCS inquiries about possible courses of action in the event truce negotiations failed. Its origins are detailed in Schnabel and Watson, *JCS History*, Vol. 3, pp. 930–934, 936.
160. Ambrose, *Eisenhower*, Vol. 2, pp. 34–35.
161. *New York Times*, January 8, 1953. The man who worried about reducing the stockpile was New York Republican Representative W. Sterling Cole, chairman-to-be of the Joint Committee on Atomic Energy.
162. Memorandum of Dulles remarks, December 11, 1952, USS *Helena* folder, subject files; Memorandum of Dulles–Selwyn Lloyd conversation, December 26, 1962, classified materials folder, subject files, Box 8, John Foster Dulles papers, Eisenhower Library.

New Delhi. If the negotiators at Panmunjom had not quickly reached a settlement acceptable to Washington, these observers have suggested, limited war in Korea might well have become nuclear.[163]

Close analysis and comparison of the Eisenhower administration's behavior in the spring of 1953 with the Truman administration's actions two years earlier, however, suggest more modest conclusions about the NSC discussions in particular and about the role of atomic diplomacy in ending the war in general. The NSC deliberations proved more discursive than decisive. They took place in relatively permissive circumstances rather than under the crisis conditions that beset the Truman administration. The enemy, rather than threatening escalation, showed signs of interest in accommodation. Late in December 1952, Moscow hinted that Stalin might welcome summit talks.[164] The dictator's death early in March 1953 revived hopes for relaxation of Soviet-American tensions and an end to the Korean fighting.[165] On March 30, Beijing, by proclaiming qualified acceptance of the principle of voluntary repatriation of prisoners of war, opened the door for removal of the key obstacle to a negotiated settlement in Korea.[166]

At home, the new administration enjoyed far more political leeway than had its predecessor in dealing with the war. While the hero-president could not mistake the public's desire to end the stalemate in Korea, he was not subjected to immediate and direct pressures to do so. Two out of three Americans were ready to take "strong steps" to stop the fighting. Polls suggested that a large majority was willing to do so unilaterally, if necessary, and less than half thought that great risks would be encountered in the attempt.[167] But popular desires did not focus on a particular solution to the Korea problem. Capitol Hill, moreover, remained strangely silent about how best to end the war, in part because of the "honeymoon" normally granted new presidents, in part because Dulles assiduously cultivated congressional

163. Keefer, "President Eisenhower and the End of the Korean War," pp. 279–280; and Callum MacDonald, *Korea: The War Before Vietnam* (New York: Free Press, 1987), pp. 177–179. Keefer and MacDonald make the link between the NSC decision and the Dulles remarks most explicit. See Ambrose, *Eisenhower*, Vol. 2, p. 98; and Burton I. Kaufman, *The Korean War* (New York: Knopf, 1986), pp. 319–320; Ambrose and Kaufman take the view that no nuclear threat was made because Beijing already knew of America's atomic strength and the possibility that Eisenhower might use it.
164. *New York Times*, December 26, 1952.
165. Kaufman, *Korean War*, p. 306.
166. *FRUS*, 1952–1954, Vol. 15, *Korea*, p. 824.
167. Rosemary Foot, *The Wrong War* (Ithaca: Cornell University Press, 1985), p. 220.

support, and in part, perhaps, because senior Republicans knew about the Truman exercises in atomic diplomacy.[168]

The bureaucratic political atmosphere early in 1953 was also much less conducive to decision and action than it had been two years earlier. Then the JCS had agreed that a dangerous situation demanded deploying atomic bombs to the Western Pacific and giving the UN Commander contingent authority to use them. Now, they rejected General Clark's request for a repeat performance. In mid-February, just when the NSC began discussing possible uses for nuclear weapons in Korea, they refused to redeploy atomic bombs and bombers across the Pacific, declined to give Clark the authority he sought, and concealed from him the fact that no complete nuclear weapons were in close physical proximity to his command.[169]

Behind those actions lay sharp disagreement within the Pentagon over how atomic arms might be used in Korea. Unable to agree on Op-Plan 8-52, the chiefs referred it to the Joint Strategic Survey Committee (JSSC) for study on a routine rather than an urgent basis. The report produced a month later bared sharp inter-service differences. While air force and navy staffers thought nuclear bombing might constitute sufficient pressure to force China into accepting reasonable armistice terms, army chief of staff Collins disagreed. In his view, only concerted ground, sea, and air operations promised success in an advance northward to the narrow waist of the peninsula or to the Yalu.[170] Division of this sort boded ill for speedy progress in NSC discussions of war termination strategies.

Those rambling conversations were more tentative and educational than decisive for several reasons. They did not always include all of those whose assent to any use of atomic weapons was essential. Only twice during the seven NSC meetings between February and May of 1953 when nuclear possibilities were discussed were President Eisenhower, his secretaries of state and defense, and the chairman of the Joint Chiefs of Staff present.[171] On

---

168. Generalizations as to the mood of Congress and the public are based on the *New York Times* for January and February 1953.
169. CINCFE to JCS, 090933Z, February 9, 1953, sec. 122; CSUSA (Chief of Staff, U.S. Army, Collins) to CINCFE, DA 93097, February 10, 1953; JCS 931744 to CINCFE, 182204Z, February 18, 1953; SM 314-53 Lalor to Generals White and Lemnitzer, and JCS 93174A to CINCFE, 182236Z, February 18, 1953, CCS 383.21 Korea (3-19-45), Sec. 123, RG 218, NA.
170. Schnabel and Watson, *JCS History*, Vol. 3, pp. 932–933, 949.
171. *FRUS*, 1952–1954, Vol. 15, *Korea*, pp. 769, 825, 892–893, 945, 975, 1013, 1064.

May 20, when some analysts argued that a contingent decision to resort to nuclear arms was taken, John Foster Dulles was in Saudi Arabia.[172]

The Pentagon and the State Department, each for reasons of its own, were content with discussion rather than decision in the NSC. JCS Chairman Bradley did not press the JSSC to complete quickly the options paper that eventually went to the NSC; and on April 8, he suggested that the "best solution for Korea" was "to drag our feet."[173] Bradley and the Joint Chiefs did so, in part, because of their continuing disagreements over how to use the atomic bomb and because they felt a political decision should precede rather than follow discussion of its military employment in Korea.[174] General Bradley also delayed NSC consideration of the nuclear options paper until General Collins, the staunchest opponent of a resort to atomic arms, returned from a Latin American tour.[175] When the document finally went to the secretary of defense for NSC consideration, Collins had loaded it with so many preconditions as virtually to preclude tactical use of nuclear weapons in Korea.[176]

Dulles held back in deference to the trepidation of the allies, especially the British, about any escalation of the fighting. On March 5, he told British Foreign Secretary Sir Anthony Eden that it might be necessary to expand the war in order to end it. If pressuring China "at the center" failed to keep Beijing from intensifying the fighting in Indochina and Korea, then operations to the Korean waist which might "as an incident" involve air action could not be ruled out. But Dulles left London without getting Eden's clear assent to that proposition.[177] Early in April, he spoke of obtaining a Korean settlement "adroitly" so as not to offend allies.[178] By the eve of his departure for the Middle East and South Asia early in May, Dulles knew that London was retreating from its earlier support for the so-called Greater Sanctions Statement.[179]

---

172. *FRUS*, 1952–1954, Vol. 9, *The Near East and Middle East*, p. 113.
173. *FRUS*, 1952–1954, Vol. 15, *Korea*, p. 893.
174. Ibid., pp. 976–977.
175. Collins schedules, May 4–16, 19, 1953; JCS meeting agendas, May 16, 19, 1953, CCS 335.14 (6-6-42), Sec. 117, RG 218, NA.
176. *FRUS*, 1952–1954, Vol. 15, *Korea*, pp. 1059–1064.
177. Ibid., pp. 805–806.
178. Ibid., p. 895.
179. Ibid., pp. 968–969.

With allies in doubt and the Pentagon divided, President Eisenhower behaved more like an owl than a hawk throughout the NSC discussions. He was not inclined to take military risks at the outset of his administration. Contemplating cuts in SAC's strength and budget, he apparently did not know, as late as the end of March 1953, the exact size of his nuclear stockpile.[180] He had commissioned but not yet seen studies on how best to deal with the Soviet Union.[181] Thus when presented on April 28 with a preliminary study of contingency plans for transferring nuclear weapons to military custody, Eisenhower concluded that there was no immediate reason to do so and sent the issue back to the NSC special subcommittee on atomic energy for further study.[182]

The president also defined narrowly the kind of bluff he might employ in Korea. On April 28 he rejected a suggestion to fake a manpower buildup there. Eisenhower, who knew something about strategic deception from planning the Normandy invasion nearly ten years earlier, then shunted aside the idea of putting nuclear weapons in military hands so as "to create an impression of strength and determination." Doing so would put too much pressure on the enemy. Instead, one could impress the foe with American resolve and avoid "unduly alarming our allies or our own people" by acting so that "a foreign G-2," piecing together bits of information about the transfer, would conclude that "he had pierced the screen" of Washington's intentions. It could be announced that the president had authorized transfer of nuclear weapons to military custody, and "indications" that some atomic arms were actually being placed under Pentagon control would then be given. "With a little handling," the president concluded, "the desired effect could certainly be secured."[183]

---

180. Office of the Historian, Strategic Air Command, Status of Strategic Air Command, January 1–June 30, 1953, frames 0476–0478, 0483, 0505, reel K4263, Office of Air Force History, Bolling Air Force Base; Cutler to Dean, March 28, 1953, atomic energy sub-series, NSC series, OSANSA files, Box 1, Eisenhower papers.
181. *FRUS, 1952–1954*, Vol. 2, *National Security Affairs*, p. 323.
182. *FRUS, 1952–1954*, Vol. 15, *Korea*, p. 947, omits this crucial portion of the minutes, the full text of which appears in Memorandum of Discussion at the 141st Meeting of the National Security Council, Tuesday, April 28, 1953 (text as partially declassified under Freedom of Information Act Request NLE 85-269), NSC summaries of discussion folder, Ann Whitman File, NSC series, Box 4, Eisenhower papers.
183. Ibid. The suggestion for faking a manpower buildup came from Undersecretary of Defense Roger Kyes.

Although this discussion ended with a decision to have the NSC special committee on atomic energy make recommendations "promptly" on the matter, Dulles, one of its key members, left for the Middle East and South Asia less than two weeks later without any action having been taken.[184] In his absence, President Eisenhower first steered the full NSC away from a firm decision on contingency plans for tactical use of nuclear weapons, then weakened the force of their approval. On May 13 he got Acting Secretary of State Walter Bedell Smith to admit that expanding the Korean fighting would temporarily disrupt NATO. Then he remarked that Washington "desperately" needed its European allies. He also spurned Vice President Richard Nixon's suggestion that drastic action might be preferable now rather than later, when Soviet nuclear strength would have grown.[185]

When the NSC on May 20, 1953, gave final consideration to nuclear contingency plans for Korea, Eisenhower qualified its approval. Informed that the plans involved nuclear strikes against China, he voiced the same concern that had stayed President Truman's hand: the possibility of retaliatory Soviet attacks on Japan. While admitting the importance of speed and surprise in launching a nuclear attack, he also hinted at his openness to a summit meeting with the new Soviet leaders. Most importantly, Eisenhower brought the discussion to a conclusion in a way that suggested that he did *not* believe the time had come to begin assembling forces for implementation of the contingency plan. He simply acknowledged that "if circumstances arose which would force the United States to an expanded effort in Korea," then the joint chiefs' plan, which required a year of preparations, was "most likely to achieve the objective we sought."[186]

That "decision," stripped of implementing actions, was not the prologue to an attempt at coercive atomic diplomacy. Instead, Washington engaged in milder, nonnuclear persuasive diplomacy. State Department officials hoped to nudge Moscow into persuading Beijing and Pyongyang to accept a compromise on the prisoner of war issue. Their plan preserved the principle of no forced repatriation and established procedures for third-party custody, interrogation, and eventual release of prisoners. Ambassador Charles Bohlen was to emphasize the scheme's importance and imply its finality when

---

184. Ibid.; *FRUS*, 1952–1954, Vol. 9, *The Near and Middle East*, p. 1.
185. *FRUS*, 1952–1954, Vol. 15, *Korea*, pp. 1015–1016.
186. Ibid., pp. 1065–1068.

informing the Soviets of its terms. But he was "to all possible [extent] to avoid ultimatum connotations." After discussing the scheme with the joint chiefs on May 18, the State Department forwarded its outlines to Dulles in New Delhi.[187]

It was in connection with this scheme rather than in response to the NSC nuclear contingency "decision" of May 20 that John Foster Dulles spoke to Jawaharlal Nehru. The Indian prime minister opened their May 21 conversation by appealing for an armistice lest the Korean fighting expand. When meeting Dulles again on May 22, Nehru twice expressed great concern about the possibility of intensified hostilities. On both occasions, however, Dulles responded mildly. He first indicated that if the Panmunjom talks failed, Washington "would probably make a stronger rather than a lesser military exertion [which] . . . might well extend the area of conflict." But he quickly added that "only crazy people" could think that America wanted to prolong a struggle which had proven enormously costly in lives and dollars. The second day Dulles simply "made no comment and allowed the topic to drop."[188]

Like Charles Burton Marshall two years earlier, Dulles expected his words to be passed on to Chinese leaders.[189] But his message was less threatening than Marshall's and constituted an appeal for support of the new American negotiating position on the prisoner-of-war issue. Indeed, Dulles's primary purpose in meeting Nehru was to persuade the Indians to drop their prisoner-of-war formula and support the American proposal.[190] If Nehru did so, China would be under all the more pressure to compromise on the last obstacle to peace in Korea.

Dulles's mild behavior on this occasion was paralleled by Ambassador Bohlen's manner in approaching the Soviets a few days later. Having previously ruled out making any explicit reference to what might happen if communist negotiators rejected the new American truce proposal, Bohlen got State Department approval to go no further than saying that failure of the armistice talks would "create a situation which the U.S. Government is

---

187. Ibid., pp. 1038–1056, 1111.
188. Ibid., pp. 1051, 1068–1069.
189. Ibid., p. 1068. Ambassador Douglas MacArthur III, who accompanied Dulles on his journey, recalled that the idea of getting the "message" to Beijing was of particular importance to Dulles. Interview with Douglas MacArthur III, June 30, 1987.
190. FRUS, 1952–1954, Vol. 15, Korea, pp. 1069, 1071. It should be noted that the initial suggestion for Dulles to visit New Delhi was made in December 1952. See ibid., Vol. 9, The Near and Middle East, p. 1.

seeking most earnestly to avoid."[191] When he met Soviet Foreign Minister Molotov on May 28, Bohlen added "most sincerely" to the approved phrase, to enhance the chances for acceptance of the latest American proposal.[192] His words in Moscow, like Dulles's in New Delhi, represented an appeal for cooperation more than a threat of atomic action in the absence of agreement.

This tactful approach may have had some effect, for a few days later the communist delegation at Panmunjom indicated willingness to accept some, and bargain over other, terms of the new American prisoner-of-war proposal.[193] But the Eisenhower administration did not, then or later, apply nuclear pressure to speed the armistice talks to conclusion.

The president did, on the eve of the truce agreement, authorize transfer of completed nuclear weapons to military custody for overseas deployment.[194] His decision, however, was not part of an atomic diplomacy scheme. It appears to have been shaped more by long-term strategic, rather than immediate Korean War–related, concerns. Early in June, 1953, the joint chiefs, through the secretary of defense, sought approval for deployment of "nuclear components" overseas "at the earliest possible date." They did not seek authorization to use the weapons, which, three weeks earlier, had been the very first item on their list of implementing actions for the contingency plans approved by the NSC. They tailored their proposal to meet State Department objections and AEC concerns about dispersal of the atomic stockpile.[195] The NSC's atomic energy subcommittee further modified the plan by reducing the number of weapons involved and postponing their deployment until surveillance of proposed sites could be completed.[196]

191. Ibid., Vol. 15, *Korea*, pp. 1095–1096, 1103–1104.
192. Ibid., pp. 1108–1111.
193. Ibid., pp. 1133–1134, 1137–1138.
194. Loper memorandum.
195. Special Assistant for National Security Affairs, memorandum for the President, April 16, 1953, atomic energy sub-series, OSANSA files, NSC series, Box 1; Secretary of Defense to Executive Secretary, National Security Council, June 8, 1953, ibid.; declassified document 3 of NLE 85-535, Eisenhower papers. Handwritten figures on the latter document put the total number of American atomic weapons at 1600. While marked "OK-Guam," the document makes no reference to Okinawa as a possible forward deployment site. The weapons were to be stored afloat or ashore at sites where the decision to place them there rested solely with the United States. The number of nuclear "hardware" kits to go overseas would presumably be somewhere between the 176 already abroad and the 386 authorized for deployment, which would put slightly less than a quarter of the American atomic stockpile outside the continental United States.
196. Executive Secretary, NSC, to the President, June 19, 1953, atomic energy miscellaneous file, OSANSA files, NSC series, Box 1, Eisenhower papers.

President Eisenhower saw the proposal for the first time on June 20, just when Syngman Rhee's release of prisoners of war threatened to destroy the final compromises on a truce being negotiated at Panmunjom. But neither Eisenhower nor any of his senior advisers thought the situation desperate enough to warrant hints of atomic diplomacy.[197] Thus while Eisenhower approved the proposed nuclear deployment, it was not immediately implemented.[198]

More than a month later, on the eve of the signature of the Korean armistice agreement, the Pentagon renewed its request for custody of complete nuclear bombs.[199] That request came to the president less than twenty-four hours after the NSC had considered how best to respond to a buildup of enemy air forces and last-minute Chinese ground offensives. But neither President Eisenhower nor Secretary of State Dulles appears to have regarded forward deployment of nuclear weapons as the appropriate reaction to those developments. The president, worried lest the armistice prove "a dangerous hoax," called for immediate dispatch of Marine reinforcements to Japan and Korea. Dulles downplayed the significance of the enemy air buildup, arguing that because the communists really wanted an armistice, their actions should be considered tactical moves rather than indications of treacherous political intent.[200]

Thus even though the Eisenhower administration approved the overseas deployment of nuclear weapons shortly before the Korean truce, its decision was not part of an atomic diplomacy scheme. Washington did not drop the hints of action that the president believed would lead the enemy to conclude that it had "pierced the screen" of American intentions.[201] Republican leaders did not go as far as their Democratic predecessors in using the movement of

---

197. Loper memorandum; *FRUS, 1952–1954*, Vol. 15, *Korea*, p. 1200–1205.
198. Loper memorandum; nearly a month later, testimony given before the JCAE suggested that neither overseas deployment site selection nor respective armed service apportionment of atomic bombs had been decided upon. See JCAE meeting minutes, July 15, 1953, Box 15, JCAE papers, RG 128, NA.
199. Loper memorandum.
200. *FRUS, 1952–1954*, Vol. 15, *Korea*, pp. 1421–1422.
201. NLE 85-269, partially declassified Memorandum of Minutes of 141st Meeting of National Security Council on April 28, 1953, NSC Summaries of Discussion folder, Ann Whitman File, NSC series, Box 4, Eisenhower papers. No indication of any SAC aircraft movements at this time is to be found in Historian, Strategic Air Command, Status of Strategic Air Command, July–December 1953, Volume 1, reel K4265, Office of Air Force History, Bolling Air Force Base. Similarly, no mention of the deployment of bombers or ships capable of delivering nuclear weapons is to be found in the *New York Times*, at, or immediately following, the time of this decision.

nuclear weapons to try to modify Chinese, Soviet, or North Korean behavior. Thus the Eisenhower administration achieved an armistice in Korea without employing atomic arms for coercive diplomatic purposes.

Conclusion

The Korean War ended, then, as it had begun, with not a single American nuclear weapon deployed within usable distance of the fighting. That state of affairs encapsulated one important truth, namely, that Washington never came close to tactical use of the atomic bomb in Korea. But it obscured another equally vital one: American statesmen repeatedly attempted to use nuclear weapons as tools with which to manage the politics and diplomacy of the war. As this article has demonstrated, they gave different answers to the question of how and when to do so.

The record of their actions reveals a story different from that traditionally told. Nuclear weapons were used politically and diplomatically by a Democratic administration long before Dwight Eisenhower and John Foster Dulles came to power. With the full record in view, it is possible to sketch a typology of their usage, ranging from verbal mention of nuclear potential only; through deployment of nuclear-configured bombers and nonnuclear weapons components and indirect disclosure of their movement; to deployment of bombers and bombs along with fuller, but still indirect, revelation of their departure from the United States. When considered in those terms, the relative seriousness and significance of the atomic diplomacy of the two administrations become much clearer. There can be no doubt that the real crisis, which triggered the most serious nuclear action, occurred in the spring of 1951. It is equally clear that Washington's actions two years later were the mildest and least threatening of the lot.

The full story also reveals the interplay of forces that conditioned the use by American statesmen of nuclear weapons as tools for conflict management. Some of those pressures prodded them into action. They were provoked by a sense of external danger: by fear of Soviet or Chinese action and British disaffection from their policies in July 1950; by enemy escalation of the fighting in the spring of 1951; and by frustration over enemy obduracy in negotiations two years later. They were also goaded toward action by pressures at home. The sense that the bomb *ought* to be useful, the fear that the public might precipitously demand its employment, and the surmise that it might help manage relations with Congress, all figured in the decisions analyzed in this essay. Analogical reasoning also made American statesmen willing to practice atomic diplomacy. Both theoretically and experientially, the movement of B-29s during the Berlin Blockade provided them with guidance on how to threaten but not provoke; how to reveal but not flaunt nuclear strength before the enemy; and how to inform yet not alarm allies.

But those same forces, in different combination and under different circumstances, also constrained the atomic diplomacy of both the Truman and Eisenhower administrations. Both administrations feared provoking the enemy. While each respected, in differing measure, the concerns of allies, those constraints did not present absolute obstacles to action. In July 1950, Dean Acheson found ways to soften and even defy British concerns; six months later, London's desire for American restraint was only one, and not necessarily the determining, factor that ruled out nuclear deployments of any kind. John Foster Dulles's behavior in the spring of 1953 suggested that, despite his tough retrospective rhetoric, he understood the importance of preserving allies' support in the Korean struggle.

Domestic political considerations also constrained American statesmen in the use of nuclear weapons as tools for managing the Korean conflict. If, at times, they were concerned about public demands for atomic action, far more often their choices were shaped by professional and bureaucratic imperatives in the Pentagon. In July 1950, General Vandenberg's desire for action was crucial in bringing about B-29 deployments; six months later, his caution, General LeMay's desire to protect the integrity of the SAC striking force, and General Collins' skepticism about the utility of bombing alone, all worked against nuclear action of any kind. It also seems clear that military professionals' understanding of the psychology of nuclear deterrence and their reluctance to weaken it through precipitate action grew during the Korean conflict. Finally, Pentagon parochialism, as manifested in the service chieftains' quarrels over shares of weapons to be deployed overseas from December 1950 through July 1953, also constrained civilian leaders' ability to use nuclear weapons in managing the Korean conflict.

The results of Washington's resort to atomic diplomacy during the war were mixed. While deployments might have strengthened deterrence, they never supported coercive diplomacy. If employed indirectly and in combination with other words and deeds indicative of strength, they might demonstrate resolve. But that sort of action, as Presidents Truman and Eisenhower both discovered, was extremely difficult to manage. Nuclear weapons were cumbersome figuratively as well as literally. No president could decide alone on their employment. It took crises, as President Truman learned, to cut through the obstacles to nuclear action of any kind. In the absence of that sense of urgency, his successor found that months were needed to build an imperfect consensus on possible uses for atomic arms in Korea.

Nuclear weapons were also slippery tools of statecraft. President Truman only with difficulty controlled the diplomatic consequences of his hint of a resort to nuclear weapons late in 1950. He could not determine as certainly as he wished the domestic politics of disclosure surrounding the April 1951 movement of atomic bombs and bombers across the Pacific. While both administrations resorted to indirect channels to communicate America's atomic strength to China, neither could be absolutely certain that the intended message had been communicated clearly to or had produced the desired effect upon the unwanted Chinese enemy in Korea.

What, then, was the significance of Washington's attempts to use nuclear weapons as tools to manage that conflict? Surely the lesson to be drawn is not the one that John Foster Dulles later touted. Nuclear weapons were not easily usable tools of statecraft that produced predictable results. One could not move from deterrence to compellence through their possession. They were more subtle instruments, whose use demanded a refined understanding of the practice of deterrence. The Korean War might be seen as an experience that schooled American statesmen in that practice. It offered not the determinative, but the first, of a series of lessons that would eventually produce full understanding of the paradox of nuclear weapons: They confer upon those who possess them more responsibility for restraint than disposable power.

Part II:
Nuclear Weapons and
Crisis Management

Nuclear Alerts and Crisis Management | *Scott D. Sagan*

An alert of nuclear forces during a superpower crisis serves two related purposes. The military purpose is to enhance one's readiness for war: alerting nuclear forces reduces their overall vulnerability to attack and prepares them for potential use. The political purpose is to enhance deterrence: nuclear alerts have been used to signal resolve in a crisis and to demonstrate how seriously a government regards the stakes involved in a potential conflict.

In theory, these two objectives are complementary. In practice, however, a number of strategic tensions may exist. Actions taken for purely military considerations may, under some circumstances, contradict or exceed the political signal that is desired. Conversely, the political restraints placed upon operational preparations in a crisis may, under other circumstances, unintentionally reduce force readiness.

In any future military crisis with the Soviet Union, American decisionmakers are likely to perceive a severe tension between the need to alert nuclear forces in order to reduce vulnerability and signal resolve and the fear that such actions could move out of control, increasing the likelihood of tragic accidents, inadvertent escalation, or nuclear preemption. A good deal of attention has been given, in both the academic and the policymaking communities, to the complex set of strategic issues surrounding a decision to use nuclear weapons if deterrence fails. Far less thought has focused on the issues surrounding a decision to alert nuclear forces if a failure of deterrence appears likely. This article seeks to examine some of these issues by looking at three cases—in May 1960, October 1962, and October 1973—in which the United States government placed its global strategic nuclear forces

Scott D. Sagan is a Council on Foreign Relations International Affairs Fellow serving in the Nuclear and Chemical Division, Plans and Policy Directorate (J-5), of the Organization of the Joint Chiefs of Staff. This article was written when he was a postdoctoral fellow on Harvard University's Avoiding Nuclear War Project.

The author would like to thank the working group of the Avoiding Nuclear War Project at Harvard University, as well as Richard K. Betts, McGeorge Bundy, Raymond L. Garthoff, Alexander L. George, Vice Admiral Jerome H. King, Jr., USN (ret.), and Major Steven R. Sturm, USAF, for their helpful comments on an earlier draft.

International Security, Spring 1985 (Vol. 9, No. 4) 0162-2889/85/040099-41 $02.50/0

on a higher state of command readiness during an international crisis.[1] An examination of what went right, and of what went wrong, when nuclear forces were alerted in the past can neither provide policymakers with effective rules of crisis management nor eliminate the inherent risks and uncertainties involved in nuclear alerts. Indeed, if nuclear alerts entailed no risks at all, they would be unlikely to contribute to deterrence at all. At the same time, an improved understanding of the problem and enhanced control over the alerting process can reduce unnecessary dangers and promote better management of superpower crises if they occur despite all efforts to prevent them.

The DEFCON System

The process by which American military forces are placed on alert is called the Defense Condition (DEFCON) system. There are five DEFCONS, or gradations of alert. It is difficult to outline with any degree of precision the preparations that take place under the five DEFCONs for three reasons. First, the complex set of military preparations that make up each of the DEFCONs varies between different unified and specified commands in the American military command system because the commanders often face different threats, plan different missions, and maintain different weapons systems. Secondly, the gradations of the system have been greatly altered over time as new weapons systems have been deployed, new communications capabilities have been created, and new strategic threats have emerged. Thirdly, and most importantly, the precise details of the DEFCON system are, with good reason, kept highly classified.

At the general level, however, it is known that most American forces are kept at the lowest alert status, DEFCON 5, in normal peacetime. The Strategic Air Command (SAC), an exception, is routinely kept at DEFCON 4. Military forces located close to areas of intense combat are often also kept at higher levels of alert. For example, the portions of the Pacific Fleet in the Western Pacific, which were not in combat, were kept at DEFCON 3 throughout most of the Vietnam War. Although the operations entailed at each level of alert

---

1. For a list of incidents prior to 1960 in which the threat of the use of strategic weapons has been raised by the United States see Barry M. Blechman and Stephen S. Kaplan, *Force Without War: U.S. Armed Forces as a Political Instrument* (Washington: Brookings, 1978), pp. 47–48. For greater detail on most of these cases see J.C. Hopkins, *The Development of the Strategic Air Command* (Office of the Historian, Headquarters Strategic Air Command, July 1, 1982).

cannot be specified, the following exercise terms, which were used for simulated DEFCONs in the North American Air Defense Command's (NORAD)
1960 exercises, can give a general sense of their relative significance:

DEFCON 5—Fade Out
DEFCON 4—Double Take
DEFCON 3—Round House
DEFCON 2—Fast Pace
DEFCON 1—Cocked Pistol[2]

The DEFCON system was created by the Joint Chiefs of Staff in November
1959 to enable them to prescribe a uniform readiness posture in various
American commands.[3] Since that time, *portions* of the American nuclear
arsenal have been placed on a higher state of alert in numerous instances
for a diverse number of reasons.[4] Yet there appear to have been only three
cases in which global American military forces have been put at DEFCON 3
or above during a crisis with the Soviet Union: DEFCON 3 was instituted on
May 16, 1960 for less than 24 hours; SAC was placed on DEFCON 2 and
other commands were placed on DEFCON 3 during the Cuban missile crisis
from October 22 until November 20, 1962; and American military forces,
nuclear and conventional, were placed on DEFCON 3 on October 24, 1973.
The focus throughout this article is on how the decision to alert forces was
made and on how the decision was implemented; in each case, alert measures
will be described in as much detail as is available in the public record. In

---

2. NORAD Regulation No. 55-1. Operations: Simulated Defense Readiness Conditions, Air
Defense Warning and Weapons Control Status. April 27, 1960, p. 2. CCS 3180 Emergency
Readiness Plans (Jan. 12, 1960), Records of the United States Joint Chiefs of Staff. Record Group
218. National Archives (hereinafter JCS).
3. Report by the J-3 to the Joint Chiefs of Staff on Operational Readiness Measures. JCS 2056/
158, June 6, 1960, p. 1463, 1472. CCS 3180 Emergency Readiness Plans (May 15, 1960), Sec. 1,
JCS.
4. Recent examples include the following: in August 1976, three B-52s were sent from Guam to
fly over South Korea, as a show of force, as American military forces cut down a tree in the
DMZ; in August 1978, a number of SAC bombers were dispersed in response to the movement
of Soviet submarines close to the American east coast; some alert measures may have been
implemented when President Reagan was shot on March 30, 1981; and, finally, in more than
one case, false warnings of attack have produced limited measures of increased nuclear command readiness. See Richard G. Head, Frisco W. Short, and Robert C. McFarlane, *Crisis Resolution: Presidential Decision Making in the Mayaguez and Korean Confrontations* (Boulder, Colo.:
Westview, 1978), pp. 189–193; David M. Alpern, "A Soviet War of Nerves," *Newsweek*, January
5, 1981, p. 21; Alexander M. Haig, Jr., *Caveat* (New York: Macmillan, 1984), pp. 157–161; U.S.
Senate, Committee on Armed Services, *Recent False Alerts from the Nation's Missile Attack Warning
System*, Report of Senators Gary Hart and Barry Goldwater, 96th Congress, 2nd Session, October
9, 1980, pp. 5, 7.

some cases, most notably the Cuban missile crisis, conventional force operations will also be examined since most imaginable scenarios for future crises would involve both nuclear and conventional forces. That nuclear war was avoided in each case is, of course, obvious; it is less clear that the nuclear alerts and conventional operations were well managed by central authorities.

May 1960: The "Unintended" DEFCON 3 Alert

On the evening of May 15, 1960, while attending the Paris Summit Conference, President Dwight D. Eisenhower and Secretary of Defense Thomas Gates received information suggesting that Soviet Premier Khrushchev might scuttle the conference on the following morning in protest against the May 1st U-2 incident. Although there were no signs of Soviet military mobilization, Gates recommended to Eisenhower that the American military alert system be tested, apparently to ensure that military commanders would be able to receive further communications if necessary. At 11:58 p.m., Gates issued an order that he later described as a "sound precautionary measure": "a quiet increase in command readiness, particularly with respect to communications . . . without public notice, if possible." As Gates later testified to the Senate Foreign Relations Committee, "it was not the intention of this order to move forces in any way":

It [the alert order] was not intended nor was it worded as a provocative message. The first word in it was "Quiet" and the last words in it were "minimum need to know."
    It was not meant as provocative. It was not meant as either an offensive or defensive alert.[5]

Within a matter of hours, however, Gates's "quiet" alert had become significantly "louder" than he had intended. By 2 a.m., the commanders in chief of each of the American military's unified and specified commands had been ordered by the Joint Chiefs of Staff (JCS) to place their forces on DEFCON 3. Within hours, newspaper and television reports announced not only that American forces were being mobilized, but even the precise level of the alert. Soon Premier Khrushchev was blustering, not only against the "provocative" U-2 overflights, but also about the "provocation" of the American alert, and Secretary Gates was forced to admit to Congress that "some

---

5. *Events Incident to the Summit Conference*, Hearings Before the Committee on Foreign Relations, U.S. Senate, 86th Congress, 2nd Session, May 27, June 1, 2, 1960, pp. 124, 133, 135.

commands went further in executing the instructions issued by the JCS as a result of my message than I had anticipated."[6]

How did this happen? The most significant misstep was Gates's failure to specify either the precise level of readiness desired or the purpose of the alert in his message to the Deputy Secretary of Defense and the Chairman of the Joint Chiefs of Staff. Indeed, the entire message read as follows:

OPERATIONAL IMMEDIATE
FROM: SEC DEF PARIS FRANCE

TO :   OSD WASH DC

NR :   EC 9-10366   152358Z MAY 60

EYES ONLY

FOR DOUGLAS AND TWINING, FROM GATES.

1. Quietly order a high state of command readiness.
2. Order all U.S. major commanders to assume immediately communications alert status.
3. Prepare, if directed, to move into a higher state of readiness for all U.S. forces.
4. Execute with minimum need to know basis.[7]

A recently declassified JCS report explained the problem well: "The Secretary of Defense stated his directive to increase readiness in words which required interpretation into a military course of action. He provided no reasons for his action and did not respond to a query asking for background information. Therefore, it was difficult for the Joint Chiefs of Staff and the commanders of the unified and specified commands to evaluate the situation in determining appropriate action. . . . "[8] Deputy Secretary of Defense Douglas and the Joint Chiefs were immediately notified by telephone. Based upon Gates's unspecific order and ambiguous incoming information suggesting that American forces in Europe were moving toward a higher state

6. See "RAF Planes on Alert," *The New York Times*, May 19, 1960, p. 9; "Test Alert Attributed to Gates," *The Washington Post*, May 17, 1960, p. 1; "Press Conference of N.S. Khrushchev in Paris on May 18, 1960," *Pravda* and *Izvestia*, May 19, 1960, pp. 1–2, in *The Current Digest of the Soviet Press*, Vol. 12, No. 2, p. 10; and *Events Incident to the Summit Conference*, p. 125.
7. Message Number EC9-10366, CCS 3180 Emergency Readiness Plans (May 15, 1960), Sec. 1, JCS.
8. Report by the J-3 to the Joint Chiefs of Staff on Operational Readiness Measures, JCS 2056/158, June 6, 1960, p. 1459. CCS 3180 Emergency Readiness Plans (May 15, 1960) Sec. 1, JCS.

of readiness,[9] they decided to place all American nuclear and conventional forces on DEFCON 3.

The speed with which the day's events progressed may be seen in the following chronology based upon the JCS records:[10]

MAY 16, 1960

12:33 a.m. (Greenwich time)	Exclusive Message—EC9-10366—arrives from SEC-DEF to Deputy SECDEF and CJCS.
1:00–1:20 a.m.	Mr. Douglas, General Twining, Admiral Burke, General White, General Lemnitzer, and General Wieseman notified by phone. Approve staff recommendation to place all commands on DEFCON 3.
1:56 a.m.	JCS orders all commands to assume DEFCON 3 and directed minimum need-to-know.
2:23 a.m.	DEPSECDEF and CJCS inform SECDEF all CINCs in DEFCON 3 and request information used as basis for his directive.
7:10 a.m.	Associated Press reports that Denver TV stations broadcast notice for fighter pilots to return to Lowry Air Force Base ("All fighter pilots F-102—attention Captain Singleton and Lt. Griffin. Code 3 alert, Hotcake One and Hotcake Six Scramble at Lowry immediately.").
7:30 a.m.	SAC contacted—they have received numerous press queries.
9:54 a.m.	DEPSECDEF to SECDEF—Recommendation for affirmative response if asked whether or not President and SECDEF advised of Communications Test.

---

9. Thirty-two minutes after Gates's message arrived, while the Deputy Secretary of Defense and the Joint Chiefs were being notified by telephone, a top secret message from CINCEUR Palmer to Chairman Twining arrived that suggested to the Joint Staff officers on duty that Palmer's forces were being placed on a "state of military vigilance" prior to JCS instructions, "apparently as (a) result of direct contact with SECDEF." Message EC 9-10368, CJCS, General Twining, Chairman's Messages, Nov. 1959–July 1960, Box 45, JCS; Report by the J-3 to the Joint Chiefs of Staff on Operational Readiness Measures. JCS 2056/155, May 25, 1960, p. 1389, CCS 3180 Emergency Readiness Plans (May 15, 1960), Sec. 1, JCS.

10. Report by the J-3 to the Joint Chiefs of Staff on Operational Readiness Measures, JCS 2056/155 25, May 1960, pp. 1389–1390. CCS 3180 Emergency Readiness Plans (May 15, 1960), Sec. 1, JCS. The television broadcast quotation is from "Test Alert Attributed to Gates," *The Washington Post*, May 17, 1960, p. 1.

8:00 p.m.	DEPSECDEF informs CJCS that SECDEF has authorized return to normal posture.
9:05 p.m.	JCS to CINCAL, CINCLANT, CINCARIB, CINCONAD, USCINCEUR, CINCPAC, CINCNELM, and CINCSAC—Assume DEFCON 5 or other DEFCON in effect prior to alert.

Although the operational details of the 1960 alert are not declassified, descriptions of DEFCON 3 exercises conducted by CINCSAC and CINCLANT in 1962 are available in the archives. These actual and simulated exercise activities demonstrate the *approximate* level of combat readiness that would have been implemented on May 16, 1960 at those two commands. The Strategic Air Command's DEFCON 3 exercise on August 16, 1962 consisted of the following activities: the implementation of sabotage alert; suspension of security readiness exercises and local security exercises; reduction of training exercises of SAC bombers, reconnaissance, and tanker units except airborne alert; increase in the number of operationally ready aircraft proportionately; alert of personnel without public announcement; reduction in training operations at missile sites in order "to preclude removing any missile from ready configuration"; and orders to be able to implement the next DEFCON in a minimum of time.[11] The Atlantic Command went through a DEFCON 3 exercise on April 30, 1962, that consisted of the following activities: recall of personnel; acceleration of loading out and repair, dispersal of forces, preparations to execute its operations plans (CINCLANT Oplan 112-60); and increase in air patrol over close-in defense sea areas.[12]

These military readiness activities, or similar actions, were not necessarily dangerous in themselves when implemented on May 16, 1960, but the level of alert—and the consequent public concern and Soviet reaction—were clearly unintended. Secretary Gates's apparent lack of familiarity with the newly instituted DEFCON system produced a "loud" rather than a "quiet" alert. The Joint Staff was clearly aware of the problem. Their draft report on the incident suggested that "a military advisor with [the Secretary of Defense] might have helped in making the wording and intent of his directive clearer"

---

11. Memorandum for the Director, Joint Staff, August 25, 1962, Random, No-Notice Practice Increase in Readiness Posture for the Strategic Air Command. CCS 3180 Emergency Readiness Plans (May 15, 1960), Sec. 2, JCS.
12. Memorandum for the Director, Joint Staff, May 9, 1962, Random, No-Notice Practice Increase in Readiness Posture for the LANTCOM. CCS, 3180 Emergency Readiness Plans (May 15, 1960), Sec. 2, JCS.

and stressed that it was simply impossible to keep high level alerts secret: "Any worldwide alerting of forces which results in a significant increase in readiness posture (DEFCON 3, 2 or 1) will invariably result in some public notice."[13]

October 1962: The Cuban Missile Crisis

American global military forces, nuclear and conventional, were placed at their highest state of command readiness in the postwar period during October 1962, an action certainly commensurate with the widespread belief that the Cuban missile crisis constitutes the closest approach to war the United States and Soviet Union have ever experienced. The dramatic events of October 16–28 are well known, and even a cursory review of the outcome of the crisis is not necessary here. It is important, however, to reexamine both the quarantine operations and the Strategic Air Command's alert and to evaluate how effectively these actions were managed.

Contingency planning and military deployments in preparation for a possible blockade or invasion of Cuba began well before the discovery of the Soviet missile sites on October 15. As early as October 1, Secretary of Defense Robert McNamara met with the Joint Chiefs of Staff to discuss contingency plans for the removal of Soviet offensive weapons systems if they were discovered and, if necessary, the removal of the Castro regime.[14] Admiral Robert Lee Dennison, the Commander-in-Chief of the Atlantic Command (CINCLANT), was then ordered to be prepared for a possible blockade of Cuba. On October 6, his forces were placed on a higher state of readiness and, on October 8, an F-4H squadron was deployed to Key West to reinforce American air defenses.[15] The purpose of these and other military preparations was to increase readiness for whatever military action may have been required and not to influence American adversaries in any way. Indeed, it was

---

13. Report by the J-3 to the Joint Chiefs of Staff on Operational Readiness Measures JCS 2056/155, May 25, 1960, p. 1384. CCS 3180 Emergency Readiness Plans (May 15, 1960), Sec. l, JCS. The statement on the advisability of a military advisor's presence was removed in the next draft of the report for two possible reasons: either the statement was considered excessively critical of the Secretary of Defense or there had in fact been a military advisor with Gates in Paris.

14. "Department of Defense Operations During the Cuban Missile Crisis," A Report by Adam Yarmolinsky, Special Assistant to the Secretary of Defense, February 13, 1963. Edited and with introduction by Dan Caldwell, in *The Naval War College Review*, Vol. 32, No. 4 (July–August 1979), pp. 84, 89.

15. Ibid., p. 84.

considered very important that such widespread preparations be "masked" by announcing that they were part of PHIBRIGLEX '62, the annual amphibious assault exercise in the area.[16] These readiness measures allowed Secretary McNamara to explain to the "Executive Committee " (Ex Comm) of the National Security Council, during the first day of its meetings after the missile sites were discovered, that "all the preparations that we could take without the risk of preparations causing discussion and knowledge of this, either among our public or in Cuba, have been taken. . . . "[17]

At this same meeting, on the evening of October 16th, Secretary McNamara first outlined the three crisis options which were to be the subject of intense discussion during the following week. The first was what McNamara called "the political course of action," a diplomatic approach to either Castro or Khrushchev, which he objected to because it was "likely to lead to no satisfactory result and it almost stops subsequent military action." A second option, which "lies between the military course" and "the political course of action" was "a blockade against *offensive* weapons entering Cuba." The third course of action was to use direct military action—an air strike, invasion, or both—to remove the threat from Cuba. In anticipation of a possible Soviet military reaction, McNamara argued that strategic forces should be placed at a high degree of readiness:

It seems almost certain to me that any one of these forms of direct military action will lead to a Soviet military response of some type some place in the world. It may well be worth the price. Perhaps we should pay that. But I think we should recognize that possibility, and, moreover, we must recognize it in a variety of ways. *We must recognize it by trying to deter it which means we probably should alert SAC, probably put on an airborne alert.* . . . "[18]

After a week of debate within the Ex Comm, decisions were made to impose a blockade (to be called a "quarantine" for both legal and political reasons), to alert American conventional forces for an air strike or invasion if necessary, and to alert American strategic nuclear forces. Although military readiness in all three areas began prior to the evening of October 22, after President Kennedy informed both the Soviet leadership and the American public that the quarantine was being imposed, the requirements for secrecy

---

16. Ibid., p. 84. Also, see Arthur M. Schlesinger, Jr., *A Thousand Days* (Boston: Houghton Mifflin, 1965), p. 803.
17. Off-the-Record Meeting on Cuba, Oct. 16, 1962, 6:30–7:55 p.m., p. 29, JFK Library.
18. Ibid., pp. 9–10. Emphasis added.

became less demanding. Indeed, contrasts in alert activities before and after the Kennedy announcement are striking. Vice Admiral Alfred G. Ward, the quarantine commander, alerted portions of his forces and sent a number of his ships out to sea prior to the President's speech, but made every effort to keep the preparations secret. For example, on the morning of October 22, destroyer captains were told to prepare for immediate action, but specifically ordered neither to place announcements on local radio and television stations for crewmen to return to ship nor to send telegrams out of the area. If there was a deficiency of personnel on any destroyer, the necessary men were to be "borrowed" from other ships in dry dock.[19] By the end of that evening, such precautions were unnecessary.

Similarly, although General Thomas S. Power, the Commander in Chief of the Strategic Air Command (CINCSAC), quietly began to move his forces toward combat readiness prior to Kennedy's announcement, he waited until the speech began to launch the airborne alert.[20] At that point, Power's concern was no longer that his preparations might be picked up by the Soviets; on the contrary, he believed, as he later wrote, that "it was most important for them [the Soviets] to know of SAC's readiness."[21] According to one source, it is with this need in mind that General Power, on his own authority at some point in the crisis, ordered that a message be sent to the Pentagon, *in the clear*, emphasizing the full strength of SAC's alert force.[22] Although, if this unusual action did actually take place, it would have ensured that Soviet intelligence would quickly learn about SAC's readiness, the high state of the American alert would have been picked up, in all likelihood, without such assistance. Soon after the President's speech, *Polaris* submarines were flushed from their ports and began moving to preassigned stations; military commands throughout the world, including the North American Air Defense Command (NORAD), were ordered to move to DEFCON 3; and SAC was

19. *Personal History or Diary of Vice Admiral Alfred G. Ward, U.S. Navy, while serving as Commander Second Fleet*, p. 8. Operational Archives, Naval Historical Center, Washington, D.C. These orders meant that when the first two destroyers left to form the quarantine line on Saturday, October 20, they were approximately one-third understaffed. Interviews with former commanders of the *U.S.S. John R. Pierce* and the *U.S.S. Stickell*.
20. "Starting on October 20, the Strategic Air Command (SAC) began dispersing its bombers and placed all aircraft on an unguarded alert—ready to take off, fully equipped within 15 minutes. On October 22, the B-52 heavy bombers started a massive airborne alert." *Department of Defense Annual Report for Fiscal Year 1963*, p. 5.
21. Thomas S. Power, *Design for Survival* (New York: Coward-McCann, 1964), p. 22.
22. According to H.R. Haldeman, Major General George Keegan was told by General Power, then his commander at SAC: "Make a little mistake. Send a message in the clear." H.R. Haldeman, *The Ends of Power* (New York: Times Books, 1978), p. 93.

placed, for the first and only time, on DEFCON 2.[23] By 6:00 a.m. Wednesday, just hours before the quarantine was to come into effect, SAC had achieved a remarkably intensive degree of readiness:[24]

1. Battle staffs were placed on 24-hour alert duty.
2. All leaves canceled and personnel recalled.
3. 183 B-47 bombers were dispersed to 33 preselected civilian and military airfields.
4. The B-52 airborne alert training program was expanded so that 1/8th of the force was airborne in a continuous series of 24-hour flights, with an immediate replacement for every bomber that landed. Fifty-seven bombers and 61 tankers were airborne. Forty-nine of the B-52s, with 182 nuclear weapons aboard, were on station, ready for execution orders.
5. Additional B-52 and B-47 bombers and tankers were placed on enhanced ground runway alert. The ground alert force totaled 672 bombers and 381 tankers, with a total of 1627 nuclear weapons on board.
6. Ninety Atlas and 46 Titan ICBMs were placed at a heightened state of readiness.

With respect to military effectiveness, narrowly defined, both the quarantine and the SAC alert were enormously well-conducted operations. The quarantine lasted from October 24 to November 20. During this time, the

---

23. *Department of Defense Annual Report for Fiscal Year 1963*, p. 5; Chester V. Clifton, Memo for the Record, "Cuba Fact Sheet" Attachment, October 27, 1962, Box 36A, Cuba General folder, 10/26/62–10/27/62, National Security Files, JFK Library; Memorandum for the Chairman, Joint Chiefs of Staff from Major General John A. Heintges, Deputy Director Joint Staff, December 3, 1962. CCS 3180 Emergency Readiness Plans (May 15, 1960), Sec. 2, JCS; NSC Executive Committee Record of Action, 11:00 a.m. Nov. 12, 1962. LBJ Library, Declassified Documents Reference System, Carrollton Press, 1980, No. 64c. An excellent contemporary account can be found in James Daniel and John G. Hubbell, *Strike in the West* (New York: Holt, Rinehart and Winston, 1963), pp. 115–120.
24. The description of SAC's alert status on October 24 is based upon Department of the Air Force, Staff Message Division, Af IN: 55634 (October 24, 1962), Box 61, Cuba Cables 10/24/62 II, JFK Library. On October 25 or 26, CINCSAC was directed to generate his remaining 804 airplanes and 44 missiles. Within 24 hours of that alert order, SAC was expected to have 172 missiles and 1200 bombers with 2858 weapons on alert. The aggregate destructive power available in this SAC-generated force alone in October 1962 was over 7000 megatons—higher than the entire American strategic arsenal today. Chester V. Clifton, Memo for the Record, October 27, 1962, "Cuba Fact Sheet" Attachment, Box 36A, Cuba General folder, 10/26/62–10/27/62, National Security Files JFK Library; and Cyrus Vance, Memorandum for the President, October 3, 1964, "Military Strength Increases Since Fiscal Year 1961," Department of Defense, 11-63, Volume 1, Tab G, Agency Files, Box 11-12, National Security Files, LBJ Library.

Defense Department estimated that U.S. naval aircraft flew 30,000 flight hours in 9,000 sorties and the ninety ships directly involved steamed for a total of 780,000 miles, all without a major accident.[25] The U.S. Navy effectively enforced the blockade, stopping surface ships when ordered to do so, again without incident.[26] The SAC airborne alert was also conducted effectively: over 2,000 B-52 bomber and tanker sorties, totalling almost 50,000 hours of continuous flight, were undertaken without a single major accident.[27]

With respect to political effectiveness, both military actions can also be seen as having been a success. The objective of the quarantine, Secretary McNamara is reported to have argued during the crisis, "was not to shoot Russians but to communicate a political message from President Kennedy to Premier Khrushchev."[28] Coupled with the "ultimatum" given to the Soviets on October 27, the quarantine in all likelihood contributed to Khrushchev's belief that the United States would attack Cuba if he did not promise to remove the missiles.[29] The objective of the SAC alert was twofold. First, as

---

25. Yarmolinsky, "Department of Defense Operations During the Cuban Missile Crisis," p. 88. The one exception was a minor collision between the *U.S.S. Wasp* and the *U.S.S. Holder* while refueling on November 14th. Memo 24 Nov. 1962. From Rear Admiral Reynold D. Hogle to CINCLANT FLT Command Information Bureau, p. 9, Operational Archives, Naval Historical Center, Washington, D.C.

26. Admiral Ward's diary of the crisis sheds some light on the questions of where the U.S. Navy set the quarantine line and whether the line was moved closer to Cuba, following President Kennedy's last-minute change of orders on the night of October 23. The diary indicates that Ward established the quarantine line as prescribed in his original CINCLANTFLT OpOrders that were *not* altered on the night of October 23: "12 destroyer stations, on an arc 500 miles from Cape MAISI at the eastern end of Cuba." However, it also states that the quarantine line was eventually moved closer to Cuba on Monday, October 29. This evidence is consistent with two theories. It is possible that President Kennedy ordered the Navy to move the line closer than 500 miles to Cuba on October 23, but that it took six days for the forces to do so. The more likely explanation, however, is that the President understood that the Navy's operational orders gave the Quarantine Commander authority to intercept ships further out than the planned 500-mile arc, if he felt it was necessary. Admiral Ward apparently had no such intentions. The result of Kennedy's order thus appears to have been only to ensure that the quarantine line was set at the point where it had originally been planned. *Personal History of Diary of Vice Admiral Alfred G. Ward*, pp. 4–6, 9–15. For contrasting accounts of the implementation of the quarantine line, see Graham T. Allison, *Essence of Decision: Explaining the Cuban Missile Crisis* (Boston: Little, Brown, 1971), pp. 127–130, and Dan Caldwell, "A Research Note on the Quarantine of Cuba, October 1962," *International Studies Quarterly*, Vol. 22, No. 4 (December 1978), pp. 625–633. Also see Phil Williams, *Crisis Management* (New York: John Wiley, 1976), pp. 128–129.

27. Power, *Design for Survival*, p. 21. SAC lost two aircraft during the crisis, both reconnaissance planes: an RB-47, on a sea-search mission, crashed at Kindly AFB Bermuda on October 27 and a U-2 was shot down over Cuba on the same day.

28. Elie Abel, *The Missile Crisis* (Philadelphia: J.B. Lippincott, 1966), p. 155.

29. The "ultimatum" was given verbally by Robert Kennedy to Soviet Ambassador Dobrynin. See Robert F. Kennedy, *Thirteen Days: A Memoir of the Cuban Missile Crisis* (New York: W.W.

was described by McNamara, it was hoped that the alert would deter Soviet military countermoves elsewhere, what would today be called "horizontal escalation." As the Soviets at no time during the crisis even threatened such action, one can only speculate on whether the alert of the enormously superior American nuclear arsenal contributed to this objective. Secondly, the alert underlined President Kennedy's public threat on October 22 to launch a "full retaliatory" nuclear strike against the Soviet Union if a single nuclear missile was launched from Cuba against any target in the Western Hemisphere.[30] Again, a judgment of the effectiveness of this action can only be highly speculative: Khrushchev's agitated conversation with William Knox on October 24—claims that missiles with nuclear warheads were already in Cuba, reassurances that the missiles would not be fired except on his personal orders, and, according to a CIA report, even a promise that "he would not be the first to fire a nuclear weapon"—may have been prompted by Kennedy's threat and the alert actions that followed.[31]

Norton, 1969), pp. 107–109. Also, see Premier Khrushchev's Supreme Soviet speech of December 12, 1962, *Pravda*, December 13, 1962, in *Current Digest of the Soviet Press*, Vol. 14, No. 51, pp. 5–6. Khrushchev's reference to information he received on the morning of Oct. 27, "directly stating that this attack (on Cuba) would be carried out in the next two or three days" (p. 87) may have been, despite the discrepancy in timing, a reference to Dobrynin's report on the meeting with Kennedy. See the account of Dobrynin's report in Nikita S. Khrushchev, *Khrushchev Remembers*, trans. and ed. Strobe Talbott (Boston: Little, Brown, 1970), pp. 497–498.

30. The speech is reprinted in Kennedy, *Thirteen Days*, pp. 163–175. At the Ex Comm meeting on the evening of October 16, Secretary McNamara proposed an even more extreme version of this nuclear threat, a warning that U.S. forces would be launched preemptively: "an ultimatum . . . particularly to Khrushchev, that we have located these offensive weapons; we're maintaining a constant surveillance over them; if there is ever any indication that they're to be launched against this country, we will respond not only against Cuba, but we will respond directly against the Soviet Union with a full nuclear strike. Now this alternative doesn't seem to be a very acceptable one, but wait until you work on the others." Off-the-Record Meeting on Cuba, October 16, 1962, 6:30–7:55 p.m., pp. 46–47, JFK Library.

31. CIA Memorandum, The Crisis USSR/Cuba, 27 October, 0600, p. III-3. Box 316-317, National Security Files, JFK Library. All the available reports on Khrushchev's comments stress his reassuring statements about his personal control over the weapons. The other contemporary accounts of the conversation with Knox do not, however, report that any form of a "no-first-use" pledge was made. See October 26, 1962 Memorandum from INR-Roger Hilsman to Secretary Rusk, Declassified Documents Reference System, Carrollton Press, 1983, No. 000254; and Telegram, American Embassy Moscow to Secretary of State, October 27, 1962, Declassified Documents Reference System, Carrollton Press, 1976, No. 61B. These latter two documents both report that Khrushchev made a specific, but extremely limited threat of a nuclear retaliation if the U.S. attacked Cuba: to destroy Guantanamo. It is important to note, however, that U.S. intelligence was not able to confirm Khrushchev's claim that "both nuclear and high explosive warheads" were already in Cuba. For evidence that Khrushchev was aware of SAC's alert, see his October 28 letter to Kennedy, reprinted in Kennedy, *Thirteen Days*, p. 210, and his December 12 speech to the Supreme Soviet, *Pravda*, December 13, 1962, in *Current Digest of the Soviet Press*, Vol. 14, No. 51, p. 5.

Yet, although the naval blockade and the SAC alert appear to have been both skillfully conducted and politically effective, the analysis of the crisis cannot end there. A number of aspects of the management of military forces deserve a closer look. For although the following set of incidents did not in actuality cause the crisis to escalate out of control, any one of them had the potential to do so. Especially when the stakes are so high, one should learn not only from the final success of crisis management, but also from the close calls.

ASW ACTIVITIES

The first example of difficulties in crisis management has to do with the U.S. Navy's anti-submarine warfare (ASW) activities in the Atlantic.[32] On Sunday, October 21, after President Kennedy decided to place a quarantine around Cuba while keeping open the air strike or invasion options to be used if necessary, Admiral George W. Anderson, Chief of Naval Operations, briefed the President and his advisers on the Navy's quarantine plans and procedures. All accounts of the briefing mention only the procedures for stopping surface ships, and none of the civilian and military participants interviewed by the author specifically remembers anti-submarine operations being discussed. That evening, Secretary McNamara formally approved the quarantine procedures and rules of engagement which had been drawn up by Admiral Anderson, and on Monday, October 22, the Joint Chiefs of Staff sent out these detailed plans to the quarantine commanders.[33]

On Tuesday evening, however, as the Ex Comm briefly met prior to Kennedy's signing of the quarantine proclamation, they were informed that Russian submarines had unexpectedly been discovered moving into the Caribbean. Immediately, according to Robert Kennedy's account of the 6 PM meeting, the President "ordered the Navy to give the highest priority to tracking the submarines and to put into effect the greatest possible safety

---

32. For three accounts which differ from each other and from the account below, see: Allison, *Essence of Decision*, pp. 136–138; John Steinbruner, "An Assessment of Nuclear Crises," in Franklyn Griffiths and John C. Polanyi, eds., *The Dangers of Nuclear War* (Toronto: University of Toronto Press, 1979), pp. 38–39; and Alexander L. George, "The Cuban Missile Crisis, 1962," in Alexander L. George, David K. Hall, and William R. Simons, *The Limits of Coercive Diplomacy: Laos, Cuba, Vietnam* (Boston: Little, Brown, 1971), pp. 112–114. For analysis of how these ASW activities influenced future Soviet naval developments, see Robert G. Weinland, "The Evolution of Soviet Requirements for Naval Forces: Solving the Problems of the Early 1960s," *Survival*, Vol. 26, No. 1 (January–February 1984), pp. 16–25.
33. Yarmolinsky, "Department of Defense Operations During the Cuban Missile Crisis," p. 84.

measures to protect our own aircraft carriers and other vessels."[34] The Navy responded with enthusiasm.

How well did the President and the members of the Ex Comm understand the orders that had just been given? How carefully were such "safety measures" managed by the central authorities? The available evidence suggests that, in the pressure of the crisis, there was inadequate time to review the rules of engagement for U.S. ASW forces and that the key decision-makers neither anticipated the vigor with which the Navy would pursue this mission nor fully understood what the operations would entail.

It is worth noting that at this Tuesday evening meeting the President specifically requested that Secretary McNamara "give a further review to the process of naval action and engagement under the quarantine."[35] The attention of the members of the Ex Comm, however, was focused on the stopping of Soviet surface ships, and the danger caused by the presence of Soviet submarines in the quarantine zone apparently became clear only on Wednesday morning. The degree of emerging apprehension is perhaps best seen in Robert Kennedy's poignant account of that morning's Ex Comm meeting:

It was now a few minutes after 10:00 o'clock. Secretary McNamara announced that two Russian ships, the *Gagarin* and the *Komiles*, were within a few miles of our quarantine barrier. . . .

---

34. Kennedy, *Thirteen Days*, pp. 61–62. Also see Pierre Salinger, *With Kennedy* (Garden City, New York: Doubleday, 1966), p. 270. Vice Admiral Ward's recollections suggest that the U.S. Navy did not anticipate finding submarines in the area: "There were submarines present. We did not know that. We discovered that. It was not known that Soviet submarines were present." Admiral Dennison's account, however, reports that there had been unconfirmed reports of Soviet submarine activity in the Western Atlantic prior to a positive sighting on Monday: "On the 22nd of October, the *Terek* was sighted not far from the Azores refueling a Zulu-type submarine, and the topside condition, and the submarines' requirement for fuel, of course, indicated that she'd been at sea for quite a long period. Considering this together with two possibly valid contact reports, she'd been on a covert patrol in the Western Atlantic near the East Coast of the United States." Vice Admiral Alfred G. Ward, *Oral History* (U.S. Naval Institute, 1972), p. 193, Operational Archives, Naval Historical Center, Washington, D.C.; Admiral Robert Lee Dennison, *The Reminiscences of Admiral Robert Lee Dennison* (U.S. Naval Institute, August 1975), p. 436, Operational Archives, Naval Historical Center, Washington, D.C.

35. Executive Committee Record of Action, October 23, 1962, 6 PM, LBJ Library, Declassified Documents Reference System, Carrollton Press, 1980, No. 64C. It is also interesting to note that McNamara rushed from the White House to a Pentagon press conference immediately following the Ex Comm meeting, and when he was asked whether the quarantine orders gave "any instructions on handling or possible escorting of Soviet submarines," he answered in the most general way: "The orders state that the US ships will protect themselves against attack during the quarantine operation." Department of Defense Press Conference of Honorable Robert S. McNamara, Secretary of Defense. The Pentagon, Tuesday, October 23, 1962, 7:30 p.m., *Public Statements of Robert S. McNamara, 1962*, Vol. IV, p. 1900, OSD Historian's Office, Washington, D.C.

Then came the disturbing Navy report that a Russian submarine had moved into position between the two ships.

It had originally been planned to have a cruiser make the first interception, but, because of the increased danger, it was decided *in the past few hours* to send in an aircraft carrier supported by helicopters, carrying antisubmarine equipment, hovering overhead. The carrier *Essex* was to signal the submarine by sonar to surface and identify itself. If it refused, said Secretary McNamara, depth charges with a small explosive would be used until the submarine surfaced.

I think these few minutes were the time of gravest concern for the President. Was the world on the brink of a holocaust? Was it our error? A mistake? Was there something further that should have been done? Or not done? His hand went up to his face and covered his mouth. He opened and closed his fist. His face seemed drawn, his eyes pained, almost gray. We stared at each other across the table. For a few fleeting seconds, it was almost as though no one else was there and he was no longer the President.

Inexplicably, I thought of when he was ill and almost died; when he lost his child; when we learned that our oldest brother had been killed; of personal times of strain and hurt. The voices droned on, but I didn't seem to hear anything until I heard the President say: "Isn't there some way we can avoid having our first exchange with a Russian submarine—almost anything but that?" "No, there's too much danger to our ships. There is no alternative," said McNamara. "Our commanders have been instructed to avoid hostilities if at all possible, but this is what we must be prepared for, and this is what we must expect."[36]

Minutes later, the intelligence report came in suggesting that the Soviets were not going to challenge the blockade: the twenty ships closest to the quarantine line had either stopped or turned around. Robert Kennedy reports that he immediately suggested that the Ex Comm "should make sure that the Navy knew nothing was to be done, that no ships were to be interfered with," and that the President gave the order to "get in direct touch with the *Essex* and tell them not to do anything. . . . "[37]

---

36. Kennedy, *Thirteen Days* (emphasis added), pp. 69–70. For a second account of this meeting see Kenneth P. O'Donnell and David F. Powers (with Joe McCarthy), *"Johnny, We Hardly Knew Ye"* (Boston: Little, Brown, 1972), pp. 331–333. Also see Executive Committee Record of Action, October 24, 1962, 10:00 AM. LBJ Library, Declassified Documents Reference System, Carrollton Press, 1980, No. 64C. The President's awareness of and concern over the Soviet submarines can also be seen in his undated Ex Comm "doodles" reproduced in Theodore C. Sorensen, *Kennedy* (New York: Harper and Row, 1965), p. 705.

37. Kennedy, *Thirteen Days*, pp. 71–72. One should also note, however, that the Record of Action for that meeting states only that "the President directed that there be no interception of any target for at least another hour while clarifying information was sought." Executive Committee Record of Action, October 24, 1962, 10:00 a.m., LBJ Library, Declassified Documents Reference System, Carrollton Press, 1980, No. 64C.

The passage displays President Kennedy's grave concern that no direct military action be taken against Soviet ships, including Soviet submarines, unless it was absolutely necessary. Although details are missing on how further decisions were made and on when orders were drafted, communicated, and executed in the fog of crisis,[38] it is known that at some point on Wednesday the authority given to the U.S. Navy to pursue Soviet submarines was clarified: specific "submarine surfacing and identification procedures" were issued by Secretary of Defense, the Soviets were informed of the operations, and Assistant Secretary of Defense Arthur Sylvester notified the press that a warning system for "unidentified submarines" in the quarantine zone had been established.[39] The reasons why it was considered necessary to force Soviet submarines to the surface were numerous and may have differed among the various participants in the crisis. The primary motivation among most civilian and military authorities was the need to protect American surface ships on the quarantine line: when the Soviet surface ships stopped on Wednesday morning, there was a fear that they were waiting to rendezvous with the submarines before attemtping to run the blockade. This fear was confirmed by Khrushchev's threat, in his conversation with William Knox, that if the U.S. Navy intercepted Soviet vessels bound for Cuba "sooner or later [the] USSR would order its subs to sink ships stopping Soviet ships."[40] It may also have been the case, as Robert Kennedy's account sug-

---

38. Vice Admiral Ward's recollections suggest that he received specific instructions on ASW activities only *after* his quarantine forces had begun to trail a Soviet submarine: "One of our ships picked up a submerged contact, trailed it for about a day and a half. . . . Meanwhile we have gotten word to the White House and to Washington and were told to trail it but to take no offensive action." It is also important to note that not every commander on the blockade line was aware of what ASW rules of engagement were in effect. For example, the Commander of the USS *Charles P. Cecil*, who held constant contact with a Soviet submarine for 35 hours before it surfaced on October 30, reports that he received no direct instructions concerning rules of engagement during the crisis and merely assumed that peacetime rules were in operation. Ward, *Oral History*, pp. 193–194; and interview with Charles P. Rozier, June 14, 1984.
39. See Jerry Greene, "Some Red Ships Alter Course, Others Go On; Hint of a Convoy," *New York News*, October 25, 1962; "U.S. Sets up a Warning System to Halt Submarines Off Cuba." *The New York Times*, October 26, 1962, p. 18; and Navy Message 252124Z October, NAVOCEANO WASH DC to Secretary of State, Box 41, Cuba Cables, 10/25/62, II, National Security Files, JFK Library. The Defense Department's "post-mortem" also notes that the American destroyer *Cecil* "forced a Soviet submarine to the surface" on October 30 and when the submarine surfaced, "it was on course 090 as prescribed in our instructions to Moscow of October 24." Yarmolinsky, "Department of Defense Operations During the Cuban Crisis," p. 87.
40. Interviews; Abel, *The Missile Crisis*, p. 154; Memorandum INR–Roger Hilsman to Secretary Rusk, October 26, 1962, Declassified Documents Reference System, Carrollton Press, 1983, No. 000254; Telegram, American Embassy Moscow to Secretary of State, October 27, 1962. Declassification Documents Reference System, Carrollton Press, 1976, No. 61B.

gests, that the ASW campaign was seen by the President as part of the tactic of applying gradual and incremental pressure on Khrushchev during the crisis.[41] In addition, there was concern that the Soviet submarines might be carrying warheads for the MRBMs and IRBMs in Cuba and at least some fear—apparently mistaken—that the submarines themselves might be armed with nuclear missiles.[42]

On the quarantine line, naval commanders reacted with enthusiasm to what Admiral Anderson later called "perhaps the finest opportunity since WWII for the U.S. naval antisubmarine forces to exercise at their trade [and] to perfect their skills": after a Soviet *Zulu*-class submarine was spotted while being refueled near the Azores on Monday, October 22, the U.S. Navy searched an area of some 3.5 million square miles, eventually receiving more than twenty possible submerged contacts and succeeding in surfacing five or six Soviet *Foxtrot*-class diesel-attack submarines in or near the quarantine zone.[43] In most of these cases—despite the Soviet submariners' use of such

---

41. Kennedy, *Thirteen Days*, p. 77. For an argument that the raising of the Soviet submarines may have been one of the essential elements in the effort to persuade Khrushchev to remove the missiles from Cuba, see George, "The Cuban Missile Crisis, 1962," pp. 113–114.

42. Interviews. The record does not state whether the *Zulu*-class submarine photographed near the Azores on October 22 was one of the *Zulus* specially altered to carry a small number of SS-N-4 missiles, which like the SS-N-3a cruise missiles deployed on E, J, and W-class submarines, could only be launched from the surface. All the Soviet submarines surfaced in the quarantine zone, however, were identified as *Foxtrot*-class diesel attack submarines. It is important to note that on October 27, the U.S. Navy set up an ASW barrier of attack submarines southeast of Newfoundland, in Admiral Anderson's words, "to intercept *possible Soviet missile-launching submarines which might have approached our coast.*" Yarmolinsky, "Department of Defense Operations During the Cuban Missile Crisis," p. 93; and Admiral George W. Anderson, Harvard Business School Club speech, The Pentagon, November 27, 1962, *Public Speeches and Published Articles of Admiral George W. Anderson, Jr.*, p. 141 (emphasis added), Mimeograph, Office of the Chief of Naval Operations, 1963. For a discussion of Soviet submarines in the early 1960s, see K.J. Moore, Mark Flanigan, and Robert D. Helsel, "Developments in Submarine Systems, 1956–1976," in Michael McGwire and John McDonnell, eds., *Soviet Naval Influence* (New York: Praeger, 1977), pp. 154–167.

43. Admiral George W. Anderson, Navy League Banquet Speech, New York, November 9, 1962, *Public Speeches and Published Articles*, p. 136. There is some uncertainty about the number of *Foxtrots* surfaced in the quarantine zone. Admiral Anderson has written that "all six diesel powered Soviet submarines in the area were detected, covered, trailed, and surfaced," which is in agreement with the accounts given by Elie Abel and Robert F. Kennedy. The Defense Department's "post-mortem," however, suggests that there were only five positive contacts made *excluding* the Z-class submarine that was *observed* in the mid-Atlantic on October 22. Vice Admiral Ward's account likewise states that five positive *Foxtrot* contacts were made in the quarantine area. Here it may be interesting to note Admiral Dennison's report that one of the Soviet submarines had one identifying number painted on the starboard side and another on the port side, apparently a clumsy effort at deception. U.S. Congress, House, Committee on Armed Services, *Hearings on Military Posture*, 88th Congress, 1st Session, 1963, No. 4, pp. 897,

evasive tactics as radical maneuvering, ejecting decoy devices to confuse sonar operators, and attempting to hide in the wake of a pursuing destroyer—U.S. naval forces simply "rode" the diesel submarines, which had to surface approximately every 48 hours to recharge batteries, or encouraged this process by using active sonar to signal the submarine to rise.[44] There is some evidence, however, that at least one zealous U.S. naval commander moved on to the next step: dropping low-level explosive charges until the submarine surfaced.[45]

The point is not that such action was unauthorized. On the contrary, the "surfacing and identification procedures" that the Secretary of Defense issued specifically permitted quarantine forces to "drop 4 or 5 harmless explosive sound signals" when in contact with unidentified submerged submarines.[46] The key point is that the central authorities, who deliberately maintained strict control over any "shot across the bow" against Soviet surface ships, permitted the ASW equivalent, in the heat of crisis, with inadequate time to review the procedures thoroughly. Although the weapons used were most likely the low explosive Practice Depth Charges (PDCs), an accepted signal device which the U.S. Navy uses to signal its own ships during exercises, the vigorous ASW activities were not entirely risk-free. Indeed, one of the Soviet submarines that the U.S. Navy forced to the surface was crippled, could not submerge again, and returned to the Soviet Union on the surface.[47]

900; Admiral George W. Anderson, Jr., "The Cuban Crisis," in Arnold Shapack, ed., *Proceedings of the Naval History Symposium: The Navy in an Age of Change and Crisis*, U.S. Naval Academy, Annapolis, Maryland, April 27–28, 1973, p. 85; Abel, *The Missile Crisis*, p. 155; Kennedy, *Thirteen Days*, p. 77; Yarmolinsky, "Department of Defense Operations During the Cuban Missile Crisis," pp. 86–87; *Personal History or Diary of Vice Admiral Alfred G. Ward While Serving as Commander Second Fleet*, p. 12; *The Reminiscences of Admiral Robert Lee Dennison*, p. 436.

44. For accounts of two of these operations see: "Fact Sheet on *Charles P. Cecil*, (DDR 835) Surfacing of Russian Submarine" and "Destroyer Forced Red Sub Up," *The Evening Capital* (Annapolis), June 14, 1963, p. 20, both located in the *Charles P. Cecil* folder, Ships Histories Archives, Naval Historical Center, Washington, D.C.; and Commanding Officer *U.S.S. Essex*, "Report Forwarding personal Accounts of ASW Barrier patrols During the Cuban Missile Crisis," December 29, 1962, Serial 0173, Operational Archives, Naval Historical Center, Washington, D.C.

45. In a "not for attribution" interview, a former senior naval officer reported that "depth charges were dropped in an isolated case" by a "zealous" commander. In a similar interview, a second source reported that one of the *Foxtrot* submarines used the evasive technique of "backing down" into its own wake and the turbulence caused by an American depth charge.

46. The procedures also indicated that the code signal "IDKCA," meaning rise to surface, was to be sent on underwater communications equipment in the 8 KC frequency range. Submarines were then to surface on an easterly course. See sources cited in Footnote 40.

47. *The Reminiscences of Admiral Robert Lee Dennison*, pp. 435–436. For an imaginative example of how such ASW activities could produce a dangerous incident, see the film *The Bedford Incident*.

In short, despite the extensive effort on the part of the Secretary of Defense, and the President himself, to manage all potentially provocative military operations in October 1962, inadequate attention appears to have been given to this key aspect of the quarantine operation. Given the complexity of such military operations and the intense pressures of crisis decision-making, such problems of management should not be unexpected. Indeed, this was not the only example of potentially dangerous military activity during the crisis.

THE ALASKAN U-2 INCIDENT

On Saturday, October 27, a U-2 aircraft under SAC's Strategic Reconnaissance Wing based at Eielson Air Force Base in Alaska took off on what has been reported to be "a routine air sampling mission" and strayed into Soviet airspace over the Chukotski Peninsula.[48] Soviet MIGs from a base near Wrangel Island scrambled to intercept the plane, the American pilot called for assistance over clear channels, and U.S. Air Force fighter aircraft in Alaska immediately scrambled, heading into the Bering Sea in an attempt to rendezvous with the U-2. Although it is not possible, of course, to report what the Soviet political and military leadership thought as they were told what their radar was picking up in the confusion, Lieutenant General David A. Burchinal, the Air Force Operations Deputy to the Joint Chiefs during the crisis, has provided the following account of Secretary McNamara's reaction:

We had a U-2 flying over the Arctic, and the kid lost his navigational system, trying to get back into Alaska he came right smack over the middle of the Kola [sic] Peninsula. We had picked him up on radar, and we got a flash report out of Alaska. They picked him up and knew where he was and he got his outbound course. . . . The word came into the "tank" where McNamara and the Chiefs were meeting. . . . He turned absolutely white, and yelled hysterically, "This means war with the Soviet Union. . . ."[49]

The U-2 found its way out of Soviet territory, and no shots were fired. When President Kennedy was told about the incident by Roger Hilsman, he

---

48. Roger Hilsman, *To Move a Nation* (Garden City, N.Y.: Doubleday, 1967), p. 221. There were five Soviet nuclear tests during the crisis: two on October 22, one on October 27, and two on October 28. *The Effects of Nuclear Weapons*, U.S. Atomic Energy Commission, revised ed. (Washington: U.S. Government Printing Office, 1964), p. 681b. Also see the account in Daniel and Hubbell, *Strike in the West*, p. 154.

49. Lieutenant General David A. Burchinal, Oral History, U.S. Army Historical Institute, Carlisle Barracks, Pa., pp. 114–115. Originally cited in David Detzer, *The Brink* (New York: Thomas Y. Crowell, 1979), p. 281.

reacted with an ironic laugh: "There is always some son of a bitch who doesn't get the word."[50] Sorensen reports, however, that the President did wonder if Khrushchev thought the United States was surveying Soviet airbases for a preemptive nuclear attack.[51] Still, at the Ex Comm meeting that afternoon, the President decided not to say anything about the incident unless the Soviets publicized it.[52]

Khrushchev did respond quickly. In his letter of October 28, 1962, in which he agreed to a withdrawal of the missiles, the Soviet leader complained about the U-2 overflight:

The question is, Mr. President: How should we regard this? What is this, a provocation? One of your planes violates our frontier during this anxious time we are both experiencing, when everything has been put into combat readiness. Is it not a fact that an intruding American plane could be easily taken for a nuclear bomber, which might push us to a fateful step; and all the more so since the U.S. Government and Pentagon long ago declared that you are maintaining a continuous nuclear bomber patrol?[53]

In response, Kennedy wrote that he regretted the incident and promised Khrushchev that he would "see to it that every precaution is taken to prevent recurrence."[54] Privately, however, the President and Kenneth O'Donnell speculated that the incident may have "frightened the hell out of Khrushchev," and could have contributed to his final decision to agree to pull the missiles out of Cuba.[55]

How could this dangerous incident have occurred? Because the SAC documents for the period are still classified, only a number of speculative points can be made.

First, it is important to note that this incident occurred despite the efforts by officials in Washington to maintain central control over all potentially provocative reconnaissance missions. The Committee on Overhead Reconnaissance (COMOR) and, at times, the whole Ex Comm paid careful attention to each U-2 flight over Cuba, but no restrictions were placed on U-2s on

---

50. Hilsman, *To Move a Nation*, p. 221, uses less colorful language. It is, however, likely that Kennedy had already been informed of the incident when he spoke with Hilsman. Interview.
51. Sorensen, *Kennedy*, p. 713.
52. NSC Executive Committee Record of Action, October 27, 1962. 4:00 p.m. meeting no. 8, JFK Library. The information that the Soviet fighters took off from a base "near Wrangel Island" is from this document.
53. Reprinted in Kennedy, *Thirteen Days*, p. 211.
54. Ibid., p. 214.
55. O'Donnell and Powers, *"Johnny, We Hardly Knew Ye,"* p. 342.

polar air sampling missions until after the October 27th incident.[56] These U-2s did not have authority to fly directly adjacent to Soviet airspace, and no one appears to have focused on them as a potential source of danger. Yet, since a U-2, on what some reports claim was a similar air sampling mission, had flown into Soviet airspace as recently as August 30, 1962,[57] the failure to anticipate problems here was a serious omission.

Second, it may be important to note that the specific cause of the incident has never been explained in detail. Why did the U-2 stray into Soviet territory? Certainly, the official story—that the pilot made a serious navigational error—is the most probable cause. There has also been, however, some speculation that the incident was not entirely "accidental,"[58] and it is at least possible that a local commander, in need of up-to-date reconnaissance in the tense atmosphere of the crisis, would give verbal orders to a pilot to fly near or into Soviet airspace. Even though analysis of American military operations in 1962 would suggest that such an occurrence is a most unlikely explanation in this specific case,[59] the Alaskan U-2 incident should serve as a reminder that the possibility of unauthorized actions in a serious crisis should not be dismissed lightly by central military or civilian decision-makers.[60]

Third, the greatest danger of immediate escalation stemming from this incident was the possibility that the American fighters sent to escort the U-2 back to Alaska would come into contact with Soviet fighters. Who gave the orders to launch the fighter aircraft rescue mission? What were their rules of engagement? It appears that such "details" were not controlled directly by the central political authorities in Washington during the brief, but dan-

---

56. On October 30th, Secretary McNamara reported to the Ex Comm that he had "ordered that no U-2 planes fly until a satisfactory system was developed to safeguard against navigational errors resulting in overflying Soviet territory." NSC Executive Committee Record of Action, October 30, 1962, 10:00 a.m., LBJ Library. The Declassified Documents Reference System, Carrollton Press, 1980, No. 64C.

57. For a Russian statement that the U-2 that penetrated Soviet airspace in August was on an air-sampling mission, see "Tass statement on Aid to Cuba and U.S. Provocation," *Pravda*, September 12, 1962, pp. 1–2, in *The Current Digest of the Soviet Press*, Vol. 14, No. 37, p. 15. Also see "U.S. Calls U-2 Overflight of Red Island Error," *The Washington Post*, September 5, 1962, p. A6.

58. Interviews. Hilsman refers to the incident as "The Dr. Strangelove Incident." Hilsman, *To Move a Nation*, p. 221.

59. U-2s would not have been aircraft used for testing Soviet air defense radars nor for gaining intelligence about Soviet bomber dispersal. Moreover, it is highly unlikely that SIOP options in 1962 could have been affected in a significant way during the crisis as a result of such last minute intelligence.

60. See the discussion of "ambiguous command" in Paul Bracken, *The Command and Control of Nuclear Forces* (New Haven: Yale University Press, 1983), pp. 227–232.

gerous incident. Robert McNamara states that he does not believe he personally ordered the fighters to scramble.[61] The most likely explanation is that the Alaskan Air Command was simply following standing orders approved prior to the crisis: if a lost plane radios for assistance, local commanders would have authority, unless specifically ordered not to, to launch fighters in an effort to escort it home.

CARIBBEAN RECONNAISSANCE MISSIONS

While conducting the blockade and preparing for a possible invasion of Cuba, commanders throughout the U.S. Navy and members of the intelligence community would desire the best possible intelligence about the adversary's forces. During the October 1962 crisis, a number of potentially dangerous incidents occurred because of this need. In the following cases, judgments by higher civilian and military authorities about appropriate actions during the crisis apparently differed from the views of individuals operating at a lower level in the chain of command.

Robert Kennedy, for example, reports that on Friday, October 26, the President learned that an American Electronic Intelligence ship (with a mission similar to the *Pueblo* or the *Liberty*) was engaged in operations just off the Cuban coast. Fearing that an attack on the ship would enormously complicate the delicate situation, Kennedy ordered the vessel to move further out to sea.[62] There were, however, other Navy ships operating close to Cuban territory. For example, the commanding officers of both the *U.S.S. John R. Pierce* and the *U.S.S. J.R. Perry* report that they trailed suspicious Soviet surface ships to within five or six miles of the Cuban coast before they moved away and state that they had the usual authority to fire at any hostile aircraft that approached them.[63] Although the commanders of the blockade certainly monitored the operations and the Secretary of Defense would have approved the standing orders and rules of engagement far in advance of the crisis, in neither case is it likely that civilian authorities reviewed or altered such procedures as the crisis evolved.

Finally, there were the uncontrolled operations undertaken during the crisis by Task Force W of Operation Mongoose, the CIA sabotage operation against Cuba. On his own authority, William Harvey, the director of Force

---

61. Interview with Robert McNamara, June 19, 1984.
62. See Allison, *Essence of Decision*, pp. 139–140, and Kennedy, *Thirteen Days*, p. 86.
63. Interviews with both commanders. Also see Daniel and Hubbell, *Strike in the West*, pp. 163–165.

W, ordered teams of covert agents into Cuba in order to support an invasion if it took place. Accounts vary over the precise details of how many agents left and how many actually landed on Cuba during the crisis. But it is known that when Robert Kennedy found out about the operation he had a harsh confrontation with Harvey, and on October 30 all of Task Force W's sabotage operations were ordered to an immediate halt.[64]

October 1973: The DEFCON 3 Alert

The only superpower crisis since 1962 in which American strategic forces have been placed at a higher state of command readiness occurred at the end of the October 1973 Middle East War.[65] In the afternoon of October 24, when the superpower-sponsored cease-fire broke down along the Suez Canal and the Egyptian Third Army was placed under the threat of destruction, Egyptian President Anwar Sadat called on the Soviets and the Americans to send forces to the Middle East to enforce the cease-fire. The American government was, Henry Kissinger reports, "determined to resist by force if necessary the introduction of Soviet troops into the Middle East regardless of the pretext under which they arrived." A Soviet military force in Egypt "might prove impossible to remove," Kissinger feared, and "there would be endless pretexts for it to intervene at any point against Israel, or against moderate Arab governments, for that matter."[66]

Ambiguous, but alarming, intelligence had come in throughout the day suggesting that the Soviets were contemplating such a military intervention: a number of previously alerted Soviet airborne divisions had been placed on an even higher state of alert that morning, an airborne forces command post had been set up that afternoon, and the Soviet airlift fleet, which had stopped

---

64. For various accounts see: *Alleged Assassination Plots Involving Foreign Leaders*, Interim Report of the Select Committee to Study Government Operations with respect to Intelligence Activities, 9th Congress, 1st Session, Nov. 20, 1975, p. 148; Thomas Powers, *The Man Who Kept the Secrets: Richard Helms and the CIA* (New York: Knopf, 1979), p. 142; and Robert F. Kennedy, Oral History Vol. 3, 4/30/64, p. 414, JFK Library.
65. For further analysis of the crisis, see Barry M. Blechman and Douglas M. Hart, "The Political Utility of Nuclear Weapons: The 1973 Middle East Crisis," *International Security*, Vol. 7, No. 1 (Summer 1982), pp. 132–156; Scott D. Sagan, "Lessons of the Yom Kippur Alert," *Foreign Policy*, No. 36 (Fall 1979), pp. 160–177; and Raymond L. Garthoff's chapter on the October War in *Détente and Confrontation: American Soviet Relations from Nixon to Reagan* (Washington D.C.: Brookings Institution, forthcoming). The following account of the crisis is also based on "not for attribution" interviews with a number of the participants.
66. Henry Kissinger, *Years of Upheaval* (Boston: Little, Brown, 1982), pp. 579–580.

transporting weapons to Egypt and Syria that morning, appeared to be preparing for another mission. Ominously, despite Kissinger's insistence that the United States "would not accept Soviet troops in any guise" to be sent to Egypt, Soviet Ambassador Dobrynin told him at 7:25 p.m. that the leadership in Moscow had "become so angry [that] they want troops."[67] Finally, at 9:35 p.m., Dobrynin called with a message from Premier Brezhnev that demanded an "immediate and clear reply." It was, Kissinger argues, "in effect an ultimatum" and "one of the most serious challenges to an American President by a Soviet leader":

> . . . Let us together, the USSR and the United States, urgently dispatch to Egypt the Soviet and American military contingents, to insure the implementation of the decision of the Security Council of October 22 and 23 concerning the cessation of fire and of all military activities and also of our understanding with you on the guarantee of the implementation of the decisions of the Security Council.
> It is necessary to adhere without delay. *I will say it straight that if you find it impossible to act jointly with us in this matter, we should be faced with the necessity urgently to consider the question of taking appropriate steps unilaterally.* We cannot allow arbitrariness on the part of Israel. . . .[68]

The Secretary of State immediately called a special meeting of the Washington Special Action Group (WSAG), which convened in the White House Situation Room at 10:40 p.m., and called Dobrynin back, repeatedly warning him: "Don't you pressure us"; "if any unilateral action is taken before we have had a chance to reply that will be very serious."[69] The participants in the WSAG meeting were Kissinger, Secretary of Defense James Schlesinger, Director of Central Intelligence William Colby, Chairman of the Joint Chiefs of Staff Admiral Thomas Moorer, Presidential Chief of Staff Alexander Haig, Deputy Assistant to the President for National Security Affairs Brent Scowcroft, and Kissinger's military assistant, Commander Jonathan Howe. They agreed that, whether the Soviets were bluffing or not, a serious American response was required. There was a deep fear among many of the participants that the Soviet leadership might be tempted to intervene unilaterally in the belief that the United States was paralyzed into inaction by the most recent events, the "Saturday Night Massacre," in the ongoing trauma of Watergate. A consensus quickly formed, therefore, behind two actions: send-

---

67. Ibid., p. 582.
68. Ibid., pp. 583–584. Emphasis added.
69. Ibid., p. 585.

ing a reply to Brezhnev that was, in Kissinger's terms, "conciliatory in tone but strong in substance," and backing up the reply with "some noticeable action that conveyed our determination to resist unilateral moves."[70]

Although the participants agreed that the American response must come immediately (if the Soviets were about to intervene unilaterally, they would begin sending airborne troops in at daybreak, only a few hours away), there was some disagreement about what kind of American military alert would send the appropriate signal to the leadership in Moscow. One position held that only an alert of conventional forces near the region was desirable. An alert of nuclear forces in the United States would not be a credible threat; alerting American conventional forces in Europe, in the Mediterranean, and in the Indian Ocean, forces more likely to be used if the Soviets moved, would be more likely to deter Soviet intervention. The opposing position called for something more dramatic: a global military alert, including the strategic nuclear forces of SAC, in order to shock the Soviets and to create time for American diplomacy to take effective action. One important rationale behind the more dramatic approach to crisis management was best expressed in Kissinger's account of the 1970 Jordanian crisis—an argument he most likely repeated in some form in the Situation Room on October 24:

In my view what seems "balanced" and "safe" in a crisis is often the most risky. Gradual escalation tempts the opponent to match every move; what is intended as a show of moderation may be interpreted as irresolution; reassurance may provide too predictable a checklist and hence an incentive for waiting, prolonging the conditions of inherent risk. A leader must choose carefully and thoughtfully the issues over which to face confrontation. He should do so only for major objectives. Once he is committed, however, his obligation is to end the confrontation rapidly. For this he must convey implacability. He must be prepared to escalate rapidly and brutally to a point where the opponent can no longer afford to experiment.[71]

This latter position, that global strategic nuclear forces should be alerted, was eventually accepted by the WSAG for a number of reasons. First, the need for quick action argued for a dramatic signal, something the Soviets would pick up quickly through the fog of the crisis. If the United States military alert could "slow down the Soviets' timetable"[72] for intervention, American diplomacy might change the situation on the ground and thereby

---

70. Ibid., p. 587.
71. Henry Kissinger, *White House Years* (Boston: Little, Brown, 1979), p. 622.
72. Kissinger, *Years of Upheaval*, p. 587.

reduce both Soviet incentives and opportunities to intervene. Second, the credibility argument in favor of alerting conventional forces was not entirely persuasive. It was estimated that the Soviets could put 5,000 airborne troops a day into Egypt; U.S. capabilities did not look particularly strong in comparison and the military was not universally sanguine about the outcome of a naval contest in the Mediterranean if it came to that.[73] Third, some participants believed that a bureaucratic factor was important: the inclusion of SAC forces in the alert would provide an opportunity to bring back to the continental United States a number of B-52s still stationed in Guam as a latent threat to the North Vietnamese. Lastly, some participants believed that a quick alert of nuclear forces would signal resolve to the Soviets without engendering domestic political turmoil in the United States.[74]

Although the precise mixture of these motives differed among the WSAG members, a consensus was reached, and at 11:41 p.m. Secretary Schlesinger and Admiral Moorer issued orders to all American military commands to place their forces at DEFCON 3 "with minimum public notice."[75] Immediately, there was a massive surge through American military communications channels, the first "signal" that the Soviet Union would have picked up. The open record does not indicate precisely what changes in the alert status of strategic submarines in port took place, but it is known that there was little change in the portion of the Pacific Fleet that was already at DEFCON 3 because of the war in Southeast Asia. At SAC, however, the following activities began, as forces were generated:[76]

1. All routine training missions were cancelled.
2. The Command and Control network was tested.
3. Although SAC keeps an airborne command post in the air at all times, CINCSAC's own airborne command post was placed on enhanced ground alert and further airborne command and control assets were readied for take-off.

---

73. According to Chief of Naval Operations Elmo Zumwalt's account, "Admiral Moorer made the point at the White House that we would lose our ass in the eastern Med under these circumstances." Elmo R. Zumwalt, Jr., *On Watch* (New York: Quadrangle, 1976), p. 446.
74. Interviews.
75. According to one account, Alaska and Panama were, or were at least planned to be, excepted. The reason apparently had nothing to do with Alaska's proximity to the U.S.S.R.: "we decided to alert everything but the kitchen sink; Alaska and Panama were the kitchen sink." Interview.
76. Interviews.

4. Some refueling tankers were dispersed.
5. An increased number of B-52s were placed on heightened ground-runway alert.
6. There was a minor increase in the alert status of the American land-based missile force.

Shortly thereafter, the WSAG received intelligence "that eight Soviet An-22 transport planes—each capable of carrying two hundred or more troops—were slated to fly from Budapest to Egypt in the next few hours." In response, further readiness measures—an alert of the 82nd Airborne Division and orders sending the aircraft carrier *Franklin Delano Roosevelt* into the eastern Mediterranean—were ordered.[77] Finally, at 5:40 a.m., the reply to Brezhnev was delivered by General Scowcroft to Ambassador Dobrynin which stated in part:

Mr. General Secretary:
I have carefully studied your important message of this evening. I agree with you that our understanding to act jointly for peace is one of the highest value and that we should implement that understanding in this complex situation.
I must tell you, however, that your proposal for a particular kind of joint action, that of sending Soviet and American military contingents to Egypt, is not appropriate in the present circumstances.
We have no information which would indicate that the cease-fire is now being violated on any significant scale. . . .
In this circumstances, we must view your suggestion of unilateral action as a matter of gravest concern, involving incalculable consequences.
Mr. General Secretary, in the spirit of our agreements this is the time for acting not unilaterally but in harmony and with cool heads. . . .
You must know, however, that we could in no event accept unilateral action. . . . As I stated above, such action would produce incalculable consequences which would be in the interest of neither of our countries and which would end all we have striven so hard to achieve.[78]

The immediate danger quickly dissipated. According to one source, a Soviet aircraft, which may have contained the advance elements of the intervention force, landed at the Cairo West airfield early in the morning, but returned almost immediately.[79] Most importantly, at 2:40 p.m. on October 25, Brezhnev sent another message to Nixon via Dobrynin that did not

---

77. Kissinger, *Years of Upheaval*, p. 589.
78. Richard M. Nixon, *RN: The Memoirs of Richard Nixon* (New York: Grosset and Dunlap, 1978), pp. 939–940.
79. Blechman and Hart, "The Political Utility of Nuclear Weapons," pp. 143–144.

mention the American alert, but stated that the Soviets would send only seventy "representatives" (apparently not military forces) to observe the cease-fire.[80] All participants felt that the crisis was significantly cooled.

Did the DEFCON 3 alert achieve its political objective? No definitive answer is possible. The first reason is that it is impossible to know what Soviet intentions were on October 24 and 25. While it is perhaps likely that Soviet leaders seriously intended to move some troops into Egypt if it appeared that the United States would not react, it is also certainly plausible to argue that Moscow's main objective was to shock the Americans into putting pressure on Israel to respect the cease-fire. Although Kissinger's account suggests that he did not begin applying such pressure until after Brezhnev's note of October 25 was received, which would be necessary so that the United States would not be seen to have been coerced by the Soviet Union, it is clear that the continued threat of Soviet intervention encouraged Kissinger's efforts in this area.[81] Thus, while the alert may have made Soviet intervention more dangerous, it was the saving of the Third Army which eventually made Soviet intervention unnecessary. This, however, does not necessarily mean that the alert was not a success, for the actions were meant to deter an immediate Soviet intervention, not to end the risk altogether.

The second reason why it is difficult to judge the alert's political effectiveness is that the WSAG sent a message, in Nixon's name, to President Sadat within minutes after alerting American forces. This message threatened to withdraw the American offer to become directly involved in the forthcoming peace talks with Israel. The Egyptian government responded early in the morning of October 25 in two messages that acknowledged the American opposition to the introduction of superpower forces into the conflict area and requested the "speedy dispatch" of a U.N. international peacekeeping force rather than a U.S.–U.S.S.R. joint force to supervise the cease-fire.[82] This change of position by Sadat significantly reduced the Soviet opportunity to intervene unilaterally, for it is unlikely that Moscow would land forces without the explicit approval of Sadat's government.

There are no known examples during the 1973 alert, in contrast to the Cuban missile crisis, of military operations exceeding the signal desired by the central authorities. The reasons are relatively straightforward. In 1973,

---

80. Kissinger, *Years of Upheaval*, p. 597.
81. Ibid., pp. 607–610.
82. Ibid., pp. 588, 592. Also see Nixon, *RN*, pp. 938–939. The precise time when the Egyptian messages arrived is not clear.

unlike 1962, neither civilian nor military authorities believed that escalation to nuclear war was at all likely. The DEFCON 3 alert was a military action intended as a political signal to the Soviet Union and was so understood by American military commanders.[83] Because there was little expectation of actual use of military force, the strategic alert was ordered at a relatively low level by the central authorities and was executed in a relatively *pro forma* fashion by the military commanders.

In one sense, however, the DEFCON 3 alert produced unintended results, which were in conflict with the objectives of at least some members of the WSAG. Just as Thomas Gates believed he had ordered a "quiet alert" in May 1960, Henry Kissinger believed that the October 1973 DEFCON 3 alert would be kept quiet, sufficiently secret that there would be no immediate public outcry in the United States and no public challenge to the Soviet Union. Apparently, none of the other participants in the decision to alert forces informed the Secretary of State that a global DEFCON 3 would quickly become known to the public.[84] Thus, Kissinger reports he was "shocked" when the global alert was in all the newspapers and on television on the morning of October 25 and alarmed because "we would now have a *public* confrontation."[85] It should not have been surprising, however, that a global DEFCON 3 alert could not be kept quiet. Indeed, Kissinger's subsequent complaint—that publicity surrounding the alert of 1973 showed "the change in discipline of our government" since the Jordanian crisis of 1970 when "similar alert measures" had been instituted without public alarm—demonstrates a lack of understanding of the operational significance of various alert procedures.[86] It may have been possible to place specific units of American conventional forces on alert, as was done in 1970, without it becoming public knowledge immediately. It is, however, exceedingly improbable that movement to a global DEFCON 3 could remain secret for a short period of time.

---

83. In stark contrast to the 1960 case, during which American military commanders did not know the reasons why they were ordered to generate their forces, in 1973 Admiral Moorer followed the DEFCON 3 order with a secure telephone call to the unified and specified commanders in order to explain the purpose of the alert in greater detail than was possible in an operational order. Interview with Admiral Thomas Moorer, April 10, 1984. Also see Steinbruner, "An Assessment of Nuclear Crises," p. 43.
84. The reasons for this "failure" probably differed among the other participants. Some most likely believed the alert could be kept secret; others probably knew otherwise, but chose not to stress that likelihood for fear that it would make a decision to alert forces less likely. Interviews.
85. Kissinger, *Years of Upheaval*, p. 591.
86. Ibid., p. 591; and Kissinger, *White House Years*, pp. 622, 628.

Conclusions

Although the nuclear alerts and conventional force deployments discussed in these cases were successfully managed and appear to have been politically effective, the analysis has also pointed to a number of potentially dangerous ways in which increases in military readiness for war can escape the control of central authorities. Any overall conclusion about nuclear alerts that focuses exclusively on one half of this equation is likely to be highly misleading. It would, on the one hand, be wrong to assume that because American nuclear alerts appear to have been successful in past crises, similar actions will be equally successful in the future. Such a simplistic lesson ignores two central facts. First, it should not be forgotten that the resolution of both the Cuban missile crisis and the October 1973 crisis came about not just because the Soviets backed down when faced with a demonstration of American resolve, but also because the United States accepted an important compromise as the risk of war increased. In 1962, President Kennedy was willing to assure the Soviets privately that the American missiles in Turkey would be withdrawn and to offer a conditional pledge on the non-invasion of Cuba. In 1973, the United States increased its effort to save the Third Army and accepted a token Soviet force of "representatives" in Egypt. In both cases, American restraint was coupled with resolve at the conclusion of the crisis bargaining.

Even more importantly, there is "a dog that didn't bark" in both cases. Certainly one of the significant reasons why both the 1962 and 1973 crises were resolved short of war is that Moscow quickly backed down rather than escalate the conflict. Especially with respect to predicting what would happen if there was a mutual high level nuclear alert in a future superpower crisis, therefore, a simple reading of the past could be highly misleading. There is no evidence that the Soviet Union alerted its nuclear forces in response to American actions in October 1973. Although no conclusive evidence is available in the open literature about the level of alert of Soviet nuclear forces in October 1962,[87] it is clear that they did not alert forces to the degree that the

---

87. The Soviet Union announced that its nuclear forces were placed at a high state of readiness during the crisis on October 24 and Khrushchev repeated the claim on December 13, 1962. The CIA intelligence summary for October 25, however, reported that "we still see no signs of any crash procedures in measures to increase the readiness of Soviet armed forces"; and Lieutenant General Burchinal's recollection was that Khrushchev "never alerted a bomber or changed his own military posture one bit." Most American participants in the crisis believe that Khrushchev's statements in this regard were bluster. Others recall, however, that the Soviets may have matched the warheads with their missiles, while not fueling them, and may have loaded bombers

United States did and that American nuclear superiority was so overwhelming at the time that the American fear of a Soviet first strike was quite low.

Whatever the causes of this relative Soviet acquiescence when confronted with American nuclear threats in the past, it cannot confidently be expected to be repeated in the future. The growth of the Soviet nuclear arsenal has raised the probability of both forces being put on a high state of alert in a very severe crisis in the future. As Lieutenant General William Odom has noted, current conditions do not always resemble the past:

> Our traditional crisis management approach to the Soviets on the nuclear level has been to escalate our threats very early to the highest level, and then negotiate our way back down. But I don't think, with the changed balance of forces today, that I would feel very comfortable about going all the way up and saying okay, we are going to bargain down. I have a feeling that they would go on up with us. Considering current Soviet force structure, if I were advising Brezhnev I think I would feel confident about staying in the bargaining on the way up a little longer than before. So that raises real questions about whether we can continue to behave the way we have in the past.[88]

A "NO-ALERTS" POLICY?

It would be equally in error, however, to believe that because the nuclear alerts and accompanying conventional force operations taken in past crises were difficult to control, they must never be used again under any circumstances. Any suggestion for a "no-alerts" policy would ignore the fact that the purposes that nuclear alerts were meant to serve in the past are likely to remain important in future crises and are unlikely to be met, in all scenarios, by other means. Any decision to place nuclear forces on alert in the future will be an extremely dangerous step, but it is by no means clear that the inherent risks involved with an alert will always be greater than the dangers

---

with nuclear weapons, while not dispersing them to forward bases. The inconclusive evidence here reflects not only the continued classification of some of the American intelligence estimates of the time, but also two other factors: the lack of hard intelligence on this matter in October 1962 and the fact that American superiority allowed senior officials to be relatively less concerned about the Soviet alert status than about the operational status of the missiles in Cuba. *Pravda* and *Izvestia*, October 24, 1964, p. 1, in *Current Digest of the Soviet Press*, Vol. 14, No. 43, p. 4; *Pravda*, December 13, 1962, in *Current Digest of the Soviet Press*, Vol. 14, No. 51, p. 5; CIA Memorandum, The Crisis USSR/Cuba, 0600 25 Oct. 1962, JFK Library, Declassified Documents Reference System, Carrollton Press, Retrospective Collection no. 19A; Burchinal Oral History, p. 116; interviews.

88. William Odom, "C³I and Telecommunications at the Policy Level," *Incidental Paper*, Guest Presentations–Spring 1980. The Seminar on Command, Control, Communications, and Intelligence, the Program on Information Resources Policy, Harvard University.

produced by refraining from alerting forces. Even if the United States could threaten a devastating retaliatory response without generating its forces, the failure to alert nuclear forces in a severe crisis, especially one in which Soviet strategic forces were moving to a higher state of readiness, might tempt the leadership in Moscow to continue escalating the crisis in the belief that the United States was willing to back down.[89]

Extremely difficult judgments would have to be made, weighing the risks of alerting versus not alerting strategic forces, in numerous unlikely but possible scenarios: if the Soviets threaten to attack NATO's Central Front in the chaotic situation produced by a disintegration of the Eastern European bloc; if the Soviets threatened a nuclear strike against China; if an invasion of Saudi Arabia appeared imminent; or if there was a replay of the Cuban missile crisis with the Soviets placing missiles in Nicaragua or Cuba. In each of these cases, the risks of escalation and war are present whether or not nuclear forces are put on alert. The 1973 case illustrates the point. Putting forces on alert was not a risk-free option; neither, however, was allowing the Soviets to put forces into Egypt. Not only would such an action have set a dangerous precedent for future crises, but Soviet intervention might have led to direct combat with the Israelis, increasing the risk of American involvement. Indeed, the risk of escalation was inherent in the situation. The alert certainly highlighted this fact, but it did not create it.

In short, wisdom begins in this area with an awareness that one can err either on the side of being excessively cautious or excessively provocative. The following observations on what can go wrong when nuclear and conventional forces are put on a higher state of readiness in a crisis do not, therefore, mean that such steps must never be taken in the future. They do suggest, however, that if military alerts are deemed necessary in a crisis, it will be essential that they be controlled with the utmost prudence and discipline.

WHAT CAN GO WRONG?

Much of the recent public concern about nuclear war has focused on the frightening "Dr. Strangelove" scenario: the danger of an unauthorized use

---

89. This is precisely the danger that developed during ABC's *Nightline*, "The Crisis Game," broadcast November 23–25, 1983. Some of the American players argued an alert of American nuclear forces in response to a Soviet invasion of Iran and Soviet nuclear alert, fearing that an American strategic reaction would be provocative. Although the "President," in the end, did order American forces to be put on alert, it is worth noting that there was strong sentiment in

of nuclear weapons by a military commander leading to nuclear war. In normal peacetime circumstances, however, the numerous mechanical devices and organizational "checks and balances" that have been developed to prevent unauthorized use of weaponry make this path of accidental nuclear war highly unlikely.[90] In a severe crisis, with nuclear forces placed on extremely high levels of alert, some of these restrictions are lifted, however, in order to reduce the probability of a Soviet first-strike successfully "decapitating" the American arsenal. For very obvious reasons, the precise details of the process by which the devolution of command authority takes place and the extent of predelegation of authority to use nuclear weapons, if any in fact exists, are kept highly classified. Although layers of secrecy surround this issue, it is unlikely that predelegation extends to the first-use of offensive strategic nuclear weapons against the Soviet Union under any circumstances. Still, any predelegated authority to launch nuclear forces in retaliation after a Soviet attack upon the United States would produce serious problems with respect to controlling or terminating a nuclear exchange once begun and at least would raise the possibility of accidental war occurring through a warning or assessment failure during a superpower crisis.[91]

It would be a mistake, however, to focus exclusively on the danger of an accidental or unauthorized use of nuclear weapons. As the Cuban missile crisis demonstrated, a variety of incidents can occur during a crisis which are neither purely accidental nor unauthorized, but which nonetheless raise the danger of inadvertent escalation. In many of the cases, actions that may have been judged inappropriate by higher political or military authorities were taken by local military commanders who have both good military reasons for taking the action and ample discretionary authority to do so. Such incidents are likely to be a permanent danger in severe crises. Crises are unique and unpredictable. Military rules of engagement and delegations of authority must all be preplanned, however, and in crises there is often insufficient time to review such procedures and tailor them to the specific

---

the Control Group to escalate the crisis further if there had been a passive American reaction to the Soviet alert. Interviews with participants.

90. For discussions of the authority to use nuclear weapons see George H. Quester, "Presidential Authority and Nuclear Weapons," in *First Use of Nuclear Weapons: Preserving Responsible Control*, Hearings Before the Subcommitte on International Relations, 94th Congress, 1st Session, Washington D.C., 1976, pp. 212–223; Bracken, *Command and Control of Nuclear Forces*, pp. 21–25, 197–203; William M. Arkin (assisted by Richard Fieldhouse), "Nuclear Weapons Command, Control and Communications," *SIPRI Yearbook 1984*, pp. 460–470.

91. See Bracken, *Command and Control of Nuclear Forces*, pp. 56–57, 227–232.

confrontation at hand.[92] These resulting dangers are further compounded when conventional and nuclear forces are placed at higher conditions of alert because rules of engagement and delegations of authority can change in ways that may be inadequately understood by central authorities.

In addition, there is a danger that a movement toward a mutual high level alert in a serious crisis could put central authorities under severe pressure to take conventional escalatory steps that they would otherwise prefer to avoid. For example, in a severe crisis, in which both superpowers have alerted their nuclear forces to unprecedented levels, the national command authorities might feel extreme pressure to relieve the strategic arsenal from the danger of quick strike decapitation. One possible conventional option would be to attack the enemy's most threatening forces such as submarines patrolling off one's coasts.[93] Moreover, in any conventional war between the Soviet Union and the United States, during which nuclear forces would be at an extremely high state of alert, American leaders could authorize what it viewed as conventional attacks against Soviet conventional forces, which Moscow might view as attacks against its strategic forces. For example, an American ASW campaign against Soviet attack submarines in "forward areas" might be seen in Moscow, correctly or incorrectly, as an attack on Soviet strategic submarines.[94] Any one of these *authorized* escalatory steps might lead to uncontrolled escalation.

Finally, in the most extreme crisis, there is the possibility that either superpower's leadership might believe that a preemptive nuclear strike on the adversary's command centers with follow-on strikes at the arsenal itself was the only option it had left.[95] This desperate choice would only be plausible if it was believed that nuclear war was almost inevitable and that striking first provided the only hope of limiting the damage to one's own side. Alerting nuclear forces, however, cuts both ways in an assessment of the attractiveness of preemption. On the one hand, movement toward a high level nuclear alert by the adversary might be seen as evidence that his forces

---

92. For discussions of the importance of rules of engagement, see Alexander L. George, "Crisis Management: The Interaction of Political and Military Considerations," *Survival*, Vol. 26, No. 5 (September–October 1984), pp. 223–234, and Captain J. Ashley Roach, "Rules of Engagement," *Naval War College Review*, Vol. 36, No. 1 (January–February 1983), pp. 46–55.
93. Bracken, *Command and Control of Nuclear Forces*, p. 65.
94. See Barry R. Posen, "Inadvertent Nuclear War? Escalation and NATO's Northern Flank," *International Security*, Vol. 7, No. 2 (Fall 1982), pp. 28–54.
95. See John Steinbruner, "Nuclear Decapitation," *Foreign Policy*, Number 45 (Winter 1981–82), pp. 16–29.

are about to attack. On the other hand, a preemptive strike would certainly be far less effective against an alerted adversary. Indeed, one danger is that preemption could become a less unattractive option in a prolonged crisis, if an adversary's nuclear force suffered severe degradation in its alert status over time. Yet, although it is difficult to predict the likelihood of various scenarios that might lead to such desperate decisions, few analysts would ignore this danger in a severe crisis with current superpower arsenals.

CONTROLLING THE RISKS IN CRISES

Among the most critical questions that an American President would ask in a future crisis with the Soviet Union is whether nuclear forces should be alerted and, if so, which forces, when, and at what level. Such questions could only be addressed intelligently in light of the unique characteristics of the crisis in question. What are the relative interests of the U.S. and the U.S.S.R. in the stakes of the conflict? What are Soviet intentions? What are the military dimensions of the situation: how vulnerable are American forces and what alternatives to a nuclear alert exist that might enhance deterrence at critical moments? Because these complex factors would be so different in each specific confrontation between the United States and the Soviet Union, however, the study of past crises is less useful in advising decision-makers on whether to alert nuclear forces in the future than on how, if an alert is considered necessary, some of the inherent risks involved might be dampened. In particular, the quite different events of May 1960, October 1962, and October 1973 illuminate four persistent problems.

The first has to do with *alert authority*. In May 1960, not only did the JCS order a higher level of alert than Secretary Gates had intended, but a number of base commanders, with ample authority to do so, advanced their alert status higher than the JCS had ordered.[96] In October 1962, Admiral Thomas Moorer, then commander of the 7th Fleet in the Pacific, did not receive JCS orders to increase his DEFCON, but when he heard that President Kennedy was about to give a nationally televised speech on Cuba, Moorer immediately placed his forces on a high state of alert and sent his ships out to sea.[97] In

---

96. For example, Secretary Gates reported in Senate testimony that there "were in one or two instances some people who interpreted the JCS order as meaning that they would have a couple of more aircraft on alert, and in that case, they, on their own, recalled, I believe some pilots who were home or off duty to have approximately two more airplanes on an alert status. But this was done on their own, testing their own alert procedures under the broad order that was issued by the Joint Chiefs of Staff." *Events Incident to the Summit*, p. 133.
97. Interview with Admiral Thomas Moorer, April 10, 1984.

October 1973, numerous military commanders were simply unable to gather the necessary personnel together to implement DEFCON 3 without taking actions that broke the spirit of the "minimum public notice" request.

These incidents are only minor demonstrations of the degree to which alert authority rests in the hands of individual military commanders, an important point that is often poorly understood by civilian leaders. It is relatively well known, for example, that if warning of a Soviet attack is received from NORAD, the Commander of the Strategic Air Command has the authority to launch the bomber force into the air in order to protect it from immediate destruction, although he lacks the authority to order the B-52s to proceed toward the Soviet Union.[98] It is less well known that the senior controller in SAC's command post has the authority to increase SAC's alert status in less dramatic ways (for example, he can order the bombers on ground alert to start their engines—which would most likely be picked up by Soviet satellites),[99] or that the JCS has the authority to order dispersal and airborne alert.[100] And many political leaders are insufficiently aware of the degree to which all unified and specified commanders have the authority, unless specifically ordered not to, to place their forces on a higher state of alert if they believe that there has been an increase in the threat of attack on the forces. Indeed, even if a commander is ordered to alert his forces to a specific DEFCON, that order only provides him a list of the minimum steps that are required.

There are certainly excellent reasons for this command arrangement. It is a long-standing tradition that military commanders can take what they judge are necessary steps to protect their forces, and it is by no means clear that one would want to tamper with that tradition. It is quite clear, however, that decentralized alert authority makes any policymaker's belief that he can "fine-tune" alerts, intricately controlling the level of American responses to increases in Soviet command readiness, quite naïve. Any future decision to

---

98. No CINCSAC has ever used his authority to order a positive control (failsafe) launch of the bomber force, although General Thomas S. Power reports that he was "close to doing so several times" when the early warning systems incorrectly reported incoming missiles. Power, *Design for Survival*, pp. 156–157.

99. On June 3, 1980 upon receipt of warning that a number of SLBMs had been launched at the United States, the SAC officer directed all alert crews to move to the alert aircraft and start their engines, a procedure which was repeated again on June 6, 1980. U.S. Senate, Committee on Armed Services, *Recent False Alerts*, pp. 5, 7.

100. U.S. House of Representatives, *Hearings on Military Posture*, 96th Congress, 1st session, part 3, book 2, p. 2464 (cited in Arkin and Fieldhouse, "Nuclear Weapons Command, Control, and Communications").

alert forces should be made with a deep awareness that keeping the alert at the desired level will be extremely difficult, and the degree of further grave escalation uncertain.

The second insight derived from the cases is the identification of the *special problem of reconnaissance:* there were numerous examples of reconnaissance activity undertaken by military commanders that would not have been approved by higher authorities for fear that the actions would appear provocative to the Soviets. Generally speaking, they fall into two categories. First, there are reconnaissance activities directly related to the military operations being threatened: the U.S. Navy's reconnaissance missions close into Cuban territory are clearly one example, and the unauthorized activities of the CIA's Task Force W are another. Second, there are espionage or other activities that are not directly related to the military operations being prepared, but that could nonetheless be provocative. Here, the Alaskan U-2 incident is the primary example.

Although improved communications have increased the technical capability of central authorities to control small-scale military or reconnaissance operations, and the advent of satellites has decreased the importance of certain kinds of potentially provocative reconnaissance activities, this problem remains a critical one. Potentially dangerous activities, which could contain elements of both categories, are numerous: certain Air Force Electronic Intelligence (Elint) missions that require penetration of Soviet airspace to gain Soviet radar signatures;[101] reconnaissance activities that a local commander would want if war appeared likely (for example, commanders of carrier task forces would desire information on enemy air bases); "Holystone" reconnaissance missions by U.S. Navy attack submarines that reportedly have included moving into Soviet territorial waters to "plug into" otherwise secure underwater Soviet military communication cables;[102] and lastly, reconnaissance aircraft which fly near Soviet territory to monitor Soviet weapons

---

101. According to two former Air Force Communications specialists, the National Security Agency (NSA) occasionally sent RC–135s on penetration missions into Soviet air space in order to activate air.defense systems. Tom Bernard and T. Edward Eskelson, *The Denver Post,* September 13, 1983, p. 3B, as cited in David M. Johnson, *Korean Airlines Incident: U.S. Intelligence Disclosures,* Incidental Paper I-84-2, Program on Information Resources Policy, Harvard University, April 1984, p. 40, fn. 118. It is also worth noting that, according to Air Force estimates, Soviet aircraft have breached American airspace six or seven times since 1961. See "Air Force's Alaska Pilots Await Call to Intercept Soviet Craft," *The New York Times,* July 8, 1984, p. 34.
102. "Submarines of U.S. Stage Spy Missions Inside Soviet Waters," *The New York Times,* May 25, 1975, pp. 1, 42; and *CIA: The Pike Report* (Nottingham, England: Spokesman Books, 1977), pp. 219–221.

testing. Again, it is not clear that one would want to stand down all potentially provocative reconnaissance missions in a crisis; some may be deemed
essential despite the danger involved. But it is clear that it would require a
very active and properly staffed Secretary of Defense to make the proper
decisions in such a matter. At a minimum, he would have to be aware of
the potential danger involved here and carefully review the lists of monthly
reconnaissance missions previously scheduled by the Joint Reconnaissance
Center as well as any new missions created by the enhanced alert status of
American forces. In extreme cases, central authorities would be required to
undergo a lengthy briefing in strategic reconnaissance activities at a moment
when time was of the essence.

The third point that the nuclear alerts of the past confirm is that the *domestic
political dimension of the problem cannot be ignored.* In two of the incidents,
policymakers incorrectly believed that the military alert could be kept secret
and therefore would not produce an immediate public reaction in the United
States. In both cases, the public reaction was probably not so great that the
desired "signal" of resolve was overwhelmed by the "noise" of domestic
opposition to the alert, although that could be a distinct possibility in other
circumstances.

The potential importance of the domestic political reaction to a nuclear
alert, however, dwarfs these considerations. In a severe superpower crisis,
if nuclear forces were placed at the highest levels of alert, the domestic
economy would be quickly affected: commercial air traffic would, at some
level of alert, most likely be grounded and the stock market might drop
precipitously. In extreme cases, a decision to put nuclear forces on a high
state of alert might trigger spontaneous evacuation from urban areas. Such
events, or even the possibility of such events, would undoubtedly influence
the decisions of policymakers in a crisis. Putting nuclear forces on alert must
not be conceived of as only a military operation with important diplomatic
and strategic implications. Particularly if a crisis lasted for a long period of
time and forces were kept at a high state of readiness, such actions could
also have grave domestic effects, which could produce critical pressures for
escalation or deescalation.[103]

---

103. For discussions of the political and strategic implications of a prolonged nuclear crisis, see
Paul Bracken, "Command and Control for a Long War," *Air Force Magazine*, April 1980, pp. 50–
54, and Paul Bracken and Martin Shubik, "Strategic War: What are the Questions and Who
Should Ask Them?," *Technology in Society*, Vol. 4, No. 3 (1982), pp. 174–175.

The final point is that many of the potentially dangerous developments in past crises occurred because *civilian authorities did not thoroughly understand the military operations they were contemplating.* This is, of course, far from being a new problem. Indeed, in the early nineteenth century, Clausewitz observed that political leaders giving military orders are often like men who are learning a foreign language; they often mean to express one idea, but actually say something quite different.[104]

The alert procedures and the rules of engagement of the American Unified and Specified Commands are exceedingly complex, and no Secretary of Defense or Ex Comm can be expected to absorb the details, or even to learn all the essential elements, in highly pressured moments of crisis. Clearly, following Clausewitz's metaphor, if we are to resolve future nuclear crises without war, it will be necessary for central civilian authorities to know the language well. Unfortunately, there are numerous reasons to be pessimistic on this score.

First, the American domestic political system produces a relatively high turnover rate in the office of the Secretary of Defense. Although each new Secretary of Defense, of course, receives briefings on this subject amid hundreds of others, it takes time and experience to understand the complexities involved. Crises, however, do not necessarily wait for this "education" to occur. Thomas Gates had been in office for only six months when he ordered a "quiet" alert in May 1960. Similarly, Casper Weinberger had been in office for approximately three months when, according to Alexander Haig's account, he did not fully understand what alert orders he had given to American military forces after President Reagan was shot on March 30, 1981.[105]

Secondly, while it is clearly the responsibility of the professional military to educate civilian authorities in these matters, there are often disincentives involved. The military's deep resentment of what they view as the "micro-management" excesses of the 1960s can often produce a reluctance to expose civilian authorities to what is seen as too much detail about alert procedures. There is a fear, which is not entirely unjustified, that if civilians know about operational aspects of alerts and other military procedures, they will be tempted to "muck-up" the process in a crisis. This is not, however, a good

---

104. Clausewitz, *On War* (Princeton, N.J.: Princeton University Press, 1976), p. 608.
105. Haig, *Caveat*, pp. 157–161. Also, see "Weinberger Quarrels with Haig's Account," *The New York Times*, March 29, 1984, p. 25.

reason for keeping authorities in the dark; it is only a good reason to educate them more thoroughly. There will always be a tendency on the part of central political authorities to improvise in crises. The dilemmas here can be made less dangerous only if civilians are made aware of them and political and military authorities together minimize potential problems.

Lastly, although the Secretary of Defense is primarily responsible for these issues, he is responsible for many other things, too. There are budgets to build, speeches to give, meetings to attend. Because crises occur so rarely, there can often be a tendency to push crisis management issues to the back of the agenda. This temptation must be resisted. Nuclear crises are not likely to be entirely avoidable in the future, and our ability to control them will be largely determined by the thought and energy given to this problem in advance.

To the Nuclear Brink

Eisenhower, Dulles, and the Quemoy-Matsu Crisis

Gordon H. Chang

Shortly after the first anniversary of the end of the Korean War, the United States confronted the possibility of renewed hostilities with the People's Republic of China. On September 3, 1954, while Secretary of State John Foster Dulles was in Manila finalizing the establishment of the Southeast Asia Treaty Organization (SEATO), Chinese Communist coastal batteries began heavy shelling of Jinmen (Quemoy)[1], one of the small Nationalist-held islands off the coast of the China mainland. Acting Secretary of Defense Robert Anderson alerted President Dwight D. Eisenhower that the intensity of the attack seemed a prelude to an all-out assault. Over the next nine months the United States, in supporting the Nationalists' defense of these islands, lurched toward disaster—in Eisenhower's own recollection, the crisis almost caused a "split between the United States and nearly all its allies" and seemingly carried the country to the "edge of war."[2]

The president's critics at the time accused him of bringing the country to the verge of war over real estate of little consequence. Much of the historical evaluation was not much kinder. Early literature on Eisenhower portrayed him as a "weak president," surrounded by advisers who wanted to use the crisis in the Strait to bring about a war with China. His administration, it was said, pursued an inflexible foreign policy that assumed, despite evidence to the contrary, a monolithic "international communism." The picture drawn by even those sympathetic to Eisenhower was one of an unimaginative president preoccupied with maintaining the status quo.[3]

The author would like to thank Barton Bernstein, David Kennedy, and John Lewis for their helpful comments on an earlier draft of this article and the MacArthur Foundation for financial support.

Gordon H. Chang is a historian at the International Strategic Institute at Stanford University and Coordinator of the Project on Peace and Cooperation in the Asian-Pacific Region.

1. The *pinyin* romanization system will be used for Chinese names in this essay, except in the title. Traditional spellings will appear in parentheses after the first use of the *pinyin*.
2. Robert Anderson to Eisenhower, September 3, 1954, Dwight D. Eisenhower Papers as President of the United States, 1953–1961 (Ann Whitman File), Eisenhower Library, Abilene, Kansas, hereafter Eisenhower Papers (AW), Dulles-Herter Series, Box 3, Dulles, Sept. 1954 (2); Dwight D. Eisenhower, *Mandate for Change, 1953–1956* (New York: Doubleday, 1963), p. 459.
3. Marquis William Childs, *Eisenhower: Captive Hero, A Critical Study of the General and the President*

In recent years, in contrast, a "revisionist" literature on Eisenhower has tried to draw an entirely different picture. Now, he is seen as a commanding chief executive, and is applauded for deft handling of the 1954–55 confrontation. One recent account characterizes Eisenhower's policy as one of "restraint and avoidance of conflict in the Taiwan Strait."[4]

But newly available documentary evidence contradicts many of the revisionist contentions and shows that Eisenhower actually brought the country to the "nuclear brink," far closer to war than a distraught public feared in 1955, closer than Eisenhower acknowledged in his own memoirs, and closer than most historians have heretofore even suspected.[5]

Among the revelations of the new evidence, three are most important: (1) the Eisenhower administration made a secret commitment to Jiang Jieshi (Chiang Kai-shek) to help defend Jinmen and Mazu (Matsu) in the event of a major Communist attack; (2) Eisenhower, despite his public ambiguity on

(New York: Harcourt, Brace, 1958), pp. 188–212, 204, 291; Townsend Hoopes, *The Devil and John Foster Dulles* (Boston: Little, Brown, 1973), pp. 262–273; Foster Rhea Dulles, *American Policy Toward Communist China, 1949–1969* (New York: Thomas Y. Crowell, 1972), pp. 130–160; Peter Lyon, *Eisenhower: Portrait of the Hero* (Boston: Little, Brown, 1974), pp. 632, 637, 853–54. Other literature on the 1954–55 crisis: O. Edmund Clubb, "Formosa and the Offshore Islands in American Foreign Policy, 1950–1955," *Political Science Quarterly*, Vol. 74, No. 4 (Dec. 1959), pp. 517–31; Morton H. Halperin and Tang Tsou, "United States Policy toward the Offshore Islands," *Public Policy*, Vol. 15 (1966), pp. 119–38; Alexander George and Richard Smoke, *Deterrence in American Foreign Policy* (New York: Columbia University Press, 1971), pp. 266–94; J.H. Kalicki, *The Pattern of Sino-American Crises: Political-Military Interactions in the 1950s* (London: Cambridge University Press, 1975), pp. 120–155; and Thomas E. Stolper, *China, Taiwan, and the Offshore Islands* (Armonk, N.Y.: M. E. Sharpe, 1985).

4. Leonard H. D. Gordon, "United States Opposition to Use of Force in the Taiwan Strait, 1954–1962," *Journal of American History*, Vol. 72, No. 3 (December 1985), pp. 637–660. See also Robert Divine, *Eisenhower and the Cold War* (New York: Oxford University Press, 1981); Stephen E. Ambrose, *Eisenhower*, Vol. II: *The President* (New York: Simon and Schuster, 1985); and Bennett C. Rushkoff, "Eisenhower, Dulles and the Quemoy-Matsu Crisis, 1954–1955," *Political Science Quarterly*, Vol. 96, No. 3 (Fall 1981), pp. 465–480.

5. Declassified material used in this essay includes memoranda of discussions between Eisenhower and his advisers and of top-level policy-making meetings, diary entries, cables, correspondence, and position papers. The federal government has released many of these documents in just the last few years, and they are kept in different locations throughout the country. The Dwight D. Eisenhower Library in Abilene, Kansas holds the Dwight D. Eisenhower Papers as President of the United States, 1953–1961 (Ann Whitman File), (hereafter Eisenhower Papers [AW]); John Foster Dulles Papers, 1951–1959 (hereafter Dulles Papers); and papers from the White House Office, Office of the Special Assistant for National Security Affairs (hereafter WHO OSANSA). The National Archives in Washington, D.C., in its Diplomatic Branch, holds papers from the Department of State and, in its Military Branch, papers from the Joint Chiefs of Staff. Many State Department documents for the period covered by this essay are reproduced in Department of State, *Foreign Relations of the United States* (hereafter *FRUS*). The Seeley G. Mudd Library of Princeton University holds the personal papers of John Foster Dulles (hereafter Princeton Dulles Papers), and the Karl Lott Rankin Papers.

the subject, was privately determined to defend the islands, and to use nuclear weapons if necessary; and (3) in April 1955, as the crisis reached its peak, Eisenhower and Dulles proposed to Jiang, if he would withdraw from Jinmen and Mazu, that the United States would establish a 500-mile blockade of China's coastal waters until the Communists renounced their intention to liberate Taiwan.

Taken together, these points make it plain that for a time in the spring of 1955, the Eisenhower administration pursued policies that could have led to war with China by either of two paths. If the Chinese Communists had attacked Jinmen or Mazu in force while Eisenhower's secret pledge to defend them was in effect, or if Jiang had accepted the evacuation/blockade plan, Washington almost certainly would have found itself in direct military conflict with Beijing. In such a conflict, Eisenhower was fully prepared to use nuclear weapons.

The fact that war was averted was due to Jiang's refusal to give up the offshore islands, thus releasing Washington from the blockade plan, and to the conciliatory gesture of Chinese Premier Zhou Enlai (Chou En-lai) to the United States in late April 1955 which dramatically reduced the tensions in the region. Ironically, it was thus the actions of the two directly belligerent parties, the Chinese Nationalists and Chinese Communists, that pulled the United States back from the brink.

The Eisenhower administration's truculence belies the picture which the revisionist historians have tried to paint of a restrained and supple president. Eisenhower was not a compliant chief executive—the revisionists have dispelled that misconception—but he must bear primary responsibility for leading the country to an untenable position in April 1955 and to the verge of military conflict with China. Moreover, the new evidence reveals that Eisenhower's leadership was not as skillful and steady as revisionists have claimed. At two critical junctures of the crisis—in late January when the administration committed itself to the defense of Jinmen and Mazu, and in April, when it proposed the evacuation/blockade plan—Eisenhower equivocated, seriously confusing his subordinates and infuriating the Nationalist government.

September, 1954: Background of the Crisis

In 1954, the United States believed that the legal status of Jinmen, Mazu, Dachen (Tachen), and several other clusters of small offshore islands under the control of the Nationalists differed from that of Taiwan and the Penghus

(Pescadores). The latter had been colonized by the Japanese after their victory over China in the war of 1895 and, even though the jurisdiction of Taiwan and the Penghus had reverted to China following World War II, the United States considered their ultimate disposition still unsettled. On the other hand, the offshore islands—some thirty in number just off the central coast of the mainland—had remained subject to China, and there was no legal question that they were Chinese territory. As the Nationalists retreated from the mainland to Taiwan in 1949, they retained control of the offshore islands for use as staging areas to harass the Communists. Jinmen, Mazu, and the others actually possessed questionable value for the defense of Taiwan, over one hundred miles away on the opposite side of the Taiwan Strait. The several thousand inhabitants of the small islands were mainly farmers and fishermen. (See map, p. 123.)

Eisenhower described many of the offshore islands as practically within "wading distance" of the mainland shore, including two important harbors. The Jinmen group is just two miles from the port of Xiamen (Amoy); the Mazu group is ten miles from the port of Fuzhou (Foochow). Both groups lie opposite Taiwan. The third main group, the Dachens, is located two hundred miles north of Taiwan.

The Communists and Nationalists had occasionally skirmished over the islands since 1949. By the start of the 1954 crisis, with American help and encouragement, Jiang had transformed them into formidable forward positions. More than fifty thousand Nationalist soldiers, many of them first-line regulars, were stationed on Jinmen alone. Apparently, Jiang was preparing the island as stepping stones for his future invasion of the mainland.[6]

The United States opposed any effort by the Chinese Communists to expand the amount of territory under their control and was fully committed to the Nationalist regime, which refused to budge from any territory it held. Since 1949, Washington had provided $1.6 billion in economic and military aid to the Nationalists.[7] Would the United States go to war with China over these insignificant specks of land? A few days after the Communists started

---

6. George and Smoke, *Deterrence in American Foreign Policy*, pp. 266–74; Stewart Alsop, "The Story Behind Quemoy: How We Drifted Close to War," *Saturday Evening Post*, December 13, 1958, pp. 26–27, 86–88; memorandum of conversation, Yu Ta-wei, Walter Robertson and others, December 6, 1955, Office of Chinese Affairs, 1948–56, Box 53, Offshore Islands, 1955, RG 59, National Archives.

7. John Foster Dulles, "Preliminary draft of possible statement of position for communication to the Republic of China," April 4, 1955, Office of Chinese Affairs, 1948–56, Box 53, Offshore Islands, 1955, RG 59, National Archives.

shelling Jinmen in September 1954, Secretary of State John Foster Dulles told the National Security Council (NSC) that the crisis was a "horrible dilemma."[8]

From the start, the administration was divided. Chairman of the Joint Chiefs of Staff (JCS) Admiral Arthur W. Radford, speaking for the majority of the JCS, advocated an all-out defense of the offshore islands as critical to the protection of Taiwan and the use of atomic weapons if the Communists launched a major assault. Radford believed that the United States had to take a stand in the interests of the global battle against communism. "If we fail to resist this aggression," Radford told a September 12 meeting of the NSC, "we commit the United States further to a negative policy which could result in a progressive loss of free world strength to local aggression until or unless all-out conflict is forced upon us."[9]

But the majority of the NSC, reluctant to face the prospect of another war with China, backed away from Radford's militarist line. Secretary of Defense Charles Wilson feared that involvement would inject the United States into the middle of the on-going Chinese civil war. Eisenhower was skeptical about the military importance of the islands for the defense of Taiwan. Though he believed their loss would be a serious blow to the morale of the Nationalists, he suspected that war would not be necessary to hold the islands. Dulles, likewise, wanted neither all-out war with China nor surrender of the islands under duress. He and the president opted to try for a way to defuse the immediate situation, while backing the Nationalists.[10]

In the following weeks, the administration publicly condemned the Communist threat and re-emphasized its support for the defense of Taiwan and the Penghus. But to keep Beijing guessing as to U.S. intentions, Eisenhower and Dulles left vague whether the commitment to the Nationalists extended to the offshore islands under their control. The two also wanted to avoid alienating European and Asian allies, who strongly opposed American involvement in the offshore area. To try to strengthen the American diplomatic position and limit the crisis, Dulles went to work with Western nations on a United Nations plan for a ceasefire, from which might develop possible

8. Memorandum of discussion at the 213th meeting of the NSC, September 9, 1954, *FRUS*: 1952–54, Vol. XIV, pp. 583–595; memorandum of discussion at the 214th meeting of the NSC, September 12, 1954, ibid., pp. 613–24.
9. 214th NSC meeting, ibid.; Radford to Wilson, September 11, 1954, *FRUS*: 1952–54, Vol. XIV, pp. 598–610.
10. Memorandum of 214th meeting of the NSC, Sept. 12, 1954, *FRUS*, 1952–54, Vol. XIV, pp. 619–624.

neutralization of the offshore islands. Simultaneously, to remove any doubt about Washington's support for the Nationalists, he concluded and signed in early December a "mutual defense" treaty with Jiang's regime. The treaty explicitly covered Taiwan and the Penghus and provided for extension to other Nationalist-held territories upon the mutual agreement of the two signatories. In return for this protection and to ensure that it would not be drawn into a precipitous war with China, Washington, however, required Jiang to pledge secretly that he would take no more offensive actions against the mainland without explicit U.S. approval.[11] Admiral Radford was so unhappy with these public and private agreements that he charged they were leading the way to the fall of all of Asia to communism.[12]

January 1955: A "Turn for the Worse"

In spite of the administration's efforts, the situation in the Taiwan Strait continued to deteriorate in late 1954, and, in Eisenhower's description, took a "turn for the worse" at the start of 1955. Both the Communists and Nationalists predicted imminent widespread hostilities. On January 10, one hundred planes from the mainland raided the Dachens, and on January 18 Communist forces overwhelmed one thousand Nationalist guerrillas (and eight American military personnel) on Yijiang (Ichiang) Island, just north of the Dachens. The Nationalists counter-attacked with air strikes on mainland ports and shipping. From Washington's vantage point, all-out war for the offshore islands and perhaps Taiwan itself seemed to loom. Eisenhower concluded that since the Dachens were too far from Taiwan's airfields, they were not as defensible militarily as Jinmen and Mazu. Nevertheless, he decided that the United States had to clarify its position. On January 19, Eisenhower agreed with Dulles and Radford that the remaining offshore islands could not be held without "U.S. interposition." As Eisenhower wrote

---

11. Dulles memorandum, September 12, 1954, *FRUS: 1952–54*, Vol. XIV, pp. 611–613; memorandum of discussion at the 215th meeting of the NSC, September 24, 1954, ibid., pp. 658–660; Dulles to Robertson, October 7, 1954, ibid., p. 708; Dulles memorandum, meeting with Eisenhower, October 18, 1954, ibid., p. 770; Dulles, report to the NSC, October 28, 1954, ibid., pp. 809–812; Mutual Defense Treaty Between the United States of America and the Republic of China, December 2, 1954, *Department of State Bulletin*, December 13, 1954, p. 899.
12. Goodpaster, memorandum, meeting of Dulles, Radford and others, October 29, 1954, *FRUS: 1952–54*, Vol. XIV, pp. 814–16; Radford memorandum, October 29, 1954, ibid., pp. 817–19; memorandum of discussion at the 221st meeting of the NSC, November 2, 1954, ibid., pp. 827–839.

in his memoirs, "the time had come to draw the line" over what territories the United States would fight for.[13] Dulles, on Eisenhower's instructions, confidentially informed Nationalist Foreign Minister George K. C. Yeh, who was visiting Washington, that the United States would publicly announce its intention to join in the defense of Jinmen, if the Nationalists withdrew from the Dachens.[14]

On the next day, January 20, 1955, the NSC argued heatedly about the path Eisenhower and Dulles had chosen. On behalf of the president, Dulles reviewed U.S. policy: the United States had obscured its public stand to confuse the enemy. This policy, though, had begun to "backfire." The Communists now seemed convinced the United States would not fight for any of the offshore islands. Dulles recommended that, while continuing to seek a ceasefire through the UN, the administration should ask Congress to grant to the president the explicit power to commit U.S. forces to the defense of Taiwan and related areas not specifically mentioned in the mutual defense treaty. These "related areas" would include Jinmen, and probably Mazu, so long as the Communists professed an intention to attack Taiwan. The United States had to remove any ambiguity about what territories it would defend. Leaving the U.S. position unclear, according to Dulles, would now create "greater risk."[15]

Robert Cutler, the president's national security adviser, Treasury Secretary George Humphrey, and Defense Secretary Charles Wilson all vehemently objected to Dulles's view. They argued that the United States would be drawn directly into war with China over territory of minimal value. Wilson said the United States should hold just Taiwan and the Penghus, and "let the others go." The president, however, vigorously endorsed everything Dulles advo-

---

13. Dulles memorandum, meeting with Eisenhower and Radford, January 19, 1955, *FRUS*: 1955–57, Vol. II, pp. 41–44; Eisenhower, *Mandate*, p. 466. Seven of the eight U.S. personnel were evacuated before Yijiang's capture. According to a historian in the Chinese Academy of Social Sciences who cites previously closed Chinese sources, Beijing employed limited military means as a political instrument to draw attention to the Taiwan question. Beijing wanted only to take Yijiang but not Jinmen or Mazu and did not want to confront the United States. After the Communists took Yijiang, in fact, Defense Minister Peng Dehuai and the Central Military Commission ordered Chinese forces to postpone their attack on the Dachens to avoid a clash with the United States. He Di, "The Evolution of the People's Republic of China's Policy Toward the Offshore Islands," unpublished paper, 1987.
14. McConaughy memorandum, meeting of Dulles, Yeh and others, January 19, 1955; Cutler memorandum, meeting of Dulles, Hoover and others, January 19, 1955; both, *FRUS*: 1955–57, Vol. II, pp. 46–48.
15. Memorandum of discussion at the 232nd meeting of the NSC, January 20, 1955, Eisenhower Papers (AW) NSC Series, Box 6, NSC Summaries of Discussion.

cated. The Dachens could be given up, he conceded, but unless the United States was prepared "completely to discount Formosa," the NSC had to make up its mind about Jinmen and Mazu, the most important remaining offshore islands. If Jiang lost these, the damage to Nationalist morale might be irreparable. Ever since many of Jiang's forces surrendered without a fight in 1949, Washington had doubted the loyalty and determination of Jiang's forces. Even a symbolic setback might undermine the entire Nationalist cause. According to Eisenhower, a statement of U.S. resolve would reduce the danger of war with China and correct the current "dangerous drift" in policy. In any case, the president said, it was clear to him that Jinmen and Mazu "were the outposts for the defense of Formosa."[16]

The NSC continued its discussion the following day. Eisenhower remained adamant in his demand that Congress give him broad general authority to defend the islands under Nationalist control. He told the NSC he was "absolutely determined" to avoid at all costs "another Yalu River sanctuary situation in any struggle over Quemoy." Eisenhower wanted no restraints if the United States became involved, and while he wished to avoid being pinned down to a permanent defense of Jinmen and Mazu, he would not abandon them as long as the Communists menaced the islands. Eisenhower said the United States might change its policy in the future after tensions eased, but at present the United States had to help hold the islands to protect Taiwan. According to the record of the discussion, Eisenhower made his point abundantly clear: everyone present, he said, should be sure of one thing—no matter how a Congressional resolution was worded, if there was an emergency during this crisis, he would do whatever had to be done to protect the vital interests of the United States, "even if his actions should be interpreted as acts of war." Eisenhower said he "would rather be impeached than fail to do his duty."[17]

Three days later Eisenhower sent his special request to Congress. On January 28, 1955, the Senate, following the House of Representatives, passed what became known as the Formosa Resolution, giving the president a virtual blank check. The resolution authorized the president to employ the armed

---

16. Ibid. A draft message for Congress, which Dulles wrote for Eisenhower following the NSC meeting, specifically mentioned Jinmen and Mazu as territories that the United States would help defend. The draft was not used. Dulles, "Draft message from the President to the Congress," January 20, 1955, ibid., pp. 83–85.
17. Memorandum of discussion at the 233rd meeting of the NSC, Jan. 21, 1955, Eisenhower Papers (AW), NSC Series, Box 6, NSC Summaries of Discussion.

forces of the United States for the protection of Taiwan, the Penghus, and "related positions and territories of that area now in friendly hands." Eisenhower, though, had changed his mind about publicly naming which offshore islands he would defend. None were specified. Eisenhower said that the United States would intervene only if a Communist attack appeared to be preliminary to an assault on Taiwan itself. James Reston of the *New York Times* called the United States line "calculated imprecision."[18] This ambiguity was selective, however: on January 31, Washington directed its ambassador on Taiwan, Karl Rankin, to inform Jiang *privately* of the U.S. intention to defend Jinmen and Mazu during the present crisis. In exchange for its commitment to Jinmen and Mazu, the United States received Jiang's agreement to withdraw his forces from the Dachens.[19] The islands' twenty-four thousand civilians and soldiers were, with the assistance of the U.S. Seventh Fleet, evacuated a few days later.[20]

Despite his compliance, Jiang was livid with Washington. His understanding, based on Dulles's talk with Foreign Minister Yeh on January 19, had been that the United States would make *public* its explicit commitment to Jinmen and Mazu. Even though Dulles and Robertson had informed the Nationalists of the administration's decision not to make its commitment public, Jiang had insisted that Washington live up to its original proposal or he would not withdraw from the Dachens. Although he felt double-crossed, he finally relented under American pressures. Just before the evacuation of the Dachens, Radford and Dulles's subordinates in the State Department

18. Public Law 4, January 29, 1955, *FRUS*: 1955–57, Vol. II, pp. 162–63; *New York Times*, April 7, 1955, p. 13. A top-secret unsigned memorandum from someone in the State Department to Eisenhower explicitly warned of the danger of a vague U.S. position. If the Communists "are left in ignorance of our intentions as to Quemoy and Matsu," read the memo, "they might stumble into a war with us, not believing that we would react. They could then allege with some plausibility that we had failed to state our position in advance and that if we had done so hostilities could have been averted." Unsigned memorandum, "Draft memorandum for the president," Feb. 1955, RG 59, Office of Chinese Affairs 1948–56, Box 53, Offshore Islands 1955, National Archives.
19. Goodpaster memorandum, meeting with Eisenhower, Hoover, Radford and others, January 30, 1955, WHO OSANSA, NSC Series, Briefing Notes Subseries, Box 17, Taiwan and Offshore Islands, Eisenhower Library; Karl Rankin, Offshore Islands Chronology of Events, June 3, 1955, Rankin Papers, Box 28, Re: Off-shore Islands, Princeton University; Hoover cable to Rankin, January 31, 1955, *FRUS*: 1955–57, Vol. II, pp. 182–184. Wellington Koo, the Nationalists' ambassador to the United States, also received the United States promise. See Koo, diary entries, January 27, 29, 31 and February 3, 1955, Wellington Koo Papers, Diaries, No. 34, January 1, 1955–August 31, 1955, Box 220, Columbia University.
20. Briscoe to Eisenhower, February 12, 1955, RG 218, Records of the Joint Chiefs of Staff, Box 6, 091 China (Feb.–Mar. 1955), National Archives.

reviewed the confused situation and concluded that Jiang's "misunderstanding" about the U.S. position was legitimate. The officials admitted that even they were unclear as to exactly what agreements the administration had reached with the Nationalists about the Dachens.[21]

February–March, 1955: U.S. Preparations for Nuclear War

Following the fall of the Dachens, the Communists continued to build their airfields, artillery emplacements, and roads on the mainland adjacent to Jinmen and Mazu in what the administration viewed as preparations for an eventual assault. Dulles feared that the United States was running out of options to end the crisis without wider hostilities. The UN ceasefire plan was getting nowhere—neither the Nationalists nor the Communists would go along with the idea; Jiang would not budge from Jinmen and Mazu; and the United States had committed itself to backing the Nationalists.[22] There was nothing else to do, Eisenhower told the NSC in mid-February, but "to watch the situation as it develops on a day-to-day basis." He reminded the NSC of his belief that the surrender of the offshore islands would result in the collapse of Jiang's government. The president coolly joked of Jiang, that the United States was now in the hands of "a fellow who hasn't anything to lose."[23]

Indeed, the United States was backing itself into a corner, helped along by Jiang who was certainly no puppet of Washington. With peacetime warmaking discretion granted by the Formosa Resolution, Eisenhower staked

21. Cable, Rankin to Department of State, January 30, 1955, *FRUS: 1955–57*, Vol. II, pp. 167–168; Scott, Memorandum of Conversation, Hoover, Radford and others, January 30, 1955, ibid., pp. 168–172; Ogburn, "U.S. Commitments to GRC," February 1, 1955, RG 59, Office of Chinese Affairs, 1948–56, Box 51, Offshore Islands 1955, National Archives. Dulles and Charles Bohlen, the American ambassador in Moscow, were uneasy with the continuing public vagueness of the U.S. position. Dulles at one point thought it would be necessary to inform the Chinese Communists about the American commitment through confidential channels. This was never done. There seem to be several reasons why Dulles and Eisenhower changed their minds about making a public commitment to Jinmen and Mazu. Pressure from the British was one reason. The British threatened to scuttle the UN effort, if an announcement was made. But Eisenhower also personally seemed to favor a vague public policy. See Cable, Dulles to Bohlen, January 22, 1955, *FRUS: 1955–57*, Vol. II, pp. 111–112; Cable, Bohlen to Dulles, January 23, 1955, ibid., pp. 114–115; Merchant, memorandum of conversation, Dulles, Makins, and others, January 20, 1955, ibid., pp. 86–89; and MacArthur, Memorandum of conversation, Eisenhower, Hoover, and others, January 30, 1955, ibid., pp. 173–176.
22. Dulles to State, February 21, 1955, ibid., pp. 299–300.
23. Memorandum of discussion at the 237th Meeting of the NSC, Feb. 17, 1955, Eisenhower Papers (AW), NSC Series, Box 6, NSC Summaries of Discussion.

his own personal reputation and the prestige of the United States on the defense of the tenuous Nationalist cause, now centered on the offshore islands. Their loss to a Communist assault would have been humiliating and devastating to American credibility.[24] Washington would not have allowed the destruction of one quarter of Jiang's best troops and the loss of Jinmen and Mazu. Undoubtedly, the United States would have joined actively in their defense, even without the secret pledge to Jiang.

During a trip to the Far East at the end of February, Dulles concluded that the situation was even more serious than he had thought. Apparently neither the mutual defense treaty with the Nationalist regime nor the Formosa Resolution had discouraged the Communists. Dulles became convinced that the Communists intended to take Taiwan by force, reversing his previous estimate that they were immediately interested only in the offshore islands. The fanaticism of the Communists, in Dulles's new view, exceeded even his original alarm.[25] Upon his return to Washington on March 6, Dulles reported to the president that if the Communists crushed the Nationalists on Jinmen and Mazu, the reaction would be catastrophic on Taiwan and for the rest of Asia. The two reaffirmed their commitment to the defense of the two island groups and concluded that this would require drastic measures, including "the use of atomic missiles," by which they evidently meant tactical nuclear weapons. To prepare public opinion, Eisenhower directed Dulles to state in a nationally televised speech on March 8 that the administration considered atomic weapons "interchangeable with the conventional weapons" in the American arsenal.[26]

On March 10, Dulles reported to the NSC what he had discussed with the president, stating that the Communists were determined to take Taiwan and the United States had to realize that a fight with them was, thus, now a question of "time not fact." He also expressed concern about the loyalty of Jiang's troops. If the Communists succeeded in landing on Taiwan, Jiang's forces might disintegrate. The United States should try to avoid involvement for the next several weeks during sensitive discussions on strengthening

24. Lawrence Freedman, "The First Two Generations of Nuclear Strategists," in Peter Paret, ed., *Makers of Modern Strategy: From Machiavelli to the Nuclear Age* (Princeton: Princeton University Press, 1986), pp. 740–43.
25. Dulles to State, Feburary 25, 1955, *FRUS*: 1955–57, Vol. II, pp. 307–10; Minnich minutes of cabinet meeting, February 11, 1955, ibid., pp. 352–53.
26. Dulles memorandum, meeting with Eisenhower, March 6, 1955, Dulles Papers, White House Memoranda, Box 3, Meetings with the President 1955 (4), Eisenhower Library.

western European unity, but the administration had to start preparing the American people for hostilities involving U.S. forces in the Taiwan area and for the use of nuclear weapons in the defense of the offshore islands. "The need for such use, to make up for deficiency in conventional forces," said Dulles, "outweighs the repercussive effect of such use upon free world nations in Europe and the Far East. United States and world public opinion must be prepared." Dulles predicted that Communist pressure would continue "until the United States decides to 'shoot off a gun' in the area."[27]

Admiral Radford heartily endorsed Dulles's position on the use of nuclear weapons, noting that the JCS had consistently advocated such a view. The JCS knew Jiang was not averse to the use of atomic weapons against the Chinese on the mainland. As long as "they were warned in advance," Jiang had told Admiral Felix Stump, Commander in Chief, Pacific Command, his countrymen would accept such attacks "as a war necessity."[28]

The rest of the NSC was practically speechless. Dulles made it clear that his conclusions had the support of Eisenhower, who was presiding over the meeting. Dulles informed the NSC that it was at the president's direction that he had included the reference to tactical nuclear weapons in his recent speech. Dulles pointed out that much more public relations work had yet to be done if the United States was to use atomic weapons within the "next month or two."

After the meeting, Eisenhower and National Security Adviser Robert Cutler reviewed top secret policy papers on nuclear warfare. The papers supported Eisenhower's personal opinion that the United States should regard nuclear weapons in the same way as any other "munition." For some time he had wanted to change public attitudes about the atomic bomb and reduce the widespread squeamishness about its use.[29]

In public statements over the next several days, the administration deliberately introduced specific comments about employing tactical nuclear weap-

27. Memorandum of discussion at the 240th Meeting of the NSC, March 10, 1955, Eisenhower Papers (AW), NSC Series, Box 6, NSC Summaries of Discussion; unsigned memo for the record of the March 10 NSC Meeting, Eisenhower Papers (AW), International Series, Box 9, Formosa Visit to CINCPAC (Commander-in-Chief, Pacific) (1955) (1).
28. Ibid.; telegram 012155Z from CINCPAC to CNO (Chief of Naval Operations), February 2, 1955, RG 218, Records of the Joint Chiefs of Staff, CCS 381 Formosa (11-8-93) (Section 19), National Archives.
29. Memorandum of 240th Meeting of the NSC, March 10, 1955; Robert Cutler, memorandum for the record, March 11, 1955, WHO OSANSA, NSC Series, Briefing Notes Subseries, Box 17, U.S. Policy toward Taiwan and the Offshore Islands.

ons if war broke out in the Taiwan Strait. Eisenhower caused a furor when, at a news conference on March 16, he said he saw no reason "why they shouldn't be used just exactly as you would use a bullet or anything else." On March 17 in Chicago, Vice President Richard Nixon echoed the president, stating that "tactical atomic weapons are now conventional and will be used against the targets of any aggressive force." He warned China against making belligerent moves.[30] These references were meant to deter the Communists as much as to prepare the American people for nuclear warfare.

Driving a Wedge Between China and the Soviet Union

In moving toward war with China, the Eisenhower administration virtually ignored the Soviet Union's potential responses. From the start of the crisis, the United States doubted the credibility of Soviet support for the Communist Chinese position. Even though Khrushchev made a blustery speech in Beijing on China's National Day, October 1, 1954, in which he condemned American interference in China's affairs and supported the liberation of Taiwan, Eisenhower labeled the performance mere "bluffing."[31] U.S. Ambassador to Moscow Charles Bohlen noted Soviet distancing from the Taiwan issue, even though Khrushchev had concluded agreements with the Chinese on other matters when he was in Beijing. American observers reported that the agreements favored China and reflected its improved position in the Sino-Soviet relationship.[32] The Soviets surrendered their last special territorial rights and privileges in China and granted further economic assistance. The Far Eastern Bureau of the State Department interpreted the accords as reflecting China's status of an almost-equal "junior partner," and noted that, while the Sino-Soviet alliance was firm, each ally clearly had its own distinct interests. The

---

30. Ambrose, *Eisenhower*, Vol. II: *The President*, p. 239; Stolper, *China, Taiwan, and the Offshore Islands*, pp. 89–90. The Chinese Communists took Eisenhower's threats seriously. In mid-January 1955 the Chinese Communists began a campaign to alert the population of the danger of nuclear attack from the United States. Previously, the Communist press had not given much attention to the subject but had minimized the destructiveness of atomic weapons. See Alice L. Hsieh, *Communist China's Strategy in the Nuclear Era* (Englewood Cliffs, N.J.: Prentice-Hall, 1962), pp. 32–33.
31. Eisenhower, *Mandate*, p. 480; Hsieh, *Communist China's Strategy*, p. 18.
32. Bohlen to Secretary of State, October 2, 1954, 793.00/10-254; Bohlen to Secretary of State, October 4, 1954, and Dulles to Bohlen, October 8, 1954, 793.00/10-454; Bohlen to Secretary of State, October 9, 1954, 793.00/10-954, all in RG 59, National Archives.

Soviets, it was believed, were uneasy about the Chinese campaign in the Taiwan Strait.[33]

The Soviet Union's attention was then focused on its own internal problems. A leadership struggle in the Kremlin had started in the latter part of 1954 and, by the end of January 1955, Director of Central Intelligence Allen Dulles could report to the NSC that "stresses and strains" in Moscow had become clearly visible. The Kremlin had assembled from abroad its largest group of ambassadors since the death of Stalin and had convened a special session of the Supreme Soviet. The CIA believed there was a dispute over economic issues and the relative importance of the military, a "guns versus butter" conflict.[34] On February 8, 1955, Moscow announced that Georgi Malenkov had been ousted and Nikolai Bulganin and Nikita Khrushchev promoted as the new top leaders. They quickly signaled their interest in improving relations with the West.

Eisenhower and Dulles believed that the Soviet influence on China was not as great as then commonly held and that China was acting largely on its own in the crisis. In executive session with the House Committee on Foreign Affairs, Dulles observed, "as far as surface appearances go, the Soviet line has been less violent than the Chinese Communist line, and when judged only by superficial impressions, one would infer that their disposition is to hold back the Chinese Communists. They have, for instance, avoided any formal, explicit endorsement of [the Chinese] position with reference to the conquest and what they call liberation of Formosa."[35] The leadership struggle in the Kremlin also confirmed for Dulles the correctness of the policy of pressure on the Communists. Dulles suspected that the Soviet Union was over-extended and was having difficulties meeting the demands of the satellite countries, especially of China. He remarked to Nationalist Foreign

---

33. O. Edmund Clubb, *China and Russia: The "Great Game"* (New York: Columbia University Press, 1971), p. 403. Department of State to all American diplomatic and consular posts, November 23, 1954, 661.93/11-2354; Bureau of Far Eastern Affairs, Briefing Paper, December 12, 1954, 793.00/12-1354; both in RG 59, National Archives.
34. Memorandum of discussion at the 234th meeting of the NSC, January 27, 1955, Eisenhower Papers (AW), NSC Series, Box 6, NSC Summaries of Discussion.
35. Transcript, press and radio background news conference, January 24, 1955, Princeton Dulles Papers, Box 96, Re: Quemoy and Matsu, p. B-2; United States Congress, House of Representatives, Committee on Foreign Affairs, *Selected Executive Hearings 1951–1956*, "U.S. Policy in the Far East, Part 2," (Washington: 1981), p. 394; Editorial Note, *FRUS*: 1955–57, Vol. II, pp. 202–203.

Minister George Yeh on February 10 that the strain on the Soviets "must be very great."[36]

Dulles openly played upon the emergent differences between the Soviets and the Chinese. In a widely publicized speech to the Foreign Policy Association on February 16, Dulles observed that the struggle in the Kremlin was not merely one for personal power. What seemed to be at issue, he said, was whether the Soviet leadership was going to sacrifice its own national interests, its security, and the welfare of its people to the expansionist ambitions of "international communism." Dulles spoke favorably of the elements in the leadership devoted to Russian concerns and offered them the prospect of "worthwhile negotiations and practical agreements between the United States and the new Russia." "Then," said Dulles, "there might be reactivated the historic friendship between our countries and our peoples."

Immediately after this overture to Moscow, Dulles turned to denouncing Beijing. Its extreme tactics and ambitions threatened the peace of Asia, he said. The Chinese Communists were "the initiators of violence" in the Taiwan Strait. The United States did not expect the Chinese Communists to surrender their claim to Taiwan but, putting on a reasonable face, Dulles asked rhetorically, "might they not renounce their efforts to realize their goals by force?" As an American news commentator soon observed, Dulles seemed to be "trying to induce Nikita S. Khrushchev or some other high Soviet leaders to become a Tito and cut loose from Peiping." In light of the long-standing interest in making Mao an "Asian Tito," Dulles's appeal to the Soviets was a novel ploy.[37]

Eisenhower himself discounted the likelihood of Soviet involvement if hostilities broke out between the United States and China. He told British Prime Minister Winston Churchill, NATO General Alfred Gruenther, and the NSC that he did not believe the Soviets would go to war over Taiwan. The Soviets would "pour supplies into China" but would not risk provoking a U.S. attack upon its own territory. The Soviets might be trying to sap American strength by involving the United States in a land war in Asia, but they were not interested in general conflict. A real shooting war, Eisenhower wrote Gruenther, would create a great dilemma for the Soviet Union.[38]

36. Koo memorandum, meeting of Dulles, Robertson, and Yeh, February 10, 1955, Koo Papers, Box 195, Notes of Conversations: Offshore Islands, Columbia University.
37. *New York Times*, February 17, 1955, p. 1; Harry Schwartz, "Moscow and Peiping: Can West Drive A Wedge?" *New York Times*, March 27, 1955, IV, p. 3.
38. Eisenhower to Churchill, February 10, 1955, Eisenhower Papers (AW), International Series,

March–April, 1955: To the Brink

Eisenhower was fully prepared, but not anxious, to use nuclear weapons. Both he and Dulles feared damaging repercussions in Europe if they were used. Secretary of State Dulles told the president on March 11 that, for the moment, U.S. involvement, "particularly involving atomic missiles," should be avoided, but after negotiations about forming a European confederation were "buttoned up," the United States would have more freedom of action in Asia.[39] Later in the day, he and the president met with other officials and decided that they had to do everything possible to improve the defense capability of the Nationalists so as to avoid the need for U.S. intervention. And if the United States were to enter the fight, Eisenhower indicated, it would do so first with conventional weapons. Atomic weapons "should only come at the end," he stipulated.[40] The administration considered the remaining days of March to be critical, as the Communists continued to augment their forces opposite the offshore islands and the Nationalists completed their fortifications. The United States blustered to put off the Communists and give more time to the Nationalists. In a speech on March 21, Dulles accused Beijing of being "dizzy with success" and an "acute and immediate threat." In the short run, China "may prove more dangerous and provocative of war" than the Soviet Union. Dulles added ominously, "the aggressive fanaticism of the Chinese Communist leaders presents a certain parallel to that of Hitler. Also, it contrasts to the *past* tactics of Soviet Communism."[41] Dulles's emotional words were clearly calculated: he classed the Chinese Communists with the Nazis but explicitly distinguished Moscow from Beijing.

On March 25 Admiral Robert Carney, Chief of Naval Operations, leaked to the press that the United States had plans to conduct an all-out attack on

Box 17, President-Churchill: January 1, 1955–April 7, 1955 (4); Eisenhower to Gruenther, February 1, 1955, Eisenhower Papers (AW), Diary Series, Box 9, Diary Feb. 1955 (1); memorandum of the 234th Meeting of the NSC, January 27, 1955.

39. Richard Betts, *Nuclear Blackmail and Nuclear Balance* (Washington, D.C.: Brookings, 1987), p. 59; Dulles memorandum, meeting with the president at 10:45 a.m., March 11, 1955, Dulles Papers, White House Memoranda Series, Box 3, Meetings with the President 1955 (6).

40. Robert Cutler memorandum, meeting with Eisenhower, Dulles, and others, March 11, 1955, WHO OSANSA, NSC Series, Briefing Notes Subseries, Box 17, U.S. Policy toward Taiwan and the Offshore Islands; Goodpaster memorandum, meeting with Eisenhower, Dulles, and others, March 11, 1955, Eisenhower Papers (AW), International Series, Box 9, Formosa—Visit to CINCPAC (1955) (1).

41. *New York Times*, April 22, 1955, p. 1 (emphasis added).

China. Carney said he himself expected war to break out by April 15, the start of the Afro-Asian Conference in Bandung, Indonesia. Eisenhower was furious with Carney's disclosure, but he privately agreed that Carney might be right about the need for the United States to fight, "because the Red Chinese appear to be completely reckless, arrogant, possibly overconfident, and completely indifferent as to human losses."[42]

As Carney had revealed, the military was planning extensive nuclear attacks on China. On March 31, General Curtis LeMay, commander of the Strategic Air Command, cabled General Nathan Twining, head of the Air Force. LeMay was personally familiar with China, having directed from the mainland the fire bombing of Japan during the Second World War. LeMay's message read in part:

Plans have been developed and are ready for immed execution by use of B-36 type acft [aircraft] based on Guam to deal with any eventuality involving Communist China. One wg [wing] is in pos at Guam now and two other wgs in the United States are on warning alert for this task. One of these two wgs can move to Guam immed. Guam has capability of supporting sixty B-36 type acft. These will have an immed capability for combat opns [operations]. . . . Target selections have been made, coordinated with other responsible comdrs and asgd [assigned] to B-36 crew.[43]

The following day, according to the Chinese, eighteen U.S. war planes in four different waves flew over Chinese territory in both the north and south. The Chinese officially condemned the flights as "military provocations." One week later, a plane carrying Chinese officials to the Bandung Conference crashed killing all aboard. There was little doubt of sabotage. The Chinese accused both the Nationalists and the United States of responsibility.[44]

Eisenhower tried to contain the American public's growing fear of war, while leaving his military options open. Disingenuously, he told a group of Senators on March 31 that he did not know and could not know in advance

---

42. Telephone call, Eisenhower and Dulles, March 28, 1955, Eisenhower Papers (AW), Diary Series, Box 9, Phone calls January–July 1955 (2). Quotation is from Ambrose, *Eisenhower*, pp. 240–241. Although he himself did not expect imminent war, Eisenhower commented in his diary on March 26 that members of the Cabinet thought hostilities would break out within the month. Diary entry, March 26, 1955, Eisenhower Papers (AW), Diary Series, Box 10, Eisenhower Diary March 1955 (1).
43. LeMay to Twining, March 31, 1955, Nathan Twining Papers, Box 100, Office File Messages, Ja–Mr 1955, Library of Congress. A wing of B-36s comprised thirty heavy bombers which could deliver atomic bombs from Guam to the mainland of China.
44. *New York Times*, April 3, 1955, p. 3.; ibid., April 12, 1955, p. 1.

if he would intervene militarily in the offshore islands if the Communists attacked. His decision, he said, would be based on whether the objective of an assault was actually Taiwan, and not limited to the offshore islands.[45]

In private, however, the adminstration was considering extreme measures to end the crisis. John Foster Dulles, his top advisers in the State Department, and his brother Allen Dulles, director of the CIA, met on March 28 to discuss what to do. They first debated the possibility of again approaching the UN, but the idea got nowhere. Talk then centered on the military options open to the United States. John Foster Dulles proposed blockading the *entire* China coast to relieve the pressure on the offshore islands. Next, he raised for discussion the threat of a "generalized" attack with conventional and nuclear weapons, in response to any Chinese assault on Jinmen and Mazu, that would destroy China's "great POL dumps" (petroleum, oil, and lubricants) and the communication and rail lines "across the length and breadth of China." If the Chinese knew that this would be the American reaction, they might not attack, he argued. Robert Bowie, head of the Policy Planning Staff, and generally one of the administration's more moderate elements toward China, suggested that the United States announce it would "from time to time" drop nuclear bombs on Jinmen and Mazu if they were captured by the Communists. Dulles thought this impractical as it would be a "considerable waste" of valuable weapons. The United States could not afford to "splurge" its nuclear arsenal, Dulles cautioned. In any case, the Secretary said, such a plan would only wind up killing harmless fishermen. But Dulles and his colleagues could not come up with any more attractive ideas.[46]

Finally, several days later, Eisenhower decided to try one other maneuver. He thought the United States might seek to convince Jiang to reduce his forces on the offshore islands—to recognize them as "outposts, not citadels"—and de-emphasize their importance to his government. If Jiang's prestige was less involved with the islands, the United States could gradually reduce its own commitment and concentrate on Taiwan and the Penghus. Under these circumstances, the impact of the loss of the offshore islands on Nationalist morale might therefore be acceptable. Eisenhower presented these ideas to Dulles in a ten-page, single-spaced memo on April 5 and urged

45. Ibid., April 1, 1955, p. 1.
46. Hanes memorandum, meeting with Dulles, Hoover, and others, March 28, 1955, Dulles Papers, White House Memoranda Series, Box 2, White House Memoranda, 1955 Formosa Strait (1). References to the use of atomic weapons are deleted from the version appearing in *FRUS: 1955–57*, Vol. II, pp. 409–415.

the Secretary of State to come up with a specific course of action. The United States, wrote Eisenhower, could no longer "remain inert awaiting the inevitable moment of decision between two unacceptable choices": an unpopular, divisive, and disadvantageous war over the islands, or retreat before a Chinese attack that could lead to the disintegration of "all Asian opposition" to communism and the loss of that continent.[47]

Over the next several days, pressures on the administration to take decisive action in the Strait continued to increase. Ambassador Rankin and General William Chase (chief of the United States Military Assistance Advisory Group on Taiwan) urged Washington to authorize the Nationalists to bomb Communist airfields and to blockade shipping along the China coast. Admiral Felix Stump also backed the Nationalist request for U.S. approval (pursuant to Jiang's secret pledge) to conduct air strikes on mainland targets.[48] Opposite proposals came from within the State Department. Robert Bowie now urged that the United States announce it would not defend the offshore islands, in order to coerce Jiang into seeing the offshore islands as "expendable outposts" and perhaps to withdraw from them altogether.[49]

Finally, Dulles flew to Augusta, Georgia on April 17 for a private two-hour meeting with the president. Dulles presented the ideas that he, Deputy Secretary of Defense Robert Anderson, Admiral Radford, Undersecretary of State Herbert Hoover, Jr., Assistant Secretary of State Robertson, and CIA chief Allen Dulles developed in response to Eisenhower's April 5 memo. Eisenhower had wanted a way to de-emphasize the offshore islands, to make them into "outposts," but Dulles and his group had concluded that such a path was self-defeating. If the United States was not going to stop on-shore Communist preparations for an attack on the islands, the islands were as good as lost. Even as "outposts," their capture would still be terribly destructive for the Nationalists. It would be better, Dulles argued, for the United States "to encourage a clean break"—get off the islands—and then blockade the China coast along the entire Taiwan Strait, some 500 miles. The position paper that Dulles showed Eisenhower said: "Unless and until the Chicoms [Chinese Communists] in good faith renounce their avowed purpose to take

---

47. Dulles memorandum, conversation with Eisenhower, April 4, 1955, *FRUS*: 1955–57, Vol. II, pp. 444–445; Eisenhower to Dulles, April 5, 1955, Dulles Papers, White House Memoranda Series, Box 2, Position Paper on Offshore Islands, April–May 1955 (5).
48. Chase to Stump, April 8, 1955, *FRUS*: 1955–57, Vol. II. pp. 465–466; Stump to Carney, April 8, 1955, ibid., pp. 471–473.
49. Bowie to Dulles, April 9, 1955, ibid., pp. 473–475.

Formosa by force, the United States and Chinats [Chinese Nationalists] will, as a measure of self-defense, institute a naval interdiction along the China Coast from and including Swatow in the south to approximately Wenchow in the north." (See map, p. 123.) The blockade would aim at stopping the Communists from building up their supplies and facilities for an attack against Taiwan, which they could not easily accomplish overland because of rough terrain. Dulles also proposed stationing nuclear weapons on Taiwan to demonstrate U.S. resolve. His plan thus combined a retreat with a wild counter-attack,[50] and envisioned the eventual creation of two Chinas effectively separated by the Taiwan Strait.

While the evacuation and blockade might have extracted the United States from the precarious situation in the offshore islands, they would have doomed the U.S. to a hell on the high seas. The Chinese Communists would never renounce their claims over Taiwan nor their option of using force to bring the island under Beijing's suzerainty. (Even today they have not ruled out such a possibility.) A naval blockade had military advantages over a static defense of small islands vulnerable to Chinese ground forces, but the United States would have had to maintain a costly act of war indefinitely. China certainly would not have let such an affront go unchallenged.

Eisenhower, after hesitation, approved Dulles's plan with a few revisions. Eisenhower emphasized that the United States must not force Jiang into anything he did not want. The Nationalists should decide whether they would retain Jinmen and Mazu or give them up. By the end of the discussion, the two men were pleased with themselves, confident their program "would immeasurably serve to consolidate world opinion" in favor of the United States. Following the meeting, Dulles spoke to reporters, saying he and the president discussed questions related to Austria, Vietnam, and the "grave implications" of the offensive buildup of the Chinese Communists in the Taiwan Strait area. The two men, he announced, had concluded that peace "is now in grave jeopardy."[51] Three days later, on April 20, Admiral Radford and Assistant Secretary of State Robertson left for Taibei (Taipei) to present the Dulles-Eisenhower plan to Jiang Jieshi.

Before meeting with the Generalissimo, Radford and Robertson conferred with Ambassador Rankin to give him details of the proposal: if the Nation-

---

50. Dulles memorandum, meeting with Eisenhower, April 17, 1955, Dulles Papers, White House Memoranda Series, Box 3, Meetings with the President 1955 (5).
51. Ibid.; *New York Times*, April 18, 1955, p. 1.

alists withdrew from Jinmen and Mazu, the United States would intercept all seaborne traffic of "a contraband or war-making character" and would "lay mine fields which would force coastwise junk traffic to come out where it also could be intercepted and controlled." Logistically, the plan was feasible—the Seventh Fleet and elements of the Fifth Air Force were present in the area and other naval forces in Okinawa and the Philippines were only twenty-four hours away. Rankin, who usually favored an aggressive policy toward the Chinese Communists and had supported the idea of a Nationalist blockade of the coast, was aghast. This proposal meant war, he told Radford and Robertson. How could the Communists accept a blockade of their coast or the mining of their own territorial waters? Radford agreed with Rankin's characterization of the proposal, adding that it would only be a matter of time before Chinese aircraft attacked American ships. Radford said he had fully informed Eisenhower of this probable outcome.[52]

Fortunately, neither the rest of the world nor the Chinese Communists were ever required to respond to the Dulles-Eisenhower ultimatum. Despite several days of talks, Jiang refused to entertain any idea of reducing his forces on the islands, let alone abandoning them to the Communists. Radford and Robertson tried to press Jiang by telling him the United States was withdrawing its secret January 31 pledge to join in the defense of Jinmen and Mazu, although Jiang could still count on U.S. logistic support. Jiang still would not budge. Rankin later surmised that Jiang rejected the blockade plan because he distrusted the Americans. After having been betrayed (as he saw it) by the United States during the evacuation of the Dachens, Jiang could hardly be expected to be receptive to a proposal that depended completely upon Washington's reliability.[53]

---

52. Rankin memorandum on the Robertson and Radford mission April 24–27, 1955, April 29, 1955, Rankin Papers, Box 26, Re: Chiang Kai-shek. The Navy immediately began planning implementation of the blockade. See Carney to Radford, April 22, 1955, *FRUS*: 1955–57, Vol. II, p. 504. Dulles also had his adviser Herman Phleger develop a "legal" rationale for the blockade. Phleger suggested that a "zone of defense" was acceptable under international law and could be imposed as part of the protection of Taiwan against the "threat of armed aggression." However, a "blockade," he cautioned, was "permissible only in time of war, or when authorized by the UN," and thus use of that term was to be avoided. Cable, Anderson to Radford, April 22, 1955, Record Group 218, Records of the Joint Chiefs of Staff, Chairman's File, Admiral Radford 1953–57, Box 7, 091 China (Apr. 1955); Admiral Carney, head of the Navy, advised Eisenhower and Radford that if the Communists challenged the proposed evacuation of Jinmen and Mazu, the United States could probably not maintain air superiority over the area solely with the use of conventional weapons. Carney to Radford, April 22, 1955, ibid.
53. Ibid., Rankin, Offshore Islands Chronology, June 3, 1955; memorandum for the record, May 5, 1955; Robertson to Dulles, April 25, 1955, *FRUS*: 1955–57, Vol. II, pp. 510–517; Goodpaster

The initiative that finally ended the crisis came not from Washington but unexpectedly from the Chinese Communists. On April 23, just before Robertson and Radford talked with Jiang, Chinese Premier Zhou Enlai dramatically announced at the Bandung Conference that his government wanted no war with the United States. He said, "the Chinese people are friendly to the American people" and that China was willing to negotiate with the United States for the reduction of tensions in the Taiwan area. On April 26, Dulles, seizing the chance to extricate the United States from its predicament, indicated that the United States would talk with Beijing about a ceasefire. The shelling of Jinmen and Mazu soon tapered off and the area quieted.

Divided Enemies?

Why did Beijing end the crisis? The Chinese may have been concerned that Washington was about to start general war, as it was no secret that Eisenhower's emissaries, with their hard-line reputations, were headed for Taiwan. The Communists may have wanted to appeal to other Asian nations fearful of a new conflagration in the Far East.[54] It is also possible that the Soviets persuaded the Chinese to end their campaign in the Strait. Washington later heard and apparently believed a rumor that Zhou Enlai secretly visited Moscow in April 1955 (perhaps before the Bandung Conference), where Khrushchev told him that the Soviet Union would not support China in a war over the offshore islands. Khrushchev reportedly said that he considered the islands a local problem and continuation of the crisis contrary to the Soviet aim of relaxing tensions with the United States.[55]

Regardless of the truth of that story, by early April 1955 it was obvious that the Chinese and Soviets were on different tracks. The contrast in their behavior was not lost on the Eisenhower administration. While the Chinese were keeping the pressure on in the Strait, and the United States was signaling its preparation for nuclear war against China, the Soviets eagerly sought improvement of relations with the West. Moscow indicated that it

---

draft memorandum, meeting of Robertson and Radford with Eisenhower on May 3, 1955, May 7, 1955, WHO OSANSA, Special Assistants Series, Chronological Subseries, Box 1, May 1955 (2).
54. Wang Bingnan, *Zhong-Mei huitan jiunian huilu* (Beijing: Shijie zhishi chubanshe, 1985), pp. 44–45.
55. Digest of Fifth Meeting, Council on Foreign Relations, March 7, 1956, Records of Groups, LXI, Group on Sino-Soviet Relations, 1955–56, p. 1.

was willing to conclude an Austrian state treaty and to end the joint occupation of Austria. For years the United States had considered the Austrian question an explicit test of Soviet intentions. On April 11 the Austrian Chancellor arrived in Moscow to receive the Kremlin's treaty proposals, and in a few short days reached agreement with the Soviets on terms described as very favorable to the West.[56] Allen Dulles privately hailed the Soviet move "as the most significant action since the end of World War II." He told the NSC that it indicated greater flexibility in Soviet policy, and perhaps a greater degree of weakness. In any case, Dulles pointed out, "it constituted the first substantial Soviet concession to the West in Europe since the end of the war."[57]

The years between Khrushchev's visit to Beijing in September 1954 and the Soviet Twentieth Party Congress in February 1956 have been called the golden period of Sino-Soviet relations,[58] but even then, the relationship was an uneasy one. Moreover, the Eisenhower administration was sensitive to signs of discord and played down the importance of the Soviet alliance with China during the entire offshore crisis. Ignoring formal communist solidarity and the Soviet Union's "nuclear umbrella" over China, the United States tried to intimidate Beijing. In their discussion about blockading the China coast, Eisenhower and Dulles did not once mention the Soviets and their possible reaction. This was not because they assumed that the Sino-Soviet relationship was monolithic, but just the opposite. Eisenhower and Dulles were reasonably confident they confronted a relatively independent actor in China. They did not believe that the source of the provocation was Moscow, nor that Moscow was even seriously interested in supporting its communist friend. In fact, Dulles subtly tried to separate the Soviets and Chinese by dangling the carrot of détente before the eyes of the new Khrushchev leadership while increasing threats against Beijing. The events of April which led to the end of the crisis suggest that Dulles's tactic may have actually had a measure of success. We now know the assumption that the administration was driven by a "mindless anti-communism" is unfounded.

---

56. Joseph L. Nogee and Robert H. Donaldson, *Soviet Foreign Policy Since World War II*, 2d ed. (New York: Pergamon, 1984), p. 112; Hoopes, *The Devil and John Foster Dulles*, p. 293; *New York Times*, April 15, 1955, p. 1.
57. Memorandum of discussion at the 245th meeting of the NSC, April 21, 1955, Eisenhower Papers (AW), NSC Series, Box 6, NSC Summaries of Discussion.
58. Franz Schurmann, *The Logic of World Power, An Inquiry into the Origins, Currents, and Contradictions of World Politics* (New York: Pantheon, 1974), p. 249.

Have Historians Misjudged Eisenhower?

Eisenhower biographer Stepher Ambrose lauds Eisenhower's handling of the crisis as a "tour de force," hailing his "deliberate ambiguity and deception" as to whether he really would have fought for the islands. Ambrose supports historian Robert Divine's praise of Eisenhower: "The beauty of Eisenhower's policy is that to this day no one can be sure whether or not he would have responded militarily to an invasion of the offshore islands, and whether he would have used nuclear weapons." Ambrose embellishes this, saying, "the full truth is that Eisenhower himself did not know."[59] But these conclusions were premature and they are contradicted by the evidence now available. Between January 31 and April 24, 1955, the United States was formally pledged to support the defense of Jinmen and Mazu. Even before the January 31 pledge, Eisenhower expressed his belief that the islands were essential to the basic morale and viability of the Nationalist government. His distinction between a Communist attack aimed at taking just Jinmen and Mazu, and an attack that was a prelude to an assault on Taiwan, may have seemed real in his own mind, but was hardly realistic. If the Communists had actually threatened to overwhelm the offshore islands, Eisenhower was clearly committed to intervene. He would not have stood aside and watched the loss of the islands.

Ambrose contends that Eisenhower successfully kept his options open through the crisis. But Eisenhower's obdurate attachment to Jiang (Jiang's suspicions of American trustworthiness notwithstanding) steadily reduced U.S. flexibility. If the Communists had committed sufficient forces to take Jinmen or Mazu in March or April 1955, the United States would have gone to war with China. On March 31 Eisenhower told the NSC not to underestimate what he called the "sanity of the Chinese Communists." He was confident that the Communists understood that he would use whatever military means was necessary to stop them. As far as Eisenhower himself was concerned, there was no question in his mind as to what he would do if the Communists attacked in force. There would have been war.[60]

Part of Ambrose's error arises from his uncritical acceptance of Eisenhower's account of the handling of the crisis. In his 1963 memoirs, *Mandate for*

---

59. Ambrose, *Eisenhower*, p. 245.
60. Memorandum of discussion at the 243rd meeting of the NSC, March 31, 1955, Eisenhower papers (AW), NSC Series, Box 6, NSC Summaries of Discussion.

Change, Eisenhower was vague in describing what his response to a Communist attack might have been. Ambrose interpreted this as reflecting Eisenhower's suppleness. But, in fact, as we now know, Eisenhower did make secret commitments to the defense of Jinmen and Mazu. Jiang himself long maintained that he received a promise from the United States that after the evacuation of the Dachens, the United States would "jointly defend Quemoy and Matsu."[61]

Eisenhower also deliberately falsified his account of the Radford-Robertson trip to Taiwan. In his memoirs, Eisenhower focused attention on the long April 5 memo to Dulles in which he recommended that the United States try to convince Jiang to de-emphasize the offshore islands. Excerpts from the memo in an appendix (subsequently cited by many historians) give the impression that it guided the Radford-Robertson mission and that Eisenhower sincerely searched for a reasonable exit from the crisis. But Radford and Robertson followed, not the April 5 memo, but the program Eisenhower and Dulles devised on April 17 for evacuation of the islands and blockade of the China coast.

After he heard of Jiang's vehement rejection of the United States proposal, Eisenhower tried to distance himself from what had been presented in Taiwan. He told Dulles that he "had never expected that the Generalissimo would give up outright on Quemoy and the Matsus," and criticized his emissaries for not understanding the "outpost" theory.[62] Eisenhower, in these afterthoughts, revealed that he was either operating on profoundly different assumptions about what Radford and Robertson were to accomplish on their important mission, or that the two men, deliberately or not, failed to carry out the president's critical instructions. Whatever the case, Eisenhower's leadership of his subordinates again appears to have been seriously flawed at a decisive moment in the offshore island crisis.

Eisenhower's memoirs state that his administration never tried to persuade Jiang to withdraw from Jinmen and Mazu. This falsehood helped corroborate statements made by Eisenhower's Vice President, Richard Nixon. During the presidential campaign of 1960, John Kennedy questioned the Eisenhower administration's commitment to Jiang, and accused it of trying to get Jiang

61. Transcript, oral history interview with Chiang Kai-shek and Madame Chiang Kai-shek, September 24, 1964, Dulles Oral History Project, Princeton University, p. 14.
62. Dulles memorandum, conversation with Eisenhower, April 25, 1955, *FRUS*: 1955–57, Vol. II, p. 517; Eisenhower to Dulles, April 26, 1955, ibid., pp. 522–523. Also see, Hoover to Robertson and Radford, April 22, 1955 and notes, ibid., pp. 501–502.

to quit the islands. Nixon's public reply was that the administration only wanted Jiang to reduce his garrisons.[63] In actual fact, Eisenhower had authorized an act of war to save Jiang's neck.

Eisenhower worked closely with Secretary of State Dulles throughout the crisis and paid close attention to the details of military deployment as well as the diplomatic problems with nervous allies. And because he was not a detached chief executive, he must bear direct responsibility for leading the country dangerously close to war. Such a war might have come in one of two ways: first, the ambiguity of his public stand on the offshore islands (in the apparent absence of any attempt to send secret messages to Beijing) might very well have allowed Communist miscalculation of American intentions and thus have invited an attack. The result, given Washington's secret commitments to Jiang and the administration's own private determination to retain the islands, would have been armed conflict between the United States and China. Second, war would certainly have come if Jiang had accepted the evacuation-blockade plan. It is inconceivable that the Chinese Communists would have acquiesced in such a violation of their sovereignty by U.S. imperialism.[64]

Lastly, it must also be said that Washington's brandishing of the nuclear cudgel during the crisis provoked not only potential disaster, but also a development that would later haunt the United States. Apparently, Eisenhower's threats helped convince the Chinese Communists that they needed nuclear weapons of their own. In January 1955, in the midst of the offshore crisis and under American pressures, Mao Zedong (Mao Tse-Tung) and other top Communist leaders decided to launch China's nuclear program.[65] The Eisenhower administration's use of nuclear deterrence to protect territory

---

63. In 1958, when the Nationalists and Communists again clashed over the offshore islands, John Foster Dulles specifically reminded Nixon that Robertson and Radford tried to get the Nationalists to give up the offshore islands in 1955. Telephone call, Dulles and Nixon, September 25, 1958, Dulles Papers, Telephone Calls Series, Box 9, Memoranda of telephone conversations, General, August 1, 1958 to October 31, 1958 (3).

64. The Indonesian ambassador to the United States explicitedly warned Washington about the dangers in the U.S. policy. In April he told a leading State Department official that Asian and European diplomats in Washington appeared "completely confused" about the administration's position on Jinmen and Mazu. The ambassador urged Washington "to announce clearly that it would resist or that it would not." The ambassador said he was "afraid that in this 'confusion' that the Chinese Communists may become reckless and decide to launch an assault on the offshore islands." Young memorandum, meeting with Notowidigdo, April 5, 1955, *FRUS: 1955–57*, Vol. II, pp. 451–452.

65. John W. Lewis and Li-tai Xue, *China Builds The Bomb* (Stanford: Stanford University Press, forthcoming 1988).

which even Dulles admitted was never considered "essential" to American interests thus came at great cost.[66]

Several months after the end of the offshore confrontation, John Foster Dulles, in a famous article in *Life* magazine, hailed the administration's handling of the crisis as a successful example of "brinkmanship." His evaluation, evidently, was myopic and much too hasty. War was avoided due more to Chinese Communist caution than to the diplomatic skills of Eisenhower and Dulles.[67]

---

66. Dulles, draft statement, April 8, 1955, *FRUS*: 1955–57, Vol. II, pp. 455–63.
67. James Shepley, "How Dulles Averted War," *Life*, January 16, 1956, pp. 70–80. There is considerable evidence to show that Beijing's actions had been limited and restrained during the crisis. Much of this information was available to American officials in 1955. See Stolper, *Offshore Islands*, pp. 86–87; Lewis and Xue, *China*; and He, "Evolution of PRC Policy Toward the Offshore Islands."

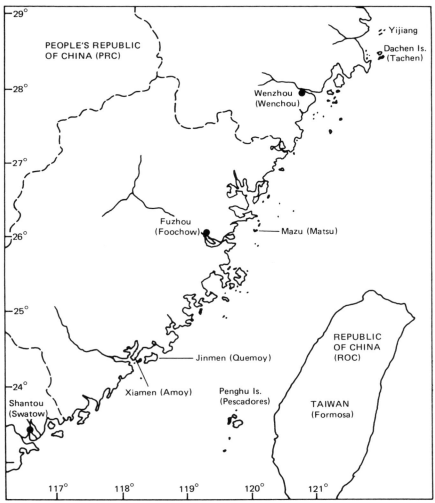

Offshore islands in the Taiwan Strait. For scale: Wenzhou to Shantou is approximately 430 miles. The proposed blockade would have extended at least that far. © *International Security* 1988.

Testing Massive Retaliation

H. W. Brands, Jr.

Credibility and Crisis Management in the Taiwan Strait

$\mathbf{F}$or eight months in 1954 and 1955, much of the world wondered whether the U.S. would go to war with the People's Republic of China over Jinmen (Quemoy) and Mazu (Matsu) in the Taiwan Strait. The crisis was an early test of the Eisenhower-Dulles doctrine of "massive retaliation." Was the American threat to protect its commitments by using anything in its arsenal, including nuclear weapons, a credible one? How should such commitments and threats be signalled, to whom, and when? Could they be effective to promote U.S. interests?

As Secretary of State John Foster Dulles recognized during the crisis, the U.S. would shortly reach the point when it would have to "face up to the question whether its military program was or was not in fact designed to permit the use of atomic weapons." He feared that the longer the U.S. went without using these weapons, the less would be their deterrent value. Dulles and Eisenhower recognized that the U.S. was thus approaching the brink of nuclear war over strategically trivial islands. However, they appeared to believe that U.S. credibility was on the line, and that if their approach didn't succeed, their entire defense policy might be undermined.

The documentary record of the decision-making process in Beijing, Moscow, and Taibei remains closed to researchers, thereby precluding a complete and balanced history of the crisis, but on the American side much of the highest-level material has recently been declassified. As a consequence it is now possible to trace the evolution of American policy in considerable detail. The documents reveal the Eisenhower administration struggling to preserve important strategic assets in the Far East in the face of competing diplomatic, political, and bureaucratic forces. To President Dwight D. Eisenhower, Secretary of State John Foster Dulles, Joint Chiefs of Staff Chairman Arthur Radford, and nearly everyone else of influence in Washington, a secure Taiwan in friendly hands represented the *sine qua non* of American policy in the Strait. Beyond this, however, opinions rapidly diverged, and considerable disagreement arose among decision-makers over the issue of the offshore islands. Much of it involved the fact that any course of action would antag-

H. W. Brands, Jr., teaches history at Texas A & M University. He is the author of Cold Warriors: Eisenhower's Generation and American Foreign Policy (New York: Columbia University Press, forthcoming in 1988) and is completing a study of American policy toward the Third World from 1945 to 1960.

International Security, Spring 1988 (Vol. 12, No. 4)

onize groups in positions to inflict damage on the administration, the United States, or both. What would please the Republic of China (ROC) would provoke, to one degree or another, the People's Republic of China (PRC), the Soviets, the NATO allies, and a significant portion of moderate-to-liberal opinion in America. Soothing the Communists and allaying the war fears of Europeans would set off Jiang Jieshi (Chiang Kai-shek) and the Nationalists on Taiwan as well as conservatives in the United States, and it might demoralize friends and clients in Asia.

Over the whole affair hung the nuclear question, more pressing than ever with the recent development of fusion devices on both sides of the cold war. Were atomic weapons necessary to defend the offshore islands? Would the threat of their use deter attack, or widen the area of conflict? Were they a special breed of armaments, or simply big bombs? Could they be utilized in a strictly tactical sense, or would escalation inevitably follow? How would American and world opinion respond to their use? To their non-use? To threats of use that were not carried out?

The story of the Eisenhower Administration's handling of this early major test of the massive retaliation doctrine is a sobering one. Eisenhower and Dulles succeeded in avoiding war while protecting the American position on Taiwan, but their success owed as much to luck as to skill, as they themselves privately admitted. They found themselves forced to the brink of a major conflict over an issue intrinsically unrelated to American security, as they also admitted. Although they repeatedly attempted to narrow the focus of the American commitment so as to exclude territory not worth defending, they ultimately failed to do so. Constrained by the demands of domestic politics, by considerations of international credibility, and not least by the limitations of their strategic policy, they felt control slipping from their hands.[1]

---

1. The literature on the general subject of crisis management is quite extensive. Representative are Glenn D. Paige, *The Korean Decision: June 24–30, 1950* (New York: Free Press, 1968); Coral Bell, *The Conventions of Crisis: A Study in Diplomatic Management* (London: Oxford University Press, 1971); Graham T. Allison, *Essence of Decision: Explaining the Cuban Missile Crisis* (Boston: Little, Brown, 1971); Charles F. Hermann, ed., *International Crises: Insights from Behavioral Research* (New York: Free Press, 1972); Alexander L. George and Richard Smoke, *Deterrence in American Foreign Policy: Theory and Practice* (New York: Columbia University Press, 1974); John R. Oneal, *Foreign Policy Making in Times of Crisis* (Columbus: Ohio State University Press, 1982); and Michael Brecher, ed., *Studies in Crisis Behavior* (New Brunswick, N.J.: Transaction Books, 1979). Oneal's book contains further titles and an overview of the literature.

On the specific issue of the Taiwan Strait crisis of 1954–55, the best-informed works are O. Edmund Clubb, "Formosa and the Offshore Islands in American Policy," *Political Science Quar-*

Retreat or Defend: First Cost Estimates

After their flight from the mainland in 1949, the Nationalist forces of Jiang Jieshi had occupied Jinmen and the other offshore islands, and the PRC had never managed to oust them. (See map, p. 123.) In fact, the Republic of China had garrisoned the islands with some 70,000 regular and guerrilla troops and had used them as bases for raids on the mainland. While Washington refrained from publicly encouraging these harassing operations, officials in the Truman administration had quietly expressed their appreciation that the raids tied down a sizable Communist force that might have caused trouble in Korea. On the whole, however, the view in Washington was that while the islands were useful, they were probably not worth fighting for.[2]

By September 1954, when the PRC began shelling Jinmen, the situation had changed considerably—or so it seemed to Eisenhower's new Chairman of the Joint Chiefs of Staff, Admiral Radford. After the stalemate in Korea

terly, Vol. 74, No. 4 (Winter 1960), pp. 517–531; Morton H. Halperin and Tang Tsou, "United States Policy toward the Offshore Islands," *Public Policy,* Vol. 15 (1966), pp. 119–138; Leon V. Sigal, "The 'Rational Policy' Model and the Formosa Straits Crisis," *International Studies Quarterly,* Vol. 14, No. 2 (June, 1970), pp. 121–156; George and Smoke, "The Taiwan Strait Crises, 1954–1955," in *Deterrence in American Foreign Policy,* ch. 9; J. H. Kalicki, *The Pattern of Sino-American Crises: Political-Military Interactions in the 1950s* (London: Cambridge University Press, 1975), ch. 6; Hungdah Chiu, "The Question of Taiwan in Sino-American Relations," in Hungdah Chiu, ed., *China and the Taiwan Issue* (New York: Praeger, 1979), ch. 6; Bennett C. Rushkoff, "Eisenhower, Dulles and the Quemoy-Matsu Crisis, 1954–1955," *Political Science Quarterly,* Vol. 96, No. 3 (August, 1981), pp. 465–480; Thomas E. Stolper, *China, Taiwan, and the Offshore Islands* (Armonk, N.Y.: M. E. Sharpe, 1985); and Leonard H. D. Gordon, "United States Opposition to Use of Force in the Taiwan Strait, 1954–1962," *Journal of American History,* Vol. 72, No. 3 (December, 1985), pp. 637–660.

The works by Rushkoff, Stolper, and Gordon are the first to utilize previously classified sources to any significant extent. None of the three authors, however, had access to the most important materials in the recently published volumes on the period in the State Department's *Foreign Relations of the United States (FRUS)* series (Washington, D.C.: U.S. Government Printing Office). The pertinent numbers are Volume XIV in the 1952–1954 set, published in 1985, and Volume II in the 1955–1957 set, published in 1986. While the *Foreign Relations* series at one time drew almost exclusively on State Department records, these volumes, like others recently published, also include material originating in the White House, the CIA, and the Defense Department. For the period of the 1954–55 crisis, as for much of the Eisenhower administration, the most significant items are the memoranda of discussions at meetings of the National Security Council. More than any other president since its creation, Eisenhower took the NSC seriously and used it as the essential instrument of policy formation. These memoranda, therefore, and the documents that support them provide extremely revealing insights into the making of foreign policy in the mid-1950s.

2. See memorandum of discussion, 213th NSC meeting, Sep. 9, 1954, *FRUS:* 1952–54, Vol. XIV, p. 581. A useful chronology of events relating to the offshore islands can be found in the Karl Lott Rankin papers at the Mudd Library, Princeton University, Princeton, New Jersey.

and the French collapse in Indochina, Radford argued, the West sorely needed a victory in Asia. Speaking for the majority of the military leadership,[3] he declared that the United States could not afford to back away from this most recent Communist challenge. He conceded that Jinmen and the other offshore islands did not possess sufficient importance to warrant, on strictly military grounds, an all-out defensive effort. But he contended that the loss of the islands would discourage, perhaps fatally, the ROC and other countries looking to America for protection. At the same time, the PRC attack provided a wonderful opportunity to knock Beijing down a few notches. An unsuccessful assault on the islands, Radford said, would constitute "a serious political and psychological reverse for the Communists and a corresponding lift for all anti-Communist forces in the Far East. The loss of 'face' on the part of Communist leadership could have far reaching consequences."[4]

The military leadership made explicit from the outset that a defense of the islands would require counterattacks on the mainland. General John Hull, Commander in Chief for the Far East, asserted that defending forces would have little alternative to such counterattacks since Jinmen lay under the guns of the PRC and within easy aircraft range of the mainland. Therefore, Hull argued, there existed a "serious likelihood that the situation would progress rather swiftly to that of general hostilities with Communist China." Under these circumstances, the United States should be prepared to act with whatever force was necessary to achieve success, "including the use of atomic weapons."[5]

The State Department contended that the disadvantages of losing the offshore islands did not overbalance the turmoil that another war with the PRC would create in the American alliance system. Since the Communist victory in 1949, European leaders, particularly the British, had looked askance at America's China policy, believing it needlessly provocative and more likely

---

3. The principal dissenter was Army Chief of Staff Matthew Ridgway, who, not coincidentally, had also advised against intervention in Indochina five months before. At that time as well, Radford had been at the fore of those calling for military action against the Communists. On the general question of intervention at Dienbienphu, see John Prados, *The Sky Would Fall: Operation Vulture: The U.S. Bombing Mission in Indochina, 1954* (New York: Dial Press, 1983); and George C. Herring and Richard H. Immerman, "Eisenhower, Dulles, and Dienbienphu: 'The Day We Didn't Go to War' Revisited," *Journal of American History*, Vol. 71, No. 2 (September, 1984), pp. 343–363.
4. In State Department to Manila (U.S. Embassy), Sep. 3, 1954, *FRUS*: 1952–54, Vol. XIV, p. 557. See also memorandum of conversation, Sep. 7, 1954, decimal file 793.00/9-754, State Department records (record group 59), National Archives, Washington.
5. Hull to JCS in Radford to Wilson, Sep. 11, 1954, *FRUS*: 1952–54, Vol. XIV, p. 598.

to drive Beijing into Moscow's arms than otherwise. Moreover, the British argued, by intervening in China's civil war the United States tended to inflame anti-Western sentiment throughout Asia, complicating the affairs of the Commonwealth and rendering the British position in Hong Kong and Malaya more precarious than it already was. Finally, they feared that American belligerence would lead to world war. British Foreign Secretary Anthony Eden told Dulles that a commitment to the defense of Jinmen might place NATO in a "terrible wicket."[6] Dulles and Eden did not always communicate well, but in this case the secretary of state got the point. Reflecting on the question, Dulles commented that a decision to defend Jinmen almost certainly "would alienate world opinion and gravely strain our alliances." He added, "This is the more true because it would probably lead to our initiating the use of atomic weapons."[7]

In the White House, Eisenhower shared Dulles's caution about outrunning the allies; at the same time, the president recognized the need to keep touch with his base of popular support. While not ignoring the influence of Asia-Firsters like Majority Leader William Knowland, the so-called "Senator from Formosa," Eisenhower believed that, at the moment, the public at large had no stomach for a war against China. Perhaps after further provocation by Beijing, perhaps after appropriate preparation by the administration—but not now. The president agreed with Dulles's assessment that popular sentiment would be "sharply divided" regarding an overt American commitment to the offshore islands and that any precipitate moves by the administration might provoke a "serious attack" in Congress. In fact, Eisenhower considered the stakes higher than Dulles realized. The president asserted that if he acted without the consent of Congress he might supply his critics with "logical grounds for impeachment."[8]

Guessing Intentions: The Soviet Union and the Two Chinas

The biggest unknowns in the administration's policy equation involved the reactions of the Soviet Union, the PRC, and the ROC to any move by the United States. The Soviets weighed in at the beginning of October when

---

6. Notes of conversation attached to O'Connor to Dulles, Sep. 19, 1954, *FRUS*: 1952–54, Vol. XIV, p. 649.
7. Dulles memorandum, Sep. 12, 1954, *FRUS*: 1952–54, Vol. XIV, p. 611.
8. Memorandum of discussion, 214th NSC meeting, Sep. 12, 1954, *FRUS*: 1952–54, Vol. XIV, p. 613.

First Secretary Nikita Khrushchev helped celebrate the fifth anniversary of the People's Republic of China by affirming the support of the Soviet people for their Chinese comrades in the latter's quest to liberate Taiwan.[9] Although American leaders could not tell whether socialist fraternalism extended to a Soviet willingness to go to war over the offshore islands,[10] Ambassador Charles Bohlen in Moscow believed that Khrushchev's speech, coming immediately in the wake of a hardline statement by PRC Premier Zhou Enlai (Chou En-Lai), put the Kremlin "solidly behind the Chinese position." Bohlen did not think the Soviets wanted a general war, but he feared what he called the "self-intoxicating effect" of Communist rhetoric, and he cautioned that an accidental war could not be ruled out.[11]

Although the Central Intelligence Agency (CIA) thought Bohlen exaggerated Khrushchev's clout with the PRC,[12] Eisenhower took the Soviet connection seriously. He recognized that the aims of Moscow and Beijing were not identical, but he believed that in this case the Russians would be forced to stand up for their largest ally. "When we talk of general war with Communist China," the President commented at a meeting of the National Security Council (NSC), "what we mean is general war with the USSR also." The Kremlin, Eisenhower argued, could not afford *not* to honor its commitments. For all the Russians' reliance on force, the Soviet system, like that of the United States, ultimately rested on credibility. "If the Soviets did not abide by their treaty with Communist China and go to war in support of their Chinese ally, the Soviet empire would quickly fall to pieces."[13]

American decision-makers could only guess regarding Beijing's designs.[14] A special national intelligence estimate (SNIE) incorporating the views of the CIA, the Army, Navy, Air Force, and the Joint Chiefs commented unhelpfully

---

9. See *New York Times,* Oct. 12, 1954, p. 1.

10. Stolper, *China, Taiwan, and the Offshore Islands,* p. 19, makes the point that Khrushchev promised the support of the Soviet *people* on the Taiwan issue, not that of the Soviet *government.* The distinction appears to have been lost on American officials.

11. Moscow (U.S. Embassy) to State Department, Oct. 2, 1954, *FRUS: 1952–54,* Vol. XIV, p. 674.

12. CIA Director Allen Dulles characterized Khrushchev as "rather a brash fellow" who for reasons unclear had received "a lot of latitude" from his associates in the Kremlin. Memorandum of discussion, 216th NSC meeting, Oct. 6, 1954, *FRUS: 1952–54,* Vol. XIV, p. 689.

13. Memorandum of discussion, 221st NSC meeting, Nov. 2, 1954, *FRUS: 1952–54,* Vol. XIV, p. 827.

14. American military intelligence did suggest that in light of a present insufficiency of PRC forces for major amphibious operations, and due to the operational advantages of springtime weather for an invasion, an attack on Taiwan itself was at least several months away. "Chinese Communist Capabilities and Intentions with respect to Formosa," Oct. 12, 1954, 091 China, Radford files, JCS records (record group 218), National Archives.

that the PRC doubtless intended to seize the offshore islands "at some time" and that the Communists would probably undertake "probing actions" to test American resolve. If they encountered no appreciable American resistance, they would continue to push. If they ran into American opposition, they might push anyway, believing that even if the U.S. didn't back off, they could portray it as an imperialist aggressor.[15]

Jiang's intentions were nearly as unfathomable. "We are always wrong when we believe that Orientals think logically as we do," Eisenhower told the NSC.[16] The logical course, it seemed, would be for Jiang to withdraw the Nationalist forces from their exposed positions on the offshore islands. As Eisenhower put it, the islands were "so small and so very close to the mainland" that sooner or later they would have to fall to the PRC.[17] But there was no guarantee that Jiang saw matters in the same light. All appearances, in fact, suggested that the ROC president intended to defend the offshore islands to the last man.[18] Whether this represented heroism or a martyr complex was hard for Eisenhower to tell, but it certainly did not suggest common sense.

Other administration officials, however, found Jiang's actions far more comprehensible. Robert Bowie, director of the State Department's Policy Planning Staff, argued that Jiang aimed to defend the offshore islands not *despite* the difficulty of the task but *because of* that difficulty. What constituted a danger to the United States, Bowie contended, represented an opportunity to the ROC president:

Chiang recognizes that his only hope of achieving his paramount ambition of returning to the Mainland lies in large-scale U.S. military involvement with the Chinese Communists. To Chiang the offshore islands are important not so much for defense of Taiwan or for demonstrating Nationalist military prowess but because they offer the most likely means for involving the U.S. in hostilities with the Chinese which could expand to create his opportunity for invasion.[19]

---

15. Special National Intelligence Estimate (SNIE 100-4-54), Sep. 4, 1954, *FRUS*: 1952–54, Vol. XIV, p. 563. The State Department's Office of Chinese Affairs thought the "current parlous state of Western unity" in the post-Geneva period would encourage testing by the PRC. Memorandum on SNIE 100-4-54, Sep. 17, 1954, CA 306.11a, State Department records, National Archives.
16. Memorandum of discussion, 237th NSC meeting, Feb. 17, 1955, *FRUS*: 1955–57, Vol. II, p. 279.
17. Memorandum of discussion, 221st NSC meeting, Nov. 2, 1954, *FRUS*: 1952–54, Vol. XIV, p. 827.
18. See Robertson to Dulles, Apr. 25, 1955, *FRUS*: 1955–57, Vol. II, p. 510.
19. Bowie to Dulles, Apr. 9, 1955, *FRUS*: 1955–57, Vol. II, p. 473.

Bowie concluded that an American commitment to the offshore islands would be dangerous. Such a commitment might or might not deter the Communists, but it certainly would encourage Jiang to further provoke them. The only solution, he contended, was a forthright declaration that the United States had no intention of participating in the defense of the islands.

Dulles's First Plan: Trading a Treaty for Mediation

While Eisenhower and Dulles pondered their options,[20] hostilities in the Taiwan Strait escalated. Artillery exchanges led to air raids; the fighting spread to the sea lanes as Nationalist ships attacked mainland coastal traffic and Communist torpedo boats responded by sinking an ROC destroyer escort.

Facing the growing possibility of a full-scale assault on the offshore islands, and simultaneously confronting the challenge of the administration's first midterm elections,[21] Dulles devised a two-part strategy for keeping a lid on the situation in the Strait. The first part involved an attempt at mediation: referring the PRC–ROC dispute to the United Nations, which presumably would call for a ceasefire. The idea had obvious attractions: by turning the issue over to the UN Security Council, the administration could spread

20. Decision-making during the crisis in the Taiwan Strait was definitely a joint Eisenhower-Dulles affair. As such, the affair suggests that both the traditional view of Dulles as prime mover of American foreign policy and the recent correction offered by the "Eisenhower revisionists," which puts the president in complete and nearly total command, provide an overly simplistic picture of the true situation. Each school defies summary in a note, but for a start on the former see Roscoe Drummond and Gaston Coblentz, *Duel at the Brink: John Foster Dulles' Command of American Power* (Garden City, N.Y.: Doubleday, 1960); and Richard Goold-Adams, *The Time of Power: A Reappraisal of John Foster Dulles* (London: Weidenfeld and Nicolson, 1962). On the latter: Robert A. Divine, *Eisenhower and the Cold War* (New York: Oxford University Press, 1981); Fred I. Greenstein, *The Hidden-Hand Presidency: Eisenhower as Leader* (New York: Basic Books, 1982); and Stephen E. Ambrose, *Eisenhower*, Vol. II: *The President* (New York: Simon and Schuster, 1984).
21. It would be too much to imply that the world revolves around the American electoral calendar, or that American leaders fabricate trouble to fit their political timetables, but the regularity with which international crises have appeared in the months before elections is striking. In the first two decades of the cold war: the Azerbaijan affair occurred in 1946; the Berlin blockade, in the summer of 1948; the outbreak of the Korean war, in June 1950; Dienbienphu and the inception of the offshore islands affair, in 1954; the Suez and Hungarian crises, in 1956; the American intervention in Lebanon and second round of the offshore islands controversy, in 1958; the U-2 fiasco, in 1960; the Cuban missile crisis, in 1962; the Gulf of Tonkin affair, in 1964. It might be argued that after 1964 Vietnam was a chronic crisis. To some degree, of course, these examples simply demonstrate that the world is a dangerous place. On the other hand, it is not so easy to create a similar list for odd-numbered years.

responsibility for finding a solution or blame for failing to do so. At the same time, referral to the United Nations would force the hand of both the Soviets and the PRC. Dulles explained:

This move could put a serious strain on Soviet-ChiCom [Chinese Communist] relations. If the S.U. vetoed the move, that would gravely impair its "peace offensive" and then the U.S. would win a measure of support from allies and world opinion now lacking. If the Soviets did *not* veto, the ChiComs could react adversely, and might, indeed, defy the U.N. In that case the ChiComs would again become an international outcast.[22]

Of course referral to the UN had disadvantages as well. Once the Council took up the issue, there was no telling quite what it would do. As Dulles admitted, the administration could not "wholly control the situation."[23] Furthermore, any ceasefire the Council might propose would almost certainly be based on the status quo. This might well touch off a strong political reaction in the United States: conservatives would probably consider acquiescence in the status quo tantamount to recognition of the Communist government in Beijing. Realizing the hazards involved, Dulles sought to keep the American hand in this UN initiative hidden. He worked through a proxy, New Zealand; he concealed the plan under the code name "Oracle"; he stamped reports and memoranda concerning the whole business—which had relatively little to do with national security per se—"top secret."

An additional problem was the distinct likelihood that Jiang would veto any ceasefire measure, because acceptance of the status quo would destroy Nationalist dreams for a return to the mainland, the very raison d'être of Jiang's regime. When Karl Lott Rankin, the American ambassador in Taibei, learned of Dulles's UN plan, he warned against it, predicting a "violently unfavorable reaction" from Jiang. Unless the United States took steps to cushion the shock, Rankin contended, Jiang would interpret referral to the UN as "another Yalta."[24]

To keep Jiang and his U.S. supporters happy, Dulles proposed the second half of his plan: a mutual-security treaty for the ROC. For many months Taibei had been pestering Washington for such a pact. The administration

---

22. Dulles memorandum, Sep. 12, 1954, *FRUS*: 1952–54, Vol. XIV, p. 611.
23. Ibid. See also various records for this period in files 793.00 and 793.5, State Department records, National Archives.
24. Taibei (U.S. Embassy) to State Department, Oct. 5, 1954, *FRUS*: 1952–54, Vol. XIV, p. 682. Rankin's retrospective account of the crisis can be found in Karl Lott Rankin, *China Assignment* (Seattle: University of Washington Press, 1964).

did not object to the idea in principle; the NSC noted that a non-Communist Taiwan in the middle of the Pacific island chain was "essential to U.S. security."[25] But first one thing and then another delayed action on a treaty: attempts to end the war in Korea, the possibility of intervention in Indochina, the formation of the Southeast Asia Treaty Organization. The outset of the crisis in the Strait threatened to stall treaty talks further,[26] but Dulles soon decided that the administration should try to swap a U.S.-ROC defense pact for Jiang's pledge not to denounce UN consideration of the dispute. Eisenhower approved Dulles's plan,[27] and during the second week of October the administration dispatched Assistant Secretary of State Walter Robertson to Taibei to persuade Jiang.

Not surprisingly, negotiations for the trade proved difficult. Robertson described to Jiang the advantages of appealing to the UN, pointing out that if the Soviets, on behalf of Beijing, vetoed a ceasefire proposal, "the Chinese Communist regime and its claim to a position in the UN would be further discredited." If the Russians chose not to veto, "the island positions would be provisionally secured, and the grave consequences of their loss would be avoided."[28]

But Jiang was not impressed. Suggesting that referral to the UN was the first step toward a sellout, he accused the Americans of abandoning him as the French had abandoned the Vietnamese. "Like all Asians," he told Robertson, "the Chinese have watched the situation in Indochina closely. After the negotiations at Geneva, all of Indochina was surely doomed. The beginnings of negotiations with the Communists will eventually lead to the loss of Formosa." Jiang declared that he had heeded American advice before, against his own better judgment, and it had only led to "disaster" for his people. Why should he listen now?[29]

Robertson responded that of course what the Republic of China chose to do was strictly its own business; but he added that American intelligence

---

25. NSC 5503, "U.S. Policy toward Formosa and the Government of the Republic of China," Jan. 15, 1955, *FRUS*: 1955–57, Vol. II, p. 30.
26. Walter Bedell Smith to Robertson, Sep. 1, 1954, *FRUS*: 1952–54, Vol. XIV, p. 555.
27. See Dulles to Robertson, Oct. 7, 1954, *FRUS*: 1952–54, Vol. XIV, p. 708; memorandum of telephone conversation, Oct. 7, 1954, ibid.; State Department to Taibei (U.S. Embassy), Oct. 18, 1954, 793.5/10-1854, State Department records, National Archives; Dulles to Robertson, Oct. 8, 1954, 793.5/10-854, State Department records, National Archives.
28. Memorandum of conversation, Oct. 13, 1954, 793.5/10-1354, State Department records, National Archives.
29. Ibid.

Nuclear Diplomacy | *238*

sources indicated a serious possibility of an all-out PRC assault against some of the offshore islands, and he predicted that no amount of skill and courage on the part of the ROC military would suffice to defend them. More to the point, he declared that it was "highly doubtful" that President Eisenhower would commit American forces to the defense of the islands and "engage in what might in fact become a major war with Communist China." This was as close as Robertson came to delivering an ultimatum, and he quickly softened the message by commenting that when the matter came before the UN the United States would want to reaffirm, "perhaps more formally," its connection with the ROC.[30]

Realizing, apparently, that they had no choice, Jiang and his associates spent much of the next two days attempting to secure this "more formal" connection on the most favorable basis possible. They sought to define the treaty area to include the offshore islands. Robertson flatly rejected the idea. They insisted that a treaty be signed *before* the UN took up a ceasefire proposal. Robertson, lacking definite instructions on this point and basically sympathetic to Jiang's position, indicated that he would relay the suggestion to Washington.[31]

The administration eventually accepted Jiang's condition,[32] and Dulles put the UN plan on hold while negotiations for a treaty took place. After considerable wrangling and some Nationalist leakage of the administration's bargaining position—which prompted grave warnings from the Americans that such indiscretions were "very harmful" to fruitful discussions[33]—Dulles on November 23 initialed a treaty specifically pledging the United States to defend only Taiwan and the nearby Penghus (Pescadores). With evident relief the secretary of state reported to Eisenhower: "This has been a difficult negotiation but the result, I believe, stakes out unqualifiedly our interest in Formosa and the Pescadores and does so on a basis which will not enable the Chinese Nationalists to involve us in a war with Communist China."[34]

Dulles's Second Plan: Pulling Jiang Back and Bringing Congress Aboard

If Dulles thought the worst was over, he soon recognized his mistake. Just as the treaty talks were ending, the PRC announced the espionage conviction

---

30. Ibid.
31. Ibid.
32. See memorandum by Douglas MacArthur Jr., Oct. 14, 1954, *FRUS: 1952–54*, Vol. XIV, p. 755.
33. Memorandum of conversation by McConaughy, Nov. 6, 1954, ibid., p. 870.
34. Memorandum by Dulles, Nov. 23, 1954, ibid., p. 929.

of thirteen American fliers shot down over China during the Korean War. Predictably, this action provoked cries of outrage in the United States; Senator Knowland went so far as to demand a blockade of the China coast.[35] Although at least a few of the individuals involved were in fact agents of the CIA,[36] the administration did not concede the point and consequently had to share, to some degree at least, the public expressions of outrage. As a result, Dulles chose to delay still further the submission of the ceasefire resolution to the Security Council, requesting New Zealand to postpone its initiative until the furor subsided.[37]

But when in January the Communists succeeded in capturing one of the offshore islands—a small member of the Dachen (Tachen) group, some two hundred miles north of Taiwan—the administration was forced to reconsider its basic approach. Heretofore, Eisenhower and Dulles had resisted making an explicit and public statement of American intentions in the Taiwan area; they preferred, as Dulles remarked, to "fuzz up" the matter and retain as much freedom of action as possible.[38] The sentencing of the American fliers, however, and the heightened pressure on the Dachens seemed to indicate that the policy of obfuscation was failing to restrain the PRC. On January 19 Dulles told Eisenhower that he was becoming increasingly concerned that doubt as to American intentions was having a "bad effect" on American prestige in the area. Fighting in the Dachens, whose fall to the Communists appeared imminent, had especially damaged American credibility. "It was in many quarters assumed that we would defend the islands, and our failure to do so indicated that we were running away when actual danger appeared."

To counter this perception, Dulles proposed to pressure Jiang to evacuate the Dachens, which were even less defensible than the other offshore islands, while simultaneously asking Congress for explicit authority to deploy American forces to defend Taiwan and such of the surrounding area as the president considered important.[39]

---

35. *New York Times*, Nov. 28, 1954, p. 1. The administration rejected the idea, but took the precaution of investigating the legal basis for a blockade. The conclusion of the State Department's Office of Chinese Affairs was that some justification could be found in the actions and directives of the United Nations relating to the Korean War—but not much. Cowles to Robert Murphy, Nov. 29, 1954, CA 230 TS, State Department records, National Archives.

36. See diary entry for Dec. 2, 1954, Robert H. Ferrell, ed., *The Diary of James C. Hagerty: Eisenhower in Mid-Course, 1954–1955* (Bloomington: Indiana University Press, 1983), p. 121; and Dulles telephone conversation, Dec. 1, 1954, Dulles papers, Eisenhower Library, Abilene, Kansas.

37. Memorandum of conversation by Bond, Nov. 30, 1954, *FRUS: 1952–54*, Vol. XIV, p. 961.

38. Memorandum of discussion, 221st NSC meeting, Nov. 2., 1954, ibid., p. 827.

39. Memorandum of conversation by Dulles, Jan. 19, 1955, *FRUS: 1955–57*, Vol. II, p. 41.

Although the Joint Chiefs objected to giving up the Dachens,[40] Eisenhower accepted Dulles's package. As soon as the new Congress convened, the secretary set to work selling his proposal to the legislature, inviting key members of the House and Senate to the State Department for an explanation of the administration's strategy. Referring to the Nationalist occupation of the offshore islands as "a matter of historic accident, rather than one of military planning," Dulles described the ROC situation on the Dachens as nearly hopeless. These islands were so close to the mainland and so far from Taiwan that PRC planes could carry out raids and return to base before ROC fighters responded. As a result, defense of the Dachens would require the use of American aircraft carriers, which, he suggested, could not be spared from more important assignments elsewhere. On the other hand, Jinmen could be covered by the ROC Air Force; in addition, its location opposite the logical staging point for an amphibious assault on Taiwan gave it a strategic value the Dachens lacked. If the United States did not take the action he proposed, Dulles said, there would occur "a falling of the islands one by one, including Jinmen, involving wiping out more than 100,000 of the best Nationalist troops, a drop in morale on Formosa so that the defense of Formosa would be extremely difficult and might require considerable replacements of Nationalist and United States troops." As to the effect on American prestige: "We would be charged with turning and running and making excuses, and the whole effect on the non-communist countries in Asia would be extremely bad."

Arthur Radford, also present at this session, underlined Dulles's argument regarding the significance of ROC morale. Should Jiang and his people come to believe that they could not rely on the United States, they might decide to throw in the towel. Since Taiwan must not fall to the Communists, Radford continued, this would leave the United States in a bad spot. "We might have to go in ourselves."

Some of the congressional leaders asked what kind of military action could result from the administration's plan. Alexander Wiley, the ranking Republican on the Senate Foreign Relations Committee, wanted to know what would happen if the Communists attacked an American aircraft carrier. The Russians, Wiley said, had the best submarines in the world, and they had "more in the Far Eastern area than we have in our total fleet."

---

40. Joint Intelligence Committee, "Intelligence Estimate of the Situation in the Tachen Islands," Jan. 22, 1955, 381 Formosa, JCS records, National Archives.

Radford responded that the situation was under control. He contended that the Soviet navy would not intervene; if it did, the American fleet could "take care of it."

Wiley asked what the administration would do if Jiang did not agree to evacuate the Dachens. "We would be in a hell of a fix," Dulles admitted. But the Secretary went on to express confidence that with proper persuasion the Nationalists would go along with the administration's plan.[41]

Dulles and Radford went from this meeting to a session of the NSC. Allen Dulles, Director of Central Intelligence, described the military buildup in the Dachen area and predicted a major assault at any moment. The ROC position there, he added, was precarious, morale was low and resupply difficult. Even retreat, should Jiang approve evacuation, might prove dangerous and costly.

Eisenhower's Special Assistant for National Security Affairs, Robert Cutler, contended that the entire offshore islands question required rethinking. Suppose Jiang consented to pull out of the Dachens; wouldn't the United States be more committed to Jinmen than ever? Was this what the administration wanted? Cutler asserted that an American guarantee for Jinmen would "almost certainly involve the United States in military actions on the mainland of Communist China." Communist aircraft, he argued, would attack American planes, which would then pursue the attackers over PRC territory. One thing would lead to another, and before long the U.S. and the PRC would be at war.

Eisenhower responded that in some respects the matter was out of American hands. If the Communists wanted war, he said, there was "nothing we could do to prevent it." But the president added that he agreed with Dulles that the proposed strategy, by making more explicit the nature of America's intentions, would actually decrease the risk of war. At the moment, the administration's China policy was in a condition of "dangerous drift." Something must be done to recapture control of the situation.

Foster Dulles conceded that drawing a line around Jinmen would involve a risk of general war with the PRC, but he gave such an outcome "less than a 50-50 chance." Beijing, the secretary asserted, did not want to "get tough with us in a big way" just yet.

Treasury Secretary George Humphrey raised the issue of Moscow's objectives. "Nothing in the world," he argued, "would please Soviet Russia so

---

41. Memorandum of conversation, Jan. 20, 1955, *FRUS: 1955–57*, Vol. II, p. 55.

much as to get the United States involved in hostilities with Communist China."

Eisenhower granted that Humphrey was probably right, but still the president chose to follow Dulles's lead. Eisenhower admitted that the offshore islands would be difficult to defend, and he understood the larger hazards their defense involved. But the "psychological consequences" of allowing a Communist takeover were too great to accept. The administration faced a "concrete test" of its resolve, and it could not back down. Adjourning the meeting, the president directed Dulles to move ahead with his proposal.[42]

On January 24 the White House sent a message to Congress explaining American policy with respect to Taiwan and the offshore islands. Describing the "pattern of aggression" by the PRC against Nationalist positions, and declaring that the seizure of Taiwan by an unfriendly power would "seriously dislocate" the Western position in the Pacific, Eisenhower asserted the necessity of taking firm measures "designed to improve the prospects for peace," including preparations for the use of American military power. Reiterating Dulles's point that the present deployment of ROC forces was the result of "historical rather than military reasons"—but without mentioning the Dachens by name—the president declared that the United States stood ready to help the ROC "redeploy and consolidate" its troops. He urged speedy ratification of the ROC mutual-security treaty. Most significantly, he requested special congressional authorization to commit American forces to the Strait, but "only in situations which are recognizable as parts of, or definite preliminaries to, an attack against the main positions of Formosa and the Pescadores."[43]

With this statement the administration sought to reassure Jiang, his congressional supporters, and everyone else who might be listening that it considered Taiwan worth a fight; at the same time it avoided an explicit commitment to the offshore islands. Dulles earlier had spoken of the desirability of clearing up confusion about American policy in the Strait, but while working on the president's message he had concluded that it would be best not "to nail the flag to the mast" regarding particular islands.[44] As a result,

---

42. Memorandum of discussion, 232nd NSC meeting, Jan. 20, 1955, *FRUS: 1955–57*, Vol. II, p. 69.

43. Eisenhower message to Congress, Jan. 24, 1955, *Public Papers of the Presidents: Dwight D. Eisenhower, 1955* (Washington, D.C.: U.S. Government Printing Office, 1959), p. 207.

44. Memorandum of discussion, 233rd NSC meeting, Jan. 21, 1955, *FRUS: 1955–57*, Vol. II, p. 89; memorandum of conversation, Jan. 21, 1955, CA 306.11a, State Department records, National Archives.

any decision on the use of American forces in the Taiwan area remained up to President Eisenhower, whose military judgment few legislators would care to challenge.

Eisenhower's Approach: Focusing the Commitment Still Further

Politically, Dulles's maneuver proved an immediate success. The House at once passed the "Formosa Resolution," authorizing the administration to commit American forces in the Strait; the Senate, despite some last-minute worries on the secretary's part,[45] concurred a few days later. For good measure, the Senate ratified the mutual-defense treaty by an overwhelming margin.[46]

On the Asian front the reaction was mixed. Jiang grumbled but went along with the Dachen evacuation, evidently believing that by doing so he was tying the United States more closely than ever to Jinmen and Mazu. Zhou Enlai publicly reaffirmed Beijing's view that Taiwan was "an inalienable part of China's territory," and he denounced the United States for shielding "the traitorous Chiang Kai-shek clique."[47] Through private channels as well, the PRC premier took a hard line, emphasizing that the American statement left little room for compromise. "It was a war message," he told a British diplomat. Obviously intending that his comments be passed along, Zhou declared that China was not afraid of the United States and would fight to defend its interests.[48]

The Russian response was harder to gauge. From Moscow, Ambassador Bohlen cabled the opinion that although the Kremlin showed "no inclination" to initiate hostilities over an area as peripheral to vital Soviet interests as Taiwan, Moscow could not allow the United States to bully a fellow socialist country. Soviet leaders, Bohlen contended, would face "a terrible dilemma" if war broke out. "Confronted with a choice between involvement in a war in which they had no direct interest and abandonment of their chief and

45. Dulles telephone conversation, Jan. 25, 1955, Dulles papers, Eisenhower Library.
46. On the Formosa Resolution, the vote in the House was 410 to 3; in the Senate, 83 to 3. The Senate ratified the treaty by a vote of 65 to 6.
47. In Noble Franklin, ed., *Documents on International Affairs 1955* (London: Oxford University Press, 1958), pp. 445–446.
48. Zhou's remarks in memorandum from British government to U.S. State Department, Jan. 28, 1955, *FRUS: 1955–57*, Vol. II, p. 157. The British chargé d'affaires, Humphrey Trevelyan, describes this conversation in greater detail in *Living with the Communists: China, 1953–5; Soviet Union, 1962–5* (Boston: Gambit, 1972), pp. 142–144.

possibly only real ally in [the] world, it is impossible in advance to say which decision would be made." Bohlen added that no matter what Moscow decided, there existed definite limits on the ability of the Kremlin to keep the PRC in line. "It seems increasingly obvious that [the] Soviet Government does not have [a] controlling influence [on] Chinese actions."[49]

In Washington, the American intelligence community sifted through these and other reports and concluded that although Beijing was probably not looking for a large war, with passing time the Communists would become "increasingly impatient and less cautious" and might "miscalculate" American responses. There existed, therefore, a significant possibility that the United States and the PRC would find themselves in a conflict neither intended. Should this happen, the analysts asserted, Beijing would probably do "all in its power" to bring in the Soviet Union. Moscow would not eagerly join the fight but would, in the last analysis, "give the Chinese Communists whatever local military support appeared necessary to preserve the Sino-Soviet alliance and prevent the destruction of the regime."[50]

Eisenhower and Dulles were no more sanguine. At a January 27 meeting of the NSC, the president said that Moscow seemed to be encouraging Chinese aggression. The Russians, he declared, were "undoubtedly doing all they could to involve the United States in Asia and in a general war with Communist China." Dulles agreed, pointing to the political and diplomatic advantages the Kremlin stood to gain, especially in Europe, from American overcommitment to the Far East. In Britain particularly, the secretary said, a wave of anti-Americanism could be expected to follow the outbreak of hostilities between the United States and the PRC.[51]

Radford, as usual, viewed the situation with greater optimism. Russia and the PRC, the JCS chairman said, were "bluffing." The administration should call the Communists' bluff. And if war with the PRC did come—well, worse could happen. The Joint Chiefs were not foolish enough to be planning a land war against the hundreds of millions of Chinese; fighting would take place only at sea and in the air, where the United States enjoyed overwhelming superiority. The worst difficulties in such a conflict would be wholly on

---

49. Moscow (U.S. Embassy) to State Department, Jan. 27, 1955, *FRUS*: 1955–57. Vol. II, p. 147.
50. Special National Intelligence Estimate (SNIE 100-3-55): "Communist Reactions to Certain Possible U.S. Courses of Action with respect to the Islands off the Coast of China," Jan. 25, 1955, *FRUS*: 1955–57, Vol. II, p. 125.
51. Memorandum of discussion, 234th NSC meeting, Jan. 27, 1955, ibid., p. 135.

Beijing's side, starting with how to "get at us if we don't choose to be got at."[52]

Through the first half of February, the administration concentrated on helping the ROC evacuate the Dachens. Unsure whether Communist forces would contest the retreat, American military officials took no chances. With Eisenhower's approval,[53] the JCS gave the commander of the Seventh Fleet authority to conduct reprisals against bases from which attacks on American forces originated.[54] At the same time, the Joint Chiefs ordered the Strategic Air Command (SAC) to begin, on an "urgent basis," target selection for an "enlarged atomic offensive" against the PRC.[55]

Although the evacuation itself went unchallenged by the PRC, the administration had no time to relax. While PRC units moved into the Dachens, Beijing maintained its propaganda offensive, increased its military buildup opposite Taiwan, and rejected an invitation from UN Secretary-General Dag Hammarskjold to send a representative to the UN to discuss a peaceful resolution of the conflict.[56]

Eisenhower found the Communists' actions downright provocative. "You know," he told Press Secretary James Hagerty, "they are certainly doing everything they can to try our patience. It's awfully difficult to remain calm under these situations. Sometimes I think that it would be best all around to go after them right now without letting them pick their time and the place of their own choosing."[57]

Although Eisenhower in this instance was essentially letting off steam, the administration began girding psychologically for war. New intelligence reports indicated that the PRC and the Soviet Union might consider a small-scale conflict to their advantage; the same reports indicated a strong possibility that such a war would not remain limited.[58] Dulles returned from Taibei,

---

52. Ibid.; memorandum of conversation, Jan. 27, 1955, CA 306.11, State Department records, National Archives.
53. Radford to Nathan Twining et al., Feb. 5, 1955, CCS 381, JCS records, National Archives; Hagerty diary, Jan. 29, 1955, Hagerty papers, Eisenhower Library.
54. Commander-in-Chief, Pacific (CINCPAC) to U.S. Army, Pacific (USARPAC) et al., Jan. 30, 1955, CCS 381, JCS records, National Archives.
55. JCS to Commander, Strategic Air Command (COMSAC), Feb. 1, 1955, CCS 381, JCS records, National Archives.
56. *New York Times*, Feb. 4, 1955, p. 1.
57. Hagerty diary, Feb. 3, 1955, Hagerty papers, Eisenhower Library.
58. Special National Intelligence Estimate (SNIE 11-4-55): "Review of Current Communist Attitudes toward General War," Feb. 15, 1955, *FRUS: 1955–57*, Vol. II, p. 273; Robert Totten for

where he had delivered the mutual-defense treaty, convinced that the problem in the Strait was "much more virulent" than he had realized. The United States, Dulles said, must prepare itself for a "quite serious showdown."[59] The secretary told the NSC that he saw "at least an even chance" that the United States would have to fight. Although the administration had avoided an explicit commitment to Jinmen and Mazu, much of the world considered the defense of those islands a test of American resolve, and if the Communists attacked, the United States might have to hit back. Dulles went so far as to declare that war was "a question of time rather than a question of fact." Having been "pretty well convinced" by the arguments of Radford and the military chiefs, he believed that such a war would quickly go nuclear. But he hoped the administration could find a way to delay the conflict, in order "to create a better public climate for the use of atomic weapons."[60]

Eisenhower concurred on the advantages of playing for time,[61] and during the next few days the administration set about trying to foster the "better climate" Dulles spoke of. On March 12 the secretary described "new and powerful weapons of precision" which American scientists had added to the free world's arsenal, explaining that these devices could "utterly destroy military targets without endangering unrelated civilian centers." Dulles added that the administration was prepared to use these weapons in the event of war in the Strait.[62] Vice President Richard Nixon offered his opinion that "tactical atomic weapons are now conventional and will be used against the targets of any aggressive force."[63] Eisenhower, asked whether such comments accurately reflected administration policy, responded, "in any combat where these things can be used on strictly military targets and for strictly military purposes, I seen no reason why they shouldn't be used, just exactly as you would use a bullet or anything else."[64] European on-lookers, especially the British, reacted strongly, feeling that the U.S. was treading far too close to war.

Joint Intelligence Group to Radford, Mar. 16, 1955, 091 China, Radford files, JCS records, National Archives.
59. Minutes of cabinet meeting, Mar. 11, 1955, Eisenhower papers, Eisenhower Library.
60. Memorandum of discussion, 240th NSC meeting, Mar. 10, 1955, *FRUS: 1955–57*, Vol. II, p. 345; memorandum for the record, Mar. 11, 1955, Dulles papers, Eisenhower Library.
61. Memorandum for the record, Mar. 11, 1955, Eisenhower papers, Eisenhower Library.
62. Townsend Hoopes, *The Devil and John Foster Dulles* (Boston: Little, Brown, 1973), pp. 278–279.
63. Ibid., p. 279.
64. Ambrose, *Eisenhower*, p. 239.

Behind the scenes, the president sent his closest personal aide, Colonel Andrew Goodpaster, to Honolulu to confer with the American Pacific commander, Admiral Felix Stump. Stump reassured Goodpaster that the Communists were not quite ready to start a war. Preparations for a full-scale assault on Mazu, Stump said, would require at least another month, while the groundwork for an invasion of Jinmen woud take twice as long. Thus, he believed, the president and the secretary would probably get the period of grace they desired.[65]

But time only strained the situation more. Through the first part of April, American intelligence sources reported continuing Communist reinforcement of the Taiwan area.[66] ROC military leaders requested American support—which Eisenhower refused—for mine-laying operations in the Jinmen channel.[67] Radford began agitating for preemptive strikes against PRC airbases, arguing that such moves made sense not only militarily but politically. In the event war came, Radford said, critics would be likely to ask "Pearl Harbor type" questions if the administration were caught at a disadvantage. Radford also asserted that the crisis in the Far East would not end until China got a "bloody nose," and he advocated a declaration to the effect that the United States would consider further strengthening of Communist positions provocative.[68] In addition, lest any confusion exist in the minds of the Communists, he advocated telling Beijing and Moscow directly that the United States would use "all means available" to defend the offshore islands.[69]

Eisenhower rejected Radford's advice, and resisted subsequent recommendations for bombing PRC radar complexes, sending nuclear-armed rocket batteries and a division of American troops to Taiwan, or shifting an additional Strategic Air Command bomber wing to the Pacific.[70] Less convinced

---

65. Goodpaster memorandum to Eisenhower, Mar. 15, 1955, Eisenhower papers, Eisenhower Library.
66. Stump to Chief of Naval Operations (CNO) Carney, Apr. 8, 1955, 381 Formosa, JCS records, National Archives; Chief, Military Assistance Advisory Group (CHMAAG) Formosa to JCS, Apr. 7, 1955, ibid.
67. Radford in memorandum for the record, Mar. 11, 1955, Eisenhower papers, Eisenhower Library; CNO to CINCPAC, Apr. 6, 1955, 381 Formosa, JCS records, National Archives.
68. Memorandum of conversation, Mar. 26, 1955, *FRUS*: 1955–57, Vol. II, p. 400.
69. Radford to Wilson, Mar. 27, 1955, 091 China, Radford files, JCS records, National Archives.
70. See CHMAAG Formosa to CINCPAC, Mar. 27, 1955, 381 Formosa, JCS records, National Archives; Ridgway to Radford, Apr. 5, 1955, *FRUS*: 1955–57, Vol. II, p. 452; Herbert Hoover, Jr., to Dulles, Apr. 1, 1955, ibid., p. 439; Gen. William Chase to Stump, Apr. 8, 1955, ibid., p. 465; Radford briefing paper, Mar. 31, 1955, 091 China, Radford files, JCS records, National Archives.

than Dulles that a war was at hand, and less eager than Radford to start one, Eisenhower refused to be rushed into anything.

All the same, the president realized that events could not be allowed to continue on their present course. As he argued in a note to Dulles, the administration was widely perceived to be committed, politically if not legally, to the defense of Jinmen and Mazu, territory it considered essentially unimportant. If the Communists decided to attack, the United States might find itself in a major war it did not wish to fight. On the other hand, he continued, for the administration to renounce a defense of the offshore islands would invite Communist adventurism abroad and conservative criticism at home. Something had to be done. "The only logical course of action is to attempt to bring about reasonable changes in the situation rather than to remain inert awaiting the inevitable moment of decision between two unacceptable choices."[71]

Eisenhower proposed a diplomatic initiative designed to persuade Jiang to reconsider the importance of the islands—to convince him that they should be treated as "outposts," which, while important, were not essential to the security of Taiwan proper. The objective, the president said, would be to "make clear that neither Chiang nor ourselves is committed to *full-out* defense of Quemoy and the Matsus, so that no matter what the outcome of an attack upon them, there would be no danger of a collapse of the free world position in the region." If Jiang agreed, the United States would step up its military aid program, increase the American air group already on Taiwan to a full wing, and send "a couple of regiments of Marines" for moral support.[72] After further consideration, Eisenhower decided to improve the offer by including a promise to deploy nuclear weapons on Taiwan and to blockade the China coast in the area of the Strait.[73]

Even so, Eisenhower recognized, Jiang might balk at giving up the offshore islands—which is what, in essence, the president's proposal amounted to[74]—

71. Eisenhower to Dulles, Apr. 5, 1955, *FRUS: 1955–57*, Vol. II, p. 445.
72. Ibid.
73. Memorandum of conversation by Dulles, Apr. 17, 1955, *FRUS: 1955–57*, Vol. II, p. 491; memorandum for record by Rankin, Apr. 29, 1955, Rankin papers, Princeton. For further details, see Gordon H. Chang, "To the Nuclear Brink: Eisenhower, Dulles and the Quemoy-Matsu Crisis," *International Security*, Vol. 12, No. 4 (Spring 1988), pp. 96–122.
74. This point came up in the 1960 election campaign, with the Democrats alleging that the Eisenhower administration had attempted to persuade Jiang to withdraw from Jinmen and Mazu, and the Republicans denying the charge. In his memoirs, Eisenhower took pains to defend his actions in the affair, reproducing part of the memorandum in which he outlined the plan to Dulles, as a means of demonstrating that he had no intention of forcing Jiang back from

and he argued that on psychological and other grounds the administration must move cautiously. "To protect the prestige of Jiang and the morale of his forces, any alteration in military and political planning should obviously be developed under his leadership; above all, there must be no basis for public belief that the alterations came about through American intervention or coercion."[75] For this delicate mission, Eisenhower first sought the services of Congressman Walter Judd, who was even more outspoken than Knowland in his devotion to the welfare of the ROC. The Minnesota Republican initially agreed, but upon reconsideration backed out.[76] Eisenhower then tapped Walter Robertson and Arthur Radford, both of whom were known for their strong support of the ROC.[77]

While the president laid plans for softening up Jiang, Dulles took advantage of the approaching Bandung conference of Asian and African nations to work the diplomatic back channels. Hoping that Zhou would want to make a peaceful impression at what was, in some respects, the PRC's coming-out party, Dulles directed the State Department to advise America's Asian friends how to encourage Zhou's conciliatory tendencies. To the governments of Japan, Pakistan, Thailand, Iran, Iraq, and Egypt, the department sent suggestions that their attitudes at Bandung might have a signal effect on whether there would be peace or war in the Far East.[78] To the Philippine government the administration provided a draft resolution for submission at Bandung calling on all parties "to renounce forthwith the use of force or the threat of force" in the Taiwan Strait.[79] To the British, whose Commonwealth connections provided a reliable communications link to India, Dulles said

---

the islands. Dwight D. Eisenhower, *The White House Years: Mandate for Change 1953–1956* (Garden City, N.Y.: Doubleday, 1963), pp. 481, 611–612. In a narrow sense, Eisenhower was right. The president did not feel he was in any position, politically or diplomatically, to force Jiang to retreat from Jinmen and Mazu. Nonetheless, he would have been delighted had Jiang made such a decision on his own, and the essential purpose of the Robertson-Radford mission was to encourage such thinking. In particular, Eisenhower wanted Jiang to begin treating the islands as "outposts," i.e., as expendable. Jiang, of course, saw where such an idea would lead, which is why he rejected it. Stephen Ambrose, in Eisenhower's defense, suggests that Robertson and Radford missed the subtlety of Eisenhower's plan. Ambrose, *Eisenhower*, p. 244. What seems more likely is that they, with Jiang, simply thought through the "outpost" notion to its logical conclusion and were willing to call a spade a spade.
75. Eisenhower to Dulles, Apr. 5, 1955, *FRUS: 1955–57*, Vol. II, p. 445.
76. Dulles telephone conversation, Apr. 11, 1955, Dulles papers, Eisenhower Library.
77. Indeed, before accepting their assignment, both men expressed doubts about the President's basic idea. Dulles telephone conversation, Apr. 13, 1955, Dulles papers, Eisenhower Library.
78. State Department to U.S. Embassy, Ankara et al., Apr. 8, 1955, *FRUS: 1955–57*, Vol. II, p. 466.
79. Attachment to memorandum of conversation, Apr. 8, 1955, ibid., p. 465.

that if assurances could be obtained through Bandung that the Communists would not attack Taiwan itself and would leave the offshore islands "to be fought for," such a guarantee would be a "considerable contribution."[80]

Jiang doubtless would have been infuriated had he learned that the administration was suggesting to other governments that the islands should be "fought for"; as it was, he found the mission of Robertson and Radford distasteful enough. Rumors had drifted from Washington to Taibei that their aim was to get Jiang to give up Jinmen and Mazu. On learning that the rumors were essentially correct, Jiang was, as Robertson described it, "visibly shaken."[81] For five hours the two emissaries tried to explain the advantages of the administration's proposal, but Jiang would have none of it. He accused the United States of reneging on the agreement he claimed it had made at the time of the evacuation of the Dachens. Robertson replied that the United States had committed itself only to the security of Taiwan, not to Jinmen and Mazu. In any event, Robertson added, the situation had changed since January; President Eisenhower was now convinced that he could not use American forces for the defense of the offshore islands without a "large loss" of public support at home and abroad. The United States government was not, Robertson continued, telling Jiang how to manage ROC affairs, and certainly was not ordering him to give up the offshore islands. It was merely saying that he had better not count on American help in defending them.

But Jiang refused to budge. Even if the United States would not stand and fight, he and his people would. They had retreated far enough. "Soldiers," he said, "must choose proper places to die. Chinese soldiers consider Quemoy [and] Matsu are proper places for them."[82]

Off the Hook—for the Moment

Jiang's rejection of Eisenhower's proposal would have left the administration in as precarious a position as before,[83] had not the Communists suddenly

---

80. Memorandum of conversation, Apr. 7, 1955, ibid., p. 453. The full extent of American pressure on allies and clients attending the Bandung conference remains unclear. A sense of that pressure can be inferred from a reference by C. D. Jackson, former White House aide and still administration insider, to "some heavy work by Allen Dulles' boys" in preparing friendly Asian states for the conference. Jackson to John Jessup, Oct. 5, 1955, Jackson papers, Eisenhower Library.
81. Taibei (U.S. Embassy) to State Department, Apr. 25, 1955, *FRUS*: 1955–57, Vol. II, p. 509.
82. Summary of conversation in Robertson to Dulles, Apr. 25, 1955, ibid., p. 510.
83. Eisenhower's initial reaction was to tell Dulles, "We are still on the horns of the dilemma." Eisenhower to Dulles, Apr. 26, 1955, ibid., p. 522.

decided to call a halt to the confrontation in the Strait. Dulles had hoped Bandung might produce motion toward a settlement, but he hardly expected Zhou's "sensational initiative," as Kenneth Young, the director of the State Department's Office of Philippine and Southeast Asian Affairs, described it.[84] At a luncheon hosted by the Prime Minister of Ceylon, and later at the closing session of the Bandung conference, Zhou declared that China did not want war with the United States, and he proposed negotiations to ease tension in the vicinity of Taiwan.[85]

Eisenhower seized the offer,[86] and within a short time the immediate crisis was over. The details of the dénouement required some time to work out, but over the next few months the shelling of the islands stopped, the PRC released the American prisoners from the Korean war, and American and PRC representatives began direct discussions.[87]

The Administration came away from the crisis congratulating itself on its skillful handling of a dangerous business. Dulles publicly asserted that the Taiwan Strait affair proved the worth of the administration's bold approach to foreign policy. "Some say we were brought to the verge of war," he declared. "Of couse we were brought to the verge of war. . . . If you run away from it, if you are scared to go to the brink, you are lost."[88] Eisenhower boasted in his memoirs that he had steered a steady course "through narrow and dangerous waters between appeasement and global war." He declared that during the eight months of the crisis "the Administration moved through treacherous cross-currents with one channel leading to peace with honor and a hundred channels leading to war or dishonor."[89]

Recent students of the Eisenhower era have concurred with this judgment, paying tribute especially to the manner in which the president kept his

---

84. Kenneth T. Young, *Negotiating with the Chinese Communists: The United States Experience 1953–1967* (New York: McGraw-Hill, 1968), p. 44. As to Dulles's expectations regarding Bandung, in the wake of Zhou's proposal the secretary of state commented that conference had come out far better than expected, that "the friendly Asian countries" had "put on an amazing performance." Minutes of cabinet meeting, Apr. 29, 1955, Eisenhower papers, Eisenhower Library.
85. *New York Times*, Apr. 23, 1955, p. 1, and Apr. 24, 1955, p. 1. Opinions differ as to why the PRC chose to back down at this time. Kalicki, for example, emphasizes the deterrent effect of American statements in prompting PRC leaders to shift to non-belligerent tactics in their quest to gain Taiwan. Kalicki, *Patterns of Sino-American Crises*, pp. 150–152. Stolper places greater weight on domestic political developments in the PRC, adding that Beijing retreated partly to prevent the issue of the offshore islands from being separated from the question of Taiwan. Stolper, *China, Taiwan, and the Offshore Islands*, pp. 98–108.
86. See Ambrose, *Eisenhower*, p. 244.
87. See Young, *Negotiating with the Chinese Communists*, p. 45 ff.
88. James Shepley, "How Dulles Averted War," *Life*, Jan. 16, 1956, p. 70 ff.
89. Eisenhower, *Mandate for Change*, p. 483.

intentions hidden at the moments of greatest stress.[90] The administration did avoid war, and it emerged from the crisis with its basic objective, a secure Taiwan, intact. Eisenhower deserves credit for resisting repeated advice from the military to draw a nuclear line around the islands.

On the other hand, one cannot escape the fact that the crisis in the Strait was largely self-inflicted. "Perhaps," Dulles said, at the March NSC meeting in which he predicted at least an even chance of war, "we should have taken this problem more seriously at an earlier time."[91] Through inattention more than anything else, the administration allowed the idea to develop that American credibility was connected to the defense of the islands. Had Eisenhower or Dulles stated plainly, before the issue became a center of world attention, that Taiwan itself was what they were interested in, events would not have taken them to the edge of war over territory they deemed fundamentally insignificant.

Further, the outcome was nothing to brag about. Taiwan was safe—but its security had never been in serious doubt, as American intelligence sources reported from the beginning. And the administration, by signing a treaty with the ROC and publicly committing itself to the defense of Taiwan, had narrowed its options for the future. In this respect Jiang, not Eisenhower and Dulles, was the big winner. As for the offshore islands, the cause of all the trouble, their future remained as uncertain as ever. They continued to be hostages to the PRC, ready for use whenever the Communists needed a pretext for confrontation with the West. Not surprisingly, when Beijing sought such a confrontation three years later, the administration was again forced nearly to war.[92]

Ratifying the New Look

These considerations raise some basic questions regarding the crisis. Why, really, did the administration make such a fuss over the islands? Why did it risk damage to friendly relations with the Europeans, whose cooperation was far more central to American security than Taiwan's ever would be?

90. See Divine, *Eisenhower and the Cold War*, pp. 65–66; and Ambrose, *Eisenhower*, p. 245.
91. Memorandum of discussion, 240th NSC meeting, Mar. 10, 1955, *FRUS: 1955–57*, Vol. II, p. 345.
92. On the second Taiwan Strait crisis, see Stolper, *China, Taiwan, and the Offshore Islands*, ch. 8 and bibliography; Gordon, *United States Opposition to Use of Force*; Kalicki, *Pattern of Sino-American Crises*, ch. 8; and George and Smoke, *Deterrence in American Foreign Policy*, ch. 12.

Why did it scare the wits out of half the world by openly threatening nuclear war?

Political and diplomatic factors played an important role, of course. No Republican administration could lightly disregard the wishes of the China bloc, a significant element of its party. And Eisenhower certainly sought to avoid the appearance of retreating in the face of aggression. Superpowers, he believed, have reputations to maintain.

But a more complete answer would seem to lie in the fundamental strategic posture of the United States in 1954. Ten months before the crisis in the Strait began, Eisenhower approved NSC 162/2, which effected a basic change in American national security policy. Asserting that a sound economy was as essential to American defense as a strong military establishment, and that the United States could not afford both a conventional and a nuclear deterrent, NSC 162/2 authorized early use of nuclear weapons in any conflict with the Communists.[93] The paper itself, of course, was top secret, but on the obvious grounds that a deterrent only deters if the other side knows about it, the administration soon made the new policy public. In a widely noted address of January 1954, Dulles described what was quickly dubbed the doctrine of "massive retaliation," declaring that the United States was prepared to make use of its "massive retaliatory power" to punish aggression by responding "vigorously at places and with means of its own choosing."[94]

From the beginning, massive retaliation ran into credibility problems. The Soviets also possessed atomic weapons; would the United States risk escalation and retaliation in circumstances not involving vital American interests? Many observers thought not. Nor did the events of the first part of 1954, when the Eisenhower administration made threatening sounds about military intervention in Indochina but, in the end, let the French lose, do anything to silence the skeptics.[95]

---

93. The operative sentence was: "In the event of hostilities, the United States will consider nuclear weapons to be as available for use as other munitions." NSC 162/2, Oct. 30, 1953, *FRUS: 1952–54*, Vol. II, p. 577. Although it is now somewhat dated, Glenn H. Snyder's "The 'New Look' of 1953," in Warner R. Schilling, Paul Y. Hammond, and Glenn H. Snyder, *Strategy, Politics, and Defense Budgets* (New York: Columbia University Press, 1962) remains in many ways the most sophisticated treatment of the revised policy.
94. Quoted in John Lewis Gaddis, *Strategies of Containment: A Critical Appraisal of Postwar American National Security Policy* (New York: Oxford University Press, 1982), p. 147.
95. For the debate over massive retaliation, see Gaddis, *Strategies of Containment*, ch. 5; Paul Peeters, *Massive Retaliation: The Policy and Its Critics* (Chicago: Henry Regnery, 1959); and Gregg Herken, *Counsels of War* (New York: Knopf, 1985), p. 103 ff.

What the administration faced, therefore, in the autumn of 1954, was an erosion of credibility of its nuclear deterrent, upon which, as cuts in conventional forces proceeded, the administration was placing more and more reliance. Popular antipathy toward nuclear weapons was growing, heightened particularly when an American hydrogen-bomb test showered lethal fallout on the crew of a Japanese fishing boat.[96] It therefore appeared to administration leaders that the longer the United States went without using nuclear weapons, or without at least making a serious show of considering their use, the less of a deterrent they would become.

That this unsettling trend played a significant role in administration thinking shows most clearly in the record of an NSC meeting at the height of the crisis. Radford, who had been advocating giving the Communists a "bloody nose" from the outset, repeated his advice, and he reminded the president that the "whole military structure" of the United States had been built around an assumption of the availability of nuclear weapons. Dulles, who often differed significantly with Radford, admitted in this case that perhaps the JCS chairman was right. The Communists, Dulles said, probably would not take the administration seriously until it decided to "shoot off a gun" in the area. He added that very shortly the United States would have "to face up to the question whether its military program was or was not in fact designed to permit the use of atomic weapons." If the Administration continued to allow popular sentiment against nuclear weapons to grow, "we might wake up one day and discover that we were inhibited in the use of these weapons by a negative public opinion." Having just returned from a visit to the Pacific, the secretary of state noted "very great concern on the part of our military people in the Formosa area with respect to this particular problem." Dulles asserted that it was a matter of "vital importance" that American leaders "urgently educate our own and world opinion as to the necessity for the tactical use of atomic weapons." If they could not make these weapons usable, he concluded, "our entire military program would have to be drastically revised."[97]

---

96. On reactions to the radioactive poisoning of the *Fukuryu Maru*, and to the broader question of nuclear testing, see Robert A. Divine, *Blowing on the Wind: The Nuclear Test Ban Debate 1954–1960* (New York: Oxford University Press, 1978).
97. Memorandum of discussion, 240th NSC meeting, Mar. 10, 1955, *FRUS*: 1955–57, Vol. II, p. 345. Although possessing considerably less influence that Dulles and Radford, Rankin agreed on the possible need for war. "A military engagement," he told Robertson, "may well be necessary to convince the enemy that we mean business." Rankin to Robertson, Mar. 13, 1955, Rankin papers, Princeton.

In view of these arguments and public statements by the administration, it seems inescapable that much of the intensity of the affair derived from a desire on the part of American officials to enhance the credibility of their basic defense posture. It would be too much to say that the administration as a whole was deliberately looking for an excuse to demonstrate its resolve to use nuclear weapons, although Radford seems to have been. But it would appear that once administration officials found themselves confronted with a challenge, their wish to prove the plausibility of the nuclear threat made them disinclined to look for a peaceful resolution. Had matters remained entirely under their control, their propensity toward escalation might not have mattered much. Dangerously, as they soon discovered, events did *not* remain under their control, and the situation eased only when the PRC chose to call off the confrontation.

Perhaps, then, the significant lesson of the Taiwan Strait affair involves the unanticipated effect in crisis situations of decisions made in other areas for other reasons. Eisenhower adopted the "New Look" of NSC 162/2 largely as a cost-cutting measure. While he obviously understood that greater reliance on atomic weapons would limit his choices in the future, he surely did not anticipate losing control of the decision whether to go to nuclear war over some inconsequential islands off China. In itself, this fact is not especially remarkable; history abounds with unforeseen consequences. Nonetheless, at present, when American leaders are debating the merits of shifts in defense planning hardly less radical than Eisenhower's New Look—the Strategic Defense Initiative, for example, or the Maritime Strategy—the example of how an analogous change three decades ago contributed materially to a close brush with war bears pondering.

The Influence of Nuclear Weapons in the Cuban Missile Crisis

Marc Trachtenberg

What role did nuclear weapons play in the Cuban missile crisis, and what does the episode tell us about the broader problem of the political utility of nuclear forces? In 1983, a number of veterans of the Kennedy Administration were brought together to look back and reflect on the affair, and in their minds these questions had very clear answers. What the crisis showed, according to Robert McNamara, who had been Secretary of Defense at the time, was that America's superiority in numbers of nuclear weapons "was not such that it could be translated into usable military power to support political objectives."[1] Dean Rusk, the Secretary of State under Kennedy, made an even stronger claim: "The simple fact is that nuclear power does not translate into usable political influence."[2] And indeed the argument is often made that the crisis demonstrates the political insignificance of the nuclear balance—or even the political irrelevance of nuclear weapons in general.[3]

On the other hand, there have always been those who maintained that America's "overwhelming strategic superiority," or simply the American willingness to risk nuclear war, had a good deal to do with the course that the

The author wishes to acknowledge an extraordinary debt of gratitude to John Mearsheimer for all the help he gave with this article.

Marc Trachtenberg is Associate Professor of History at the University of Pennsylvania.

1. Transcript of a Discussion about the Cuban Missile Crisis, June 28, 1983, pp. 1–2, Alfred Sloan Foundation, New York; hereinafter cited as "Sloan transcript, June 28, 1983." I am grateful to Mr. Arthur Singer for allowing me to view the videotapes of these discussions. McGeorge Bundy, who in 1962 had been Kennedy's national security adviser, elaborated the point: America's superiority, it was felt at the time, "was not a usable superiority in the sense that we would ever want to go first because if even one Soviet weapon landed on an American target, we would all be losers." Sloan transcript, January 27, 1983, reel 6, take 1, p. 7.
2. Sloan transcript, January 27, 1983, reel 6, take 1, p. 40.
3. See, for example, the joint statement by six veterans of the crisis (McNamara, Bundy, Rusk, Sorensen, Gilpatric, and Ball) in *Time* magazine, September 27, 1982: "The Cuban missile crisis illustrates not the significance but the insignificance of nuclear superiority in the face of survivable thermonuclear retaliatory forces" (Rusk et al., "The Lessons of the Cuban Missile Crisis," p. 85). See also Walter Slocombe, *The Political Implications of Strategic Parity*, Adelphi Paper No. 77 (London: Institute for Strategic Studies, May 1971), pp. 18–20 (although his Appendix 2, where he sets out his argument in greater detail, is more modest in tone); and Benjamin Lambeth, "Deterrence in the MIRV Era," *World Politics*, Vol. 24, No. 2 (January 1972), pp. 230–234.

International Security, Summer 1985 (Vol. 10, No. 1) 0162-2889/85/0137-27 $02.50/1

crisis took.[4] Bernard Brodie, for example, took it for granted that America's "nuclear superiority" had been crucial in 1962. It was, he said, "a mischievous interpretation" of the crisis "to hold that its outcome was determined mostly by our conventional superiority."[5]

In the twenty years that have passed since the confrontation took place, claims about the Cuban missile crisis have played an important role in the discussion of strategic issues. Theories are tested by events, and people have looked to the sharpest crisis of the nuclear age for answers: how much of a political shadow do nuclear weapons cast? These debates, however, have always had a rather abstract and speculative character. But thanks to the release in the last few years of an extraordinary series of documents on the crisis, it is now possible to study these issues on the basis of hard empirical evidence.[6]

What does the missile crisis tell us about the way nuclear weapons affect international politics? The problem will be approached here by examining three schools of thought—about the crisis, and about the political utility of nuclear forces in general.

There is first the thesis that nuclear weapons played no political role at all in 1962—that is, that their sole function was to deter their use by others. Thus General Maxwell Taylor, the Chairman of the Joint Chiefs of Staff at the time, once flatly stated that "the strategic forces of the United States and the U.S.S.R. simply cancelled each other out as effectual instruments for influencing the outcome of the confrontation."[7] And claims of this sort are

---

4. See, for example, Arnold Horelick, "The Cuban Missile Crisis: An Analysis of Soviet Calculations and Behavior," *World Politics*, Vol. 16, No. 3 (April 1964), pp. 387–388; and Jerome H. Kahan and Anne K. Long, "The Cuban Missile Crisis: A Study of its Strategic Context," *Political Science Quarterly*, Vol. 87 (December 1972), esp. pp. 579–581, 586; and especially Thomas C. Schelling, *Arms and Influence* (New Haven: Yale University Press, 1966), pp. 95–96.
5. Bernard Brodie, "What Price Conventional Capabilities in Europe?," Rand Paper P-2696 (Santa Monica, Calif.: Rand Corporation, February 1963), pp. 24–25; also published in *The Reporter*, May 23, 1963. Note also Brodie's comment in a letter to the French strategist Pierre Gallois of July 21, 1965: "I do not think gross superiority matters as little as you suggest. The Cuban affair of 1962 does not bear you out. . . . The reasons are several, but it is mostly that neither side threatens the other with total war. Instead they simply threaten actions which *could* escalate" (Box 1, Brodie Papers, UCLA).
6. Some of the most interesting material—extracts from the transcript of two secretly taped meetings held at the White House on October 16, and the minutes of two ExCom meetings held on October 27—is reproduced below. But the recently declassified material represents only a small portion of the Kennedy Library's holdings on the crisis. And there are important, but still unavailable, sources in other archives, and in private hands as well—for example, the extensive, almost verbatim notes that Paul Nitze took of meetings during the crisis.
7. Maxwell D. Taylor, "The Legitimate Claims of National Security," *Foreign Affairs*, Vol. 52, No.

often linked to more general arguments about the "uselessness" of nuclear forces. "Nuclear weapons," McNamara recently argued, "serve no military purpose whatsoever. They are totally useless—except only to deter one's opponent from using them."[8] From this point of view, it was the balance of conventional forces that was decisive.

A second major school of thought argues that nuclear weapons did matter, because the *risk* of nuclear war was bound to affect political behavior. This argument takes two basic forms. On the one hand, there is the notion of "existential deterrence": the mere existence of nuclear forces means that, whatever we say or do, there is a certain irreducible risk that an armed conflict might escalate into a nuclear war. The fear of escalation is thus factored into political calculations: faced with this risk, states are more cautious and more prudent than they would otherwise be.

On the other hand, there is the notion that risk is not simply an inescapable fact of life. The level of risk is instead seen as something that can be deliberately and consciously manipulated. As Thomas Schelling laid out the argument: international politics in the nuclear age often takes the form of a "competition in risk taking, characterized not so much by tests of force as by tests of nerve." The "manipulation of risk" was therefore the means of getting the upper hand in what was ultimately a kind of bargaining situation.[9] The missile crisis was Schelling's prime example: "The Cuban Crisis was a contest in risk taking, involving steps that would have made no sense if they led predictably and ineluctably to a major war, yet would also have made no sense if they were completely without danger."[10]

A third school of thought claims that it was the balance of nuclear capabilities, and not the balance of resolve or conventional capabilities, that proved decisive. This interpretation is not logically inconsistent with the approach that emphasizes risk, since a government's ability to manipulate risk might depend largely on the military power at its disposal. But those

---

3 (April 1974), p. 582. Taylor here denied that America's "strategic superiority" played a meaningful role in the crisis. But at the time he had taken a radically different line: "We have the strategic advantage in our general war capabilities," he wrote McNamara on October 26, 1962. ". . . This is no time to run scared." Quoted in John Lewis Gaddis, *Strategies of Containment* (New York: Oxford University Press, 1982), p. 229n.
8. Robert S. McNamara, "The Military Role of Nuclear Weapons: Perceptions and Misperceptions," *Foreign Affairs*, Vol. 62, No. 1 (Fall 1983), p. 79. Note also his comments on the role of nuclear forces in the missile crisis in Gregg Herken, *Counsels of War* (New York: Knopf, 1985), p.167.
9. Schelling, *Arms and Influence*, p. 94.
10. Ibid., p. 96.

who emphasize the strategic balance tend to assume that its effects are virtually automatic: the Soviets were outgunned in 1962, and they had no choice but to accept the terms the United States insisted on.

No Role at All?

Is it true that the strategic forces of the United States and the Soviet Union "simply cancelled each other out" during the crisis? This claim is generally based on the notion that nuclear weapons are "unusable" weapons—that they are good only for deterring their use by others. This implies, with regard to the crisis, that nuclear forces neutralized each other and thus had no real effect on either side: it was as though they had been simply swept off the board, and that matters proceeded as though they did not exist. The effect of this line of argument, therefore, is to emphasize the importance of conventional forces—that is, of America's conventional predominance in the Caribbean.

The notion that nuclear forces cannot be harnessed to political purpose is thus often based on the assumption that the President of the United States would never deliberately start a nuclear war.[11] But if war could come without such a deliberate and conscious decision on the part of either the President or his Soviet counterpart, then the risk of war would be real and would therefore inevitably affect political behavior. The evidence in fact shows that: 1) leading officials believed that nuclear war could come without either side having to make a cold-blooded decision to start one; 2) these officials were willing during the crisis to accept a certain risk of nuclear war; and 3) the risk of nuclear war was consciously manipulated in order to affect Soviet options in the crisis.

First, McNamara, for example, in the postmortem he gave to a Congressional committee in February 1963, demonstrated a clear grasp of the logic of escalation—that is, of how one's actions could set off a chain of events over which one could exercise only limited control. If America had invaded Cuba, he said, thousands of Soviet soldiers would have been killed, and the Soviets "probably would have had to respond." Some of the Soviet missiles

---

11. Note, for example, the logic of McGeorge Bundy's argument in "To Cap the Volcano," *Foreign Affairs,* Vol. 48, No. 1 (October 1969), pp. 9–11—how he moves from the point about the impossibility of "any sane political authority" consciously starting a nuclear war to the conclusion about the irrelevance of the strategic balance; or the kind of argument McNamara makes in the Sloan transcript, June 28, 1983, pp. 1–2.

in Cuba might have been armed and operational, and if they were, "they might have been launched," so there was a danger of nuclear war. "In any event," he continued, Soviet leader Nikita Khrushchev "knew without any question whatsoever that he faced the full military power of the United States, including its nuclear weapons." McNamara's conclusion was chilling: "we faced that night the possibility of launching nuclear weapons and Khrushchev knew it, and that is the reason, and the only reason, why he withdrew those weapons."[12]

The general point that a nuclear war was possible because events could have a momentum of their own, quite apart from the conscious intent of statesmen, has been a staple of the strategic literature since the late 1950s. Even those who base claims about the irrelevance of the nuclear balance on the argument that no rational government would ever deliberately start a nuclear war have frequently argued along these lines. "The gravest risk in this crisis," according to McGeorge Bundy, McNamara, and four other former members of the Kennedy Administration, "was not that either head of government desired to initiate a major escalation but that events would produce actions, reactions or miscalculations carrying the conflict beyond the control of one or the other or both."[13]

Second, the highest officials in the American government clearly recognized that a confrontation with the Soviet Union would entail a certain risk of nuclear war. But they felt that this was a risk that simply had to be accepted. As Rusk put it on October 16: "I think we'll be facing a situation that could well lead to general war." The case of Secretary McNamara is again particularly interesting in this connection. On October 16, he argued that an attack on Cuba, after any of the missiles there were operational, would pose too great a risk: some of those missiles might survive an attack and be launched, and this could lead to a thermonuclear holocaust. But by October 27—that is, after the CIA had reported that some of the missiles on

12. U.S. Congress, House of Representatives, Committee on Appropriations, Subcommittee on Department of Defense Appropriations, "Department of Defense Appropriations for 1964," February 6, 1963, p. 31. Note also the discussion of the escalation problem on pp. 152–156 below.
13. For the point about the strategic literature, see Bernard Brodie, *Strategy in the Missile Age* (Princeton: Princeton University Press, 1959), p. 355; and Albert Wohlstetter, "Nuclear Sharing: NATO and the N + 1 Country," *Foreign Affairs*, Vol. 39, No. 3 (April 1961), pp. 378–379. Note also Bundy, "To Cap the Volcano," p. 18; and his "Strategic Deterrence After Thirty Years: What Has Changed?," *Atlantic Community Quarterly*, Vol. 17, No. 4 (Winter 1979–80), p. 486. The quotation is from Rusk et al., "Lessons of the Cuban Missile Crisis," p. 86.

the island were indeed operational—McNamara declared that "we must now be ready to attack Cuba. . . . Invasion had become almost inevitable." In other words, even he, who was quite conservative in this regard, was willing by this point to accept what by his own reckoning was a serious risk of nuclear war.[14]

Finally, there is the point that the specter of nuclear war was deliberately manipulated to support American objectives in the crisis. McNamara, for example, pointed out on October 16 that American military action would probably lead to a Soviet military response "some place in the world." The United States, he argued, should recognize that possibility "by trying to deter it, which means we probably should alert SAC, probably put on an airborne alert, perhaps take other s-, alert measures. These bring risks of their own, associated with them."[15] (McNamara here was probably referring to the danger that too much might be read into these preparations, and that they might touch off a Soviet preemptive attack. The fear of preemption was widely viewed at the time as lying at the heart of a semi-automatic process of escalation.)

Note that McNamara's assumption was that nuclear preparations would serve to deter Soviet responses *in general*; that is, the implied nuclear threat was not directed simply at the possibility that the U.S.S.R. might consider using its *nuclear* forces. If the missiles in Cuba were attacked, the Soviets would very much want to take some kind of counteraction—in Berlin, most probably, or against Turkey, or maybe even in Iran or Korea—and the United States had to take "a whole series of precautionary measures. . . . All of our

---

14. For Rusk, see Presidential Recordings, Transcripts, Cuban Missile Crisis Meetings, October 16, 1962, first meeting (11:50 a.m.–12:57 p.m.), p. 10, President's Office Files, John F. Kennedy Library, Boston. Henceforth this source will be cited as "October 16 transcripts, I" (for the 11:50 meeting) or "II" (for the second meeting, which lasted from 6:30 to 7:45 p.m.). Extracts are published below. For McNamara, see October 16 transcripts, I, pp. 11, 13; "Summary Record of NSC Executive Committee Meeting No. 8, October 27, 1962, 4:00 PM," p. 5, Box 316, National Security Files, John F. Kennedy Library (and also published below)—cited hereinafter as "ExCom Minutes" with number and date; CIA Report, "Major Consequences of Certain U.S. Courses of Action in Cuba," October 20, 1962, reporting that 16 MRBMs were then operational, and arguing that it was "prudent to assume" that nuclear warheads for them would be available, Declassified Documents Collection, 1975, 48E.

15. October 16 transcripts, II, p. 10; see also Dillon's remarks, ibid., I, p. 27. The same kind of point might be made about the effect of American military preparations during the Berlin crisis the previous year. In a letter to Chancellor Adenauer of October 13, 1961, President Kennedy remarked cryptically, "The Soviets have been warned and they appear to have taken cognizance of the warning that our present course is dangerous to them" (Box 117, Folder "Germany. Security. 8/61–12/61," President's Office Files, John F. Kennedy Library). Note, finally, General Burchinal's remarks, quoted below, p. 157.

forces should be put on alert, but beyond that, mobilization, redeployment, movement and so on."[16] The threat of general war—in fact, the threat of any U.S.–Soviet war, because of the risk of escalation it would inevitably entail—would be the means of dealing with these possible Soviet countermoves. These deterrent threats, by reducing the probability of any direct Soviet retaliation, would thus increase America's freedom of action in Cuba.

It is clear, therefore, that the risk of nuclear war did play a role. Indeed, this risk was overtly and deliberately exploited. But this was a deadly game, played reluctantly and without any trace of enthusiasm. Political necessity—the logic of the confrontational situation—prevailed over the government's horror of nuclear war and led it to adopt tactics of this sort.

The Balance of Resolve

The specter of nuclear war influenced both Soviet and American policy. But did these nuclear fears and anxieties simply make both sides equally cautious, or were the effects uneven?

The fear of a Soviet countermove against Berlin weighed heavily on American policy during the crisis. This was what McNamara wanted to prevent by taking his "series of precautionary measures." But why was it assumed that the prospect of nuclear war would have such a one-sided effect? The Soviets would be deterred from moving against the city (even though their forces in the Caribbean might already have been attacked); but the Americans presumably would not be deterred by the same threat of war from following through with their policy of defending the city. It was taken for granted that the same risk would have unequal effects.

The situation in the Caribbean was the mirror image of the situation around Berlin. The Americans had conventional predominance, but (given that the missiles had already been put in) the United States was the power that was threatening to alter an existing situation. If the nuclear threat had perfectly symmetrical effects, American power should have been as stalemated around Cuba as Soviet power was around Berlin. But the fact that this was not the case shows that fears and anxieties were not perfectly in balance: the balance of resolve favored the United States.

---

16. October 16 transcripts, II, pp. 49–50. For discussion of the measures that were in fact taken, see Scott D. Sagan, "Nuclear Alerts and Crisis Management," *International Security*, Vol. 9, No. 4 (Spring 1985), pp. 106–122.

Thus an invasion of Cuba might lead to a general war. This put pressure on the Soviets to head off that invasion and accept terms. The Americans, for similar reasons, were also under pressure to settle the crisis before matters came to a head. But the pressures were not equal: if a settlement had not been reached, the United States, in spite of the risks that U.S. leaders themselves recognized, would almost certainly have invaded Cuba at the end of October.

How much of an imbalance was there? And what determines the level of tolerable risk? One way to test this issue is to examine the case of the Jupiters—that is, the question of an arrangement involving the withdrawal of the American Jupiter missiles from Turkey in exchange for a withdrawal of the Soviet missiles from Cuba.

Kennedy, according to his close adviser Theodore Sorensen, was "quite amazed" when Treasury Secretary Douglas Dillon (who had also served under Eisenhower) told him during the crisis that "everyone knows that those Jupiter missiles aren't much good anyway. We only put them in there during the previous Administration because we didn't know what else to do with them, and we really made the Turks and the Italians take them."[17] Could the Jupiters therefore be removed in exchange for a withdrawal of the Soviet missiles in Cuba? It is well known that the idea was seriously considered by American officials during the crisis, well before the Soviet government even formally proposed a "deal" of this sort.[18]

What has not been clear, however, is the degree to which the President was personally in favor of such an arrangement. In fact, there were from the outset very precise assurances to the contrary. When McNamara, for example, was asked during his Congressional testimony in February 1963 about a trade involving the missiles in Turkey, he said that "the President absolutely refused to discuss it at the time, and no discussion took place."[19] Taking such claims at face value, historians and political scientists have constructed many arguments on the basis of President Kennedy's supposed refusal to consider a trade.[20]

---

17. Transcript of oral history interview of Theodore Sorensen, by Carl Kaysen, March 26, 1964, pp. 65–66, Kennedy Library.
18. See *The New York Times*, December 6, 1962, p. 3:1; Arthur M. Schlesinger, Jr., *Robert Kennedy and His Times* (Boston: Houghton Mifflin, 1978), p. 515; and Abram Chayes, *The Cuban Missile Crisis* (New York: Oxford University Press, 1974), pp. 81–82, 98–99.
19. U.S. Congress, "Department of Defense Appropriations for 1964," p. 57; see also p. 74. Note also the passage in Theodore Sorensen, *Kennedy* (New York: Harper & Row, 1965), p. 714.
20. See for example Jack Snyder, "Rationality at the Brink: The Role of Cognitive Processes in

On the other hand, a number of scholars have argued, essentially on the basis of Robert Kennedy's memoir on the crisis, that there in fact was a "deal."[21] According to Robert Kennedy, the Soviet Ambassador was told on October 27 that the President "had been anxious to remove those missiles from Turkey and Italy for a long period of time. He had ordered their removal some time ago, and it was our judgment that, within a short time after this crisis was over, those missiles would be gone."[22] On the basis of these assurances, so the argument goes, the Soviets agreed to withdraw their missiles from Cuba. And within the space of a few months, the Jupiters were in fact dismantled. Did this mean that a "bargain" had been struck?

There are two ways in which the documents throw some light on this issue. First of all, the Executive Committee minutes published here show very clearly that at the peak of the crisis, on October 27, with an invasion of Cuba imminent, President Kennedy was in fact the strongest advocate of a trade in that high policymaking group. Repeatedly, he returned to the theme that some kind of trade involving the Jupiters would eventually be necessary. What he plainly wanted was to get the Russians to stop working on the missile sites in Cuba and maybe also make the missiles there inoperable; this would then be followed by a negotiation involving the missiles in Turkey. But he was opposed on this issue by all of his chief advisers. Rusk, Bundy, and his brother Robert all came out against the idea. Even McNamara was arguing by this point that an invasion of Cuba, which the President was then defining as the only alternative to a trade, was "almost inevitable."

The second point is that what Robert Kennedy told the Soviet Ambassador that very evening was not quite accurate: although the government had been interested in withdrawing the Jupiters for some time, their removal had not actually been *ordered* prior to the crisis.[23] What Dobrynin was told was thus

---

Failures of Deterrence," *World Politics,* Vol. 30, No. 3 (April 1978), esp. pp. 354–355; and Barton J. Bernstein, "The Cuban Missile Crisis: Trading the Jupiters in Turkey?," *Political Science Quarterly,* Vol. 95, No. 1 (Spring 1980), pp. 97–125.

21. Graham T. Allison, *Essence of Decision: Explaining the Cuban Missile Crisis* (Boston: Little, Brown, 1971), p. 218, 228–230; Chayes, *The Cuban Missile Crisis,* p. 98; and Schlesinger, *Robert Kennedy,* pp. 520–524.

22. Robert F. Kennedy, *Thirteen Days* (New York: W.W. Norton, 1969), pp. 108–109.

23. Roger Hilsman, a high State Department official at the time, claimed in his memoirs that the President had "ordered—in August 1962—that steps be taken immediately to remove the American missiles from Turkey." *To Move a Nation* (Garden City, N.Y.: Doubleday, 1967), p. 203; repeated in Schlesinger, *Robert Kennedy,* p. 519, and Allison, *Essence of Decision,* p. 226. But the document Hilsman evidently had in mind, National Security Action Memorandum 181 of August 23, 1962, merely stated that "in the light of evidence of new bloc activity in Cuba," the President

not just a simple statement of fact: a concession of sorts was being made, but it was a disguised concession. In view of the President's attitude about a trade and the more hostile attitude of his advisers, what all this implies is that the settlement that emerged after the assurances were given to Dobrynin should probably be understood as the conflation of a negotiation—as an "imposed negotiated solution," so to speak.

Thus Kennedy had not ruled out an arrangement involving the Jupiters, and McNamara's recent comment about the President's attitude rings true: "I recall him saying very well, 'I am not going to go to war over worthless missiles in Turkey. I don't want to go to war anyhow, but I am certainly not going to go to war over worthless missiles in Turkey.'"[24]

But the implication here is that it was taken for granted that the level of risk should be commensurate with the political importance of the issues in dispute. If ultimately the issue came down to whether America was willing to withdraw the "worthless" Jupiter missiles from Turkey, then, no matter what the strategic balance was, the President was not going to dig in his heels and risk a nuclear holocaust over that. Kennedy's eagerness for something like a political settlement was therefore rooted not in a conviction that nuclear forces were politically impotent, but rather in the notion that the main obstacle to a solution was too trivial to warrant any serious risk of nuclear war. The same logic, however, implies that his attitude about the kind of risk worth running might have been very different if the political issues at stake had been viewed as basic—as in fact they had been during the Berlin crisis the previous year.

Thus one is struck, on the one hand, by the President's aversion to risk: he certainly did not view the crisis as a "contest in risk taking" in which the goal was to outbid the other side. But on the other hand, Kennedy's aversion to risk was by no means absolute: during the crisis, the Soviets were after all under enormous pressure. In fact the new evidence about the final settlement supports the idea that the basic situation was not one of simple parity. If the settlement was not tantamount to a Soviet capitulation, it was not really a bargain either—and above all, not a bargain between equals.

---

had directed that the Defense Department study the question of "what action can be taken to get Jupiter missiles out of Turkey?" (Box 338, Folder "Cuba(4). 8/23/62," National Security Files, Kennedy Library). On the myth of the presidential "order," see in particular Bernstein, "Trading the Jupiters," pp. 102–104, and esp. fn. 24.
24. Sloan transcript, June 28, 1983, p. 63.

The Role of the Strategic Balance: The American Side

Political concerns therefore played an important role in determining the kind of risk the American government was willing to take on. But how did military factors affect the course of the crisis? Would it in particular have made a difference in 1962 if "the relative strategic positions of the Soviet Union and the United States had been reversed"? In 1969 McGeorge Bundy said no: "A stalemate is a stalemate either way around."[25] But what does the historical evidence suggest?

In theory, the strategic balance could have played a role by influencing either American policy or Soviet policy or both. This section will be concerned mainly with how the Americans might have been affected; the Soviet side will be examined in the next section. Three issues in particular will be considered here: 1) did people at the time think that America's strategic superiority would be decisive? 2) how did people deal with the narrower problem of the military significance of the Soviet missiles in Cuba? 3) how was the problem of escalation handled, and how does this bear on the problem of the strategic balance?

To begin with the crudest way in which the balance might have played a role: was the American government more willing to face the prospect of general war with the Soviet Union because it knew that damages, even in the worst case, could be limited to a certain "tolerable" level of devastation? Actually, there is no evidence that President Kennedy and his advisers counted missiles, bombers, and warheads, and decided on that basis to take a tough line. The veterans of the crisis have often denied that any calculation of that sort had been made, and there is no reason to dispute them on this point.[26] Few assumed at the time that the strategic balance in itself meant that the U.S.S.R. would almost automatically back down; and there is no evidence at all in the documents that anyone believed that the United States could face a war with confidence because of its vast nuclear power.

In fact, one of the most striking things about the October 16 transcript is that no one even touched on the issue of what exactly would happen if the

25. Bundy, "To Cap the Volcano," p. 11.
26. See, for example, Rusk in Sloan Transcript, January 27, 1983, reel 6, take 1, p. 40; or Paul H. Nitze, "Assuring Strategic Stability in an Era of Détente," *Foreign Affairs*, Vol. 54, No. 2 (January 1976), pp. 214–216.

crisis escalated to the level of general war—although of course everyone might have learned all they felt they needed to know about the issue in some other way. But one does come away from the transcript with the sense that even rough calculations of this sort were not terribly important. No one discussed what American counterforce capabilities were—that is, how well the United States might be able to "limit damage" in the event of an all-out war. It was as though all the key concepts associated with the administration's formal nuclear strategy, as set out for example just a few months earlier in McNamara's famous Ann Arbor speech—in fact, the whole idea of controlled and discriminate general war—in the final analysis counted for very little. One of President Kennedy's remarks on October 16 seems to capture this feeling: "What difference does it make? They've got enough to blow us up now anyway."[27]

But the absence of a crude belief in the decisiveness of the strategic balance does not in itself mean that the issue was not present in less direct ways. People were in fact concerned with the problem of whether the deployment of missiles in Cuba would make an important difference in military terms. The positions taken on this question reflect, in a rather crude and imperfect way to be sure, basic attitudes about the significance of shifts in the strategic balance. They thus can function as something of a surrogate for more direct notions about the role of the nuclear balance.

It is sometimes claimed that the general belief among high administration officials was that the deployment would not count for much from a strictly military point of view. And the chief document used to support this argument is a Sorensen memorandum of October 17, which claimed that it was "generally agreed that these missiles, even when fully operational, do not significantly alter the balance of power—i.e., they do not significantly increase the potential megatonnage capable of being unleashed on American soil, even after a surprise American nuclear strike."[28] But Sorensen was simply wrong

27. October 16 transcripts, II, p. 15.
28. In Box 48, Folder "Cuba. General. 10/17/62–10/27/62," Sorensen Papers, Kennedy Library. This document is the basis for Bernstein's claim, in "Trading the Jupiters," that the missiles "did not alter the strategic balance" (p. 118). In an earlier article, he developed this point at greater length, arguing, on the basis of the Sorensen memorandum, that most ExCom members agreed (among other things) that the deployment of the missiles in Cuba "did not add to the likelihood of a Soviet first strike." But there is *nothing at all* in the Sorensen document that even remotely deals with this question. Bernstein's claim was made in his "The Week We Almost Went to War," *Bulletin of the Atomic Scientists*, Vol. 32, No. 2 (February 1976), p. 16. It is of course

on this point: there was in fact no consensus on the issue of whether the deployment of the missiles really mattered in strategic terms. The transcript of the October 16 discussions makes this very clear. "What," Bundy asked, "is the strategic impact on the position of the United States of MRBM's in *Cuba*? How gravely does this change the strategic balance?" And McNamara answered as follows: "Mac, I asked the Chiefs that this afternoon, in effect. And they said, substantially. My own personal view is, not at all."[29]

What the military, and for that matter the CIA as well, were worried about was that the missiles currently in Cuba might just be an opening wedge, preparing the way for a more massive buildup there. The larger the force, the more the Soviets would be able, in the words of the CIA assessment, "to blunt a retaliatory attack,"[30] and thus to threaten the United States with a

---

odd that Sorensen in this document takes megatonnage as the basic index of strategic power—and this a couple of years after the total megatonnage of the American nuclear arsenal had begun its long and dramatic decline. The Kennedy Administration, in fact, wanted other things besides sheer destructive power from its strategic forces. In one typical document, Rusk called for improvements in the American strategic force "which would increase its survivability, its flexibility, and its ability to be used under a wide range of contingencies" (Rusk to McNamara, enclosed in Rusk to Bundy, October 29, 1961, Box 275, Folder "Department of Defense. Defense Budget FY 1963. 1/16–10/61," National Security Files, Kennedy Library). A shift in the strategic balance could be meaningful if it affected any of these things; and Rusk later recalled that in 1962 "we were concerned on the military side that substantial numbers of missiles in Cuba . . . could knock out our Strategic Air Command bases with almost no advance warning—they were so close" (Sloan transcripts, January 27, 1983, reel 1, take 1, p. 18).

29. October 16 transcripts, II, p. 12.

30. Gen. Taylor in October 16 transcripts, II, p. 13; CIA Report, "Soviet Reactions to Certain US Courses of Action on Cuba," October 19, 1962, Annex B ("Military Significance of Ballistic Missiles in Cuba"), Declassified Documents Collection, 1975, p. 48D. Note also Raymond Garthoff's analysis, written at the end of the crisis: his memorandum on "The Military Significance of the Soviet Missile Bases in Cuba" of October 27, 1962 was published (with commentary) in his article "The Meaning of the Missiles," *Washington Quarterly*, Vol. 5, No. 4 (Autumn 1982), pp. 78–79, and again in his "A Retrospective Look at a 1962 Evaluation of the Soviet Missiles in Cuba," an addendum to *Intelligence Assessment and Policymaking: A Decision Point in the Kennedy Administration* (Washington, D.C.: Brookings, 1984), pp. 32–33. In his commentary, Garthoff asserted that the question of how the deployment affected the military balance was not "an issue of contention," and that in fact "it was not even fully analyzed in the hectic week of initial decisions" (*Intelligence Assessment*, p. 28; with some minor variations of wording, also in "The Meaning of the Missiles," p. 76). But the evidence just cited shows that these claims have to be taken with a grain of salt. There is additional evidence as well. The issue of the "effect of the missiles on the overall balance of power" was, for example, considered by the "main policy group" at its meeting at the White House on October 18, according to p. 46 of the recently declassified Sieverts Report, "The Cuban Crisis, 1962," an in-house history written mainly on the basis of interviews and completed in mid-1963 (Box 49, National Security Files, Kennedy Library). Indeed, the issue of the military significance of missiles in Cuba had been around ever since the administration had begun to worry about a possible deployment during the summer. For example, National Security Action Memorandum No. 181 of August 23, 1962 specifically

first strike. Neither President Kennedy nor anyone else at the meeting, however, seemed much concerned with how such a deployment would affect the vulnerability of America's strategic forces. But Kennedy did seem concerned that the initial deployment might be followed by a more massive one. He in fact linked this point to McNamara's argument about how the United States could not contemplate military action against the island once the missiles there were operational. No one could be sure an air strike would destroy all the missiles, and if any remained, some of them might be launched against America:

let's just say that, uh, they get, they get these in there and then you can't, uh, they get sufficient capacity so we can't, uh, with warheads. Then you don't want to knock 'em out ['cause?], uh, there's too much of a gamble. Then they just begin to build up those air bases there and then put more and more. I suppose they really. . . . Then they start getting ready to squeeze us in Berlin, doesn't that. . . . You may say it doesn't make any difference if you get blown up by an ICBM flying from the Soviet Union or one that was ninety miles away. Geography doesn't mean that much.[31]

The President was clearly thinking out loud: he was not really sure how he stood on this issue. A little later in the meeting, he veered toward the McNamara line. The real issue now, he said, was a political or psychological one. He had said the previous month that we would not tolerate the deployment of Soviet missiles in Cuba, and now he had to follow through: "Last month I said we weren't going to. Last month I should have said . . . that we don't care. But when we said we're *not* going to and then they go ahead and do it, and then we do nothing, then . . . I would think that our risks increase."[32] What perhaps made this line attractive was that it freed him from the need to agonize over the more difficult problem of whether the deployment was militarily important. It provided a straightforward rationale for the American decision to resist the deployment of the missiles, sparing the President from any need to resolve the perplexing issues of nuclear strategy.

At other times, however, Kennedy's remarks point in the other direction: "In his view the existence of fifty planes in Cuba [the IL-28 bombers] did not

requested an analysis "of the probable military, political and psychological impact of the establishment in Cuba of either surface-to-air or surface-to-surface missiles which could reach the U.S." (Box 338, National Security Files, Kennedy Library). It is unclear whether such a study was ever written; an attempt to locate it via the Freedom of Information Act proved unsuccessful.
31. October 16 transcripts, II, p. 13 (for JFK), and I, p. 11 (for McNamara).
32. October 16 transcripts, II, p. 15.

affect the balance of power, but the missiles already in Cuba were an entirely different matter."[33] Or, on October 27, when he was making a case for a trade involving the Jupiters: "The President recalled that over a year ago we wanted to get the Jupiter missiles out of Turkey because they had become obsolete and of little military value. If the missiles in Cuba added 50% to Soviet nuclear capability, then to trade these missiles for those in Turkey would be of great military value."[34]

One of the ways that President Kennedy tried to get a handle on the issue of the military significance of the missiles was by raising the question of Soviet motivation. If they did not matter strategically, why would the Russians put them in? Were they unhappy with their ICBMs? Khrushchev was running a major risk. What did he think he could get out of deploying these missiles in Cuba? "It's just as if we suddenly began to put a major number of MRBMs in Turkey," he said. "Now that'd be goddam dangerous, I would think." "Well, we *did*, Mr. President," Bundy replied. "Yeah, but that was five years ago."[35] They had been warned, the President said, and still they put the missiles in: "I don't think there's any record of the Soviets making this direct a challenge, ever, really . . . since the Berlin blockade."[36] But then Bundy placed this issue in its proper perspective by pointing out that the Soviets had made their decision *before* the President had issued his warning; they could have drawn back later, of course, but proceeding with a decision that had already been made was not quite the same as an outright act of defiance.

One therefore has the sense that President Kennedy's feelings on this issue had not really taken definite shape: it was as though he was groping for answers. Indeed, it seems that the administration in general, ever since it took office, was being pulled in two opposite directions: by intellectual argument, and by its extreme distaste for the idea of massive retaliation, it was drawn toward notions of discriminate and controlled war-fighting, and in fact nuclear war-fighting, strategies; but revolted by the very idea of nuclear war, and convinced that matters would in all probability very quickly get out of hand as soon as nuclear weapons began to be used in a major way, the

---

33. Schlesinger, *Robert Kennedy*, pp. 510–511. Since one of the basic differences between bombers and missiles relates to warning time, this quotation suggests that by this point Kennedy was concerned with how the missiles might affect Soviet first strike capabilities.
34. ExCom Minutes No. 7, October 27, 1962, p. 4.
35. October 16 transcripts, I, p. 13, and II, p. 26.
36. Ibid., II, p. 32.

most important people in the Kennedy Administration found it hard to take such notions seriously. As a result, the nuclear strategy of "controlled response" never really cut very deep under Kennedy[37]; and a certain ambivalence about these basic issues was very characteristic of that administation's approach to military policy.

Thus the administration was still sorting out its views on this issue: it was unclear exactly what the strategic significance of the Soviet deployment was, and people's attitudes were so uncertain, and so divided, that the discussion tells us very little about more fundamental beliefs about the political meaning of the strategic balance.

But views about escalation throw a much sharper light on the problem. What is striking here is the sense that peace was hanging on a thread, that it did not take much to touch off a nuclear holocaust—attitudes that would have been inconceivable if the sense was that the Soviets were simply outgunned and would have to back down, or even if the assumption was just that they were desperately anxious to avoid war and would draw back in a simple test of will. General David Burchinal, the Director of Plans on the Air Staff in 1962, later recalled how during the crisis an American U-2 spy plane had gotten lost and turned up over Soviet territory. Word of this "came into the 'tank' where McNamara and the Chiefs were meeting: 'We've got a U-2 at 75,000 feet over the Kola Peninsula.'" McNamara, he said, "turned absolutely white and yelled hysterically, 'This means war with the Soviet Union. The President must get on the hot line to Moscow!' And he ran out of the meeting in a frenzy."[38]

Whether this story is true or not, it is clear from other sources that McNamara was very sensitive to the danger of things spinning out of control. But President Kennedy also, in some comments on the crisis he gave to the National Security Council in January 1963, stressed the importance of having time to work out policy: if the Russians had had to react in only "an hour or

---

37. It is now well known that the influence of declaratory strategy on actual planning for general war is much slighter than many people used to assume. Note in this connection the testimony, for example, of Air Force General Bruce K. Holloway. What role did McNamara's strategy of "assured destruction" play in the elaboration of the Single Integrated Operational Plan (SIOP)—the basic plan for general war? "This is one place I can certainly say something nice about McNamara," Holloway remarked. "He never reversed us to my knowledge while I was JSTPS on the SIOP as it was presented to the JCS and as it was approved" (Holloway oral history interview, August 16–18, 1977, p. 359, Office of Air Force History, Bolling Air Force Base, Washington, D.C.).
38. Transcript of oral history interview of General David Burchinal, April 11, 1975, pp. 114–115, Office of Air Force History, Bolling Air Force Base, Washington, D.C.

two, their actions would have been spasmodic and might have resulted in nuclear war."[39]

Fears of this sort had an important effect on policy: there was in particular a great concern about the risk of escalation within the Cuban theater. With regard to the air strike option, Taylor and McNamara argued on October 16 that it was crucial to take out every target that might have any nuclear capability. The Joint Chiefs, Taylor said, unanimously believed that an attack should not be limited to the missile sites:

it would be a mistake to take this very narrow, selective target because it invited reprisal attacks and it may be detrimental. Now if the, uh, Soviets have been willing to give, uh, nuclear warheads to these missiles, there is every, just as good reason for them to give nuclear capability to these [air] bases. We don't think we'd ever have a chance to take 'em again, so that we lose this, the first strike surprise capability. Our recommendation would be to get complete intelligence, get all the photography we need, the next two or three days, no, no hurry in our book. Then look at this target system. If it really threatens the United States, then take it right out with one hard crack.[40]

McNamara fully accepted the basic argument about the risk of retaliation from surviving forces on the island, and in fact developed it in a number of ways. One point was that if military action was to be undertaken, it had to be done quickly, before the missile sites became operational. Otherwise, since there was no guarantee a strike would destroy all the missiles, some of the surviving ones might be launched against American cities: once any missiles became operational, he argued, the risk of an attack would be too great.[41] Another point was that there could be no warning: "if you are going to strike, you shouldn't make an announcement."[42] If you went the political route, that meant giving a warning, and hence a chance for an adversary to prepare his missiles for launch, thus effectively preventing the U.S. from taking military action: the political approach "almost *stops* subsequent military action"; "once you start this political approach, I don't think you're gonna *have* any opportunity for a military operation."[43]

39. "Notes on Remarks by President Kennedy before the National Security Council, Tuesday, January 22, 1963," National Security Files, Box 314, Kennedy Library.
40. October 16 transcripts, II, p. 8.
41. Ibid., I, pp. 11, 13, 14.
42. Ibid., II, p. 17
43. Ibid., II, pp. 9, 44.

Note how this kind of reasoning thus tends to draw one to the extremes: either a full-scale surprise attack or no direct military action at all, but not the brandishing of threats to coerce an adversary. Military power is viewed primarily as a way of affecting an enemy's capabilities rather than as a means of influencing his will. And this is based on the notion that once the ball starts rolling, things may very well become uncontrollable; the enemy cannot be counted on to behave rationally and control his own behavior.

But it was precisely this set of assumptions that was attacked by Rusk and Bundy. There were great political advantages to limiting the attack to the missile sites; there was no reason to assume that the Soviets would retaliate with whatever they had left, since such behavior would be suicidal for them. Rusk, for example, did not believe that "the critical question" was whether, in the event of an attack, every missile could be destroyed before it went off, because if the remaining missiles were launched, "we are in general nuclear war": "In other words, the Soviet Union has got quite a different decision to make."[44] And Bundy refuted the notion that if the United States attacked the missiles, the other side would retaliate with bombers, some of which might have nuclear capability: if their bombers attacked America in retaliation, then *they* were opting for general war—"it then becomes much more *their* decision."[45] President Kennedy himself saw both sides of the argument—one again has the sense that he was thinking out loud—but on balance it seems he favored the more limited form of attack: he just did not believe that if the missiles were destroyed, there might be a reprisal with nuclear weapons dropped from bombers, "because obviously why would the Soviets permit nuclear war to begin under that sort of half-assed way?"[46]

This argument turned to a certain degree on the technical issue of Soviet command and control: how automatic retaliation would be would depend to a considerable extent on whether the decision to strike back would be made in Moscow or by some low-level Soviet commander in charge of a missile battery in Cuba. McNamara's disagreement with Rusk focused on this point: "We don't know what kinds of communications the Soviets have with those sites. We don't know what kinds of control they have over the warheads."[47]

The problem of command and control thus relates to the broader question of whether the deployment of nuclear missiles in a given country deters all

---

44. Ibid., I, p. 13.
45. Ibid., II, p. 18. See also I, p. 25, and II, p. 43.
46. Ibid., I, p. 25. See also I, p. 17, and II, pp. 10, 17.
47. Ibid., I, p. 13.

forms of attack on that country—an issue that bears on the current debate over the deployment of intermediate-range missiles in Europe. The deterrent effect in 1962 seems real enough, even if in the final analysis the presence of operational missiles would not in itself have been sufficient to prevent an American attack on Cuba. But was this effect rooted solely in assumptions about the possible looseness of an enemy's control apparatus? While the evidence on this point is not very strong, it does seem that a sense for the danger of attacking Cuba after nuclear weapons were deployed there had a somewhat broader base than uncertainty about Soviet command and control. For one thing, one is struck by the casual way in which people referred to *Cuban* control over the missiles.[48] And this was linked to a visceral fear that the missiles might be *deliberately* launched if, for example, the United States sent troops to Venezuela: Robert Kennedy was worried about an implicit Cuban threat "that if you go there, we're gonna fire it."[49]

From McNamara's point of view, the air strike option clearly had its problems: for political reasons, a "bolt from the blue" was obviously unattractive, but to give warning would allow the other side to take actions that could effectively paralyze the United States. He therefore proposed a blockade as an alternative. The missiles in Cuba posed, to his mind, not a military problem, but rather a "domestic political problem."[50] America had said it would act if missiles were brought in, and now it had to do something—not necessarily enough to force the withdrawal of the missiles, but measures that would prevent their use: a continuous surveillance of Cuba and a permanent naval blockade to prevent any more missiles from coming in. The United States would declare to the world that, "if there is ever any indication that [the missiles in Cuba were] to be launched against this country, we will respond not only against Cuba, but we will respond directly against the Soviet Union with, with a full nuclear strike." This was not "a perfect solution by any means," and he said he did not want to argue for it; but if this alternative did not seem very acceptable, "wait until you work on the others."[51]

The fear of escalation thus went a long way toward neutralizing whatever advantages might have accrued to the United States by virtue of its "strategic superiority"—at least from the point of view of the American government.

48. Ibid., II, pp. 14, 46.
49. Ibid., II, pp. 14–15.
50. Ibid., II, pp. 46, 48.
51. Ibid., II, pp. 46–48.

This was most true in the case of McNamara, but to one degree or another, these fears were shared by most of his colleagues, and the American government was very cautious during the crisis.[52] The Kennedy Administration did not plunge eagerly into the poker game of risk manipulation, encouraged by a sense that strategically it had the upper hand.

But it is also important to remember that its fear of escalation did not drive the threshold of acceptable risk down to zero. On both the air strike and the blockade, McNamara's initial views were not accepted. The blockade did in fact eventually function as a political instrument—that is, as a "first step," raising the prospect of further, more extreme steps if a settlement was not reached. If the blockade did not "achieve the removal of the missiles," the President seemed ready, on October 20, to approve an air strike "against a minimum number of targets to eliminate the main nuclear threat."[53] And of course at the peak of the crisis, the United States was ready to invade Cuba, even though some of the missiles there were by then considered operational: even McNamara at that point thought that an invasion was "almost inevitable."

The Strategic Balance: The Soviet Side

There were two possible ways in which the strategic balance could have influenced the course of the crisis: through its effect on American policy or through its effect on Soviet behavior. We have already seen that its direct

---

52. Note in this context General Burchinal's later account of how the blockade was actually implemented: "So about that time, also, we decided to impose a blockade, and we put our naval vessels out on picket—no more ships coming into Cuba. They would be challenged on the high seas regardless of flag, and they'd be searched, and if they had anything that falls under war materiel they will be turned around or they will be sunk. So, we set it up. And, there was control in detail, so there was a phone from the Secretary of Defense's office right to the deck of the damn destroyer on patrol in this blockade. So, the first ship comes up to the blockade line. He's a Swede. They give him the signal 'heave-to.' 'Standby, what is your cargo?' And he said, 'Go to hell!' Full steam ahead and right through the damn blockade and right on into Havana. Nobody stopped him. He just said, 'The hell with you—nobody tells me what to do on the high seas with my ship.' So, they just looked at each other, these people who were now learning to 'manage crises' and run wars. 'That didn't work very well. What do we do now?' And so our signal caller had said, 'Don't shoot,' and the destroyer had said, 'I'm ready to stop him.' 'No, no, let him go, let him go.' So the next ship comes along and he's Lebanese—he's flying a Lebanese flag. So, they challenge him. And he said, 'Oh, I'm very happy to comply. I'll stop, come aboard, here I am, I'm just a poor Lebanese out here running my ship into Cuba.' So they went aboard and opened up his hatches, and he's got a bunch of military electronic gear, and they shut the hatches down, pretended it wasn't there, and said, 'Pass friend.' And he steamed merrily into Havana. That was our naval blockade. And that's the way it was being run under the kind of civilian control we had." Burchinal oral history, pp. 116–117.
53. Sieverts Report, p. 75.

effect on the United States was apparently minimal. But a strong, although somewhat speculative, case can be made that Soviet policy was very much influenced by the strategic balance. This case rests on a study of what was going on in the area of military preparations during the crisis.

One of the most striking features of the Cuban missile crisis, in fact, is an extraordinary asymmetry in the area of general war preparations. On October 22, President Kennedy announced the presence of the missiles and the measures the United States was taking to force their removal, and every day, from that point on, the Central Intelligence Agency prepared a memorandum outlining the military measures the Soviet Union was taking in response. The first order of business at each morning ExCom meeting was a briefing by the CIA Director, John McCone, essentially summarizing the latest intelligence memorandum. Day after day, the theme was the same: the U.S.S.R. was not making preparations for war. Thus, the CIA, on October 24, did not believe that "measures to achieve a higher degree of action readiness for Soviet and bloc forces are being taken on a crash basis." The same point was made in the October 25 memorandum; and still on October 27, at the climax of the crisis, the CIA said it simply had not been able to detect any "significant redeployment" of Soviet forces.[54]

The United States, on the other hand, was making very serious preparations for a general nuclear conflict: America's ICBMs were put on alert, and the Strategic Air Command as a whole, as one writer put it, was "fully mobilized for war."[55] "We increased the airborne alert force of B-52's up to a third of the force," General Burchinal recalled. "We had SAC bombers on nuclear alert with weapons in the bomb-bays on civilian airfields all over the US. We dispersed the air defense force, with nuclear weapons, also on civilian airports all over the country." But the point that Burchinal stressed was that "all these moves were signals the Soviets could see and we knew they could see them. We got everything we had, in the strategic forces, nuclear forces, counted down and ready and aimed and we made damn sure they saw it without anybody saying a word about it."[56]

How is Soviet inaction to be understood, and what inferences from the disparity between Soviet and American military measures might have plausibly been drawn at the time? Military preparations, of course, strengthen

---

54. Both the CIA memoranda and the Executive Committee minutes are in Boxes 315 and 316, National Security Files, Kennedy Library.
55. See David Detzer, *The Brink: Cuban Missile Crisis, 1962* (New York: Thomas Crowell, 1979), p. 164.
56. Burchinal oral history, p. 115.

one's bargaining position. They are an indication of resolve, a hint of what one might actually do, a means perhaps of preventing the enemy from making certain countermoves and thus of preemptively increasing one's own freedom of action. It is clear that these bargaining advantages of preparing for war were understood at the time.[57] But if taking these measures can have such effects, it is even clearer that a *refusal* to make serious preparations during a confrontation, when one's adversary has put his strategic forces on full alert, can have important political effects. It is a question here not just of the Soviets' reluctance to declare an official alert of their own. This might be explained by the specific character of what an alert might have meant in the Soviet system. For instance, the Soviets might have been unable for technical reasons to hold their strategic force on alert for more than a short period of time, and therefore might have been reluctant to place their forces on alert unless they were certain a war was coming.[58] The more important point is that the Soviets evidently did nothing, even in the way of major ad hoc measures (such as putting some of their bombers on strip alert), to reduce the vulnerability of their strategic forces. A national leader like Khrushchev may take a tough position in diplomatic contacts, in effect threatening war if his opponent perseveres with his policy; but how seriously can such threats be taken if what is going on in the military sphere is giving exactly the opposite signal?[59]

It can be taken for granted that the Soviet Union of Nikita Khrushchev was not oblivious to considerations of this sort. Khrushchev had tried over the past few years to extract political advantages by brandishing the specter of nuclear war. If anything, he had tended to overestimate the bluff value of nuclear weapons, and to overlook the ways in which the tactic of exploiting the nuclear threat could backfire.[60] But during the Cuban crisis, the Soviets

57. October 16 transcripts, I, p. 27, and II, p. 10.
58. The Soviet missile guidance system evidently used gyroscopes with metal ball bearings that would fail if they were subject to continuing stress—that is, if the missile were held ready for launch over a prolonged period. See Robert P. Berman and John C. Baker, *Soviet Strategic Forces: Requirements and Responses* (Washington, D.C.: Brookings, 1982), p. 88.
59. See the Khrushchev–Kennedy correspondence published in the Department of State *Bulletin*, November 19, 1973, and republished in Ronald R. Pope, ed., *Soviet Views on the Cuban Missile Crisis: Myth and Reality in Foreign Policy Analysis* (Washington, D.C.: University Press of America, 1982), pp. 28–67. Note also the account of Khrushchev's interview with the American businessman W.E. Knox in Hilsman to Rusk, October 26, 1962, Box 36a, Folder "Cuba. General. 10/15/62–10/23/62," National Security Files, Kennedy Library.
60. Arnold L. Horelick and Myron Rush, *Strategic Power and Soviet Foreign Policy* (Chicago: University of Chicago Press, 1966), is the classic study.

backed away from a strategy of bluff: something more compelling had intervened, leading them to pay the price, in bargaining terms, of not seriously
preparing for war.

It is reasonable to suppose that their view of the United States had a good
deal to do with the choices they made. For they saw a country whose whole
way of thinking about nuclear issues had focused on the question of how
much an advantage there might be to getting in the first blow; where responsible officials, from the President on down, had stressed how the United
States would not rule out the option of striking first in certain circumstances;
and where the logic of preemptive action—of semi-unintended war, resulting
from the fear of surprise attack—was very widely recognized.[61]

The important volume on *Soviet Military Strategy* (1962), edited by Marshal
Sokolovskii, shows just how sensitive the Soviets were at this time to the
American emphasis on the logic of preemption. The Americans, the Soviet
authors pointed out, understood that "the one who strikes first will undoubtedly gain an important advantage." This was why the United States was so
afraid of surprise attack. But the Americans assumed that the fear of surprise
attack—and here the Soviet authors were quoting directly from a U.S. Senate
document—"gravely increased the temptation to strike first in a nuclear war."
The Americans thought they might have to attack simply because they felt
their enemy was about to strike: "a pre-emptive blow . . . is defensive,
according to American military theorists, since it is dealt to an enemy who
is ready to attack (to initiate a preventive war or deal a first blow). It is
considered to be the final and only means of avoiding disaster."[62]

It is clear that the Soviet authors understood some of the basic arguments
American strategists were making during the period; official doctrine, and
the capabilities with which it was linked, would naturally be viewed in this
context. The most disturbing thing here, from their point of view, would be
the notion of "damage limitation" and the American counterforce capabilities
that supported it. "Damage limitation," whatever official attempts were made

61. See especially Khrushchev's July 10, 1962 speech, published in *Pravda* the next day, and in
English in the *Current Digest of the Soviet Press*, Vol. 14, No. 28 (August 8, 1962), esp. pp. 3–4,
for the Soviet leader's reaction to President Kennedy's refusal to rule out a first strike option.
Kennedy's remarks were originally made in an interview with Stewart Alsop, "Kennedy's Grand
Strategy," *Saturday Evening Post*, March 31, 1962, p. 14. See also Michael Brower, "Nuclear
Strategy of the Kennedy Administration," *Bulletin of the Atomic Scientists*, Vol. 18, No. 8 (October
1962), esp p. 38f.
62. V.D. Sokolovskii, ed., *Soviet Military Strategy* (Englewood Cliffs, N.J.: Prentice Hall, Rand
edition, 1963), pp. 160–162. The original Soviet edition was published in 1962.

to rationalize it in "second-strike" terms, must have struck them as a code term for preemption. This certainly was how Carl Kaysen, Bundy's aide during the Kennedy Administration, explained it a few years later: "Should sufficient warning of preparations for a Soviet strike or actual launching of one be available, U.S. missiles could be launched against Soviet missile sites and airfields, thus limiting to an extent depending on warning time the damage the Soviet strike would inflict."[63]

Given all this, Soviet leaders might have viewed war preparations as very dangerous—and quite possibly because of the disparity in force levels and in degrees of force vulnerability, risky in a way that the corresponding American alert simply was not. Indeed, the famous remark of Soviet Deputy Foreign Minister Kuznetsov to John McCloy shortly after the crisis—"You Americans will never be able to do this to us again"—suggests that the Soviets drew back because of a relative, but remediable, weakness, and obviously their conventional inferiority in the Caribbean was not what Kuznetsov had in mind.[64]

But however the asymmetry in military preparations is to be explained, the important thing to note is that people in Washington were aware of it during the crisis. What conclusions might they have realistically drawn from it? Could they have felt that the lack of parallelism reflected a Soviet sense of their own strategic inferiority? This is why speculation about the Soviet motivation for the deployment can be so revealing: did anyone feel that the Soviets had made what was assumed to be the very risky move of introducing missiles into Cuba out of weakness—for example, because they had been so uncomfortable with the existing strategic balance during the Berlin crisis the previous year? And what conclusions were drawn from the fact that the deployment had been carried out in such a furtive and deceptive fashion, tactics of this sort being traditionally associated with the weak?[65]

63. Carl Kaysen, "Keeping the Strategic Balance," *Foreign Affairs*, Vol. 46, No. 4 (July 1968), p. 668.
64. The quotation is from Charles E. Bohlen, *Witness to History, 1929–1969* (New York: W.W. Norton, 1973), pp. 495–496. There is also the related question, about which there has been so much conjecture, of the connection between the Cuban missile crisis and the development of Soviet strategic capabilities after 1962. It is hard to believe there is no connection at all, but it is still too early for firm conclusions on this subject.
65. This is no accident, since everyone knows that one pays a price for deceptive or devious behavior: the risk of embarrassment if one is found out, a discrediting of one's future claims and promises, possibly increased self-righteousness on the part of one's adversary and the bargaining advantages this gives him. For these reasons it is pointless to lie or cheat without sufficient cause: the disadvantages have to be offset by some other consideration, and the most natural candidate is a sense of one's own relative weakness.

These certainly are the kinds of things to look out for as more evidence is released. It is already clear that some people close to the crisis did in fact draw these sorts of inferences. General Burchinal, for example, later stressed that Khrushchev "never alerted a bomber or changed his own military posture one bit. We had a gun at his head and he didn't move a muscle"; and Burchinal implied that this issue was discussed at the time with his civilian superiors.[66] One would like to see how the arguments were played out and what effect they had on policy. In any event, the mere fact of asymmetry does not seem consistent with the picture that Bundy painted in 1969. It suggests in itself that the nuclear situation was not one of simple "stalemate" in 1962.

What then was the role of the strategic balance in 1962? America's "superiority" apparently did not have much of a direct effect on American policy during the crisis—or at least this is what the limited evidence now available seems to indicate. But with regard to the Soviets, the evidence points in the opposite direction: their strategic "inferiority" appears to have had a profound effect on their behavior in the crisis.

Conclusions

What role did nuclear forces play during the Cuban missile crisis? We began by considering three different lines of argument: 1) the claim that nuclear weapons played no role at all, that they just cancelled each other out; 2) the set of arguments that emphasize the notion of risk; and 3) the strategic balance interpretation, which asserts that America's nuclear superiority played a crucial role in determining the course and outcome of the crisis. How well have each of these interpretations held up in the light of the evidence examined here?

There is first the argument that nuclear forces simply neutralized each other—that nuclear forces were "unusable," and that because they were militarily useless, they could not be harnessed to any political purpose, beyond simply deterring their use by others. Of all the arguments considered here, this is the most difficult to sustain. It is obvious that the fear of nuclear war affected both Soviet and American behavior in the crisis; and indeed these fears were consciously manipulated, most notably by the American

66. Burchinal oral history, p. 116.

strategic alert. For such anxieties to have a real effect on political behavior, there was no need for the President to decide consciously that he would under certain circumstances start a nuclear war: escalation could be largely inadvertent. It was sufficient, as Brodie pointed out in a 1963 talk on the crisis, that the government was able simply to "threaten the next in a series of moves" that seemed to tend in the direction of general war.[67]

The risk of nuclear war could therefore affect behavior. But the threshold of acceptable risk could vary, and nuclear anxieties in fact did not have an equal effect on both sides. The "balance of resolve" was therefore crucial. The balance was not so completely lopsided that the crisis was ended by a total Soviet capitulation. Nor, on the other hand, was the final arrangement a bargain negotiated between equals. The balance was unequal, but not so unequal that it makes sense to view the crisis as a simple "contest" with a clear victor.

It would therefore be a bit too extreme to view the crisis as a "competition in risk-taking" à la Thomas Schelling. "Until we can manipulate the risk of general war and engage in competitive risk-taking with the Soviets," Schelling said a few months after the crisis, ". . . I don't think we are going to learn to take care of Berlin, much less to take care of Indonesia and Finland, when the time comes."[68] But this kind of attitude is really not reflected in the documents on the Cuban crisis. To be sure, people felt they had to act. Both for foreign policy reasons—the Soviet deployment was in direct defiance of an American warning—and for reasons of domestic politics as well, the administration knew that it could not sit this one out. But no one wanted to keep upping the ante, to keep outbidding the Soviets in "resolve," as the way of triumphing in the confrontation.

As for the argument about the strategic balance, the evidence at this point suggests that it did not have an important direct influence on American policy. The Kennedy Administration's fears of escalation substantially cancelled out, in its own mind, whatever benefits it might have theoretically been able to derive from its "strategic superiority." The American ability to "limit damage" by destroying an enemy's strategic forces did not seem, in American eyes, to carry much political weight. Thus in practice the more

---

67. Bernard Brodie, "AFAG Talk: Political Impact of U.S. Force Postures," May 28, 1963, p. 7 (recently released by Rand).
68. David Abshire and Richard Allen, eds., *National Security: Political, Military, and Economic Strategies in the Decade Ahead* (New York: Praeger, 1963), p. 646.

subtle official theories about nuclear war-fighting evidently did not have much of an effect on American policy.

But the Soviets seem to have been profoundly affected by their "strategic inferiority." The ironic thing is that they probably took American ideas about "damage limitation" and "discriminate and controlled general war," and the capabilities with which they were linked, far more seriously than the Americans did. And this was in spite of the fact that just a few months earlier, after the Ann Arbor speech, they had contemptuously dismissed the McNamara strategy as absurd. It really does seem that "we had a gun to their head and they didn't move a muscle"—that their failure to make any preparations for general war was linked to a fear of provoking American preemptive action. And this meant that it was more essential than it otherwise might have been to head off an invasion of Cuba through a political settlement. The danger of provoking an American preemptive strike tended to rule out countermeasures—or even the serious threat of countermeasures, around Berlin or elsewhere—that would significantly increase the risk of war. The effect therefore was to tie their hands, to limit their freedom of maneuver, and thus to increase their incentive to settle the crisis quickly.

This implies that the strategic balance mattered in 1962. Does this conclusion have "hawkish" or "pro-nuclear" implications? Its real meaning is more complex: the point that nuclear forces can carry political weight in itself tells us very little about basic issues of policy—about whether, or in what ways, nuclear power *should* be used to support political objectives. The lessons of history are rarely clear-cut.

The historical analysis of the Cuban missile crisis is still in its infancy. The new documents on the crisis, as revealing as they are, represent just the tip of the iceberg. It is only as more material is released that the full meaning of the crisis can begin to unfold. If this material is approached correctly—if questions are framed so that answers turn on what the archival evidence shows—the historical study of the crisis can be of real value. It is one of the best ways we have of bringing the problem of the political utility of nuclear forces into focus—of going beyond speculation and reaching some solid conclusions about one of the most basic problems of the nuclear age.

White House Tapes and Minutes of the Cuban Missile Crisis

ExCom Meetings
October 1962

Introduction to Documents

Until the partial and gradual opening of the archives in the last few years, people interested in studying the Cuban missile crisis had to rely almost exclusively on accounts given by the participants. But the picture that came through in the memoir literature was almost bound to be distorted: after President Kennedy's assassination, and the series of national traumas that followed in rapid succession, it was inevitable that recollections about the early 1960s would be filtered through many layers of emotion, and in fact the prevailing interpretation of the period came to have an almost mythic quality. But what this meant to a historian is that the archives were certain to contain some real surprises.

In 1973, in the context of the Watergate scandal, it was revealed that during the Kennedy Administration a number of recordings had been made of White House meetings, and there is little doubt that the taping had been done secretly. Indeed, some of President Kennedy's closest associates were surprised—even incredulous—at the disclosure. "I know nothing about it," McGeorge Bundy told the *New York Times*; he added "that he did not recall seeing any recording equipment at meetings he attended." And Arthur Schlesinger, Jr., "described the idea of secret recordings during the Kennedy Administration as 'absolutely inconceivable.' " "It was not the sort of thing Kennedy would have done," he told a news agency. "The kind of people in the White House then would not have thought of doing something like that."[1]

There are in fact 127 audiotapes of White House meetings on deposit at the Kennedy Library in Boston. They cover the period from July 30, 1962 to November 8, 1963; eighteen tapes, including eight tapes of official "ExCom" meetings, relate directly to the missile crisis. There is also a dictabelt containing the President's reflections on the crisis—the only known evidence, according to the register in the Kennedy Library, of "this sort of reflective diary-keeping" by Kennedy during his presidency.

The first missile crisis tape—or actually extracts from it, together with an 87-page "sanitized" transcript—was released last year by the Kennedy Library. The transcript, sections of which are presented here, covers what was

---

1. *The New York Times*, July 19, 1973, p. 20.

International Security, Summer 1985 (Vol. 10, No. 1) 0162-2889/85/0164-40 $02.50/1

in effect the first day of this thirteen-day crisis. It represents about two and a half hours of conversation recorded in the White House on October 16, 1962. President Kennedy had just found out about the missiles earlier that morning.

The other documents presented here are not quite as unusual, but are still very revealing. After President Kennedy gave his famous speech on October 22 announcing the existence of the missiles and outlining the measures the United States was taking to deal with the problem, the group of advisers he had brought together at the beginning of the crisis was officially designated the "Executive Committee of the National Security Council," or "ExCom" for short. There were no formal minutes kept of its first four meetings, but Bromley Smith prepared minutes beginning with its fifth meeting on October 25, and "sanitized" versions are available in Boxes 315 and 316 of the National Security Files at the Kennedy Library. Published here are the minutes of two meetings held at the climax of the crisis, and excerpts from the minutes of a third: an invasion of Cuba was imminent, and the confrontation was clearly coming to a head.

How exactly does this material bear on accepted notions about the crisis? The first major revision relates to the issue of a trade involving the American missiles in Turkey. Many writers have assumed, on the basis of very explicit claims by the participants, that President Kennedy refused to countenance a trade involving the Jupiters in Turkey. Perhaps the most important scholarly study of this issue is Barton Bernstein's article, "The Cuban Missile Crisis: Trading the Jupiters in Turkey?" Although Bernstein here backed away from the more extreme claims he had made in earlier articles, he still tended to minimize the degree to which the President was committed to the idea of a trade. He presented Kennedy as "wavering" on October 27 between war and peace, as "prepared to countenance a trade" only "at a few points" when "he seemed desperate."[2] The ExCom minutes published here, however, show that the President's attitude at this point was quite consistent; he wanted to freeze work on the missile sites, and then enter into negotiations with the Russians: "we have to face up to the possibility of some kind of a trade."

Moreover, there is no evidence in the minutes of ExCom session no. 8 (cited by Bernstein to support his claim) of Kennedy at any point "opting for a course toward war."[3] Kennedy's proposal to consult the NATO allies, which

2. Barton J. Bernstein, "The Cuban Missile Crisis: Trading the Jupiters in Turkey?," *Political Science Quarterly*, Vol. 95, No. 1 (Spring 1980), pp. 119, 117.
3. Ibid., p. 119.

Bernstein alludes to in this context, might in fact be viewed as a maneuver to shore up his less belligerent position. There is some evidence that the British, in particular, took a dovish line: according to notes of the National Security Council meeting held on October 22, the President commented that a message just received from Prime Minister Macmillan "contained the best argument for taking no action."[4] Compare this with Bernstein's claim, based on Macmillan's memoirs, that the British Prime Minister "had been a strong supporter of the quarantine and worried, especially in the early days, that Khrushchev would wring concessions that would weaken the alliance."[5]

A second point relates to Robert Kennedy's role. According to Arthur Schlesinger, Jr., Robert Kennedy "was a dove from the start. If you bomb the missile sites and airports, he said on the first day, 'you are covering most of Cuba. You are going to kill an awful lot of people and take an awful lot of heat on it.' If the Americans said they were bombing because of the missiles, 'it would be almost [incumbent] upon the Russians to say that we are going to send them in again and, if you do it again, we are going to do the same thing in Turkey.' "[6] But actually, as the transcript makes clear, Robert Kennedy was arguing for an invasion. The passage Schlesinger alludes to was introduced by Robert Kennedy raising the issue of an invasion, and in fact practically every time he spoke in the course of these October 16 meetings, his comments seemed to point in that direction.[7] His argument was that an air strike would be insufficient since six months later the Soviets could just rebuild the missile bases: "if you're going to get into it at all," you might as well take your losses "and get it over with."[8] At one point, he even asked whether the United States might be able to engineer some pretext for a war against Cuba—whether we could "sink the *Maine* again or something."[9]

The same kind of point comes out when we examine Robert Kennedy's feelings about the blockade option. In his memoir on the crisis, he claimed

4. In box 313, folder "NSC Meetings 1962, No. 507," National Security Files, John F. Kennedy Library, Boston.
5. Bernstein, "The Cuban Missile Crisis," p. 114.
6. Arthur M. Schlesinger, Jr., *Robert Kennedy and His Times* (Boston: Houghton Mifflin, 1978), p. 507.
7. Presidential Recordings, Transcripts, Cuban Missile Crisis Meetings, Off-the-Record Meeting on Cuba, October 16, 1962, first meeting, p. 21 (for the passage Schlesinger refers to) and p. 31, and second meeting, pp. 24–25, 27—from the President's Office Files, JFK Library, Boston. Henceforth cited as "October 16 transcripts, I [for the first meeting] or II [for the second]." Extracts are published below; the full transcript and an audiocassette containing extracts from the original tape are both available by mail from the Kennedy Library.
8. October 16 transcripts, II, p. 25.
9. Ibid., II, p. 279

to have supported McNamara's position in favor of a blockade.[10] But when McNamara said on October 16 that the Soviets could be prevented from redeploying missiles after an air strike by a blockade, Robert Kennedy in effect argued against this: "Then we're gonna have to sink Russian ships." That to his mind meant risking war; and, he seemed to think, you might just as well face the risk of war then (through an invasion) as later.[11] His opposition to the blockade was also reflected in the ExCom minutes. On October 25, for example, he "repeated his view that we may decide that it is better to avoid confronting the Russians by stopping one of their ships and to react by attacking the missiles already in Cuba."[12] And he made the same point, but perhaps even more strongly, during the morning ExCom meeting on October 27, the minutes of which are published below.

All of this, perhaps, may force us to reconsider some traditional judgments about Robert Kennedy's moderation and moral sensibilities. When people talk about the role that moral considerations play in shaping foreign policy, Robert Kennedy's Pearl Harbor analogy is often the first example cited. For this reason alone, some standard claims about his attitude during the crisis merit close examination. "Listening to the war cries of the hawks," Schlesinger wrote, Robert Kennedy "sent his famous note to Sorensen: 'I now know how Tojo felt when he was planning Pearl Harbor.'" [13] But perhaps this was meant quite literally—although it was certainly an ironic way of putting things: he really did understand how it felt to be contemplating a large-scale military attack, because that was precisely what he at this point wanted.

A third point has to do with the military significance of the missiles in Cuba. There is the claim, made most recently by Raymond Garthoff, that even McNamara "did not deny that there was military significance to the deployment," and that the "question of the actual impact on the military balance, therefore, did not become an issue of contention."[14] In fact, it is

10. Robert F. Kennedy, *Thirteen Days* (New York: New American Library, Signet Books, 1969), p. 37.
11. October 16 transcripts, II, pp. 24–25.
12. "Summary Record of NSC Executive Committee Meeting No. 5, October 25, 1962, 5 p.m.," p. 5, National Security Files, Box 315, JFK Library.
13. Schlesinger, *Robert Kennedy*, p. 507. These claims about Robert Kennedy's moderation from the very outset were made even more strongly in the televised series based on Schlesinger's biography that was shown early in 1985. In fact the script for the episode dealing with the Cuban missile crisis showed both of the Kennedy brothers as eager from the start for a negotiated solution. But, as the transcript shows, not only was this not true of Robert, but the President himself thought at this time that an air strike was the very least that should be done (I, p. 27).
14. Raymond Garthoff, "A Retrospective Look at a 1962 Evaluation of the Soviet Missiles in

clear from the transcript that McNamara did flatly deny that the deployment would have any effect on the strategic balance; the Joint Chiefs of Staff, on the other hand, felt that the effect would be substantial.[15] And it is clear that the issue did play a certain role in the discussion. In particular, McNamara's view was the basis for his belief that the missiles posed not a "military problem" but simply a "domestic, political problem"—and this assumption lay at the heart of his thinking about what should be done.[16]

These are all fairly narrow points. But it is not simply because they force us to make specific revisions of this sort that these documents are so valuable. They are fascinating because they give us such a direct and unfiltered sense for these events—a rare glimpse, for example, at the disorderly, unsystematic but not necessarily inefficient way in which things were worked out. Myths are easy enough to deflate, and some of the hyperbole lavished on this episode—"this combination of toughness and restraint, of will, nerve and wisdom, so brilliantly controlled, so matchlessly calibrated"[17]—is almost embarrassing to read in the light of the evidence. But the detailed analysis of the crisis, which documents of this sort will eventually permit, can take us well beyond simple revisionism: their real value is that they permit us to bring into focus questions about the wellsprings of policy, about exactly how things developed and why. How was it, for example, that McNamara, who at the outset of the crisis had been unwilling to sanction an attack on Cuba if any of the missiles there were operational, came at the end to view an invasion of the island as "almost inevitable," even though some of the missiles by that time had reached operational status? Does this shift in attitude suggest anything of a general nature about political behavior in time of crisis?[18]

And then there is the question of the time constraint—that is, the deadline for action—and the closely related issue of how long it would take before the missiles became ready to fire. On the one hand, there was the assumption

Cuba," addendum to his *Intelligence Assessment and Policymaking: A Decision Point in the Kennedy Administration* (Washington, D.C.: Brookings, 1984), p. 28; or, in slightly different form, in his article "The Meaning of the Missiles," *Washington Quarterly*, Vol. 5, No. 4 (Autumn 1982), p. 76.
15. October 16 transcripts, II, p. 12.
16. Ibid., II, pp. 45–46.
17. This is from the concluding paragraph in the chapter on the missile crisis in Arthur Schlesinger, Jr., *A Thousand Days* (Boston: Houghton Mifflin, 1965), p. 841.
18. October 16 transcripts, I, pp. 11, 13; "Summary Record of NSC Executive Committee Meeting No. 8, October 27, 1962, 4:00 PM," p. 5, Box 316, National Security Files, JFK Library (and reprinted below).

on October 16 that the missiles in question were "field-type" weapons, and if the equipment had been checked out and the site surveyed, the missiles could be "fielded, placed and fired in six hours."[19] But at other times, people spoke of a two-week period. General Marshall Carter, the Deputy Director of Central Intelligence, said that the CIA estimate was "that these could be fully operational within two weeks," although maybe a single missile would be operational much sooner.[20] All this strikes the reader as very unclear; and even at the time, McNamara, it seems, was uncertain about whether the crucial time constraint was six hours or two weeks.[21] Is it conceivable that the notion of a two-week period took hold in an almost arbitrary way, that the deadline for final action was determined on the basis of this assumption even before this issue was satisfactorily ironed out, and that the deadline so set persisted, as much by default as by anything else, even after it had become known that a number of the missiles were operational?

A document as complete as this transcript evidently is, recording a free and fairly unstructured discussion, can be revealing as much for what it does not contain as for what it does. Everyone has heard the story about Sherlock Holmes and the significant episode of the dog in the night. "But the dog," Watson said, "did nothing in the night." That, Holmes replied, was the significant episode. The October 16 transcript is full of "significant episodes" of this sort. One wonders, for example, why no one even explicitly broached the issue of how the transformation of Cuba into a base for Soviet missiles would affect the vulnerability of America's strategic forces: when McNamara denied that the deployment would have any effect on the strategic balance, no one forced him to back up his opinion and deal directly with issues of this sort.

Similarly, there is the question of what the U.S. government knew about Soviet command and control. McNamara's unwillingness at this point to attack Cuba once any of the missiles there became operational was rooted in his fear that Soviet control over the missile sites might be loose, and in the event of an attack the local commander might decide on his own initiative to launch his missiles against American cities. But his comment that we just "don't know" what kinds of communication and control system the Soviets had over the missiles in Cuba scarcely seems adequate. No one pressed him

---

19. October 16 transcripts, I, pp. 3–4, and II, p. 3.
20. Ibid., II, p. 2; see also I, p. 23, and II, p. 42.
21. Ibid., II, p. 11.

on this issue, but it is hard to believe that the government knew nothing of a general nature about Soviet command and control that was relevant to the situation in Cuba—how closely in their system, for example, control over warheads was integrated with control over delivery systems. One wonders whether there was any reaching down into the bureaucracy for answers to questions of this sort.

Historical analysis in fact proceeds largely by focusing on these little issues, and practically any project worth doing involves scores of such second-order problems. This mode of operation reflects as much as anything else the prejudice of the professional historian—or really the intellectual style of the discipline. From experience one comes to take it for granted that the process of sorting out the more prosaic kinds of problems gives one, often in the most unexpected ways, a "feel" for what was going on: as the French say, "le bon Dieu est dans le détail."

—Marc Trachtenberg

Editor's Note:

PUNCTUATION. The following conventions are used:

[?]   When the transcriber is not certain of what is said on the recording.
. . . .   To indicate a sentence that the speaker trails off without completing.
. . .   When a speaker is interrupted before a sentence is completed.
[   ]   Used to enclose tentative interpretations or editorial comments of the transcriber.
[Deleted]   To indicate material removed by the sanitizers of the documents.
. . . . . .   A line of ellipses between sections represents material in the documents not selected for reprint here.
(pp.   )   Page numbers at end of sections refer to pages in original transcriptions in Kennedy Library.

NAMES. "JFK" and "RFK" are used for President Kennedy and Robert Kennedy, respectively. When the identity of a speaker is unknown, "Speaker?" is used; when the identification of a speaker is uncertain, a question mark follows the name.

Participants in the meetings were:

President John F. Kennedy
Dean Rusk, Secretary of State
Robert McNamara, Secretary of Defense
General Maxwell Taylor, Chairman of the Joint Chiefs of Staff

McGeorge Bundy, Special Assistant to the President for National Security Affairs
Douglas Dillon, Secretary of the Treasury
General Marshall Carter, Deputy Director of the C.I.A.
Robert F. Kennedy, Attorney General
Edwin Martin, Assistant Secretary of State for Latin America
George Ball, Under Secretary of State
U. Alexis Johnson, Deputy Under Secretary of State

Excerpts from:
OFF-THE-RECORD MEETING ON CUBA
October 16, 1962
11:50 A.M.–12:57 P.M.

JFK:	Secretary Rusk?
Rusk:	Yes. [Well?], Mr. President, this is a, of course, a [widely?] serious development. It's one that we, all of us, had not really believed the Soviets could, uh, carry this far. Uh, they, uh, seemed to be denying that they were going to establish bases of their own [in the same?] [words unintelligible] with a Soviet base, thus making it [essential to or essentially?] Cuban point of view. The Cubans couldn't [word unintelligible] with it anyhow, so. . . . Now, uhm, I do think we have to set in motion a chain of events that will eliminate this base. I don't think we [can?] sit still. The questioning becomes whether we do it by sudden, unannounced strike of some sort, or we, uh, build up the crisis to the point where the other side has to consider very seriously about giving in, or, or even the Cubans themselves, uh, take some, take some action on this. The thing that I'm, of course, very conscious of is that there is no such thing, I think, as unilateral action by the United States. It's so [eminently or heavily?] involved with 42 allies and confrontation in many places, that any action that we take, uh, will greatly increase the risks of direct action involving, uh, our other alliances and our other forces in other parts of the world. Uhm, so I think we, we have to think very hard about two major, uh, courses of action as alternatives. One is the quick strike. The point where we [make or think?], that is the, uh, overwhelming, overriding necessity to take all the risks that are involved doing that. I don't think this in itself would require an invasion of Cuba. I think that with or without such an invasion, in other words if we make it clear that, uh, what we're doing is eliminating this particular base or any other such base that is established. We ourselves are not moved to general war, we're simply doing what we said we would do if they took certain action. Uh, or we're going to decide that this is the

time to eliminate the Cuban problem by actual eliminate the island [*sic*].

The other would be, if we have a few days—from the military point of view, if we have the whole time—uh, then I would think that, uh, there would be another course of action, a combination of things that, uh, we might wish to consider. Uhm, first, uh, that we, uh, stimulate the OAS[1] procedure immediately for prompt action to make it quite clear that the entire hemisphere considers that the Rio Pact has been violated [and actually?] what acts should [we take or be taken?] in, under the terms of the Rio Pact. The OAS could constitute itself an organ of consultation promptly, although maybe, it may take two or three days to get, uh, instructions from governments and things of that sort. The OAS could, I suppose, at any moment, uh, take action to insist to the Cubans that an OAS inspection, uh, team be permitted to come and, itself, look directly at these sites, provide assurance[s?] to the hemisphere. That will undoubtedly be turned down, but it will be another step in building up the, uh, building a position.

I think also that we ought to consider getting some word to Castro, perhaps through the Canadian ambassador in Havana or through, uh, his representative at the U.N. Uh, I think perhaps the Canadian ambassador would be the best, the better channel to get to Castro [apart?] privately and tell him that, uh, this is no longer support for Cuba, that Cuba is being victimized here, and that, uh, the Soviets are preparing Cuba for destruction or betrayal.

You saw the *Times*[2] story yesterday morning that high Soviet officials were saying, "We'll trade Cuba for Berlin." This ought to be brought to Castro's attention. It ought to be said to Castro that, uh, uh, this kind of a base is intolerable and not acceptable. The time has now come when he must take the interests of the Cuban people, must now break clearly with the Soviet Union, prevent this missile base from becoming operational.

And I think there are certain military, uhm, uh, actions that we could, we might well want to take straight away. First, to uh, to call up, uh, highly selective units [no more than?] 150,000. Unless we feel that it's better, more desirable to go to a general national emergency so that we have complete freedom of action. If we announce, at the time that we announce this development—and I think we do have to announce this development some time this week—uh, we announce that, uh, we are conducting a surveillance of Cuba, over Cuba, and we will enforce our right to do so. We reject the mission of secrecy

1. Organization of American States
2. *New York Times*

in this hemisphere in any matters of this sort. We, we reinforce our forces in Guantanamo. We reinforce our forces in the southeastern part of the United States—whatever is necessary from the military point of view to be able to give, to deliver an overwhelming strike at any of these installations, including the SAM sites. And, uh, also, to take care of any, uh, MIGs or bombers that might make a pass at Miami or at the United States. Build up heavy forces, uh, if those are not already in position.

[Deleted]

I think also that we need a few days, uhm, to alert our other allies, for consultation with NATO. I'll assume that we can move on this line at the same time to interrupt all air traffic from free world countries going into Cuba, insist to the Mexicans, the Dutch, that they stop their planes from coming in. Tell the British, who, and anyone else who's involved at this point, that, uh, if they're interested in peace, they've *got* to stop their ships from Cuban trade at this point. Uh, in other words, isolate Cuba completely without at this particular moment a, uh, a forceful blockade.

I think it would be important to use the, uh, consider, uh, calling in General Eisenhower,[3] giving him a full briefing before a public announcement is made as to the situation and the [forcible?] action which you might determine upon.

But I think that, by and large, there are, there are these two broad alternatives: one, the quick strike; the other, to alert our allies *and* Mr. Khrushchev that there is utterly serious crisis in the making here, and that, uh. . . . Mr. Khrushchev may not himself really understand that or believe that at this point. I think we'll be facing a situation that could well lead to general war; that we have an obligation to do what has to be done but do it in a way that gives, uh, everybody a chance to, uh, put the [word unintelligible] down before it gets too hard. Those are my, my reactions of this morning, Mr. President. I naturally need to think about this very hard for the next several hours, uh, what I and what my colleagues at the State Department can do about it.

McNamara: Mr. President, there are a number of unknowns in this situation I want to comment upon, and, in relation to them, I would like to outline very briefly some possible military alternatives and ask General Taylor to expand upon them.

But before commenting on either the unknowns or outlining some military alternatives, there are two propositions I would suggest that

---

3. Dwight D. Eisenhower

we ought to accept as, uh, foundations for our further thinking. My first is that if we are to conduct an air strike against these installations, or against any part of Cuba, we must agree now that we will schedule that prior to the time these missile sites become operational. I'm not prepared to say when that will be, but I think it is extremely important that our talk and our discussion be founded on this premise: that any air strike will be planned to take place prior to the time they become operational. Because, if they become operational before the air strike, I do not believe we can state we can knock them out before they can be launched; and if they're launched there is almost certain to be, uh, chaos in part of the east coast or the area, uh, in a radius of six hundred to a thousand miles from Cuba.

Uh, secondly, I, I would submit the proposition that any air strike must be directed not solely against the missile sites, but against the missile sites plus the airfields plus the aircraft which may not be on the airfields but hidden by that time plus all potential nuclear storage sites. Now, this is a fairly extensive air strike. It is not just a strike against the missile sites; and there would be associated with it potential casualties of Cubans, not of U.S. citizens, but potential casualties of Cubans in, at least in the hundreds, more likely in the low thousands, say two or three thousand. It seems to me these two propositions, uh, should underlie our, our discussion.

Now, what kinds of military action are we capable of carrying out and what may be some of the consequences? Uh, we could carry out an air strike within a matter of days. We would be ready for the start of such an air strike within, within a matter of days. If it were absolutely essential, it could be done almost literally within a matter of hours. I believe the chiefs would prefer that it be deferred for a matter of days, but we are prepared for that quickly. The air strike could continue for a matter of days following the initial day, if necessary. Uh, presumably there would be some political discussions taking place either just before the air strike or both before and during. In any event, we would be prepared, following the air strike, for an air, invasion, both by air and by sea. [Deleted] after the start of the air strike, that would be possible if the political environment made it desirable or necessary at that time. [Fine?] Associated with this air strike undoubtedly should be some degree of mobilization. Uh, I would think of the mobilization coming not before the air strike but either concurrently with or somewhat following, say possibly five days afterwards, depending upon the possible invasion requirements. The character of the mobilization would be such that it could be carried out in its first phase at least within the limits of the authority granted by Congress. There might have to be a second phase, and then it would require a declaration of a national emergency.

Now, this is very sketchily the military, uh, capabilities, and I think you may wish to hear General Taylor, uh, outline his choice.

Speaker ?:   Almost too [words unintelligible] to Cuba.

Speaker ?:   Yes.

Taylor: Uh, we're impressed, Mr. President, with the great importance of getting a, a strike with all the benefit of surprise, uh, which would mean *ideally* that we would have all the missiles that are in Cuba above ground where we can take them out. Uh, that, that desire runs counter to the strong point the secretary made if the other optimum would be to get every missile before it could, becomes operational. Uh, practically, I think the, our knowledge of the timing of the readiness is going to be so, so, uh, difficult that we'll never have the, the exact permanent, uh, the perfect timing. What we'd like to do is to look at this new photography, I think—and take any additional—and try to get the, the layout of the targets in as near an optimum, uh, position as possible, and then take 'em out without any warning whatsoever. That does not preclude, I don't think, Mr. Secretary, some of the things you've been talking about. It's a little hard to say in terms of time how much I'm discussing. But we must do a good job the first time we go in there, uh, pushing a 100 percent just as far, as closely as we can with our, with our strike. I'm having all the responsible planners in this afternoon, Mr. President, at four o'clock, to talk this out with 'em and get their best judgment.

I would also mention among the, the military actions we should take that once we have destroyed as many of these offensive weapons as possible, we should, should prevent any more coming in, which means a naval blockade. So I suppose that all. . . . And also a reinforcement of Guantanamo and evacuation of dependents. So, really, the, in point of time, I'm, I'm thinking in terms of three phases.

One, a, an initial pause of some sort while we get completely ready and get, get the right posture on the part of the target, so we can do the best job. Then, virtually concurrently, a air strike against, as the secretary said, missiles, airfields, uh, nuclear sites that we know of. At the same time, naval blockade. At the same time, reinforce Guantanamo and evacuate the dependents. I'd then start this continuous reconnaissance, the list that you had, continue over Cuba.

Then, then the decision can be made as we, as we're mobilizing, uh, with the air strike as to whether we invade or not. I think that's the hardest question militarily in the whole business—one which we should look at very closely before we get our feet in that deep mud in Cuba.

Rusk: There are st-, one or two things, Mr. President, uh. Gromyko[4] asked to see you Thursday. Uh, it may be of some interest to know what he says about this, if he says anything. He may be bringing a message on this subject. Uh, but that. . . . I just want to remind you that you are seeing him and that may be relevant to this [topic?]. I might say incidentally, sir, that you delay anything else you have to do at this point.

Secondly, I don't believe, myself, that the critical question is whether you get a particular missile before *it* goes off because if they shoot *those* missiles we are in general nuclear war. In other words, the Soviet Union has got quite a different decision to make. If they, if they shoot those missiles, want to shoot 'em off before they get knocked out by aircraft. . . . So, I'm not sure that this is, uh, necessarily the precise [critical?] element, Bob.

McNamara: Well, I would strongly emphasize that I think our time should be based on the assumption it is, Dean. We don't know what kinds of communications the Soviets have with those sites. We don't know what kinds of control they have over the warheads.

Rusk: Yes, [words unintelligible] . . .

McNamara: If we saw a warhead on the site and we knew that that launcher was capable of launching that warhead, I would. . . . Frankly, I would strongly urge against the air attack, to be quite frank about it, because I think the danger to this country in relation to the gain that would accrue with the excessive [time?]. . . . This is why I suggest that if we're talking about an air attack, I believe we should consider it *only* on the assumption that we can carry it off before these become operational.

JFK: What is the, uh, advant-. . . . Must be some major reason for the Russians to, uh, set this up as a. . . . Must be that they're not satisfied with their ICBMs. What'd be the reason that they would, uh. . . .

Taylor: What it'd give 'em is primary, it makes the launching base, uh, for short range missiles against the United States to supplement their rather defective ICBM system, for example. There's one reason.

JFK: Of course, I don't see how we could prevent further ones from coming in by submarine.

Taylor: Well, I think that that thing is all over . . .

JFK: I mean if we let 'em blockade the thing, they come in by submarine.

---

4. Andrei A. Gromyko, Soviet Foreign Minister

McNamara: Well, I think the only way to prevent them coming in, quite frankly, is to say you'll take them out the moment they come in. You'll take them out and you'll carry on open surveillance and you'll have a policy to take them out if they come in. [Deleted]

Bundy: Are you absolutely clear of your premise that an air strike must go to the whole air complex?

McNamara: Well, we are, Mac . . .

Bundy: . . . air complex? [Appears to be a repeat of the words above.]

McNamara: . . . because we are fearful of these MIG 21s. We don't know where they are. We don't know what they're capable of. If there are nuclear warheads associated with the launchers, you must assume there will be nuclear warheads associated with aircraft. Even if there are not nuclear warheads associated with aircraft, you must assume that those aircraft have high explosive potential. [Deleted]

Rusk: Still, about why the Soviets are doing this, uhm, Mr. McCone[5] suggested some weeks ago that one thing Mr. Khrushchev may have in mind is that, uh, uh, he knows that we have a substantial nuclear superiority, but he also knows that we don't really live under fear of his nuclear weapons to the extent that, uh, he has to live under fear of ours. Also we have nuclear weapons nearby, in Turkey and places like that. Uhm. . . .

JFK: How many weapons do we have in Turkey?

Taylor?: We have Jupiter missiles . . .

Bundy?: Yeah. We have how many?

McNamara?: About fifteen, I believe it is.

Bundy?: I think that's right. I think that's right.

Speaker?: [Words unintelligible]

Rusk: But then there are also delivery vehicles that are, could easily . . .

McNamara: Aircraft.

Rusk: . . . be moved through the air, aircraft and so forth.

Speaker?: Route 'em through Turkey.

Rusk: Uhm, and that Mr. McCone expresses the view that Khrushchev may feel that it's important for us to learn about living under medium-range missiles, and he's doing that to sort of balance that, uh, that political, psychological [plank?]. I think also that, uh, Berlin is, uh, very much involved in this. Uhm, for the first time, I'm beginning really to wonder whether maybe Mr. Khrushchev is entirely rational about Berlin. We've [hardly?] talked about his obsession with it. And

---

5. John A. McCone, Director of the C.I.A.

I think we have to, uh, keep our eye on that element. But, uh, they may be thinking that they can either bargain Berlin and Cuba against each other, or that they could provoke us into a kind of action in Cuba which would give an umbrella for them to take action with respect to Berlin. In other words like the Suez–Hungary combination. If they could provoke us into taking the first overt action, then the world would be confused and they would have, uh, what they would consider to be justification for making a move somewhere else. But, uh, I must say I don't really see the rationality of, uh, the Soviets' pushing it this far unless they grossly misunderstand the importance of Cuba to this country.

Bundy: It's important, I think, to recognize that they did make this decision, as far as our estimates now go, in early summer, and, this has been happening since August. Their *Tass* statement of September 12, which the experts, I think, attribute very strongly to Khrushchev himself, is all mixed up on this point. It has a rather explicit statement, "The harmless military equipment sent to Cuba designed exclusively for defense, defensive purposes. The president of the United States and the American military, the military of any country know what means of defense are. How can these means threaten United States?"

Now there, it's very hard to reconcile *that* with what has happened. The rest, as the secretary says, has many comparisons between Cuba and Italy, Turkey and Japan. We have other evidence that Khrushchev is, honestly believes, or, or at least affects to believe that we have nuclear weapons in, in Japan, that combination, [word unintelligible] . . .

Rusk: Gromyko stated that in his press conference the other day, too.

Bundy: Yeah. They may mean Okinawa.

Speaker?:   Right.

McNamara: It's not likely, but it's conceivable the nuclear warheads for these launchers are not yet on Cuban soil.

Bundy: Now that seems to me that's. . . . It's perfectly possible that this, that they are in that sense a bluff. That doesn't make them any less offensive to us . . .

McNamara: No.

Bundy: . . . because we can't have proof about it.

McNamara: No, but it does possibly indicate a different course of action . . .

Bundy: Yeah.

McNamara: . . . and therefore, while I'm not suggesting how we should handle this, I think this is one of the most important actions we should take: to ascertain the location of the nuclear warheads for these missiles.

Later in the discussion we can revert back to this. There are several alternative ways of approaching it.

JFK: Doug, do you have any. . . .

Dillon: No. The only thing I'd, would say is that, uh, this alternative course of, of warning, getting, uh, public opinion, uh, OAS action and telling people in NATO and everything like that, would appear to me to have the danger of, uh, getting us wide out in the open and forcing the Russians to, uh, Soviets to take a, a position that if anything was done, uh, they would, uh, have to retaliate. Whereas, uh, a, a quick action, uh, with a statement at the same time saying this is all there is to it, might give them a chance to, uh, back off and not do anything. Meanwhile, I think that the chance of getting through this thing without a Russian reaction is greater under a quick, uh, strike than, uh, building the whole thing up to a, a climax then going through. . . . [It will be a lot of debate on it?]

Rusk: That is, of course, a possibility, but, uh. . . .

Bundy: The difficulties—I, I share the secretary of the treasury's feeling a little bit—the difficulties of organizing the OAS and NATO; the amount of noise we would get from our allies saying that, uh, they can live with Soviet MRBMs, why can't we; uh, the division in the alliance; the certainty that the Germans would feel that we *were* jeopardizing Berlin because of our concern over Cuba. The prospect of that pattern is not an appetizing one . . .

Rusk: Yes, but you see . . .

Bundy: . . . [words unintelligible]

Rusk: . . . uh, uh, everything turns crucially on what *happens.*

Bundy: I agree, Mr. Secretary.

Rusk: And if we go with the quick strike, then, in fact, they *do* back it up, then you've exposed all of your allies [word unintelligible], ourselves to all these great dangers without . . .

Bundy: You get all these noises again.

Rusk: . . . without, uh, the slightest consultation or, or warning or preparation.

JFK: But, of course, warning them, uh, it seems to me, is warning everybody. And I, I, obviously you can't sort of announce that in four days from now you're going to take them out. They may announce within three days they're going to have warheads on 'em; if we come and attack, they're going to fire them. Then what'll, what'll we do? Then we don't take 'em out. Of course, we then announce, well, if they do that, then we're going to attack with nuclear weapons.

(pp. 8–17)

. . . .

JFK:	The advant-, what is. . . . . The advantage of taking out these airplanes would be to protect us against a reprisal . . .
Taylor:	Yes.
JFK:	. . . by them. I would think you'd have to pre-, assume they'd be using, uh, iron bombs and not nuclear weapons because obviously why would the Soviets permit nuclear war to begin under that sort of half-assed way?
McNamara:	I think that's reasonable.
Speaker?:	But they still . . .
Speaker?:	But they have . . .
Speaker?:	. . . have ten IL-28s and twenty . . .
Speaker?:	Yes. Yes. They may carry out [words unintelligible]. Yes.
Speaker?:	. . . twenty-five big ones.
JFK:	So you think that if we're going to take out the, uh, missile sites you'd want to take out these planes at the same time?
Carter?:	There are eight airfields that are capable of mounting these jets. Eight [words unintelligible] . . .
Bundy:	But politically, if you're trying to get him to understand the limit and the non-limit and make it as easy for him as possible, there's an enormous premium on having a small, as small and clear-cut an action as possible, against the hazard of, uh, going after all the operational airfields becomes a kind of . . .

(pp. 25–26)

. . . .

Dillon:	I would think this business about the Soviet reaction, that there, that might be helpful, uh, if we could maybe take some, uh, general war preparation type of action that would show them that we're ready if they want to start anything, without what you might, with starting anything.
Bundy:	One. . . .
Dillon:	You just don't know.
Bundy:	On this track, one obvious element on the political side is do we say something simultaneously or, uh, to the Cubans, to the Soviets, or do we let the action speak for itself?

Rusk:	This point whether we say something to the Cubans and the Soviets before any, before . . .
JFK:	I think we ought to, what we ought to do is, is, uh, after this meeting this afternoon, we ought to meet tonight again at six, consider these various, uh, proposals. In the meanwhile, we'll go ahead with this maximum, whatever is needed from the flights, and, in addition, we will. . . . I don't think we got much time on these missiles. They may be. . . . So it may be that we just have to, we can't wait two weeks while we're getting ready to, to roll. Maybe just have to just take *them out*, and continue our other preparations if we decide to do that. That may be where we end up. I think we ought to, beginning right now, be preparing to. . . . Because that's what we're going to do *anyway*. We're certainly going to do number one; we're going to take out these, uh, missiles. Uh, the questions will be whether, which, what I would describe as number two, which would be a general air strike. That we're not ready to say, but we should be in preparation for it. The third is the, is the, uh, the general invasion. At least we're going to do number one, so it seems to me that we don't have to wait very long. We, we ought to be making *those* preparations.
Bundy:	You want to be clear, Mr. President, whether we have *definitely* decided *against* a political track. I, myself, think we ought . . .
Taylor?:	Well, we'll have . . .
Bundy:	. . . to work out a contingency on that.

(pp. 27–28)

Excerpts from:
OFF-THE-RECORD MEETING ON CUBA
October 16, 1962
6:30–7:55 P.M.

Taylor:	This is a point target, Mr., uh, President. You're never sure of having, absolutely of getting everything down there. We intend to do a great deal of damage because we can [words unintelligible]. But, as the secretary says here, there was unanimity among all the commanders involved in the Joint Chiefs, uh, that in our judgment, it would be a mistake to take this very narrow, selective target because it invited reprisal attacks and it may be detrimental. Now if the, uh, Soviets have been willing to give, uh, nuclear warheads to these missiles, there is every, just as good reason for them to give nuclear capability to these bases. We don't think we'd ever have a chance to take 'em again, so that we lose this, the first strike surprise capability. Our

	recommendation would be to get complete intelligence, get all the photography we need, the next two or three days, no, no hurry in our book. Then look at this target system. If it really threatens the United States, then take it right out with one hard crack.
JFK:	That would be taking out the, uh, some of those fighters, bombers and . . .
Taylor:	Fighters, the bombers, uh, IL-28s may turn up in this photography. It's not that all unlikely there're some there.
JFK:	Think you could do that in one day?
Taylor:	[Deleted]
McNamara:	Mr. President, could I outline three courses . . .
JFK?:	[Yes?].
McNamara:	. . . of action we have considered and speak very briefly on each one? The first is what I would call the political course of action, in which we, uh, follow some of the possibilities that Secretary Rusk mentioned this morning by approaching Castro, by approaching Khrushchev, by discussing with our allies. An overt and open approach politically to the problem [attempting, or in order?] to solve it. This seemed to me likely to lead to no satisfactory result, and it almost stops subsequent military action.
	[Deleted]
	A second course of action we haven't discussed but lies in between the military course we began discussing a moment ago and the political course of action is a course of action that would involve declaration of open surveillance; a statement that we would immediately impose an, uh, a blockade against *offensive* weapons entering Cuba in the future; and an indication that with our open-surveillance reconnaissance which we would plan to maintain indefinitely for the future, [Deleted]
Bundy:	[Deleted]
McNamara:	[Deleted]
	But the third course of action is any one of these variants of military action directed against Cuba, starting with an air attack against the missiles. The Chiefs are strongly opposed to so limited an air attack. But even so limited an air attack is a very extensive air attack. It's not twenty sorties or fifty sorties or a hundred sorties, but probably several hundred sorties. Uh, we haven't worked out the details. It's very difficult to do so when we lack certain intelligence that we hope to have tomorrow or the next day. But it's a substantial air attack. [Deleted]

This is the very, very rough plan that the Chiefs have outlined, and it is their judgment that that is the type of air attack that should be carried out. [Deleted]

It seems to me almost certain that any one of these forms of direct military action will lead to a Soviet military response of some type some place in the world. It may well be worth the price. Perhaps we should pay that. But I think we should recognize that possibility, and, moreover, we must recognize it in a variety of ways. We must recognize it by trying to deter it, which means we probably should alert SAC, probably put on an airborne alert, perhaps take other s-, alert measures. These bring risks of their own, associated with them. It means we should recognize that by mobilization. Almost certainly, we should accompany the initial air strike with at least a partial mobilization. We should accompany an, an invasion following an air strike with a large-scale mobilization, a *very* large-scale mobilization, certainly exceeding the limits of the authority we have from Congress requiring a declaration therefore of a national emergency. We should be prepared, in the event of even a small air strike and certainly in the event of a larger air strike, for the possibility of a Cuban uprising, which would force our hand in some way. Either force u-, us to accept a, a, uh, an unsatisfactory uprising, with all of the adverse comment that result; or would, would force an invasion to support the uprising.

Rusk: Mr. President, may I make a very brief comment on that? I think that, um, uh, any course of action involves heavy political involvement. Um, it's going to affect all sorts of policies, positions, uh, as well as the strategic situation. So I don't think there's any such thing as a nonpolitical course of action. I think also that, um, uh, we have to consider what political preparation, if any, is to occur before an air strike or in connection with any military action. And when I was talking this morning, I was talking about some steps which would put us in the best position to crack the . . .

JFK: I think the difficulty . . .

Rusk: . . . the strength of Cuba.

JFK: . . . it seems to me, is. . . . I completely agree that there isn't any doubt that if we announced that there were MRBM sites going up that that would change, uh, we would secure a good deal of political support, uh, after my statement; and, uh, the fact that we indicated our desire to restrain, this really would put the burden on the Soviet. On the other hand, the very fact of doing that makes the military. . . . We lose all the advantages of our strike. Because if we announce that it's there, then it's quite obvious to them that we're gonna probably do something about it. I would *assume*. Now, I don't know, that, it seems to me what we ought to be thinking about tonight is if we made an announcement that the intelligence has revealed that there are, and if we [did the note?] message to Khrushchev. . . . I don't think, uh, that Castro has to know we've been paying much attention to it any more than. . . . Over a period of time, it might have some effect, [have settled?] back down, change. I don't think he plays it that way. So [have?] a note to Khrushchev. . . . I don't. . . . It seems to me, uh, my press statement was so *clear* about how we *wouldn't* do anything under these conditions and under the conditions that we *would*. He must know that we're going to find out, so it seems to me he just, uh . . .

Bundy: That's, of course, why he's been very, very explicit with us in communications to us about how dangerous this is, and . . .

JFK: That's right, but he's . . .

Bundy: . . . the TASS statement and his other messages.

JFK: He's initiated the danger really, hasn't he? He's the one that's playing [his card, or God?], not us. So we could, uh . . .

Rusk: And his statement to Kohler[6] on the subject of his visit and so forth, completely hypocritical.

                                (pp. 8–11)

. . . .

Bundy: But, the, uh, question that I would like to ask is, quite aside from what we've said—and we're very hard-locked onto it, I know—What is the strategic impact on the position of the United States of MRBMs in *Cuba?* How gravely does this change the strategic balance?

McNamara: Mac, I asked the Chiefs that this afternoon, in effect. And they said, substantially. My own personal view is, not at all.

Bundy: Not so much.

McNamara: And, and I think this is an important element here. But it's all very . . .

Carter: The reason our estimators didn't think that they'd put them in there because of . . .

McNamara: That's what they said themselves . . .

Bundy: That's what they said themselves . . .

McNamara: . . . in TASS statement.

Bundy: Yeah.

6. Foy D. Kohler, U.S. Ambassador to the Soviet Union

Carter:	But then, going behind that . . .
JFK:	[But why? Did it indicate? Being?] valuable enough?
Bundy:	Doesn't prove anything in the strategic balance [overall?].
Carter:	Doesn't prove anything. That was what the estimators felt, and that the Soviets would not take the risk. Mr. McCone's reasoning, however, was if this is so, then what possible reason have they got for going into Cuba in the manner in which they are with surface-to-air, uh, missiles and cruise-type missile. He just couldn't understand while their, *why* the Soviets were so heavily bol-, bolstering Cuba's defensive posture. There must be something behind it, which led him *then* to the belief that they *must* be coming in with MRBMs.
Taylor:	I think it was [old-blooded?] . . .
Carter:	[Words unintelligible]
Taylor:	. . . point of view, Mr. President. You're quite right in saying that these, these are just a few more missiles, uh, targetted on the United States. Uh, however, they *can* become a, a very, a rather important adjunct and reinforcement to the, to the strike capability of the Soviet Union. We have no idea how far they will go. But more than that, these are, uh, uh, to our nation it means, it means a great deal more. You all are aware of that, in Cuba and not over in the Soviet Union.
Bundy:	Well, I ask the question . . .
Taylor:	Yeah.
Bundy:	. . . with an awareness [laughter?] of the political . . .
JFK:	I will say, my understanding's that . . .
Bundy:	[Words unintelligible]
JFK:	. . . let's just say that, uh, they get, they get these in there and then you can't, uh, they get sufficient capacity so we can't, uh, with warheads. Then you don't want to knock 'em out ['cause?], uh, there's too much of a gamble. Then they just begin to build up those air bases there and then put more and more. I suppose they really. . . . Then they start getting ready to squeeze us in Berlin, doesn't that. . . . You may say it doesn't make any difference if you get blown up by an ICBM flying from the Soviet Union or one that was ninety miles away. Geography doesn't mean that much.
Taylor:	We'd have to target then with our missiles and have the same kind of, of pistol-pointed-at-the-head situation as we have in the Soviet Union at the present time.
Bundy:	[Deleted]
JFK:	That's why it shows the Bay of Pigs was really right. [We've, or We'd?] got it right. That was better and better and worse and worse.

Taylor:	[Deleted]

[Faint laughter]

Taylor:	[We've changed?] our evaluations well.
RFK:	Of course, the other problem is, uh, in South America a year from now. And the fact that you got, uh, *these* things in the hands of Cubans, here, and then you, say your, some problem arises in Venezuela, er, you've got Castro saying, You move troops down into that part of Venezuela, we're going to fire these missiles.
Taylor:	Well, I think you've [words unintelligible].
RFK:	I think that's the difficulty . . .
Speaker?:	[Words unintelligible].
RFK:	. . . rather than the [words unintelligible].
Speaker?:	[Words unintelligible].
RFK:	I think it gives the [word unintelligible] image.
JFK:	It makes them look like they're coequal with us and that . . .
Dillon:	We're scared of the Cubans.
RFK:	We let the, uh. . . . I mean like we'd hate to have it in the hands of the Chinese. [Possibly words unintelligible]
Dillon:	[Right?] I agree with that sort of thing very strongly.
Martin:	It's a psychological factor. It won't reach as far as Venezuela is concerned.
Dillon:	Well, that's . . .
McNamara:	It'll reach the U.S. though. This is the *point*.
Speaker?:	That's the point.
Dillon:	Yeah. That is the point.
Martin:	Yeah. The psychological factor of our having taken it.
Dillon:	Taken it, that's the best.
RFK:	Well, and the fact that if you go there, we're gonna fire it.
JFK:	What's that again, Ed? What are you saying?
Martin:	Well, it's a psychological factor that we have sat back and let 'em do it to us, that is more important than the direct threat. Uh, it is a threat in the Caribbean . . .
JFK:	[Words unintelligible] I said we weren't going tò.
Martin:	. . . [words unintelligible].
Bundy?:	That's something we could manage.
JFK:	Last month I said we weren't going to.

[Laughter]

JFK: Last month I should have said we're . . .

Speaker?: Well . . .

JFK: . . . that we don't care. But when we said we're *not* going to and then they go ahead and do it, and then we do nothing, then . . .

Speaker?: That's right.

JFK: . . . I would think that our risks increase. Uh, I agree. What difference does it make? They've got enough to blow us up now anyway. I think it's just a question of. . . . After all this is a political struggle as much as military. Well, uh, so where are we now? Where is the. . . . Don't think the message to Castro's got much in it. Uh, let's just, uh, let's try to get an answer to this question. How much. . . . It's quite obviously to our advantage to surface this thing to a degree before. . . . First to inform these governments in Latin America, as the secretary suggests; secondly to, uh, the rest of NATO [Deleted] Uh, how much does this diminish. . . . Not that we're going to do anything, but the existence of them, without any say about what we're gonna do. Let's say we, twenty-four hours ahead of our doing something about it, [deleted] we make a public statement that these have been found on the island. That would, that would be notification in a sense that, uh, of their existence, and everybody could draw whatever conclusion they wanted to.

Martin?:   I would say this, Mr. President, that I would, that if you've made a public statement, you've got to move immediately, or they, you're going to have a . . .

JFK: Oh, I . . .

Martin?:   . . . a [words unintelligible] in *this* country.

JFK: . . . oh, I understand *that*. We'll be talking about. . . . Say, say we're going to move on a Saturday and we would say on Friday that these MRBMs, that the existence of this presents the gravest threat to our security and that appropriate action must be taken.

RFK: Could you stick planes over them, until you made the announcement at six o'clock Saturday morning? And at the same time or simultaneously put planes over to make sure that they weren't taking any action or movement, and that you could move in if they started moving in the missiles in place or something, you would move in and knock, that would be the trigger that you would move your planes in and knock them out. Otherwise you'd wait until six o'clock or five o'clock that night. I don't, is that, uh, is that. . . .

Taylor: I don't think anything like that. . . . I can't visualize doing it, uh, doing it successfully that way. I think that, uh, uh, anything that shows, uh, our intent to strike is going to place the airplanes and,

	and the missiles into, these are por-, really mobile missiles. They can be . . .
RFK:	[You mean they can just?] . . .
Taylor:	They can pull in under trees and forest and disappear almost at once, as I visualize.
McNamara:	And they can also be readied, perhaps, between the time we, in effect, *say* we're going to come in and the time we *do* come in. This, this is a very, very great danger to this, this coast. I don't know exactly how to appraise it because . . .
Speaker?:	I don't know.
McNamara:	. . . of the readiness period, but it is *possible* that these are field missiles, and then in that case they can be readied very promptly if they choose to do so.
Carter:	These *are* field missiles, sir. They are mobile-support-type missiles.
Taylor:	About a forty-minute countdown, something like that's been estimated.

(pp. 12–16)

. . . .

JFK:	I'm not completely, uh, I don't think we ought to abandon just knocking out these missile bases as opposed to, that's much more, uh, defensible, explicable, politically or satisfactory-in-every-way action than the general strike which takes us . . .
Speaker?:	Move down . . .
JFK:	. . . us into the city of Havana . . .
Speaker?:	. . . those two.
JFK:	. . . and [it is plain to me?] takes us into much more . . .
Speaker?:	[Words unintelligible]
JFK:	. . . hazardous, shot down. Now I know the Chiefs say, Well, that means their bombers can take off against us, uh, but, uh . . .
Bundy:	Their bombers take off against us, then *they* have made a general war against Cuba of it, which is a, it then becomes much more *their* decision. We move *this* way. . . . The political advantages are, are *very* strong, it seems to me, of the small strike. Uh, it corresponds to the, the punishment fits the crime in political terms, the we are doing only what we *warned* repeatedly and publicly we would *have* to do. Uh, we are *not* generalizing the attack. The things that we've already recognized and said that we have *not* found it necessary to attack and said we would not find it necessary to attack . . .

(pp. 17–18)

. . . .

RFK:	Mr. President, while we're considering this problem tonight, I think that we should also consider what, uh, Cuba's going to be a year from now, or two years from now. Assume that we go in and knock these sites out, uh, I don't know what's gonna stop them from saying, We're gonna build the sites six months from now, bring 'em in . . .
Taylor:	Noth-, nothing permanent about it.
RFK:	Uh, the, what, where are we six months from now? Or that we're in any better position, or aren't we in worse position if we go in and knock 'em out and say, uh . . .
Speaker?:	[We sure are?]
RFK:	. . . Don't do it. Uh, I mean, obviously they're gonna *have* to do it then.
McNamara:	You have to put a blockade in following any . . .
Speaker?:	Sure.
McNamara:	. . . limited action.
RFK:	Then we're gonna have to sink Russian ships.
McNamara?:	Right.
RFK:	Then we're gonna have to sink . . .
McNamara?:	Right.
RFK:	. . . Russian submarines. Now whether it wouldn't be, uh, the argument, if you're going to get into it at all, uh, whether we should just get into it and get it over with and say that, uh, take our losses, and if we're gonna. . . . If he wants to get into a war over *this*, uh. . . . Hell, if it's war that's gonna come on this thing, or if he sticks those kinds of missiles in, it's after the warning, and he's gonna, and he's gonna get into a war for, six months from now or a year from now, so. . . .
McNamara:	Mr. President, this is why I think tonight we ought to put on paper the alternative plans and the probable, possible consequences thereof in a way that State and Defense could agree on, even if we, uh, disagree and put in both views. Because the consequences of these actions have *not* been thought through clearly. The one that the attorney general just mentioned is illustrative of that.
JFK:	If the, uh, it doesn't increase very much their strategic, uh, strength, why is it, uh, can any Russian expert tell us why they. . . . After all Khrushchev demonstrated a sense of caution [thousands?] . . .

Speaker?:   Well, there are several, several possible . . .

JFK: . . . Berlin, he's been cautious, I mean, he hasn't been, uh . . .

Ball?:   Several possibilities, Mr. President. One of them is that he has given us word now that he's coming over in November to, to the UN. If, he may be proceeding on the assumption, and this lack of a sense of *apparent* urgency would seem to, to support this, that this *isn't* going to be discovered at the moment and that, uh, when he comes over this is something he can do, a ploy. That here is Cuba armed against the United States, or possibly use it to try to trade something in Berlin, saying he'll disarm Cuba if, uh, if we'll, uh, yield some of our interests in Berlin and some arrangement for it. I mean, that this is a, it's a trading ploy.

Bundy: I would think one thing that I would still cling to is that he's not likely to give Fidel Castro nuclear warheads. I don't believe that has happened or is likely to happen.

JFK: Why does he put these in there though?

Bundy: Soviet-controlled nuclear warheads [of the kind?] . . .

JFK: That's right, but what is the advantage of that? It's just as if we suddenly began to put a major number of MRBMs in Turkey. Now that'd be goddam dangerous, I would think.

Bundy?:   Well, we *did*, Mr. President.

U.A. Johnson?: We *did* it. We . . .

JFK: Yeah, but that was five years ago.

U.A. Johnson?: . . . did it in England; that's why we were short.

JFK: What?

U.A. Johnson?: We gave England two when we were short of ICBMs.

JFK: Yeah, but that's, uh . . .

U.A. Johnson?: [Testing?]

JFK: . . . that was during a different period then.

U.A. Johnson?: But doesn't he realize he has a deficiency of ICBMs, needs a PR capacity perhaps, in view of. . . . He's got lots of MRBMs and this is a way to balance it out a bit?

Bundy?:   I'm sure his generals have been telling him for a year and a half that he had, was missing a golden opportunity to add to his strategic capability.

Ball?:   Yes, I think, I think you, you look at this possibility that this is an attempt to, to add to his strategic capabilities. A second consideration is that it is simply a trading ploy, that he, he wants this in so that he could, he could [words unintelligible]

(pp. 24–26)

. . . .

RFK: . . . one other thing is whether, uh, we should also think of, uh, uh, whether there is some *other* way we can get involved in this through, uh, Guantanamo Bay, or something, er, or whether there's some ship that, you know, sink the *Maine* again or something.

(p. 27)

. . . .

Bundy: I think there's an *enormous* political advantage, myself, within these options, granting that *all* the Chiefs didn't fully agree, taking out the thing that gives the trouble and not the thing that doesn't give the trouble.

McNamara?:   This, as opposed to, uh, is it an air attack on . . .

Bundy: Supplementary to an air attack. I mean, how're you gonna know that you've got 'em? And if you haven't got 'em, what've you done?

(p. 43)

. . . .

McNamara: . . . I, let me answer Mac's question first. How do we know we've got them? We will have photo recon [militarily?] with the strike. Sweeney[7] specifically plans this, and . . .

Bundy: Proving a negative is a hell of a job.

(p. 43)

. . . .

McNamara: It seems to me that there are some *major* alternatives here that I don't think we discussed them fully enough today, and I'd like to see them laid on the paper, if State agrees. The first is what I, I *still* call it the political approach. Uh, let me say it a nonmilitary action.

[Laughter]

McNamara: It doesn't start with one and it isn't gonna end with one.

Speaker?:   Yeah.

McNamara: And I, for that reason I call it a political approach.

---

7. General Walter C. Sweeney, Commanding General, Tactical Air Command

Speaker?:	Right . . .
McNamara:	And I say it isn't gonna end with one because once you start this political approach, I don't think you're gonna *have* any opportunity for a military operation.

(p. 44)

. . . .

McNamara:	Now, the second alternative, I, I'd like to discuss just a second, because we haven't discussed it fully today, and I alluded it to, to it a moment ago. I, I, I'll be quite frank. I don't think there *is* a military problem here. This is my answer to Mac's question . . .
Bundy:	That's my honest [judgment?].
McNamara:	. . . and therefore, and I've gone through this today, and I asked myself, Well, what is it then if it isn't a military problem? Well, it's just exactly *this* problem, that, that, uh, if Cuba should possess a capacity to carry out offensive actions against the U.S., the U.S. would act.
Speaker?:	That's right.
Speaker?:	That's right.
McNamara:	Now, it's that problem, this . . .
Speaker?:	You can't get around that one.
McNamara:	. . . this, this is a domestic, political problem. The announcement— we didn't say we'd go in and not, and kill them, we said we'd *act*. Well, how will we act? Well, we want to act to prevent their use, and it's really the . . .
Bundy:	Yeah.
McNamara:	. . . the act. Now, how do we pre-, act to prevent their use? Well, first place, we carry out open surveillance, so we know what they're doing. All times. Twenty-four hours a day from now and forever, in a sense indefinitely. What else do we do? We prevent any further offensive weapons coming in. In other words we blockade offensive weapons.
Bundy:	How do we do that?
McNamara:	We search every ship.
Taylor:	There're two kinds of, of blockade: a blockade which stops ships from coming in and, and simply a seizure, I mean a, simply a search.
McNamara:	A search, that's right . . .
Taylor?:	Yeah.
McNamara:	. . . and . . .

Speaker?:	Well, it would be a search and removal if found.
Bundy:	You have to make the guy stop to search him, and if he won't stop, you have to shoot, right?
Speaker?:	All [words unintelligible] up . . .
Speaker?:	And you have to remove what you're looking for if you find it.
Speaker?:	That's right.
McNamara:	Absolutely. Absolutely. And then an ul-, I call it an ultimatum associated with these two actions is a statement to the world, particularly to Khrushchev, that we have located these offensive weapons; we're maintaining a constant surveillance over them; if there is ever any indication that they're to be launched against this country, we will respond not only against Cuba, but we will respond directly against the Soviet Union with, with a full nuclear strike. Now this alternative doesn't seem to be a very acceptable one, but wait until you work on the others.

(pp. 45–47)

. . . .

Ball?:	. . . How're you gonna survey 'em during the night? Uh, I mean, it seems to me that they're some gaps in the surveillance.
McNamara:	Oh, well, it's really the, yes, it isn't the surveillance, it's the ultimatum that is . . .
Ball?:	Yeah.
McNamara:	. . . the key part in this.
Ball?:	Yeah.
McNamara:	And really what I tried to do was develop a little package that meets the action requirement of that paragraph I read.
Speaker?:	Yeah.
McNamara:	Because, as I suggested, I don't believe it's primarily a military problem. It's primarily a, a domestic, political problem.
Ball:	Yeah, well, as far as the American people are concerned, action means military action, period.
McNamara:	Well, we have a blockade. Search and, uh, removal of, of offensive weapons entering Cuba. Uh, [word unintelligible] again, I don't want to argue for this . . .
Ball:	No, no, I . . .
McNamara:	. . . because I, I don't think it's . . .
Ball:	. . . I think it's an alternative.

McNamara:	. . . a perfect solution by any means. I just want to . . .
Bundy:	Which one are we [still on?] would you say?
McNamara:	Still on the second one, uh . . .
Ball:	Now, one of the things we look at is whether any, the actual operation of a blockade doesn't, isn't a greater involvement almost than a . . .
McNamara:	Might well be, George.
Ball:	. . . military action.
Speaker?:	I think so.
McNamara:	It's, it's a search, not a, not an embargo, uh. . . .
Speaker?:	Yeah.
Ball:	It's a series of single, unrelated acts, not by surprise. This, uh, come in there on Pearl Harbor just frightens the hell out of me as to what's going beyond. [Yeah, well, anyway?] the Board of National Estimates have been working on this ever since . . .
Bundy:	What, what goes, what goes beyond what?
Ball:	What happens beyond that. You go in there with a surprise attack. You put out all the missiles. This isn't the *end*. This is the *beginning*, I think. . . .

(pp. 47–49)

Excerpts from:

Summary Record of NSC Executive Committee Meeting No. 6
October 26, 1962, 10:00 AM

Secretary Rusk summarized political actions now under way. He said the object of the talks with U Thant[8] today was to set up some form of negotiations with the Russians in New York. The objective would be to obtain a commitment from the Russians that there would be no further construction at the missile sites in Cuba, no further Soviet military shipments, the defuzing [sic] of existing weapons in Cuba, UN inspection of all nuclear-capable missiles, and an observer corps on the ground in Cuba of 350 technically able inspectors. The U.S. quarantine would continue until a UN quarantine is in place. UN teams would be put into specified Cuban ports. U.S. Navy ships would stay close to all Cuban ports to ensure that there were no landings unknown to the UN inspectors and no cargoes landed anywhere which UN inspectors did not see.

(p. 3)

. . . .

8. Secretary General of the United Nations

The President said work on the missile sites has to cease and we have to verify what is going on at the sites every day during the talks in New York. As to the message to Castro, he agreed in general, but wanted to have another look at it. He doubted that it would do any good, but it might be undertaken if done now with the greatest urgency.

Ambassador Stevenson[9] discussed the immediate negotiations now under way with U Thant and the longer talks which would follow if agreement can be reached with the Russians in New York. He said the immediate talks were aimed at getting a 24–48-hour standstill on the missile buildup in Cuba. He acknowledged that in these talks it would be impossible to obtain an agreement to make the weapons inoperable. He wanted to know whether he should seek a standstill on all Soviet arms or only offensive weapons. He would seek to get a commitment that there be no further construction, but it would not be possible to set up a system to ensure that the weapons were made inoperable and kept inoperable. In addition, he needed to know whether in return we would be prepared to suspend the quarantine.

Ambassador Stevenson said the aim of the longer term talks would be the withdrawal from this hemisphere of the strategic missiles and the dismantlement of existing sites. He predicted that the Russians would ask us for a new guarantee of the territorial integrity of Cuba and the dismantlement of U.S. strategic missiles in Turkey.

Mr. McCone disagreed with Ambassador Stevenson's linking of Soviet missiles in Cuba to U.S. missiles in Turkey. He said the Soviet weapons in Cuba were pointed at our heart and put us under great handicap in continuing to carry out our commitments to the free world. He urged that we do not drop the quarantine until the Soviet missiles are out of Cuba. He believed that we must keep up the momentum so far achieved by the quarantine.

The President said we will get the Soviet strategic missiles out of Cuba only by invading Cuba or by trading. He doubted that the quarantine alone would produce a withdrawal of the weapons. He said our objective should be to prevent further military shipments, further construction at missile sites, and to get some means of inspection.

Mr. McCone urged that any inspectors sent to Cuba be U.S. inspectors knowledgeable about strategic missiles.

The President said he understood Ambassador Stevenson to be asking for time during which he would try to negotiate the withdrawal of the missiles.

Secretary Rusk doubted that we could get any pre-conditions to negotiation.

Secretary Dillon agreed that the Soviets could not back down merely in return for dropping the quarantine.

---

9. Adlai Stevenson, U.S. Ambassador to the United Nations

Mr. Nitze[11] called attention to the importance of obtaining a guarantee that the nuclear missiles would be disassembled from their launchers.

Mr. Bundy said negotiations for a standstill or a standdown were not enough for our security because we must press, in addition, for guaranteed inspection of Cuba.

Secretary Dillon said we could not negotiate for two weeks under the missile threat which now exists in Cuba.

The President noted that there appeared to be little support for Ambassador Stevenson's plan. If the quarantine would not result in the Soviets withdrawing the missiles, what will we do if negotiations break down?

Mr. Bundy said when the interim 24–48-hour talks fail, then our choice would be to expand the blockade or remove the missiles by air attack.

General Taylor urged that we increase our reconnaissance activity in order to keep informed as to what was happening in Cuba.

The President decided to delay night reconnaissance missions, at least until the Soviets turn down U Thant's proposal. He also agreed that we should announce publicly that construction work at the missile sites in Cuba was going on and that, therefore, we will continue our aerial reconnaissance flights. The President also wanted attention called by a White House spokesman to his earlier speech which insisted that work at the missile sites in Cuba cease. The President decided that a presentation of the current situation should be made to the Congressional Leaders.

Bromley Smith[10]

(pp. 5–7)

Summary Record of NSC Executive Committee Meeting No. 7 October 27, 1962, 10:00 AM

Director McCone highlighted the intelligence information contained in the first two pages of the attached CIA Cuba Crisis Memorandum.

Secretary McNamara reported on the positions of Soviet Bloc ships moving toward Cuba. He said we do not know yet whether any such ships will enter the interception area. He recommended that we be prepared to board the Graznyy, which is now out about 600 miles. We would put ships alongside her and follow along for about 200 miles. [Deleted]

Under Secretary Ball pointed out that the Soviets did not know the extent of our quarantine zone.

The President agreed that we should ask U Thant to tell the Russians in New York where we are drawing the quarantine line. The Russians would then be in a position to decide whether to turn back their tanker or allow her to enter the quarantine zone sometime later today.

---

10. Author of minutes of Ex Com meetings
11. Paul Nitze, Assistant Secretary of Defense

Secretary McNamara recommended, and the President approved, two daylight reconnaissance missions, one in the morning and one in the afternoon. Secretary McNamara also recommended that a night reconnaissance mission be flown—Secretary Rusk recommended against a night flight. The President instructed the Defense Department to place the night reconnaissance planes on the alert and to prepare a public announcement of the mission in order that a final decision to be taken this afternoon could be promptly implemented.

The discussion then turned to the question of U.S. missiles in Turkey. Mr. Nitze said it would be an anathema to the Turks to pull the missiles out. He feared the next Soviet step would be a demand for the denuclearization of the entire NATO area. He urged us to focus attention on Cuba rather than on U.S. bases in other countries.

Under Secretary Ball reported [Deleted].

At this point in the meeting the partial text of a Soviet public statement was read by the President as it was received in the room. The President commented that the statement was a very tough position and varied considerably from the tone of Khrushchev's personal letter to the President received last night. The President felt that the Soviet position would get wide support and said we should consider making public the Khrushchev private letter.

Secretary Rusk returned to the question of U.S. missiles in Turkey and pointed out that this subject must be kept separate from Soviet missiles in Cuba. The Turkish missile problem should be dealt with in the context of NATO vs. Warsaw Pact.

Mr. Bundy said we could not accept the Soviet proposal on Turkish missiles because the Soviet missiles were not out of Cuba.

The President recalled that he had asked that consideration be given to the withdrawal of U.S. missiles from Turkey some days previously.

Under Secretary Ball replied that the Department had decided it could not raise this question with the Turks at this time for fear of a disastrous Turkish reaction. He said the question had been raised with Finletter[12] in Paris and study was being given to whether any method could be worked out to reassure the Turks if we were going to offer to withdraw the Jupiter missiles.

Mr. Bundy said we cannot get into the position of appearing to sell out an ally, i.e. Turkey, to serve our own interests, i.e. getting the Soviet missiles out of Cuba.

The President commented that the Russians had made the Turkish missile withdrawal proposal in the most difficult possible way. Now that their proposal is public, we have no chance to talk privately to the Turks about the missiles, which, for a long time, we have considered to be obsolete.

Secretary Dillon said that it was possible that the Russians had made their public statement as part of a stalling tactic to provide them with sufficient time for a full-fledged confrontation with us.

---

12. Thomas Finletter, U.S. Ambassador to NATO

The President read a draft statement telephoned from New York by Ambassador Stevenson commenting on the Soviet statement. Ambassador Stevenson argued for releasing his statement in an effort to keep the "peace offensive" from going to the Soviets.

The President left the meeting at this point with Mr. Sorensen.[13] There ensued a discussion of how to handle the discrepancy between the Khrushchev private letter and the Russian offer made public in the Soviet statement. A suggestion was made that the Russian proposals contained in the private Khrushchev letter be made public.

The President returned to the meeting. He said we must ensure that the construction work on the missile sites in Cuba be stopped at once. He suggested that we talk to the Turks about the missiles, pointing out to them the great peril facing them during the next week. He acknowledged that the Turks were now in no position to make a statement to the effect that they would ask that the Jupiters be withdrawn.

Secretary Rusk suggested that we tell the Turks they must say that the Jupiter problem is a NATO problem and is not associated with the Cuban missile problem.

Secretary McNamara called attention to the fact that the missiles belonged to Turkey and that only the nuclear warheads are under our total control.

The President returned to a discussion of where we now find ourselves, i.e. we now have Soviet public proposals and Khrushchev's private proposals. What we must seek is an immediate cessation of the work on offensive missiles in Cuba. Once this work stopped we could talk to the Russians.

Mr. Bundy reiterated the view that the threat to us in Cuba [*sic*]. One explanation for the varying Soviet proposals is that the hard line Russians wanted to make public their preferred demands in order to make impossible progress toward the Khrushchev private offer which may have been drafted by those who are less hard-nosed.

The President noted that it appeared to him that the Russians were making various proposals so fast, one after the other, that they were creating a kind of shield behind which work on the missile sites in Cuba continued. He said we had a perfectly defensible position, i.e. work on the missile sites must stop. Secretary McNamara added the thought that these offensive weapons must be made inoperable.

Mr. Bundy suggested that we tell Khrushchev privately that the position in their public statement was impossible for us, but that the position Khrushchev took in his private letter was different and we were studying these proposals. In the meantime, however, time is running out.

The President interrupted to take a telephone call from Ambassador Stevenson in New York. He resumed the discussion by saying that Khrushchev obviously is attempting to limit our freedom of action in Cuba by introducing the question of the missile bases outside this hemisphere.

---

13. Theodore Sorensen, Special Counsel to the President

Mr. Bundy read a draft press statement and Mr. Gilpatric[14] read a statement which he had prepared.

Mr. Alexis Johnson reported that he had just been informed that the Turkish Government had issued a press statement saying that the Russian proposal with respect to Jupiters in Turkey was not conceivable.

(As the remainder of the Soviet public statement was received in the Cabinet Room, it appeared that the Russian base proposal involved not merely Turkey but all of NATO.)

Mr. Sorensen introduced a draft statement which was read by the group.

Revisions were made in the Gilpatric draft, which was issued shortly thereafter in the form attached. This statement emphasized the offensive weapons buildup in Cuba.

The Attorney General said that the statement might make people think that if the Russians stopped the missile buildup in Cuba, we would be willing to withdraw our missiles from Turkey. He desired that we make doubly clear that Turkish NATO missiles were one problem and that Cuba was an entirely separate problem.

Mr. Gilpatric stated that it was crucial for us to stand on the position that we will not negotiate with the Russians while the Soviet missile threat is growing in Cuba.

The President recalled that over a year ago we wanted to get the Jupiter missiles out of Turkey because they had become obsolete and of little military value. If the missiles in Cuba added 50% to Soviet nuclear capability, then to trade these missiles for those in Turkey would be of great military value. But we are now in the position of risking war in Cuba and in Berlin over missiles in Turkey which are of little military value. From the political point of view, it would be hard to get support on an airstrike against Cuba because many would think that we would make a good trade if we offered to take the missiles out of Turkey in the event the Russians would agree to remove the missiles from Cuba. We are in a bad position if we appear to be attacking Cuba for the purpose of keeping useless missiles in Turkey. We cannot propose to withdraw the missiles from Turkey, but the Turks could offer to do so. The Turks must be informed of the great danger in which they will live during the next week and we have to face up to the possibility of some kind of a trade over missiles.

The President left the meeting to meet the State Governors who had been waiting for one-half hour to see him.

The discussion continued in the President's absence. It was not possible to say with certainty whether the Soviet public offer included all NATO bases or referred specifically to Turkey.

The Attorney General expressed his concern as to what our position would be if we talked to the Russians for sixty days and then the Cubans refused to permit UN inspectors to continue to ensure that missiles in Cuba were inoperable. The reply was that we could then decide to attack the bases by air.

There was discussion of a second statement to be put out but this proposal was later abandoned.

A draft message to Khrushchev, which had been prepared by Ambassador Thompson,[15] was read and a final version was to be completed for the President's consideration later in the day. The group agreed to meet at the State Department without the President at 2:30 PM and meet with the President again at 4:00 PM.

(Note: At the meeting at the State Department, the Attorney General repeated his view that we should keep the focus on the missile bases. He preferred to let the Soviet tankers through the quarantine line in order to avoid a confrontation with the Soviets over one of their ships. He said if we attack a Soviet tanker, the balloon would go up. He urged that we buy time now in order to launch an air attack Monday or Tuesday.

Secretary McNamara expressed his view that before we attack Cuba we must notify the Cubans.

Bromley Smith

Summary Record of NSC Executive Committee Meeting No. 8 October 27, 1962, 4:00 PM

Secretary McNamara reported on today's daylight reconnaissance mission. One mission aborted for mechanical reasons, according to preliminary reports. One plane is overdue and several are said to have encountered ground fire.

Secretary McNamara again recommended night reconnaissance missions. The President delayed a decision on night flights pending a full report on today's daylight mission (the night mission was later called off).

There followed a discussion of a draft letter from the President to Khrushchev. The President added to the draft an offer to discuss with the Russians the proposals they had made public. He predicted that Khrushchev would say we had rejected his proposal. The formulation included a comment that Khrushchev must realize that matters relating to NATO must be discussed at a later time. The letter was approved in a revised form.

A message to U Thant was discussed and approved. The purpose of the message was to obtain the halting of work on the bases in Cuba as a condition to discussion of various other problems.

Secretary Rusk reported that one of our U-2 planes had overflown the Soviet Union by accident due to navigational error. Soviet fighters were scrambled from a base

---

15. Llewellyn Thompson, adviser on Soviet affairs

near Wrangel Island. The Secretary thought that the Russians would make a loud fuss about this incident.

The President decided not to make the incident public, but be prepared to do so as soon as the Soviets publicized it.

The President asked whether we wanted to continue to say that we would talk only about the missiles in Cuba. He believed that for the next few hours we should emphasize our position that if the Russians will halt missile activity in Cuba we would be prepared to discuss NATO problems with the Russians. He felt that we would not be in a position to offer any trade for several days. He did feel that if we could succeed in freezing the situation in Cuba and rendering the strategic missiles inoperable, then we would be in a position to negotiate with the Russians.

Mr. Bundy pointed out that there would be a serious reaction in NATO countries if we appeared to be trading withdrawal of missiles in Turkey for withdrawal of missiles from Cuba. The President responded that if we refuse to discuss such a trade and then take military action in Cuba, we would also be in a difficult position.

The President left the room to talk to General Norstad[16] on the KY-9 secure telephone to Paris.

In the President's absence the message to U Thant was further discussed. The Attorney General felt we should say to U Thant: "While these and other proposals are being discussed, would you urgently ascertain whether the Soviet Union is prepared to cease work on the bases and render the missiles inoperable?" U Thant would be asked to convey the President's message to the Russians in New York most urgently.

Secretary Rusk questioned whether the Russians are trying at the last minute to obtain more of a quid pro quo from us or whether they are introducing new elements in the picture merely to weaken our public position worldwide.

Secretary McNamara pointed out, in connection with the current military situation, that a limited airstrike on Cuba was now impossible because our reconnaissance planes were being fired on. He felt that we must now look to the major airstrike to be followed by an invasion of Cuba. To do so he said we would need to call up the reserves now.

Secretary McNamara [deleted]. If we could do this he felt that the Soviets would not attack Turkey when we invaded Cuba. Our objective should be to seek to avoid any Soviet attack in Europe as a response to our invasion of Cuba.

Ambassador Thompson commented that it was impossible to draw any conclusions from the fact that one of our reconnaissance planes over Cuba had been shot at.

The President returned to the meeting, accompanied by General Lemnitzer.[17]

The President approved the final revision of the statement to U Thant, which was to be phoned to U Thant and released here publicly. (Copy attached)

---

16. General Lauris Norstad, Supreme Allied Commander, Europe
17. General Lyman Lemnitzer, former Chairman of the Joint Chiefs of Staff

The President asked whether we should call together the representatives of NATO to report to them what we had done and were planning to do. If we reject Soviet efforts to tie in NATO problems to the Cuban situation, then we could persuade NATO to take the same position. An additional reason for a NATO meeting then is that if the Russians do attack the NATO countries we do not want them to say that they had not been consulted about the actions we were taking in Cuba.

Secretary McNamara said that current military planning [deleted].

The President expressed his concern that the alternatives we are facing have not been presented to NATO. NATO does not realize what may be coming and the Europeans do not realize that we may face a choice of invading Cuba or taking the missiles out of Turkey.

Secretary McNamara urged that a NATO meeting be held tomorrow only if we have decided to launch our strike tomorrow. He repeated his hope that we can act in such a way as to reduce the pressure on the Russians to hit Turkey.

Secretary Rusk recommended that mobilization measures be authorized immediately.

The President suggested that we talk immediately to the Turks, explaining to them what we were planning to do with our missiles and then explain the entire situation to the North Atlantic Council.

Secretary Rusk then read a Stevenson draft of a letter to Khrushchev.

The President said that the key to any letter to Khrushchev was the demand that work cease on the missile sites in Cuba. He predicted that if we make no mention of Turkey in our letter, Khrushchev will write back to us saying that if we include Turkey, then he would be prepared to settle the Cuban situation. The President said this would mean that we would lose twenty-four hours while they would continue to work on the bases and achieve an operational status for more of their missiles. He suggested that we would be willing to guarantee not to invade Cuba if the Soviet missiles were taken out.

Secretary Rusk returned to the Stevenson draft, which the President approved as revised. The phrase "and assurance of peace in the Caribbean" was discussed and the reference to no invasion of Cuba was omitted. The President also agreed not to call a meeting of the North Atlantic Council.

The Attorney General commented that in his opinion the Stevenson draft letter was defensive. It sounded as if we had been thrown off balance by the Russians. The State Department draft merely said that we accepted Khrushchev's offer.

General Taylor summarized the conclusions of the Joint Chiefs. Unless the missiles are defused immediately, the Chiefs recommended implementation on Monday [deleted].

Secretary McNamara asked what we should do about air surveillance tomorrow. He stated his recommendation, i.e. if our reconnaissance planes are fired on, we will attack the attackers. General Taylor noted that in order to be ready to invade on Monday, we must continue intensive air surveillance.

The President directed that our air reconnaissance missions be flown tomorrow without fighter escort. If our planes are fired on, we must be prepared for a general response or an attack on the SAM site which fired on our planes. We will decide tomorrow how we return fire after we know if they continue their attacks on our planes and after we hear from U Thant the Russian reply to our offer.

The President considered a draft message to the Turks about their missiles. His objective was to persuade the Turks to suggest to us that we withdraw our missiles. He noted that negotiations with the Turks were very difficult if there was any life left in the proposal which we had asked U Thant to make to the Russians.

General Taylor read a late report of the shooting down of the U-2 reconnaissance plane in Cuba which said that the wreckage of the U-2 was on the ground and that the pilot had been killed. He felt that we should make an air attack tomorrow on the SAM site responsible for shooting down the U-2 plane.

Secretary McNamara said that we must now be ready to attack Cuba [deleted]. Invasion had become almost inevitable. If we leave U.S. missiles in Turkey, the Soviets might attack Turkey. If the Soviets do attack the Turks, we must respond in the NATO area. [Deleted] However, we should make every effort to reduce the chance of a Soviet attack on Turkey.

In an informal discussion following the formal end of the meeting, the Vice President asked why we were not prepared to trade the withdrawal of U.S. missiles from Turkey for the withdrawal of the Soviet missiles from Cuba, if we were prepared to give up the use of U.S. missiles in Turkey. Under Secretary Ball responded that last week we thought it might be acceptable to trade the withdrawal of the missiles in Turkey if such action would save Berlin. He felt that we could accept the Soviet offer and replace the missiles in Turkey by assigning Polaris submarines to the area.

Bromley Smith

The Political Utility of Nuclear Weapons

The 1973 Middle East Crisis

Barry M. Blechman and Douglas M. Hart

$\mathbf{E}$ver since the Eisenhower Administration's policy of massive retaliation failed to stem either the tide of left-leaning nationalist revolutions in the third world or continuing Soviet pressures on Central Europe, mainstream American opinion has tended to view the potential of nuclear weapons to support U.S. foreign policy rather skeptically. Because of the tremendous risks associated with the use of nuclear weapons, most observers agree, a threat of nuclear war is credible only in certain situations—those in which the nation's most important interests are evidently at stake. As such, nuclear weapons can serve only narrow and distinct purposes. The threat of nuclear retaliation, of course, serves to deter attacks on, or coercion of, the United States itself. Also, it is widely believed that this nuclear umbrella can be extended to those few nations, primarily the industrialized democracies, for which—for reasons of history and ethnic, cultural, economic, and political affinities—an American threat to risk nuclear holocaust on their behalf may be credible. Beyond that, however, since the late 1950s few have been willing to argue publicly that other important political or military purposes can or should be served by the nation's nuclear arsenal.

There is reason to question whether this common perspective on the utility of nuclear weapons is complete, however. There is a minority view which maintains that nuclear weapons (that is, the threat of nuclear war which they imply) actually have served the nation's policymakers more often and in more ways than are generally recognized. (Interestingly, this view is held by some on both the extreme right and the extreme left of the American political spectrum.) Indeed, there is at least some reason to believe that U.S. decisionmakers have turned to nuclear threats in support of policy in more than 20 specific incidents. Upon closer investigation, many of these incidents prove to be inadvertent, or misunderstood, or simply false; yet, there is some core number of cases—roughly one-half dozen—for which it can be documented that the nation's leaders consciously employed nuclear threats, or at least deliberately drew attention to the risk of nuclear war, as a means of bolstering American policy.

Barry Blechman is a resident associate at the Carnegie Endowment for International Peace. Douglas Hart is a defense analyst for the Pacific-Sierra Corporation.

International Security, Summer 1982 (Vol. 7, No. 1) 0162-2889/82/010132-25 $02.50/0

Most of these incidents took place in the 1950s, but the 1960s and 1970s have not been devoid of them. The most recent took place early in 1980, when the credibility of President Carter's commitment to defend the Persian Gulf came into question, and there was reason to believe that the Soviet Union was preparing to move into Iran. Within ten days of the President's statement, U.S. officials made clear nuclear threats on three separate occasions in a desperate attempt to put a real sanction behind the President's words.[1]

Given the tumultuous state of world affairs, the deteriorating character of Soviet–American relations, and the problems continuing to beset U.S. conventional military forces, the temptation to turn to nuclear threats as a means of emerging triumphant from tense international situations is likely to remain with both the present and future U.S. administrations. Indeed, the crosscutting political pressures of the budget balancers and supply-side economists alone may lead the Reagan Administration, like the Eisenhower Administration before it, to seek "more bang for the buck" in the defense area by relying more on nuclear threats.[2]

For these reasons alone it makes sense to analyze past nuclear incidents in some detail in order to understand the thinking of those who turn to nuclear threats, the psychological and political mechanisms set in motion when such threats are made, and the consequences of these actions both for the specific situation of concern and for broader considerations.

Perhaps the most relevant of the past nuclear threats took place during the Arab–Israeli War in October 1973. For the first time when both had mature and robust strategic nuclear forces, there was a serious threat of military conflict between the United States and the Soviet Union. By 1973, both superpowers had deployed nuclear forces that, on paper at least, seemed likely to be able to survive a first strike and retaliate with devastating force against the attacker. According to Western theories of nuclear deterrence, theories upon which we have staked our survival, such a balance of

---

1. See Barry M. Blechman and Douglas M. Hart, "Dangerous Shortcut," *The New Republic*, July 26, 1980, pp. 13–15.
2. Indications of the new administration's thinking about the possibility, and possible necessity, of nuclear war were first revealed during Secretary of State Alexander Haig's confirmation hearings. At the time, he indicated that the United States may have to resort to the threat of nuclear war in order to avoid having to prosecute one: "Clearly in the nuclear age responsibilities in this area become all the more awesome. But the point I wanted to make is there are things worth fighting for. We must understand that. We must structure our policy under that credible and justified premise." See *The New York Times*, January 10, 1981.

strategic capabilities should have inclined both sides to avoid any move that might have precipitated escalation and led to a greater risk of confrontation and nuclear war. In short, the balance of strategic nuclear forces should have led to stable political relations. This did not prove to be the case, however; in October 1973 both the United States and the Soviet Union took military steps in the Middle East of some significance. Moreover, for the first time since the Cuban missile crisis in October 1962, U.S. policymakers perceived a need to manipulate the risk of nuclear war overtly with the objective of influencing Soviet behavior.

Why was this done? What was expected to be accomplished? And how? To answer these questions, we interviewed several of the five principal participants in the Washington Special Action Group (WSAG)—the forum for crisis management during the Nixon Administration—and additional members of their senior staffs.[3] These interviews, and supplementary material found in published sources, can make an important contribution to the current debate on the utility of nuclear weapons in the conduct of American foreign policy.

The Crisis

The superpower confrontation in 1973 lasted less than 48 hours, beginning early in the morning of October 24th. There was no time for extensive deliberations, for the formulation of sophisticated policy options, for debate. Decision-makers were occupied almost entirely with keeping abreast of a rapidly changing situation and formulating necessarily *ad hoc* reactions to unfolding events. Given the capabilities of modern communications and control systems, this compression of decision-making time is likely to characterize most future crises and will have to be a fundamental consideration in crisis management.

As the Washington Special Action Group met on the morning of October 24th, fighting between Israel and Egypt continued in the Middle East, despite two UN Security Council cease-fire resolutions in as many days. By this time Israel had repulsed the Syrian and Egyptian incursions which started the war

---

3. Participants in the WSAG included Secretary of State Henry A. Kissinger, Secretary of Defense James R. Schlesinger, Director of Central Intelligence William E. Colby, the President's Deputy National Security Advisor General Brent Scowcroft, and Chairman of the Joint Chiefs of Staff Admiral Thomas Moorer; President Nixon took no part in the WSAG's deliberations. The ground rules governing our interviews preclude direct quotations.

and at considerable cost had begun to move deep into Arab territory. A cease-fire had been declared and was holding on the Syrian front, but fighting continued on the west bank of the Suez Canal, where Israeli forces had trapped an entire Egyptian army. Although the United States put consider-able pressure on Israel to abide by the cease-fire, it was clear that American concerns were not decisive. At a minimum, the Israelis seemed determined to retain the encircled Egyptian Third Army as a bargaining chip in any future disengagement talks. Israeli policymakers might also have contem-plated destroying the Third Army as a "lesson" to any future would-be aggressors. Despite contrary orders from Cairo, the commander of the Third Army persisted in attempts to break out of the trap his forces were in, but succeeded only in giving Israel an excuse for continuing operations against the beleaguered units. Israeli troops refused to allow UN observers to reach the surrounded Egyptian divisions. And in Tel Aviv, General Chaim Herzog stated that the Third Army's only option was "surrender with honor."[4]

KISSINGER AND THE DOUBLE-CROSS RISK

The extent to which Israel's belligerent attitude may have resulted from deliberate or inadvertent signals from Henry Kissinger is uncertain. Kissinger flew to Moscow and agreed with the Russians to seek a cease-fire on October 20th. Two days later he was in Israel. He spent three and a half hours closeted with Prime Minister Golda Meir and members of her cabinet trying to persuade them to accept the cease-fire terms he had negotiated with the Soviets. Mrs. Meir and her "kitchen cabinet" were quite unhappy, to say the least, with the deal. In effect, the Israelis were being asked to forgo destruc-tion of the Third Army in return for the promise of face-to-face talks with the Egyptians "aimed at establishing a just and durable peace in the Middle East." To add insult to injury, the terms of the deal had been delivered with the instructions that no changes, substantive or semantic, could be made in the language of the agreement.

Accounts of Kissinger's performance in Israel vary. Some observers claim that the Secretary encouraged Israel to believe that the twelve-hour deadline for implementation of the cease-fire, stated in the agreement, was actually flexible. The Israelis reportedly interpreted this statement as a sign that Washington was prepared to allow them to complete the encirclement of the

---

4. The London Sunday Times Insight Team, *The Yom Kippur War* (Garden City, NY: Doubleday and Co., 1974), pp. 403–404.

Third Army. Another version holds that Kissinger pressed Mrs. Meir and her advisers for an immediate cease-fire and strict adherence to the terms of the agreement. According to this view, Kissinger repeatedly stressed that both the United States and the Soviet Union opposed the destruction of the Egyptian Third Army.

Exactly what the Secretary of State told Mrs. Meir on the 22nd, however, is not nearly as important as the results of the meeting. Kissinger left Israel believing that the end of the war was near and that with careful diplomacy in the weeks ahead the situation could be defused. The Israelis, on the other hand, thought that they had some time left to fulfill their military objectives. And the Soviets thought that Kissinger had taken them to the cleaners. By the time the Secretary's plane had returned to Washington on the 23rd, the tactical situation had deteriorated; Israel seemed to be ignoring the cease-fire. A hotline message from Brezhnev to Nixon late on October 23rd, the eve of the crisis, confirmed that Moscow felt betrayed:

. . . the words were hard and cold, he urged that the U.S. move decisively to stop the violations. He curtly implied that we might even have colluded in Israel's action.[5]

This feeling of betrayal seems to have been central in determining Moscow's subsequent behavior. Kissinger himself apparently empathized. Upon learning that Israel had completed surrounding the Third Army after the cease-fire deadline, he is reported to have exclaimed, "My God, the Russians will think I double-crossed them. And in their shoes, who wouldn't?"[6]

SOVIET PREPARATIONS FOR INTERVENTION

The Soviets moved decisively to rectify the situation. By October 24th, signs of Soviet preparations for military intervention in Egypt had become a source of serious concern. All seven Soviet airborne divisons were then on alert; three had been placed on alert as early as October 11, the rest in the early morning hours of the 24th. An airborne command post had been established in Southern Russia and Soviet Air Force units were also on alert. Together these forces represented some 40,000 combat troops. According to some reports, preparations for imminent departures were visible at several bases used by the airborne divisions. Indeed, one source reports that one of the

---

5. Richard Nixon, *RN, The Memoirs of Richard Nixon* (New York: Grosset and Dunlap, 1978), Volume II, p. 495.
6. Insight Team, *The Yom Kippur War,* p. 399.

seven divisions had been moved from its base outside Moscow to an airfield near Belgrade the week before. On the 17th of October, a unit of 30 *Antonov* transports (the same squadron that spearheaded the invasion of Czechoslovakia in 1968) was said also to have been moved to Belgrade.[7]

In addition, seven Soviet amphibious assault vessels, some possibly with naval infantrymen on board, and two helicopter carriers were deployed in the Mediterranean. The Soviet Mediterranean fleet itself numbered some 85 ships, a figure that Bernard and Marvin Kalb refer to as "unprecedented."[8]

There was also a nuclear specter in the midst of the Soviet naval activity. U.S. intelligence had been tracking a Russian ship carrying radioactive materials since it had entered the Mediterranean via the Bosporus on the 22nd. Our interviewees confirmed that the U.S. intelligence community was quite positive that there was nuclear material aboard the ship, even though the reason for the radioactivity could not be defined. When the ship docked at Port Said on the 25th, there was some speculation that it was transporting warheads for a brigade of Soviet SCUD missiles previously deployed near Cairo. This rumor was never confirmed, and the radioactive emissions could have come from naval weapons with nuclear warheads or from something else. Still, these reports about the movement of nuclear materials on the Soviet ship heightened concern among the members of the WSAG that a Soviet intervention was imminent and introduced a new dimension to the crisis.[9]

Early in the morning of the 24th, an apparent standdown in Soviet airlift of weapons and supplies to Egypt and Syria had been welcomed as a sign that Moscow was prepared to move in concert with the United States to limit arms transfers to the belligerents.[10] But by noon, this pause appeared more ominous. A large portion of the Soviet airlift fleet could not be located by U.S. intelligence systems, electronic intercepts indicated that Soviet flight plans for the next day were being changed, and certain "communications

7. These moves could have been in anticipation of a need to shore up Syria. An Israeli attempt to capture Damascus had appeared likely on the 17th. The staff of the division said to be outside Belgrade was reported in one source to actually have moved to Syria. Bernard and Marvin Kalb, *Kissinger* (Boston: Little, Brown and Co., 1974), pp. 470–471; *The New York Times*, October 27, 1973; Nixon, *RN*, Vol. II, p. 480; Insight Team, *The Yom Kippur War*, p. 409.
8. Walter Laqueur, *Confrontation: The Middle East War and World Politics* (New York: Bantam Books, 1974), p. 200; Kalb and Kalb, *Kissinger*, p. 488; Henry S. Kissinger, *Years of Upheaval* (New York: Little, Brown and Co., 1982), p. 584.
9. *Aviation Week and Space Technology*, November 5, 1973, pp. 12–13, 15; Kalb and Kalb, *Kissinger*, pp. 493–494.
10. Laqueur, *Confrontation*, p. 199.

nets" showed a surge in activity, indicating that a major change in Soviet operations could be expected soon.

In the afternoon of the 24th, events began to accelerate even more dangerously. At 3:00 p.m., amid signs of increasing panic in Cairo, President Sadat appealed to the United States and the Soviet Union to impose a joint peacekeeping force between Egyptian and Israeli units. At the UN, a group of nonaligned countries began to circulate informally a draft Security Council resolution calling on the superpowers to separate the combatants. Around 7:00 p.m., Soviet Ambassador Dobrynin informed Kissinger that their UN Ambassador had orders to support such a proposal. About this same time, President Nixon's reply to Sadat's public appeal for joint intervention was received in Cairo. The note, drafted by Kissinger, rejected the proposed joint intervention and stressed the risks of superpower involvement:

Should the two great nuclear powers be called upon to provide forces, it would introduce an extremely dangerous potential for great-power rivalry in the area.[11]

Perhaps Kissinger hoped that this blunt refusal would reach the Politburo in time to head off the coming showdown. But a phone call to Dobrynin about fifteen minutes later dashed whatever hopes might have existed for containing events at this juncture. The Soviet Ambassador informed the Secretary that the USSR might not wait for the nonaligned proposal in the UN; it might introduce a similar motion itself. Kissinger warned Dobrynin that the situation was becoming very dangerous: "I urged him not to push us to the extreme. We would not accept Soviet troops in any guise. Dobrynin replied that in Moscow, 'they have become so angry, they want troops.'"[12]

Around 9:00 p.m., a message from Brezhnev arrived blaming the Israelis for continued fighting on the west bank of the Suez Canal. This note, however, appears to have been only a preamble to a second Brezhnev message, delivered over the telephone by Dobrynin to Kissinger a half-hour later. The second note is the key to the crisis, but its full text has not been released. Henry Kissinger recently claimed it constituted "one of the most serious challenges to an American President."[13] Senator Fulbright referred to the

---

11. Nixon, *RN*, Vol. II, p. 497.
12. Kissinger, *Years of Upheaval*, p. 582.
13. *Ibid.*, p. 583.

text as "urgent." Senator Jackson called it "brutal, rough." Publicly, the President described the message as "very firm," and added that it left very little to the imagination. The British Ambassador to the United States at the time was also impressed with the toughness of the language. The note reportedly blamed Israel once again for violating the cease-fire resolutions and called on the United States to send forces in conjunction with the Soviet Union to Egypt. In the crucial passage, Brezhnev warned that if the U.S. was unwilling to participate in such a joint undertaking, the Soviets would be forced to consider unilateral action.[14]

Kissinger assembled a team of Kremlinologists to examine the two Soviet messages. These experts found the second communication "totally different" and more threatening than the first.[15]

At 11:00 p.m. on October 24th, the Secretary of State again convened the Washington Special Action Group. All the individuals interviewed for this article agree as to the essence of the situation they faced at that time. All evidence pointed to serious preparations by the Soviets for an intervention in Egypt in the very near future—within 24 hours. Brezhnev's second note, a continuing increase in traffic on relevant communications nets, the nuclear specter alluded to previously, and growing evidence of the actual loading of transport aircraft at Soviet airborne division bases led the group to request presidential authority to place U.S. forces on a higher level of alert. As one participant put it, "They [the Soviets] had the capability, they had the motive, and the assets (i.e., transport aircraft) had disappeared from our screens." If the United States had not reacted to these military preparations, all participants agree, it would have been imprudent in the extreme. The only question concerns the form that the reaction took.

THE UNSPOKEN MESSAGE: THE AMERICAN MILITARY ALERT

Nixon gave his concurrence to the alert and the Chairman of the Joint Chiefs of Staff ordered the alert status of U.S. forces advanced to DEFCON III[16] around midnight. By 2:00 a.m., the alert status of all major U.S. commands

---

14. Nixon, *RN*, Vol. II pp. 497–498; Kissinger, *Years of Upheaval*, p. 584.
15. Kalb and Kalb, *Kissinger*, p. 491.
16. There are five defense readiness conditions (DEFCONs), of which DEFCON I indicates a state of war. Although parts of the strategic forces, such as the Strategic Air Command and parts of the Polaris and Poseidon fleets are regularly kept at DEFCON III, the measures taken in the early morning hours of October 25th moved all forces up one level of readiness. See Secretary of Defense Schlesinger's statement in *Department of State Bulletin*, Vol. 69, No. 1795 (1973), p. 617.

had been advanced, including the Strategic Air Command—the component charged with nuclear missions. In a key action, fifty to sixty B-52 strategic bombers—a long-standing symbol and central component of U.S. nuclear capabilities—were moved from their base on Guam to the United States. Aerial refueling tankers assigned to the Strategic Air Command were dispersed to a larger number of bases and began non-routine operations. Marginal changes also were made in the status of U.S. strategic submarines and land-based intercontinental missiles. Finally, the aircraft carrier *John F. Kennedy* was dispatched toward the Mediterranean from just west of the Straits of Gibraltar, and the 82nd Airborne Division (about 15,000 troops) was told to be ready to move by 6:00 a.m.[17]

The intent was that these military actions themselves would carry the message to the Soviets. There was no public announcement of the alert and, despite Dobrynin's request for an "immediate" reply to Brezhnev's second note, there were no private communications with the Soviets until 5:00 a.m. In a move calculated to show the Administration's displeasure with the Soviets' implied threat and to raise their apprehension about U.S. plans, Kissinger refused any contact with Dobrynin despite the latter's repeated requests, by telephone, for a response. Kissinger and others believed that it would be helpful if the initial signals of the American response picked up by the Kremlin were the indicators of U.S. military activity intercepted by Soviet intelligence systems. The unusual coolness in the Kissinger–Dobrynin relationship also was deliberate and was meant to show the Administration's displeasure with Brezhnev's last message. When a written response finally was given to Dobrynin at 5:40 a.m. on the 25th, it was passed to the Ambassador by Brent Scowcroft, Kissinger's deputy—again, an unusual and deliberate move. The whole manner with which these early morning exchanges were held was meant to show that, even so far as personal relationships were concerned, as long as the Soviets' threat of intervention remained valid, it could no longer be "business-as-usual."

The text of the message delivered to Dobrynin reflected the Administration's concern and contained hints of the potentially serious military confrontation threatened by U.S. military forces:

---

17. Kalb and Kalb, *Kissinger*, pp. 491–492; Insight Team, *The Yom Kippur War*, pp. 413–415; Kissinger, *Years of Upheaval*, p. 589.

Mr. General Secretary:

I have carefully studied your important message of this evening. I agree with you that our understanding to act jointly for peace is one of the highest value and that we should implement that understanding in this complex situation.

I must tell you, however, that your proposal for a particular kind of joint action, that of sending Soviet and American military contingents to Egypt, is not appropriate in the present circumstances.

We have no information which would indicate that the cease-fire is now being violated on any significant scale. . . .

In these circumstances, *we must view your suggestion of unilateral action as a matter of gravest concern, involving incalculable consequences.*

It is clear that the forces necessary to impose the cease-fire terms on the two sides would be massive and would require closest coordination so as to avoid bloodshed. This is not clearly infeasible, but it is not appropriate to the situation.

It would be understood that this is an extraordinary and temporary step, solely for the purpose of providing adequate information concerning compliance by both sides with the terms of the cease-fire. If this is what you mean by contingents, we will consider it.

Mr. General Secretary, in the spirit of our agreements [i.e., the 1973 Agreement on the Prevention of Nuclear War] this is the time for acting not unilaterally, but in harmony and with cool heads. *I believe my proposal is consonant with the letter and spirit of our understandings* and would ensure a prompt implementation of the cease-fire. . . .

You must know, however, that we could in no event accept unilateral action. . . . As I stated above, such action would produce *incalculable consequences* which would be in the interest of neither of our countries and which would end all we have striven so hard to achieve.[18]

Nuclear threats or even allusions to nuclear weapons were absent from the note, save for the oblique reference to the 1973 agreement on preventing nuclear war in the penultimate paragraph. References to matters "of the gravest concern" and repeated use of the phrase "incalculable consequences," however, could only be taken as hints of the possibility of nuclear war if the situation were not contained quickly.

Cleverly, the note also contained a face-saving gesture for Moscow, by permitting the introduction of a small number of observers. This gave Brezh-

18. Nixon, *RN*, Vol. II, pp. 498–499. The complete text of the U.S. reply has never been released. Nixon's version, reproduced here, is the most extensive, but it has evident gaps; the sixth paragraph refers to a proposal to permit Soviet observers to monitor the cease-fire.

nev a way out of the crisis and eventually resulted in the dispatch of 70 Soviet "representatives" to monitor the cease-fire.

More importantly, the United States sought to placate Soviet concerns by simultaneously reining in its recalcitrant ally. Shortly after the alert was in place, Kissinger informed Israeli Ambassador Simcha Dinitz of Soviet preparations for an intervention and of the U.S. response. His purpose was to impress Jerusalem with the gravity of the situation and the imminent danger of catastrophe should Israel force the Soviets' hand by annihilating the Third Army. Clearly, the Secretary of State hoped to convince Israel to spare the Egyptian unit by demonstrating that further hostilities would have far more than a regional impact. In short, the U.S. adopted a dual approach. On the one hand, it stood tough in the face of the threatened Soviet intervention. On the other hand, more privately, it tried to alter the conditions that had led to the Soviet threat to begin with.

Among the reasons why the Washington Special Action Group selected the alert as the most appropriate response to the threat of Soviet intervention was the group's belief that this type of move would send a clear and immediate signal to the Soviets without engendering a serious public debate in the United States, at least during the crisis itself. This expectation proved to be naive, however, and eventually harmed the Administration's political position at home.

By the 7:00 a.m. news on the 25th, the alert was the lead story in all national media. Most Americans awoke on that Saturday to TV footage of U.S. preparations for war—soldiers returning from leave, B-52s taking off and landing, war ships preparing to go to sea. As the public had gone to sleep unaware of the Soviet preparations for intervention in the Middle East, the reasons for this U.S. military activity were unclear. In the political atmosphere that had resulted from, first, years of increasingly strained efforts to present a favorable picture of the war in Vietnam and, second, the revelations of Presidential misdeeds associated with Watergate, the U.S. military activity was viewed, if not cynically, at least skeptically. Indeed, by the time the Special Action Group reconvened in the morning of October 25th, its primary task was to prove that the crisis was real and not an outrageous attempt to distract attention from Watergate.

The burden of proof then fell on Secretary Kissinger, who had previously scheduled a press conference for noon of the 25th. Perhaps for this reason— to emphasize the gravity of the situation for domestic purposes—but also perhaps to reinforce the message of nuclear danger which already had been communicated to the Soviets by word and deed—the Secretary chose to stress the nuclear aspects of the crisis. In an opening statement during which he departed from a prepared text, glared at the cameras, and intoned in his most ominous voice, Dr. Kissinger dealt extensively with the dangers of superpower confrontations:

The United States and the Soviet Union are, of course, ideological and to some extent political adversaries. But the United States and the Soviet Union also have a very special responsibility.

We possess, each of us, nuclear arsenals capable of annihilating humanity. We, both of us, have a special duty to see to it that confrontations are kept within bounds that do not threaten civilized life.

Both of us, sooner or later, will have to come to realize that the issues that divide the world today, and foreseeable issues, do not justify the unparalleled catastrophe that a nuclear war would represent.

The Secretary returned to the theme of the horrendous consequences of nuclear conflict at several points during the question period (". . . humanity cannot stand the eternal conflicts of those who have the capacity to destroy.").[19] The performance was quite impressive and—regardless of its effect on the American press—delivered a clear message to the Soviet Union.

The crisis ended within hours. In the early afternoon of the 25th, the Soviet Ambassador to the UN, acting on new instructions, stopped his efforts to secure the inclusion of U.S. and Soviet troops in the UN peacekeeping force. The dispatch of an international force excluding both Soviet and U.S. troops was ratified by the Security Council soon afterwards. Coincidentally, Israeli military activity also ceased, although what steps, if any, the United States took to ensure Israeli compliance with the cease-fire have never been made clear. Also around this time, a message arrived from Brezhnev taking advantage of the conciliatory gesture contained in the U.S. note, informing the United States that the Soviet Union was sending a small number of observers to monitor Israeli compliance with the cease-fire.

Participants' memories of when the crisis ended in fact, if not formally, differ, however. Some maintain that it was clear early in the morning of the 25th that the U.S. had achieved its objective. One Soviet aircraft touched down at the Cairo West airfield in the early morning hours, but returned home almost immediately. It was as if this aircraft, containing the lead element of the interventionary force, had been caught en route when the

19. *The New York Times*, October 26, 1973.

Kremlin decided the risk was too great and reversed course. Other signs that Soviet military forces were returning to normal activities soon followed. If this analysis is accurate, Kissinger's statements at the press conference alluding to nuclear risks could only have been intended to be sure these favorable developments were continued and to emphasize how grave the situation had been for domestic purposes. Others, however, maintain that it was not clear at the time of the press conference that the crisis had been resolved successfully. If so, then Kissinger's remarks were intended primarily to draw a line for the Kremlin, to indicate in the strongest terms that the U.S. was not prepared to tolerate unilateral Soviet intervention in the Middle East and that it was prepared to undertake very grave risks to prevent it.

Communications, or signals, intelligence not only provided the most important warnings that the Soviet Union was preparing to intervene in Egypt in October 1973, but also was the major medium chosen by the United States to transmit the threat designed to thwart the possibility of such a move. Yet the inability of even key participants to identify a distinct end to the crisis illustrates the vagaries of confrontations in which nations communicate primarily through this netherworld of the technology of eavesdropping. As Secretary of Defense Schlesinger stated on October 26th, it was easier to determine when the Soviets had gone on alert than when they had reduced their level of readiness.[20]

Analysis

If the 1973 crisis is to help analysts to understand the potential future role of nuclear weapons, or nuclear threats, in American policy, it is essential to deduce the answers to two crucial questions: Why did American decision-makers decide to stress the nuclear dimension of the crisis? And what were the consequences of this decision?

Reasons for the decision to advance the state of alert of American military forces itself are fairly clear. There was sufficient evidence to believe that a

---

20. *The New York Times*, October 27, 1973. For an analysis of the role of U.S. intelligence during the 1973 Middle East conflict (among other subjects), see U.S., Congress, House, Hearings Before the Select Committee on Intelligence, *U.S. Intelligence Agencies and Activities*, 6 parts (Washington D.C.: Government Printing Office, 1976). The Report of the Committee was not published in the United States, but it can be found in *CIA: The Pike Report* (Naughtingham, England: Southend Press, 1977); see also *The Village Voice*, February 16, 1976, pp. 78–79.

Soviet intervention was likely. There was agreement that such a move left unopposed would have had a major adverse impact, not only on the American position in the Middle East but, given then-recent history (particularly in Southeast Asia), on the U.S. position worldwide. Individuals present at the WSAG meetings agree that the shift to DEFCON III was seen as a clear, unambiguous, and prompt way to convey the gravity with which the United States viewed the situation and of its intent to combat any Soviet move, if necessary, with military force. Most to the point, the alert had the benefit that it would be detected virtually immediately by Soviet intelligence systems through the changes it would cause in U.S. military communications patterns, while it was expected these signals would be relatively invisible to most of the world for some period of time.

At the same time, the alert had the added benefit that, as one participant put it, ". . . [it was] not so desperate a signal as to get the two nations past the point of no return." As such, particularly when combined with the "out" left to the Soviets in the telegraphed response to Brezhnev's message, it allowed both nations sufficient maneuvering room so that they would be able to defuse the situation before things got too far out of hand.

Another participant explained that the alert fit closely with Kissinger's approach to crisis management. Rather than matching Soviet actions "tit for tat," the Secretary believed, it was necessary to do something more dramatic, something which would get the attention of Soviet decision-makers because it was several times more alarming than their own action. The point, he stressed, was to do something unmistakably above the noise level, something that would make unambiguously plain how seriously the United States viewed the situation and, thus, how grave were the risks of not reaching accommodation.

It was this reasoning which led to inclusion of the nuclear dimension in the American response. A conventional response would not have been sufficient to quickly and forcefully make clear the U.S. position. The war in the Middle East had been going on for several weeks and, as a result, U.S. and Soviet conventional military capabilities had already been enhanced. The U.S. Sixth Fleet in the Mediterranean had already been beefed up, U.S. airlift aircraft were already heavily engaged, U.S. equipment in Europe had already been tapped for use in the Middle East. Given the perceived imminence of the Soviet intervention, and given these previous military preparations, only escalation to the nuclear level, symbolically of course, was seen as dramatic and threatening enough to make absolutely clear the gravity with which the United States perceived the situation and its determination to do whatever was necessary to stop it.

It should be noted that this view is not unanimous. Others, even among the participants, believe that the nuclear aspects of the crisis were unimportant. Much of the activity involving strategic forces, they argue, occurred inadvertently; the orders were given for the alert and, virtually automatically, all components of the armed forces advanced their readiness for war, including SAC. As for the shift of B-52s from Guam to the United States, the most visible and clearly deliberate move involving nuclear forces, this, it is argued, was simply the Defense Department's taking advantage of the crisis to carry out a long-sought shift of military assets for reasons of economy. Secretary of Defense Schlesinger had sought permission to make such a move for some time, it is noted, but was denied authorization because the State Department feared the political consequences of further reductions in U.S. military forces in the Pacific. When the crisis erupted, it is said, the Defense Department saw a new opportunity to justify a move.

Those who hold to this view assert that none of the key participants in the crisis took the possibility of nuclear war seriously. That is likely to be the case; nonetheless, it does not detract from the role played by the *risk* of nuclear war in resolving the crisis, nor the perception by at least some American decision-makers that emphasizing these dangers could help to achieve the U.S. objective. To appreciate this, it is important to understand the character of the threat made by the United States. American decision-makers were not threatening to unleash nuclear war, to launch its nuclear-armed missiles and bombers at the USSR if Soviet troops landed in Egypt; something much more subtle was involved.

Changes in the alert status, disposition, and activity patterns of U.S. nuclear forces, as well as the hints in Nixon's response to Brezhnev and the much clearer statements in Kissinger's press conference, served both to stress the dangers of confrontation and to emphasize the stake which the United States perceived in the situation. In effect, these actions constituted manipulation of the risk of nuclear war; they both drew attention to the ultimate dangers of confrontation and advanced U.S. preparations to fight a nuclear conflict. As such, they carried a clear message. In effect, the U.S. actions said to Soviet decision-makers: "If you persist in your current activity, if you actually go ahead and land forces in Egypt, you will initiate an interactive process between our armed forces whose end results are not clear, but which could be devastating. Moreover, the United States feels so strongly about this issue that it is prepared to participate in this escalatory process until our objectives are achieved. The United States is prepared to continue escalating the confrontation up to and including a central nuclear exchange between us, even though we understand that the consequences of such an interaction potentially are 'incalculable.''" In short, in its nuclear moves and statements, the United States was demonstrating and making credible the vital stake it perceived in the situation. It indicated that it understood what might result from confrontation, but that it was prepared to carry on in any event. And it posed the choice to the Soviets of cutting short the crisis before the escalatory process went too far, or continuing in awareness that the risks could grow to terrifying proportions.

INFLUENCING FRIENDS AND DETERRING ADVERSARIES
The U.S. actions served one additional purpose as well. They camouflaged the fact, and thus made it politically acceptable, that although the United States had achieved its objective—halting the threatened Soviet intervention—the ostensible Soviet objective in contemplating the intervention also had been achieved: Israeli actions against the encircled Egyptian Third Army were halted. The central difficulty throughout the crisis was the need to influence the behavior of an adversary and the behavior of an ally at the same time. If the United States simply had countered the Soviet threat, and done nothing about Israeli efforts to dismember the Egyptian army, Sadat's regime would have been imperiled and the chances for a negotiated settlement in the Middle East destroyed. Moreover, had Washington put its forces on alert without pressing Israel to comply with the cease-fire, Russian suspicions of a double-cross would have been confirmed and the situation could easily have gotten out of control. On the other hand, the United States could have attempted to halt the Israelis while ignoring the Soviet threat, on the assumption that such a course of action would remove the cause of Moscow's displeasure. However, this would have set a dangerous precedent for future crises by signalling to the Soviets that coercive threats could be invoked without fear of reciprocal counter-threats.

DOMESTIC AND THIRD PARTY AUDIENCES
It is irrelevant that the survival of the Third Army (and thereby Sadat's regime) was also in the United States' and Israel's long-term interests (witness the current excellent relations between the United States and Egypt, and the

Egyptian–Israeli peace treaty). Politically, the U.S. could not be seen to be stopping the Israelis in response to Soviet pressures. Use of the word "politically" here refers to both domestic politics and to the consequences of such an action for political relations between the United States and a number of nations. For example, the 1973 War marked one of the most divisive moments in the history of NATO. The oil embargo, which began on October 18, created an atmosphere of panic and disunity in Western Europe. Deliveries of arms purchases made by Israel in several European countries months before the outbreak of hostilities were held up, and the U.S. resupply effort was denied various forms of support by many NATO allies. Emotions were running high. Any sign of U.S. weakness *vis à vis* the Soviet Union during this tense period, Kissinger and others feared, could have permanently crippled the alliance.

Similarly, American prestige in the third world was waning in the aftermath of the Vietnam conflict. One of the central themes of the "Nixon Doctrine" was that the United States would no longer fight its allies' wars for them, but should an American client be threatened by a nuclear power, the U.S. would act to counterbalance such a move. If the United States had appeared to back down in the face of the Soviet challenge in the Middle East, it was feared that the whole edifice of U.S. relations with its non-European allies could have collapsed.

Domestically, the Nixon Administration faced the problems of assuaging supporters of Israel, and dealing with charges that the President was so overwhelmed by the Watergate scandal that he could no longer adequately attend to the pressing issues confronting the nation. By putting U.S. armed forces in a higher state of alert and, particularly, by emphasizing its willingness to contemplate even nuclear war to achieve its ends, the Administration established the image of responding in a very forceful manner. This served to minimize the potentially adverse political consequences of, in fact, not fully supporting Israel in the course of action it wished to pursue.

THE AFTERMATH OF CRISIS

Finally, the alert gave the United States added leverage in its relations with Israel immediately following the crisis. Although they halted offensive military operations against the Third Army on October 25, the Israelis were reluctant to grant passage to convoys carrying food, water, and medical supplies to the trapped unit. On the afternoon of the 26th, Kissinger made another *démarche* to Dinitz. The crisis had demonstrated quite dramatically how seriously both superpowers viewed the current situation, he said, and it could be a harbinger of future disaster if "humanitarian convoys" were not allowed to reach the Third Army. Kissinger skillfully portrayed the Israelis as holding the key to regional and world stability. The following day Jerusalem bowed to American pressure and agreed to allow the convoys to reach the Egyptian troops.

The import of the U.S. manipulation of the risk of nuclear war was not lost on the Russians. Initially, the Soviets were taciturn about the crisis. Following Kissinger's press conference, *Tass* merely noted the new cease-fire and the dispatch of 7,000 peacekeeping troops to the battle zone. On the following day, however, Brezhnev delivered a polemical address in which he accused "some NATO countries" of formulating an "absurd" response in the wake of "fantastic speculation" as to Soviet intentions. This line became the standard Soviet public interpretation of the events of October 24th and 25th.

According to one member of Kissinger's senior staff, however, the Soviets took a very different tack in private conversations. He noted that the Soviets never tried to belabor their American interlocutor with protests that the United States had misinterpreted their actions, or that it had overreacted. Such contrasting behavior, our interviewee believes, confirms that the Soviets were seriously contemplating an intervention and that they understood the seriousness of the American signals sent by the nuclear threat.

Given, then, that the United States did deliberately draw attention to the risk of nuclear war in October 1973 and that this message was received clearly by the Soviets, what was its effect? How important was the nuclear alert? The answer to this question, of course, is unknown and unknowable short of public testimony by Leonid Brezhnev and other Soviet decision-makers. And even then, one could not be certain that their answers were honest nor their memories clear. Moreover, as was the case with the American participants in the crisis, it may be that the perceptions of those Soviets that were involved would differ—that different individuals would stress different aspects of the U.S. response as decisive.

1962/1973: ANALOGIES TO THE CUBAN MISSILE CRISIS
This question mirrors a more well-known debate over the importance of nuclear forces to the U.S. success in the 1962 Cuban missile crisis. Many observers of that earlier confrontation, perhaps most, conclude that the Soviet Union withdrew its missiles from Cuba in that incident because the United

States had overwhelming nuclear superiority. Faced with the certainty that they would "lose" if the situation escalated to a central nuclear exchange, those holding to this viewpoint argue, the USSR decided to terminate the confrontation early. Many others, however, including each of President Kennedy's three senior advisors during the crisis (Secretary of State Dean Rusk, Secretary of Defense Robert McNamara, and National Security Advisor McGeorge Bundy), argue that the decisive factor was U.S. naval superiority in the Atlantic and Caribbean and the huge buildup of conventional forces in the Southeastern United States in preparation for an invasion. According to these individuals, even though the United States had a clear-cut advantage in long-range nuclear forces, a threat to go to nuclear war if the missiles were not removed would not have been credible because no president could have deliberately taken a move that would have resulted in even the few million casualties that would have been expected in 1962. While a threat of nuclear retaliation against the Soviet Union if missiles were launched from Cuba *was* made, this was a deterrent threat, aimed at forestalling the Soviets from shifting the focus of the confrontation elsewhere, particularly to Berlin. The effective compellent mechanism—that which brought about the withdrawal of Soviet missiles—it is argued, was the demonstration of conventional military capabilities.

Our analysis of the 1973 confrontation sheds some light on this debate; it demonstrates that both views are incorrect, or perhaps that both are partially correct.

It is clear that, on October 24, 1973, the Soviets had made all the preparations necessary for them to intervene in Egypt within 24 hours. All of the members of the WSAG believed that the possibility of intervention was serious enough to require a decisive American response. Yet the Soviets chose not to, finding a way, instead, of ending the confrontation and, thus, of appearing to yield to American pressures.[21] Why? The Soviet Union clearly did not back down because the United States had an edge in strategic weaponry and could "win" a nuclear exchange. There was a rough balance of strategic forces between the superpowers in the early 1970s. Neither side possessed the capability for a disarming first strike, and each would have expected to suffer devastating retaliation if it launched nuclear war. On the

---

21. Soviet achievement of their tactical objective—final Israeli acceptance of the cease-fire—was a factor, but irrelevant to considerations of the political consequences of the superpower confrontation.

other hand, it is hard to believe that the alert of U.S. conventional forces, at least in terms of the specific military threat implied by that move, was decisive either. It was probably unclear to both sides which nation would have come out ahead in a naval battle in the Mediterranean or in a contest between their respective interventionary forces in Egypt itself. Indeed, our interviewees noted that there was no time to even contemplate what military steps would have been taken if the alert had failed to dissuade the Soviets from their proposed course.

DEMONSTRATING INTEREST, CAPABILITY, AND WILL

The Soviets chose not to land troops in Egypt because of more fundamental considerations. The United States was able to convince Soviet leaders that strategic parity, an uncertain conventional balance, and domestic problems notwithstanding, the President was willing to risk war with the USSR to block the contemplated Soviet action. This resolve was made credible by three related and mutually reinforcing components of the American response.

First, there was the historical context in which the October 1973 crisis took place. This component is at once the most important and least tangible. For more than 20 years, statements by U.S. decision-makers had made clear the importance which they attached to stability in the Middle East. Moreover, on literally dozens of occasions, the United States had acted in specific situations to ensure that the *status quo* in the Middle East was not changed by force. At times these actions included the deployment of American military forces. Some of these actions stemmed from the long-standing commitment to Israel, but it went well beyond that. Throughout the 1950s, 1960s, and into the 1970s, U.S. armed forces and diplomacy had been used to counter threats to Middle Eastern stability, whether in an Arab–Israeli or intra-Arab context, and whether the threat was posed by local powers, the Soviet Union, or even—on one occasion—by NATO allies. Given this history, the U.S. threat to risk war in order to prevent Soviet intervention in the Middle East sounded genuine; it fit the historic pattern of U.S. behavior and reflected long-standing American perceptions of its vital interests.

Second, there were the actions taken involving conventional U.S. forces. Apart from their direct effects on U.S. military preparedness, indicators of preparations for the use of conventional forces, such as the alert of the 82nd airborne division, communicated American resolve and seriousness to Soviet decision-makers. It signalled that the United States was contemplating realistic and feasible moves in this early stage of the crisis, and that a number of credible options would be available to the American president if the Soviet intervention took place. Moreover, the conventional alert added credibility to the nuclear threat. It indicated that steps would be taken that would begin and facilitate the escalatory process. It showed that the United States would not have to choose between accepting the Soviet *fait accompli* and initiating nuclear war, in which case, Soviet leaders would reason, the nuclear decision would be unlikely. Rather, American decision-makers would have to choose only between accepting the Soviet intervention and a military action whose worst immediate consequences were calculable. It made the U.S. position and the risk of escalation to nuclear war seem credible.

Third, there was the nuclear threat itself. But it is essential to keep in mind the character of the threat. It was not to unleash nuclear war, but to get involved in the situation militarily and to pursue an escalatory process despite awareness that its potential consequences were incalculable. The nuclear threat, in short, served to make clear just how importantly the United States viewed the stakes in the situation and the ultimate cost which could be suffered by the Soviet Union if it initiated a process of military interaction.

Lessons

The divergence of views among the participants in the 1973 crisis as to the importance of nuclear threats in successfully terminating the confrontation mirrors the larger debate over the utility of nuclear weapons in the conduct of American foreign policy. The 1980 presidential election elevated this 35-year-old controversy to the forefront of national security issues. The subject is complex and almost completely abstract. No matter how arcane, however, these theological speculations can have an enormous impact on more tangible issues like the trade-off between resources devoted to conventional units and those allocated to strategic forces, the type of arms control agreements, if any, which should be sought, and the manner in which the nation should define its vital interests.

It is always difficult and sometimes misleading to derive lessons from the past. Yet, it has been demonstrated on numerous occasions that statesmen can ignore history only at their peril. Nuclear weapons and the threats they imply can be used, at times, to help protect American interests in difficult situations. Raising the risk of nuclear war obviously is not without its dangers, however. The 1973 crisis can tell us something about both the ways in which nuclear threats can be used to support policy, and the dangers of turning to such desperate tactics.

Today and into the foreseeable future, as in 1973, both the United States and the Soviet Union maintain sizable forces of nuclear-armed missiles and bombers capable of withstanding an attack and retaliating with tremendous destruction against the military forces, economy, and population of the attacker. Under such circumstances, a statesman cannot actually threaten nuclear war more credibly than to draw attention to the fact that a process has been set in motion which, unless stopped, could lead to nuclear war. Such deliberate manipulation of the opponent's assessment of the likelihood of a nuclear exchange can be used to define, and to make clear to the opponent, that one perceives a vital stake in the situation. For such an attempt to define a vital stake in a situation to be credible, however, circumstances must be appropriate. The nation making the nuclear statement must have an evidently vital interest in the situation, such as its geostrategic location or its economic value. And there must be some historical continuity to its interest there. For the United States to manipulate the risk of nuclear war to compel the withdrawal of Cuban forces from Angola would be as inappropriate and ineffective as would Soviet nuclear threats in defense of the Sandinista regime in Nicaragua. Only in certain places and very special circumstances might attempts to manipulate the risk of nuclear war be credible. For the United States, these probably include military contingencies involving Europe, Japan, and Korea, for which a willingness to make first use of nuclear weapons has long been articulated policy. Elsewhere, such U.S. threats probably would only be credible in the Middle East (including the Persian Gulf), and only when taken in response to Soviet, not local, actions. For the Soviet Union, military challenges to its position in Eastern Europe would no doubt trigger credible threats of nuclear war, as would a serious military confrontation with China in Central Asia. In all other places, Soviet nuclear threats would only be credible in the context of direct military confrontation with the United States and, even then, would depend on the circumstances which had precipitated the conflict to begin with.

This view of the character of nuclear threats in an age of substantial nuclear retaliatory capabilities on both sides also suggests that within fairly permissive boundaries, the effectiveness of nuclear threats may not be influenced by the *aggregate* strategic balance. The threat is not so much to go deliberately to nuclear war as it is to participate and persevere in an escalatory process, even though it might *result* in nuclear war. Accordingly, the credibility of the threat would not, from a first approximation, be influenced by calculations of just how badly off each side would be if the escalation ran its course, presuming, of course, that both sides had maintained substantial forces. Its credibility would depend on the ability of the nation making the threat to demonstrate convincingly that it perceived such vital interests at stake that it was even prepared to fight a nuclear war, if that became necessary.

On the other hand, this analysis emphasizes the vital importance of maintaining adequate conventional military forces. For one, in those situations in which the nation's non-nuclear military capabilities are obviously dominant, there is no need for nuclear threats, and thus no need either to run the risks implied by such actions. It would, moreover, be unwise to tarnish this potentially crucial instrument of foreign policy by overuse. But even in more ambiguous situations, adequate conventional forces are necessary to make credible the message contained in nuclear threats. The risk of nuclear war can only be emphasized credibly when one can demonstrate how the initial stages of the escalatory process might take place.

What would have happened if Soviet forces had attempted to land in Egypt despite the U.S. nuclear alert is difficult to say; the risks, though, were tremendous. Say, for example, that coincident with its alert, the United States had not been able to persuade Israel to refrain from attacking the beleaguered Egyptian Third Army—and, as a result, that the Soviet Union had felt compelled, despite its awareness of the dangers, to intervene. What then?

In an optimistic scenario, Soviet airborne forces would have been deployed so as to defend Cairo and the Egyptian heartland in a gesture of greater political than military import, thus avoiding actual conflict with Israeli forces. In response, the United States could have made a comparable deployment of American troops in Israel, well away from the battle area, and the crisis could have been resolved at that point.

But what if the Soviets had decided to intervene in a more direct way in the war? Or what if the Israelis, fearing that such a direct intervention might occur, chose to attack Soviet transports as they entered the war zone? (Note that Israeli aircraft deliberately provoked a battle with Soviet aircraft in 1970, when Soviet air defense units were deployed in Egypt.) Or what if the Soviets, believing that the United States would interfere with Soviet transports during their vulnerable landing period, chose to attack the U.S. Sixth Fleet preemptively, perhaps along with Israeli Air Force facilities? What then?

Where would the conflict have ended? Moreover, given that the United States already had introduced the possibility, perhaps likelihood, that the confrontation would escalate to the nuclear level, would not the Soviets have chosen to initiate the use of nuclear weapons, thus gaining whatever advantage might reside in the side that strikes first?

Speculation like this is open-ended. But it serves to illustrate that once the threshold of active military involvement is crossed, finding a stopping point becomes far from easy. By raising the specter of nuclear war at the onset of the confrontation, the United States made more difficult the termination of any escalatory process which might have ensued short of the use of nuclear weapons. Of course, this is precisely what made the nuclear threat so effective. The two go hand in hand; one cannot have the ostensible benefit of a nuclear threat without running its risks. Good reason to turn to nuclear threats only in the most desperate situations.

Finally, we might view the October 1973 crisis in the broader perspective of relations between each of the superpowers and their clients in the third world, and the consequences of those ties for U.S.–Soviet relations. In the 1973 incident, first Egypt and then Israel, through actions of their own, actions which their patrons were powerless to prevent, brought the United States and the Soviet Union to the edge of catastrophe. Evidence that the Soviet Union did not support President Sadat's decison to go to war is persuasive. Similarly, there is no question that the United States sought to prevent an all-out Israeli military victory so as to facilitate a longer-lasting political settlement and to enhance the U.S. position in the Middle East. Yet, the two ostensibly dependent nations dominated the situation. Egypt began the war; Israel continued to act against the Third Army in the face of U.S. protests. The result was the Soviet–American confrontation.

Similar incidents in which clients of the superpowers have forced them into confrontation have occurred in the past; they will occur again in the future. How many can occur without the two great powers actually fighting one another is impossible to say. And where that fighting might end is even more difficult to gauge. What seems clear is that it is in the interest of both the United States and the Soviet Union to begin a dialogue about their respective behaviors in the third world, about what each perceives as legitimate and illegitimate behavior in crisis situations, and about possible ways of managing the risks of superpower confrontation growing out of these local conflicts. Such a dialogue obviously cannot begin soon, given the state of political relations between the United States and the Soviet Union, but it should be high on the agenda if and when relations between the two superpowers improve to the point where constructive negotiations can be resumed.[22]

---

22. Professor Alex George at Stanford University presently is completing a study of reasons for, and means through which, the United States and the Soviet Union might reduce the risks of confrontation in the third world. It is entitled *Toward a U.S.–Soviet Crisis Prevention Regime: History, Status, Requirements.*